MONTROSE LIBRARY DISTRICT
1 11 0001268046

PATRICK HENRY:

PATRIOT AND STATESMAN

PATRICK HENRY:

PATRIOT AND STATESMAN

"Time, only, brings increase to greatness."—

By

NORINE DICKSON CAMPBELL

ILLUSTRATED

THE DEVIN-ADAIR COMPANY
Old Greenwich, Connecticut

The Devin-Adair Company, Old Greenwich, Conn. 06870

ISBN No. 0-8159-6501-X
Library of Congress Catalog Card Number 75-96808

Printed in the U.S.A.

Second Printing, 1975

Dedicated

To the memory of my Mother

Carrie Warnock Dickson

and my Sister

Louise

and to my forebear

Colonel Roger Gordon, Jr.

and his company

who fought under

General Francis Marion

and

gave their all

in 1781

ACKNOWLEDGEMENTS

I WISH TO express my warmest appreciation to Mrs. James P. Lucier, who helped to reduce the length of this volume by making manuscript changes and assisting in implementing them.

I am also most grateful to the following for their kind assistance:

Miss Anna Brooke Allan, The University of North Carolina Library, Chapel Hill, North Carolina; the late Honorable Leon M. Bazile, Historian, Hanover County, Virginia; Mrs. John Beaty, Barboursville, Virginia; Dr. Carl Bridenbaugh, Professor of History, Brown University; Miss Dorothy Thomas Cullen, Curator and Librarian, The Filson Club, Louisville, Kentucky; Miss Frances Coleman, Librarian, Kentucky Historical Society, Frankfort, Kentucky; Miss Georgia R. Coffin, Rare Books Department, Cornell University Library, Ithaca, New York; Miss Norma Cuthbert, Department of Manuscripts, Henry E. Huntington Library, San Marino, California; Mrs. Clara Hill Carner, Marion, Virginia; the late Adjutant-General Sheppard Crump, Richmond, Virginia; C. B. Dickson, Hanover County, Virginia; Miss Betsy Fleet, Greenmount, King & Queen County, Virginia.

The late Miss Mary Elizabeth Goodwyn, Walter Hines Page Library, Randolph-Macon College, Ashland, Virginia; Mrs. Herbert Gregory, The Jefferson, Richmond, Virginia; Richard G. Hensley, Chief Librarian, Division of Reference and Research Services, Boston, Public Library; Mrs. Dorothy D. Herrick, Librarian, Pamunkey Regional Library, Hanover, Virginia; James L. Jennings, Chief Clerk, Matriculation Office, University of Edinburgh, Edinburgh, Scotland; Mrs. Flavia Reed Owen, Librarian, Walter Hines Page Library, Randolph-Macon College, Ashland, Virginia; Miss Kathryn Owen, Winchester, Kentucky; Colonel A. E. Potts, Hampton, Virginia; William S. Powell, Researcher, State of North Carolina Department of Archives and History, Raleigh, North Carolina; Milton C. Russell, Head, Reference and Circulation, Virginia State Library, Richmond; Russell M. Smith, Assistant in Manuscripts, University of Virginia, Charlottesville, Virginia; Hugh Wheeler, Sussex, England, and Mrs. Charles M. Darling, Ashland, Virginia, and Miss Virginia Lee Hall, Beaverdam, Virginia, who undertook the task of typing this work.

My sincere gratitude to the following descendants for their kind response and encouragement:

The late Reverend Patrick Henry Fontaine, Jackson, Mississippi; John Winston Fontaine, Paces, Virginia; Mrs. J. B. Fontaine, Pontotoc, Mississippi; Mrs. Edward F. Fulwider, Beaverdam, Virginia; John E. Fontaine, Way, Mississippi; Miss Mary L. Garland, Richmond, Virginia; the late Mrs. Elizabeth Fontaine Harris, St. Augustine, Florida; the late Miss Nelly Preston, Seven Mile Ford, Virginia, and the late Miss Mary Winn Shelton, Rural Plains, Ellerson, Virginia.

And finally I wish to thank Mr. Edmund C. Burnett and the W. W. Norton & Co., Inc. for their kind permission to include material from Mr. Burnett's book, *The Continental Congress*, Copyrighted 1941 by The Macmillan Company.

CONTENTS

INTRODUCTION

LIVING IN THE COUNTRYSIDE near "Scotchtown," the home of Patrick Henry, I naturally became interested in the great patriot. I had remembered him from school days as being the most colorful of all the men in the Revolution, but I seemed to recall only the hackneyed phrase, "Give me liberty, or give me death!" I longed to know more. . .

I was often drawn to visit Scotchtown, the abode of Henry from the year 1771 until the spring of 1778, "during the prime years of his service to the Colony and the Nation." Everything about this place fascinated me. But most of all I liked to walk the great hall that he had many times walked, and to hold the doors that once had known his touch. From here he had gone many times in his efforts to establish the Republic.

From Scotchtown he had journeyed to the House of Burgesses; to the first and second Continental Congresses; to St. John's Church; down the peninsula to retrieve the powder taken from the Powder Horn; to the Virginia Conventions, where in 1776 he was elected the first Governor of an American colony under a constitutional republic.

Maintaining his residence here while awaiting the renovation of the governor's palace, Scotchtown became the bailiwick from which Patrick Henry governed Virginia—a vast and powerful colony, in its infantine state—stretching to the great regions of the Mississippi. Traveling back from Williamsburg to Scotchtown when he could be spared from duties, he jogged along in his stick gig, or rode horseback over the red clay roads, which can still be seen in the wooded shade, worn and sunken. During this time Patrick Henry bore upon his shoulders a great share of the responsibility of establishing, out of chaos, the first independent state under a written constitution in the annals of the world; finally to govern the colony, finance its war, and exert unbelievable perseverance in supplying Washington's army. Here, at Scotchtown, he dreamed upon the rights of mankind—God's laws.

Here, then, was the challenge that caused me to take up my research. I desired to know how Patrick Henry, "plebeian, born in obscurity," and supposedly unlearned, (as has been stated by some writers of history) had attained the heights of leadership among his countrymen. Here was a man who, in a period of crisis throughout the colonies, kept up a regular correspondence with such leading men in Congress as John and Samuel Adams, Richard Henry Lee, George Mason, Washington and other patriots. Could it have been only his oratory, rather than the powerful faculties of his mind, that caused the eyes of his countrymen to be focused upon him? What was his relationship with his contemporaries? And why had he taken up the fight in the first place?

Here began my study. Turning to the Henry orations in the *Selections from Speeches of Eminent Americans*, published one hundred years after the birth of Patrick Henry, and purchased by a forebear in 1840 for the small sum of seven shillings, six-pence, Patrick Henry's speeches were to become the nucleus from which I would form my thinking.

It has been long recognized by scholars of history that William Wirt, Patrick Henry's first biographer, had not done justice to the fame and genius of this great patriot. Beginning his work with apologies, Mr. Wirt, a practicing lawyer, wrote his dismal sketches, which were published in 1817. He stated that the materials which he had been able to collect "are scanty and meager, and utterly disproportionate to the great fame of Mr. Henry." Why, then, did he attempt to write the biography of Patrick Henry—*Sketches of the Life and Character*, so much in demand that as early as 1859 it had reached its fifteenth edition? Did he write in haste because he knew it would sell? Col. John Henry, who was only four years old when his father died, said he was "chagrined" when he read William Wirt's book. He felt that Wirt should have visited Red Hill before writing it, and that he should have talked with two of Patrick Henry's sisters who were then living. He also realized that "Jefferson had unduly influenced Wirt." Wirt's appraisal, made at the behest of Jefferson, was not in keeping with the facts. Jefferson "misled Wirt, who misapprehended the whole matter, and thereupon proceeded to moralize on the evil results of neglecting one's books when one is in school," attempting to prove that Patrick Henry had little learning. Wirt did not trouble himself to find out that Patrick's tutor, Col. John Henry, had attended one of the finest Aberdonian colleges.

Mr. Wirt showed poor judgment in trusting his queries to the vague memory of Mr. Jefferson's declining years. As one lawyer writing of another, he could have been more generous. Instead, he is seen "placing Henry on a pinnacle of greatness, and then casting him down, and again elevating him only to denounce him later on." Some present-day writers have done likewise.

Apology cannot remove reprehension. The injustice to Patrick Henry has been done. I was prompted to write a new appraisal. It seems Wirt's informants had little knowledge of the true Patrick Henry. His biography might have waited. "The obscurest epoch always is today. Contemporary estimates rarely are those of posterity. Time, only, brings increase to greatness."

It fell to William W. Henry, Patrick Henry's grandson, to clear his grandfather's records. His three-volume work, *Life, Correspondence and Speeches*, supplies the most complete and valuable information, covering the whole period of Mr. Henry's achievements. William Henry, like his grandfather, was also useful in the affairs of his state. He was state's attorney, a member of Virginia's legislature for four sessions, and was the orator at the centennial of the laying of the cornerstone of the Capitol in Washington. The source of his biography of Patrick Henry is pure. Unfortunately, it had a limited edition of only 1,100 copies. Published in 1891, the volumes of this fine work are not easily accessible. Every generation should have this appraisal of Patrick Henry. The author had access to Governor Henry's executive papers and the legislative papers at the Capitol in Richmond, and to the papers in the State Department at Washington, as well as those of the Continental Congress and many private letters and documents. Thus, a new light has been shed upon the patriot and his struggle to place his country on a free and independent basis.

From W. W. Henry's three volumes, Dr. Moses C. Tyler did a revised edition of the *American Statesman*, drawing from these texts and from a great many papers placed in his hands by this grandson of Patrick Henry. In the preface, Dr. Tyler recorded his grateful acknowledgement to the author, "not alone for his unstinted generosity . . . but for another sort, also, which is still more rare, and which I cannot easily describe,—his perfect delicacy, while promoting my more difficult researches by his invaluable help, in never once encumbering that help with the least effort to hamper my judgment, or to sway it from the natural conclusions to which my studies might lead."

The research that I have undertaken led me by a stroke of

good luck to discover some valuable information. I was also given some traditional data by a former teacher in the Woman's College, Richmond, whose forebear purchased Scotchtown (Henry's home) 22 years after Governor Henry had moved to Williamsburg.

In undertaking this biography, I hope to answer Patrick Henry's critics and to better inform those who might think of him as an orator only. Thus, it has been my purpose to make a comprehensive compilation and comparison of all the facts regarding Patrick Henry and to shed a present-day light upon the achievements and predictions of this famous Virginian. Old truths are being slowly unearthed which must re-establish this patriot, orator and statesman in the first rank of the nation. It is fitting that we point to a man who gave meaning to America.

"We must not allow ourselves to lose contact with the past; on the contrary, we must feel it under our feet, because we have raised ourselves upon it."

"God grants liberty only to those who love it, who are always ready to guard and defend it."

Norine Dickson Campbell

Beaverdam, Va.

PATRICK HENRY:

PATRIOT AND STATESMAN

Important Dates in the Life of Patrick Henry

1736–May 29	Born at "Studley", Hanover County, Va.
1751	Employed as clerk in store
1752	Storekeeper
1754	Married Sarah Shelton
1754–59	Storekeeper and farmer
1760	Admitted to the bar
1763	First great speech, "Parson's Cause"
1764	Moved to "Roundabout" in Louisa County
1765–May 29	Second speech, Stamp Act
1769	Returned to Hanover County
1769	Practicing at bar of General Court
1771	Moved to "Scotchtown"
1765–1774	A popular leader and Burgess
1774–1775	In Continental Congress
1775–March 23	"Liberty or Death" speech at St. Johns Church, Richmond
1775	Leader of Gunpowder Expedition
1775	Colonel and Commander-in-Chief
1775	Death of Sarah Shelton Henry at "Scotchtown"
1776	Champion of Independence and Religious Liberty
1776–79	First Governor of Virginia 3 one-year terms
1777–October 9	Married Dorothea Dandridge
1779	Moved to "Leatherwood", Henry County
1779–1784	Leader of the General Assembly
1784–86	Governor of Virginia 2 one-year terms
1786	Moved to Prince Edward County
1788	Opposed Federal Constitution
1791–93	Argued British Debt Case
1794	Retired to "Red Hill", Charlotte County
1794	Refused offer of U. S. Senatorship and service on Mission to Spain
1795	Refused offer to serve as Secretary of State for President
1796	Refused offer to serve as Chief Justice of Supreme Court
	Refused offer to serve as Governor
1799	Refused offer to serve on Mission to France
1799–March 4	Last public appearance
1799	Elected to General Assembly
1799–June 6	Died at "Red Hill", Charlotte County
	Buried at "Red Hill"

I

ANCESTRY

> *. . . . Freedom is thought*
> *Men kneel before,*
> *And thought men stand before*
> *And lift their eyes to catch the summit of,*
> *And climb at last through blood to reach. . . .*
> —Marion Louise Bliss

THE STORM CLOUDS were gathering over St. John's Church. The time was March 20, 1775. It was the meeting of the Second Virginia Convention in Richmond. The colonies had received with alarm the King's speech on opening Parliament; yet hope still lingered in the hearts of some of the convention delegates. But there was one member who was certain there would be no change of policy in England, and that the colonies would never see a return to the "halcyon days of old."

"*There is no longer any room for hope*. If we wish to be free . . . we must fight! An appeal to arms and to the God of Hosts, is all that is left us. Sir, we are not weak, if we make the proper use of those means which the God of nature hath placed in our power. Three millions of people, armed in the holy cause of liberty, and in such a country as that which we possess, are invincible by any force which our enemy can send against us. . . ."

It was Patrick Henry speaking. His words epitomized the spirit and sturdiness of the early Scotch patriots, especially the Dissenters whom he had known in the backwoods country; such as had gathered at Studley, the home of his Dissenter mother; at the Morris Reading House, and at the lower Fork Church—the followers of Samuel Davies who held to the principles and doctrines of Calvin and Knox.[1]

But what of this delegate who was rousing his country and fusing bands of patriots together to hurl defiance at the tyranny of Great Britain? What of his heritage, his influence? Was he "plebeian, born in obscurity, poor, without the advantages of literature," as was charged by some of his Tory colleagues?[2]

Patrick Henry's mother was Sarah Winston; his father John Henry. His mother, by a previous marriage, had become Sarah Winston Syme. She and her first husband, Col. John Syme, lived at Studley, in Hanover County, Virginia. Colonel Syme was the first member from Hanover to the House of Burgesses and served his coutrymen for over a decade until his death. Their son, and only child, John Syme, Jr., Patrick Henry's half-brother, was also a Burgess and remained with this body for about 15 years.

Colonel Syme was a well-to-do planter. He was purportedly one of the largest property holders in the county. His lands extended from Studley and Retreat to New Castle; into King William and Goochland Counties. At his death in 1731, Sarah Syme, like Martha Custis, became the mistress of a large plantation. John Syme, Jr. about the year 1750, married Mildred Merriweather and built the house called Rocky Mills, on the South Anna River, which was later moved to its present site on the James and rechristened Fairfield.

---

[1] Henry's father was an Episcopalian, his mother a Presbyterian. Henry, *Henry*, I, pp. 15–16;

The Reverend Samuel Davies was the advocate of civil rights and liberties among the nonconformists in Hanover County in the neighborhood of Studley. (See Meade, I, p. 435 n. *Old Churches Ministers and Families.*)

On August 17, 1775, he preached in Hanover on "The Constituents of a Good Soldier," in which he referred to "that heroic youth Colonel Washington. . . ." Five days later this item appeared in the *Williamsburg Gazette:*

> We hear from Hanover that 50 men have offered themselves as volunteers to range on the Frontiers of this Colony, and have recommended Mr. Samuel Overton to the Governor as their captain; his Honor has been pleased to give him a commission and furnished the company with ammunition and provisions.

For eleven years Patrick Henry listened to the sermons of Samuel Davies. At the age of eleven he heard the Dissenting Ministers at the Morris' reading house and at the Hanover Church, later known as Pole Green Presbyterian Church. Mr. Davies preached in Hanover and the surrounding counties until 1758, until Patrick Henry was twenty-two. The patriotism of Samuel Davies could have greatly influenced Patrick Henry's thinking on civil and religious liberties.

[2] Henry, *Henry*, op. cit., I, p. 260. Randolph's Ms. *History of Virginia.*

Among the guests at Studley was Colonel Syme's cousin, John Henry, and his friend, Robert Dinwiddie, later Governor. John Henry was a second cousin[3] of Eleanor Syme of Edinburgh and was a welcomed guest at Studley where the three Scotsmen were said to be a jolly company.

Following the death of John Syme, the elder, John Henry married the widow Syme, by whom there were nine children—two sons and seven daughters, Patrick Henry being the second son. He was born at Studley May 29, 1736.

Sarah Winston Syme Henry, Patrick Henry's mother, was the daughter of Isaac Winston and Mary Dabney of Hanover County. Another daughter, Lucy Winston Coles, was the grandmother of Dolley Madison. The Winstons were an eminent family of Yorkshire, England, who emigrated from Wales to the Colony of Virginia. It is said that through the Gloucestershire branch the Winstons were related to the Duke of Marlborough.[4] The Dabneys were prominent Huguenots who settled the upper James.

John Henry, Patrick's father, was the son of Alexander Henry and Jean Robertson of Aberdeen, Scotland. He emigrated to Virginia sometime early in 1723. Jean Robertson, Patrick Henry's grandmother, was the aunt of Dr. William Robertson, the noted minister and scholar. Because of his relationship to Patrick Henry, and their similarity of gifts, it might be interesting to glance at this first cousin once removed of Patrick Henry:

> Dr. Robertson was first appointed minister of Gladsmuir, in Haddingtonshire, Scotland. Afterwards he was appointed chaplain of Stirling Castle; two years later he was appointed one of his majesty's chaplains in ordinary for Scotland; and afterward, principal of the University of Edinburgh. He distinguished himself by his eloquence as a preacher, and in debate in the General Assembly as leader of the moderate party in the Church of Scotland. After the publication of his "*History of Scotland*," Dr. Robertson was appointed Historiographer-Royal of Scotland. Later when he published the "*History of the Reign of Charles V*" in three volumes, he received from the booksellers the

---

[3] Moses Coit Tyler declared:

> Patrick Henry's father was second cousin to the beautiful Eleanor Syme of Edinburgh, who in 1777, became the wife of Henry Brougham of Brougham Hall, Westmoreland. Their eldest son was Lord Brougham, who was thus the third cousin of Patrick Henry.

Tyler, *Patrick Henry*, p. 3. Henry, *Henry*, I, p. 3.

[4] Henry, *Henry*, I, p. 1, n.

princely sum of £4500. It reached its fourteenth edition before his death.[5]

In 1777, Dr. Robertson published his *History of America*, which, it is said, "no history of this continent can ever supplant." Dr. Robertson's essay on "Chivalry" gave inspiration to Patrick Henry and deeply imprinted on his mind the principles of honesty, generosity, courage and loyalty.

Most noticeable in these two cousins is their similarity of mind and of oratory. It is said of Dr. Robertson that he "evinced in the General Assembly a readiness and eloquence in debate which his friend Gibbon might have envied in the House of Commons."[6] The "pomp and strut" which the poet Cowper imputed to Dr. Robertson was acknowledged in his "real dignity and power," that sprang from "the true elevation of intellectual and moral character."[7]

Greatness seems to follow the Robertson family. Dr. Robertson's great-nephew, Henry, Lord Brougham, with his powerful forces of speech, did much to destroy the slave-trade of Great Britain. It was to his grandmother that he considered himself indebted for his talents. She was Dr. Robertson's sister, the niece of Patrick Henry's grandmother.[8]

"To some it will perhaps seem not a mere caprice of ingenuity to discover in the fiery, eccentric, and truculent eloquence of the great English advocate and parliamentary orator a family likeness to that of his renowned American kinsman; or to find in the fierceness of the champion of Queen Caroline against George IV, and of English antislavery reform and of English parliamentary reform against aristocratic and commercial selfishness, the same bitter and eager radicalism that burned in the blood of him who, on this side of the Atlantic, was, in popular oratory, the great champion of the colonies against George III, and afterward of the political autonomy of the State of Virginia against the all dominating centralization which he saw coiled up in the projected Constitution of the United States."[9]

---

[5] Chambers' *Cyclopaedia of English Literature*, Vol. IV, pp. 297–298–299.

[6] *Ibid.*, Vol. IV, p. 298.

[7] *Ibid.*, Vol. IV, p. 299.

[8] Morgan, *Henry*, p. 21. Henry, *Henry*, I, p. 3.

[9] Tyler, *Patrick Henry*, *American Statesman*, pp. 3–4.

Professor Tyler pointed out:

> I have, from private sources, information that Brougham was aware of his relationship to Patrick Henry, and that in recognition of it he showed

Patrick's great-uncle, Donald Robertson, emigrated to Virginia and was tutor to George Rogers Clark, the conqueror of the Great Northwest; also to John Tyler, the father of President Tyler; and to John Taylor of Caroline. He also prepared James Madison for Princeton at the Robertson Academy in King and Queen County. From January, 1762, until September, 1767, James Madison was in the hands of this Scotch classicist. Subjects included Latin, Greek, French, Spanish, miscellaneous literature, arithmetic, geometry, algebra, geography and astronomy. The curriculum was said to resemble in form that of Robertson's first three years at the University of Edinburgh. The schoolmaster pronounced in broad Scottish accent and sometimes entered his account books in Latin, suggesting that he did much of his "financial thinking" also in the Latin.[10] Madison afterwards entered Princeton University, but he is reported to have declared in his latter years concerning his early tutor: "All that I have been in life I owe largely to that man."[11]

The list of Donald Robertson's pupils, taken from his notebook and reassembled[12] from the volumes of the *Virginia Magazine of History and Biography*, shows that Professor Robertson taught 221 pupils in his academy from 1758–1773. Although the list does not contain the name of George Rogers Clark, it was noted by Madison's biographer that "George Rogers Clark, with his elder brother, Jonathan, had been sent to stay during their school career at the nearby home of their maternal grandfather."

Mr. Robertson married Rachel Rogers, the daughter of John Rogers of King and Queen County, September 21, 1764. She was the aunt of George Rogers Clark. That Robertson was a classicist,

---

marked attention to a grand-nephew of Patrick Henry, the late W. C. Preston, of South Carolina, when the latter was in England. Moreover, in his *Life and Times*, I, pp. 17–18, Brougham declares that he derived from his maternal ancestors the qualities which lifted him above the mediocrity that had always attached to his ancestors on the paternal side. p. 4 n.

[10] Brant, *James Madison, The Va. Revolutionists, 1751–1780*, pp. 58–59–60–65. Donald Robertson, born in 1717, was 19 years older than Patrick Henry. Robertson "received his education in Aberdeen and Edinburgh and came to Virginia in 1753." "He first became a tutor in the home of Colonel John Baylor of Caroline County, establishing his own school in King and Queen County on the banks of the Mattaponi four miles above Dunkirk in 1758." a. Tuition for a year's enrollment in the Robertson Academy; *To* Master Jamie's (Madison) year, £5. Brant, *James Madison, The Va. Revolutionist*, 1751–1780, p. 59.

[11] *Ibid.*, p. 60. Gwathmey, *Twelve Virginia Counties*, p. 126.

[12] Miss Elizabeth S. Gray, *The Bulletin of the King and Queen Historical Society*, January, 1963.

and a patriot, will not be questioned. He had superlative influence in shaping the minds of his pupils in the cause of the Revolution. Hearing that the peace treaty between Great Britain and the Colonies had been signed, he remarked that "the principles which he taught and fought for so hard had finally seen fruition, and he could now rest at ease. He died a few hours later."[13]

Through the Rev. William Robertson of Edinburgh, the father of Jean Robertson, Patrick Henry is descended from Alfred the Great.[14] The Robertson relatives in Virginia were kinsmen of George Robertson, Chief Justice of Kentucky.[15]

The Henrys throughout Europe were men of eminence. Although John Henry was of Scottish extraction, the Henry family originally was Norman, and their forebears fought under William the Conqueror. Patrick Henry's grandson, the historian, mentioned the influential Henrys in England, Ireland and the North of Scotland.[16] He pointed to John Henry's kinsman, David Henry, associate editor for more than half a century of the *Gentleman's Magazine,* who wrote of his kinsmen in Scotland as being "more respected for their good sense and superior education than for their riches."[17]

It cannot be doubted, then, that Patrick Henry's genius sprang from a long line of orators and educators. The name, Henry, like Robertson, was distinguished and carried with it responsibility.

Patrick Henry's father, John Henry, was, like Peter Jefferson, a surveyor. He laid off the boundaries of Hanover and Louisa Counties and prepared a map of Virginia in 1770 which was published in London. John Henry was also the presiding magistrate of the court and a colonel of the militia. While he was commanding officer of the regiment, he called his men together and celebrated the coronation of George the Third by burning a large quantity of gunpowder, and they all declared their allegiance to the King.

John Henry at one time owned several plantations. The 348-

---

[13] *Ibid.*

[14] Patrick Henry is 30th in descent from Alfred the Great.

Reg. C. 9484 C. H. Browing, *Some Colonial Dames of Royal Descent.*

John S. Wurts, *Magna Carta,* Part 8, p. 2672, shows Patrick Henry's descent from King Edward III of England.

[15] Henry, *Henry,* I. p. 4.

[16] *Ibid.*

[17] *Ibid.,* I. pp. 2–3.

acre Mount Pleasant, one of his homes, was sold as a glebe when Patrick Henry was an infant, and the family moved to Mount Brilliant, later known as the Retreat, in the same county, on the South Anna River.[18] He had "considerable estate" and was sufficiently prosperous. He was a devout member of the Established Church and was sworn a vestryman of St. Paul's Parish April 11, 1738. John Henry was a man of "irreproachable integrity and exemplary piety, and won the full confidence of the community in which he lived."[19]

John Henry's brother, the Rev. Patrick Henry, was made a rector a few days after his namesake's birth. The Rev. Patrick Henry attained prominence and leadership as the beloved rector of St. Paul's Parish and for 40 years ministered to the spiritual needs of the parish at Hanover.

John Shelton of Rural Plains, whose daughter, Sarah, became Patrick Henry's first wife, was descended from King Edward the First. Some of his forebears were knighted for valor and were people of renown in England. Sarah Shelton was a cousin of Thomas West, the first Lord Delaware, whose daughter, Jane, married Sir Ralph Shelton as her fourth husband.[20]

John Shelton's wife, Ellen Parks, was the daughter of William Parks, founder and editor of the *Williamsburg Gazette*, a famous first journal of the Virginia Colony.

Patrick Henry's second wife, Dorothea Dandridge, was the granddaughter of Governor Alexander Spotswood. Through her father she descended from Capt. John West, the brother of Lord Delaware and kinsman of Patrick Henry's first wife. The children of Patrick Henry and Dorothea Dandridge shared the heritage of Martha Washington and Robert E. Lee. Dorothea Dandridge was a first cousin of Martha Washington, and the niece of the great-grandmother of Gen. Robert E. Lee.[21] Mrs.

---

[18] *Ibid.*, I. pp. 4–8.

[19] *Ibid.*, I. pp. 8–122.

Note also Meade, *Henry*, pp. 23–32–33.

[20] Sarah Shelton forebears in the *National Society Magna Charta Dames*, 1215–1908. Sir Ralph Shelton, born November 1, 1560, married first, Jane West, eldest daughter of the first Lord Delaware, who died December 30, 1595. Ralph Shelton was her fourth husband. John S. Wurts, p. 9. 2563 *Magna Charta*, Vol. VIII.

[21] Morgan, *Henry*, p. 319.

The True Patrick Henry tells us:

> Dorothea's sister Kate, famed as a beauty, was the great-grandmother of General Robert E. Lee; and Colonel Nathanial West Dandridge, the father

Bernard Moore of Chelsea, who was Anne Katherine Spotswood, was Dorothea Henry's aunt. It was in the home of Dorothea's father, Col. Nathaniel West Dandridge, that Thomas Jefferson first met Patrick Henry. Colonel West Dandridge was a cousin of John Dandridge, the father of Martha Washington. It could hardly be said of Patrick Henry that he lived in "obscurity."

On April 1, 1741, William Byrd and Mrs. Byrd, of Westover, spent the night at Colonel and Mrs. John Henry's. Colonel Byrd was several times a guest in the Henry home, as well as in the home of Parson Henry.[22] He was also the friend and guest of Col. John Syme. Colonel Byrd was 58 when he made this visit in the Syme home. He described Patrick Henry's mother as a dignified and gracious person. It was the year after Colonel Syme's death, October 7, 1732, that Colonel Byrd mentioned the attractive widow in his *Progress to the Mines*. He recorded:

> In the evening Tinsley conducted me to Mrs. Syme's house, where I intended to take up my quarters. This lady, at first suspecting I was some lover, put on a gravity which becomes a weed, but as soon as she learned who I was, brightened up into an unusual cheerfulness and serenity . . . .this widow is a person of a lively and cheerful conversation, with much less reserve than most of her country women. It becomes her well, and sets off her other agreeable qualities to advantage.[23]

Nathaniel Pope of Chilton, a gallant horseman of the Revo-

---

of Dorothea Henry, was a brother of John Dandridge, the father of Martha Washington. p. 318;

See R. H. McIlwaine's *Official Letters of the Governors of Virginia*, Vol. I, *The Letters of Patrick Henry*.

[22] Another *Secret Diary of Wm. Byrd of Westover*, 1739–1741, Edited By Maude H. Woodfin. In William Byrd's diary of March 5, 1740 he mentioned eating fowl and bacon at Major Henry's; after dinner, played cards till ten and then retired. p. 45. On April 1, 1741, William Byrd wrote that he and Mrs. Byrd spent the night at Major Henry's. (Byrd called him Major, but John Henry was colonel of the militia and was usually addressed as Col. Henry.) On the second of April, Byrd wrote: We dined with Parson Henry* and ate fowl and bacon. After dinner, he stated, we had tea and then went to Major Henry's, played cards, and about ten retired and prayed. p. 147.

* Patrick Henry, who had the King's Bounty in 1732, followed his brother, John Henry, to Virginia. After an earlier charge (at Fredericksburg), he became minister of St. Paul's Parish in Hanover County, 1737–1777. He was the uncle of the Revolutionary orator, Patrick Henry. (*Vestry Book of St. Paul's Parish*; Goodwin, p. 278.)

[23] Henry, *Henry*, I, p. 5.

lution, in a letter to William Wirt, had the following to say of the brother of Patrick Henry's mother, William Winston:

> I have often heard my father, who was intimately acquainted with William Winston, say that he was the greatest orator whom he had ever heard, Patrick Henry excepted . . . that during the last French and Indian War, William Winston was a lieutenant of a company whose men were indifferently clothed, without tents, and exposed to the rigour and inclemency of the weather, discovered great aversion to the service, and were anxious and even clamorous to return to their families; when this same William Winston addressed them with such keenness of invective, and declaimed with such force of eloquence on liberty and patriotism, that when he concluded the general cry was: 'Let us march on! Lead us against the enemy!' And they were now willing, nay anxious, to encounter all those difficulties and dangers, which, but a moment before, had almost produced a mutiny.[24]

"Mr. Henry was thoroughly well born, and on both sides of his family there was a lineage of which he might well be proud."[25]

---

[24] *Ibid.*, I, pp. 6–7.

[25] Chandler and Thames, *Colonial Virginia*, p. 333.

II

EDUCATION AND EARLY LIFE

Henry, the forest-born Demosthenes,
Whose thunder shook the Philip of the seas
—Byron's Works, The Age of Bronze

WE ARE TOLD that young Patrick Henry "was sent to a common English school until about the age of ten years, where he learned to read and write and acquired some little knowledge of arithmetic." It has been said that a Professor Jarratt taught school in Hanover about this time, but whether he was Patrick's early tutor is not known.[1]

When Colonel Henry thought his son had properly advanced, he took him under his own supervision for more serious study.[2] Colonel Henry was well qualified as a teacher, having attended King's College in Aberdeen, Scotland, 1720–1724.[3]

The great divine, Samuel Davies, himself a scholar, stated that John Henry had a classical education and that he was more familiar with his Horace than with his Bible.[4] Of both, he seems to have had superlative knowledge, as shown in his analysis of the Greek text during a discussion with Col. Richard Bland and Commissary Blair (as recorded in *Evangelical Magazine*).[5]

Later, about the time of the Stamp Act, John Henry had a

[1] Morgan, *Patrick Henry*, p. 25.
[2] John Adams *Diary*, (Works II,) p. 396.
[3] Meade, *Patrick Henry*, I, p. 15; A Johannes Henry, perhaps Patrick Henry's kinsman, was graduated from the University of Edinburgh on 24th February, 1703. Chief Clerk, Matriculation Office, University of Edinburgh, James L. Jennings.
[4] Grigsby's *Virginia Convention of 1776*, p. 145.
[5] Henry, *Henry*, I, p. 4. "Evangelical Magazine," III, p. 173.

class of about ten or twelve young boys whom he taught for about a year with the help of a Scotsman named Walker. He continued to teach school for four or five years, having about twenty scholars.[6]

"From his father young Henry learned enough Latin to read with ease the great Roman classics the rest of his life; and there was an atmosphere of eighteenth-century culture both at Mount Brilliant and at the rector's home."[7] In speaking of Henry's education, Judge Spencer Roane declared:

> I do not believe that he had a regular academical one, but I do believe that he had some knowledge of the Latin tongue, and acquaintance with some of the principal branches of Science. These, a man of Mr. Henry's genius could not fail to acquire in a considerable degree, if not in the schoolroom, at least at the dinner table of his father, who was a well educated man. If other men could not catch an education under these circumstances, it does not follow that Mr. Henry could not, though it is said in some of the statements that he was taught by his father.
>
> His genius was as far-soaring above those of ordinary men as is the first qualified land of Kentucky beyond the sandy barrens of Pea Ridge (a barren ridge in King and Queen).[8]
>
> That he was acquainted with Ancient History and Mythology needs no further proof than the eloquent parallel used by him in his argument on the British Debt Case, between Rhadamanthus, Nero, and George III. I believe he was very fond of History, Magazines, good poetry or plays (say Shakespeare's) and I think was a very good geographer. He was particularly well acquainted with geography, rivers, soil, climate, etc. of America. His speeches show that he was well acquainted with English History. I think he had some acquaintance with Mathematics and Natural Philosphy.[9]

Judge Roane noted that:

> The advantage of Mr. Henry's education consisted in this, that it arose from some reading which he never forgot, and much observation and reflection. It was remarked of Montesquieu's *Spirit of Laws* that it was a good book for one traveling in a stage-coach, for that you might read as much of it in half an hour as would serve you to reflect upon a whole day. Such

[6] Colonel Samuel Meredith to William H. Cabell. Morgan, *Henry*, p. 434.
[7] *Dictionary of American Biography*, Vol. III, signed by William E. Dodd.
[8] Judge Spencer Roane's *Memorandum*. Morgan, *Patrick Henry*, p. 440.
[9] *Ibid.*, p. 441.

> was somewhat the proportion between Mr. Henry's education as drawn from reading and from observation and reflection.[10]

Whatever Colonel Henry taught or did not teach his son, one thing is certain: John Henry did teach him the meaning of patriotism.

Biographer William Wirt must have harbored a grudge against young Patrick Henry from the start. He is critical of the boy's escape into the the regions of imaginative thought; his boyhood haunts; his canoe rides down the Pamunkey; his bobbing cork and his singing brook. "It was to learn the language of the birds" that he made his solitary rambles into the Hanover woods, Patrick Henry told his half-Indian servant at Red Hill in later life.[11] Perhaps it was this rapture of the woods and the song of the brook that put music in his voice and molded his career.

Judge William H. Cabell wrote a short narration from Col. Samuel Meredith's description of the boy Patrick Henry and sent it to Mr. Wirt. Wirt might have used some of Colonel Meredith's information in writing his sketches. Colonel Meredith was Patrick Henry's brother-in-law, having married his sister, Jane. He was four years Patrick's senior, and lived within four miles of the Mount Brilliant plantation.

Wrote Colonel Meredith:

> He was sent to a common English school until about the age of ten, where he learned to read and write, and acquired some little knowledge of arithmetic. He never went to any other school, public or private, but remained with his father, who was his only tutor; with him he acquired a knowledge of the Latin language, and a smattering of the Greek. He

---

[10] *Ibid.*, p. 448.

[11] Morgan, *Henry*, p. 31. The Biographer, George Morgan, tells us that Colonel John Henry (grandson of the schoolmaster), was four years old when his father (Patrick Henry) died. He was chagrined when he first read William Wirt's book. He felt that Wirt should have visited Red Hill before writing it, and that he should have talked with two of Patrick Henry's sisters, who were still living. He also realized that Jefferson had unduly influenced Wirt. On the other hand, John Henry admired the "Sketches" for the qualities that popularized them; and showed his gratitude to Wirt in many ways. William Wirt Henry inherited the duty of clearing his grandfather's record. His first notable paper, "Character and Public Career of Patrick Henry," was published in the Richmond, Va., Dispatch in 1867; other papers followed; and in 1891 he published his three-volume *Patrick Henry: Life, Correspondence, and Speeches.* It is a work of 1,946 pages. William Wirt Henry was a thorough student of early Virginia history. He was never in robust health. He died in 1900.—Morgan, *Henry*, pp. 29–30, n.

> became well acquainted with mathematics, of which he was very fond. At the age of fifteen he was well versed in both ancient and modern history. . . .[12]

As to Patrick Henry's own assertion that "naterial parts is better than all the larnin' upon yearth,"[13] this should not be considered as proof of his illiteracy. Such expression seems to have been the mode of his day. Richard Henry Lee's niece, Nancy Shippen, the daughter of the director-general of military hospitals during the Revolutionary War, in speaking of a certain young man, wrote in *Nancy Shippen, Her Journal Book*, of "a youth of good natural parts . . ."

Many of Patrick Henry's words seem grounded in traditional usage. It should be remembered also that his father persistently pronounced in the Scottish. No doubt it was this vernacular, coupled with his jokes and witticisms, that occasioned these remarks. Henry emphasized that his name was Pähtrick, not Pat. "I am not Irish," he said.

Patrick Henry had a zest for intellectual exploration and became an avid reader. It is said that "without much labor he acquired that information which in the case of other men is the result of painful research."[14] As to his reading, one may quote his numerous volumes of the classics.[15] "His quick apprehension placed him ahead of his fellows, and he could easily afford to spend in sport the time which others were compelled to devote in reaching a point which he had already attained.[16]

Jefferson wrote Patrick Henry's first biographer, William Wirt, that "I have been often astonished at his command of proper language; how he obtained the knowledge of it I never could find out, as he read little, and conversed little with educated men."[17] The answer can be found by "pointing to that painful drill in Latin which the book-hating boy suffered under his uncle and his father when, to his anguish, Virgil and Livy detained him anon from the true joys of existence."[18] Patrick Henry read Virgil and Livy in the original when fifteen years old. One must be *adept* in the Latin, indeed, in order to translate the latter, since there

---

[12] Henry, *Henry,* I, pp. 8–9.
[13] Morgan, *Henry,* p. 33; George Morgan quoting John Page.
[14] Henry, *Henry,* op., cit. I, p. 123; Judge Edmund Winston.
[15] Meade, *Henry,* I, pp. 57–362, 34 n.
[16] Grigsby, *The Virginia Convention of 1776,* p. 145.
[17] Tyler, *Henry,* pp. 13–14. (Revised edition)
[18] *Ibid.,* pp. 14–15.

are many omissions that have to be supplied. Judge Hugh Nelson stated that when Patrick Henry was older he made it a habit of reading a translation of Livy once a year.[19]

Jefferson, to whom Patrick Henry's first biographer sent the pages of his manuscript for correction, dealt the severest blow to the reputation of Henry. From Monticello, Sept. 4, 1816, Jefferson noted:

> . . . . pa. 11, line 17. to bottom. I think this whole passage had better be moderated. That Mr. Henry read Livy thro' once a year is a known impossibility with those who knew him. He may have read him once, and some general history of Greece, but certainly not twice. A first reading of a book he could accomplish sometimes, and on some subjects; but never a second. He knew well the geography of his own country, but certainly never made any other his study. So as to our ancient charters. He had probably read those in Stith's history. But no man ever more undervalued chartered titles than himself. He drew all natural rights from a purer source, the feelings of his own breast. He never, in conversation or debate, mentioned a hero, a worthy, or a fact in Greek or Roman history, but so vaguely and loosely as to leave room to back out, if he found he had blundered. The study and learning ascribed to him in this passage would be inconsistent with the excellent and just picture given of his indolence thro' the rest of the work.[20]

Jefferson wanted to make sure that the picture of *indolence* followed throughout Wirt's story of Patrick Henry. And though Mr. Jefferson would deny Henry any knowledge of history, he would declare that Henry's "rhetoric exhibited Gothic magnificence," and that "he seemed to him to speak as Homer wrote." Jefferson also informed Wirt that "his (Henry's) imagination was copious, poetical, sublime; but vague also"; and that he said "the strangest things in the finest language, but without logic, without arrangement, desultory."[21]

But it is no new thing in the course of human events for one great man to be envious of another. Wirt, in writing to Mr. Jefferson and "begging the aid of his memory in collecting memoirs of the late Patrick Henry," stated:

---

[19] Wirt, *Henry*, p. 31. (1836 edition).

[20] *The Confidential Letters from Thomas Jefferson to William Wirt. Jefferson's Recollections of Patrick Henry*, p. 25.

[21] *Ibid.*, Privately Printed by John Gribbel of Philadelphia (1912).

> His faults as well as his virtues will be instructive, and I propose to myself to be his biographer; not his panegyrist.

Wirt added:

> ". . . . you will believe the assurance which I now give you *on my honor*, that any communication which you shall be pleased to confide to me, shall be seen by no eyes, but my own, and that they shall be returned to you as soon as I have used them.[22]

Fortunately for Patrick Henry, the letters were never returned to Monticello, and now it is possible for the student of history to see how Jefferson maligned him. (Copies of these letters, printed by John Gribbel of Philadelphia in 1912, are in the Virginia State Library. Photostats are available to the student through the generosity of Mr. Gribbel. Stan. V. Henkels has written an introduction.)

Further evidence of Mr. Henry's education is given by Dr. Moses Coit Tyler:

> Patrick Henry is said to have told his eldest grandson, Colonel Patrick Henry Fontaine, that he was instructed by his uncle, "not only in the catechism, but in the Greek and Latin classics." It may help us to realize something of the moral stamina entering into the training which the unfledged orator thus got that, as related, his uncle taught him these maxims of conduct:
>
> "To be true and just in all my dealings. To bear no malice nor hatred in my heart. To keep my hands from picking and stealing. Not to covet other men's goods: but to learn and labor truly to get my own living, and to do my duty in that state of life unto which it shall please God to call me."
>
> Under such a teacher Patrick Henry was so thoroughly grounded, at least in Latin and Greek grammar, that when, long afterward, his eldest grandson was a student in Hampden-Sydney College, the latter found "his grandfather's examination of his progress in Greek and Latin" so rigorous that he dreaded them much more than he did his recitations to his professors.[23]

That Patrick Henry made a critical study of English prose can be found in his letters "which are far more elegant than those of Pendleton and Wythe, and fully equal to those of Lee. His farewell letter to the officers of the army, and his letter to the Convention accepting the office of Governor, written on the spur

---

[22] Introduction, *The Confidential Letters from Jefferson to William Wirt.*

[23] Tyler, *Henry*, pp. 15–16.

of the moment, are faultless models of what letters ought to be."[24]

An outstanding judge of his time, Judge Peter Lyons, the King's Attorney, said of him:

> . . . whenever he arose, although it might be on so trifling a subject as a summons and petition for twenty shillings, I was obliged to lay down my pen, and could not write another word until the speech was finished.[25]

We are also told: "No man comparable to Henry has been seen in this country; he was close to nature, and drew much of his power from her; but he had in addition a matchless felicity, and intuition and insight, and a power of rising to any required height of passion and inspiration which rendered men helpless before him."[26] Patrick Henry's speeches, conversation, his method of writing in correspondence and in official documents; his resolves, and his ten amendments to the Constitution, all bespeak the intellect of the man.

"Wirt's and Jefferson's estimate vanishes into thin air when we contemplate the great mind of Patrick Henry as he rises to the peak of forensic power and bitterly assails injustice before the highest authorities of jurisprudence in this country."[27]

---

[24] Grigsby, *The Virginia Convention of 1776*, p. 146.

[25] Wirt, *Henry*, p. 56.

[26] The World's Great Classics, *Orations of American Orators*, I, p. 56.

[27] Attorney General J. Lindsay Almond, Speaking at Hanover Court House, October, 1956.

III

TESTING YEARS

PATRICK HENRY was also given careful religious training by his pious parents. Colonel Henry, good Episcopalian that he was, tried to guard his son against doing those things that he ought not to do. His mother, a woman of remarkable intellectual gifts, used firmness and gentleness in the management of her son and in moulding his character.

Sarah Henry belonged to that group of independent thinkers known as Scotch-Irish Presbyterians. These Hanover Dissenters organized and built the Morris reading house near Studley. Here, ministers of faiths other than the Church of England were welcomed and invited to preach; the Rev. William Robinson, and later Samuel Davies, the great divine, being among the first. The law of the times required the colonies to attend and support by taxes the established (Anglican) church. When the Dissenters failed to do so, they and their leaders were fined and jailed. No service was tolerated except that by the ministers of the Church of England unless licenses were first obtained.[1] Perhaps these restrictions on freedom of conscience and movement influenced Patrick Henry's career, initiated by the celebrated Parson's Cause.

At this time we see the young Patrick Henry with his mother, traveling over the red clay roads in a double gig to hear Samuel Davies preach at the Fork Church. We have a glimpse of this young fellow, sitting erect in one of the high-back pews,

[1] In Eastern Virginia the Scotch-Irish settlers were required to register their meeting-houses and only a limited number were permitted. The Dissenters were required to contribute to the support of the parish church and marriages were not considered legal unless performed by a minister of the established church until 1781.—Chandler and Thames, *Colonial Virginia*, p. 305.

"The defection from the established church was so great, and the growth of dissenting bodies so rapid, that at the time of the Revolution two-thirds of the population were members of the dissenting churches, mainly of the Presbyterian, Baptist, and Quaker denominations."—*Ibid.*, p. 205.

as he listened intently to the minister. Later, as they drove homeward, his mother would ask him to give her the text and a summary of Mr. Davies' discourse. Said her great-grandson, the historian:

> She could have done her son no greater service. Young Patrick from the first showed a high appreciation of this preacher. His sympathetic genius was not only aroused by the preacher, who he ever declared was the greatest orator he ever heard, but he learned from him that robust system of theology which is known as Calvinism, and which has furnished to the world so many of her greatest characters . . .[2]

The boy was twelve when in 1748 Mr. Davies delivered his greatest sermon, "The Curse of Cowardice." Young Henry was present on the court green when Mr. Davies addressed Captain Overton's company, entreating them "to be of good courage."

General Braddock, whom the British had sent to America with an army of grenadiers, had with him a Virginia regiment in the French and Indian War; word came from the Ohio Country that Braddock had been killed and his army defeated. In his sermon, Mr. Davies mentioned young George Washington, saying: "I may point out to the public that heroic youth, Colonel Washington, whom I cannot but hope Providence has hitherto preserved in so signal a manner, for some important service." Mr. Davies' sermon on patriotism fired young Patrick's spirit, and whenever possible he went to hear him preach.

It was this "apostle of Virginia," Samuel Davies, who rode down to Williamsburg to consult with lawyers about reviving the Toleration Act. His reasoning opened the way to religious liberty and secured for him a right to preach. Later Mr. Davies went to London to solicit money for Princeton University, of which he was later president. King George II was attracted by his reputation and went to hear him preach. Greatly impressed by his eloquence, the King arose, saying, "This is a worthy cause presented by a worthy man. . . ." But Mr. Davies fixed his eyes on His Majesty and said: "When the lion roareth, the beasts of the forest tremble; when the Lord speaketh, let the Kings of the earth keep silence." His rebuke was taken good-naturedly, however, and the King next day sent for the parson and gave him fifty pounds for the college. It was, no doubt, the eloquent Samuel Davies who helped to shape the thinking and oratory of Patrick Henry.

---

[2] Henry, *Henry*, I, p. 15.

When Patrick reached the age of fifteen, his father placed him with a merchant in the country to learn the mercantile business. A year later, Colonel Henry bought some goods from a British trader and put his sons, Patrick and William, in business. They had in stock such things as spices from India, coffee, tea, molasses, woolens, silks, homespun calico and other cotton goods. Also, one could purchase copper, tin, iron ware, and many household items needed in those days. The Henry boys, however, did not do the business they had hoped for. Occasionally a planter's coach would be seen stopping in front of their store, but the wealthy did not often buy from the Henrys. These rich traded with the British merchants who came in shallops up the river to their own wharves, exchanging hogsheads of tobacco and bales of cotton with the merchants, getting a year's supply of goods at a time. The slaves did not buy anything, because they were fed and clothed by their masters. It was mostly the people on small farms, and poor whites who lived from hand to mouth, who dealt with the Henrys. Unable to turn them away, the brothers indulged them too freely in credit and often did not have money to pay for new stock. By the end of the first year, they were without profits with which to buy more goods and had to close up their business.[3]

It was in 1754, while Patrick Henry was in the thick of these affairs, that he married Sarah Shelton. Like John Marshall and Edmund Pendleton, Henry married young. He was not quite nineteen, and Sarah just sixteen. They were married at the Shelton home, Rural Plains, which was in that part of the county known as the Forks. Completed in 1670, Rural Plains is said to be the oldest home in Hanover County, and America's oldest residence to be continuously owned and occupied to the present day by the male line of descent of the owner.[4] Here one may still see where the altar was erected in the parlor for the ceremony and where candles and fires were lighted to illuminate the grandeur. "Guests in powdered wigs, high stocks, hoopskirts and furbelows; silk stockings and silver buckles, gathered for the occasion. Feasting and dancing followed in the basement dining room where mint julep and eggnog added to the delight of all present, marking Rural Plains, the symbol of History and Romance."[5]

After several days of merriment, Patrick Henry and his

[3] Henry, *Henry*, I, p. 16.

[4] Information, Miss Mary Winn Shelton, Rural Plains, Hanover County.

[5] *Ibid.*, As described by the descendant, Miss Mary Winn Shelton.

young bride took themselves to their honeymoon cottage, known as Pine Slash, given to them by the bride's father, and adjoining the Shelton place. We are told it was poor land, but with the tract of three hundred acres went six negroes. Patrick Henry's father also gave him a little property, and he started out to support his wife by farming.[6]

From his efforts, it appears that he was not the easygoing Patrick that biographer Wirt would have us believe. There were, perhaps, days with the hunt and the chase, but in the manuscript of Judge Winston to Mr. Wirt, he told him that Patrick Henry was forced to labor on his farm with his own hands; that the negroes given him were young and inexperienced and Patrick had to lead them into the fields to show them what to do. These were the "sweat and blood years" as he grubbed away, clearing more ground for salable tobacco, plowing, sowing and reaping.[7]

Mr. Wirt would also have us believe that the daughter of Captain Shelton, and the son of the magistrate and surveyor of the county, were threatened with obscurity and starvation; that Patrick Henry was made the laughing-stock of the wealthy who rolled along the highway and saw him in his coarse garb as laborer in the field. He spoke of the young couple as being "obscure, unknown, and almost unpitied."[8] He wrote of Sarah Shelton as the daughter of an honest farmer, too poor to contribute effectually to her support.[9] The fact is, however, that the Sheltons and Henrys were as prominent as any of their neighbors.

Before three years had passed, a fire destroyed most of the Henry cottage and the greater part of the furniture. Patrick Henry had to start all over again. So it was that in 1757 he sold some of his negroes and added rooms to that part of his original home still standing. He also replaced the lost furniture and bought a small stock of goods, hoping with the farm and the store to be able to support his family. He hired a clerk to assist him during the hours he had to work on the farm. It appears that he kept a varied stock in his store, for in the carefully kept record of his 111-page account book, written in clear hand, he listed such

---

[6] Henry, *Henry*, I, pp. 16–17.

[7] Ms. Letter of Judge Edmond Winston to William Wirt. Henry, *Henry*, I, p. 17. Patrick Henry's recent biographer, Dr. Meade, tells us that Patrick Henry had an overseer while living in Hanover.

[8] Wirt, *Henry*, (1836) p. 29.

[9] *Ibid.*, p. 29.

articles as shoe-buckles, buckram, and hair pins—"sticks hair,"[10] he called them.

Weighing the knowledge he gained in these experiences, his losses now seem comparatively trivial. Running a store gave him a thorough insight into human nature. We are told it mattered not to Patrick Henry if he were grinding coffee, cutting plug tobacco or challis, he made it a habit to scrutinize the characteristics of his customers.[11] When they talked, he listened; when silence set in, he drew them into controversy, noting their reactions to given ideas and situations. At other times, he joined in their discussions, swayed them in argument and influenced their opinions. Later, as he weeded or burned brush on his farm, he thought about their arguments and weighed their statements: Were the overseers right in their criticisms of the Navigation Act? Was there truth in the ferrymen's gossip about the peddlers from New York? Had the full story been told about the Indians on the frontiers by the trappers who stopped with their packs? What of the French War? Would George Washington and General Forbes capture the forts? These and other questions Patrick Henry probably pondered as he plowed or looked after his store.

In June came a drought, causing the tobacco crops to fail for a second time, so that by the end of the year 1759 Patrick Henry's total cash sales were only 39 pounds 6 shillings 3d. Being unable to collect from the small planters who were depending on their crops, and with his capital gone, he was obliged, for the second time, to close his business, though he was not insolvent.

It was about this time and under these circumstances that he met Thomas Jefferson. Both men were excellent with the fiddle and flute. They celebrated the Christmas festivities in the home of Patrick Henry's friend and neighbor, Captain Nathaniel West Dandridge, formerly an officer in the British Navy. In giving an account of the meeting with Patrick Henry, Thomas Jefferson made this statement to Wirt:

> My acquaintance with Mr. Henry commenced in the winter of 1759–1760. On my way to the college I passed the Christmas holidays at Colonel Dandridge's, in Hanover, to whom Mr. Henry was a near neighbor. During the festivity of the season I met him in society every day, and we became well acquainted,

[10] Morgan, *Henry*, p. 39.
[11] *Ibid.*, p. 37.

> although I was much his junior, being then in my seventeenth year and he a married man. His manners had something of coarseness in them; his passion was music, dancing, and pleasantry. He excelled in the last, and it attracted every one to him. You ask some account of his mind and information at this period, but you will recollect that we were almost continually engaged in the usual revelries of the season. The occasion, perhaps, as much as his idle disposition, prevented his engaging in any conversation which might give the measure either of his mind or information. Opportunity was not, indeed, wholly wanting, because Mr. John Campbell was there, who had married Mrs. Spotswood, the sister of Colonel Dandridge. He was a man of science and often introduced conversation on scientific subjects. Mr. Henry had a little before, broken up his store—or, rather, it had broken him up; but his misfortunes were not traced, either in his countenance or conduct.

Mr. Jefferson is mistaken in saying that "Mr. Henry had a little before, broken up his store—or, rather, it had broken him up." The closing-out sale of Mr. Henry's store goods, as shown in his ledger to the firm of Crenshaw & Grant, was not until September 19, 1760, nine months after the Christmas festivities at the Dandridge's.[12] Patrick Henry was not bankrupt, nor was he ever sued for a debt. His cheerfulness during this adverse period was due in part to his determination and self-reliance. Years later he wrote to a young friend who had also been unfortunate in business:

> Adversity toughens manhood, and the characteristic of the good or the great man, is not that he has been exempted from the evils of life, but that he has surmounted them.

---

[12] Henry, *Henry*, I, p. 19.

IV

DECISIONS AND EVENTS

PATRICK HENRY decided at the age of 23 to prepare himself for the practice of law. He secured a "Digest of the Virginia Acts" and a "Coke Upon Littleton," and set to work. A volume of forms of declarations and pleas was furnished him by Peter Fontaine, and in it he wrote: "Le don de Pierre de la Fontaine," and "Patrice Henry le Jeune, son livre. Avrille 18th, 1760."[1] So it appears that he had some knowledge of the French language.

The exact time he spent in preparation for the law is not given. Colonel Meredith stated that "he was not more than six or eight months engaged in the study of the Law, during which time he secluded himself from the world, availing himself of the use of a few Law books owned by his father. . . ."[2] Henry was an apt student, of retentive mind and rapid apprehension, and he was quick to grasp the fundamentals of law. Acting upon the advice of Mr. Lewis, he rode down to Williamsburg and appeared before the examiners. From the evidence it seems that he was not fully equipped, and had some difficulty in procuring a license. Thomas Jefferson, in the same letter furnishing William Wirt information about his meeting with Patrick Henry at this time in the home of Captain Dandridge, concludes by saying:

> The spring following he came to Williamsburg to obtain a license as a lawyer, and he called on me at the college. He told me he had been reading law only six weeks. Two of the examiners, however, Peyton and John Randolph, men of great facility of temper, signed his license with as much reluctance as their dispositions would permit them to show. Mr. Wythe absolutely refused. Robert C. Nicholas refused also at first, but on repeated importunity and promises of future reading, he

---

[1] Henry, *Henry,* I. p. 24.

[2] Colonel Samuel Meredith's Statement (as taken down by Judge William H. Cabell.)

signed. These facts I had afterwards from the gentlemen themselves, the two Randolphs acknowledging he was very ignorant of the law, but that they perceived him to be a man of genius and did not doubt he would soon qualify himself.[3]

This letter, written to Mr. Wirt by Mr. Jefferson in his latter years, no doubt accounts for his confusion in naming the examiners. A few years later, in talking to Daniel Webster and the Ticknors at Monticello, his account varies somewhat; he said:

> There were four examiners, Wythe, Pendleton, Peyton Randolph and John Randolph. Wythe and Pendleton at once rejected his application; the two Randolphs, were, by his importunity, prevailed upon to sign the license; and having obtained their signatures, he again applied to Pendleton, and after much entreaty and many promises of future study, succeeded also in obtaining his. He then turned out for a practicing lawyer.

Patrick Henry gave his own account of the experience at Williamsburg to his friend Judge John Tyler, who later gave it to Mr. Wirt. It seems that he appeared before John Randolph in country clothes, no doubt wrinkled and dusty from the long ride on horseback. Judge Randolph was reluctant at first to make the examination. Here we have Judge Tyler's account to Mr. Wirt:

> A very short time was sufficient to satisfy him of the erroneous conclusion which he had drawn from the exterior of the candidate with evident marks of increasing surprise (produced, no doubt, by the peculiar texture and strength of Mr. Henry's style, and the boldness and originality of his combinations), he continued the examination for several hours; interrogating the candidate, not on the principles of municipal law, in which he no doubt discovered his deficiency, but on the laws of nature and of nations, on the policy of the feudal system and on general history, which last he found to be his stronghold. During the very short portion of the examination which was devoted to the common law, Mr. Randolph dissented or affected to dissent, from one of Mr. Henry's answers, and called upon him to assign the reasons for his opinions. This produced an argument; which he himself had so often practiced on his customers, drawing him out by questions, endeavoring to puzzle him by subtleties, assailing him with declamation, and watching continually the defensive operation of his mind. After

[3] Henry, *Henry*, I, p. 22.

> a considerable discussion, he said: "You defend your opinions well, sir, but now to the law and to the testimony." Hereupon he carried him to his office and opening the authorities he said: "Behold the force of natural reason; you have never seen these books, yet you are right and I am wrong; and from this lesson which you have given me (you must excuse me for saying it), I will never trust to appearances again. Mr. Henry, if your industry be only half equal to your genius I augur that you will do well, and become an ornament and an honor to your profession."[4]

With his license in his pocket, the prospects for the future looked bright for the young lawyer. But what of Attorney General Randolph? He undoubtedly lived to regret his signature on Patrick Henry's license, particularly when he heard Henry's "Liberty or Death" speech at St. John's Church. The young lawyer's "industry" probably speeded John Randolph's decision to desert the colony for England.

Thus Patrick Henry, at the age of 24, became a barrister. It was the spring of 1760, according to Mr. Jefferson, but he did not "then turn out for a practicing lawyer," as Jefferson stated. He was an avid reader and studied law at night. In the same ledger that Patrick Henry used in his mercantile business is an entry dated September 19, 1760, which is the date of the sale of the remnant of his store goods to Crenshaw & Grant. On the next page he started his law accounts, charging his fees by the year; his first clients being Coutts & Crosse Merchants. Even though his business was not sold until September, the young lawyer had 60 clients and charged 175 fees by the end of the year 1760 (excluding those clients who had been charged on the first page, which had been lost from the book.)[5]

Had Mr. Henry not been skilled in his practice, it would have been impossible for him to have enjoyed such a large clientele. Anyone examining his accounts will find them neatly and accurately kept, and the fees moderate. Judge Tyler called attention to the number of Mr. Henry's cases for the first three years as shown in his fee books, which were 1,185, contrasted with those of Mr. Jefferson, as shown in Randall's *Life of Jefferson*, who had but 504 cases for the first four years.[6] Henry left a fortune; Jefferson died in debt.

---

[4] Henry, *Henry,* I, pp. 21–22.

[5] *Ibid.*, p. 25.

[6] Tyler, *Henry,* p. 31.

Patrick Henry must have been quite busy, too busy in fact to have often gone hunting and to have been a "barkeeper" at the same time, as some of his critics have stated. Mr. Tyler denies this latter story, although Patrick Henry's father-in-law, Mr. Shelton, ran the tavern at Hanover at this time and the courthouse was across from the tavern; it is possible that on court days Mr. Henry sometimes assisted Mr. Shelton with his guests. Colonel Meredith and Judge Tyler both deny vehemently such statements as were sent to Mr. Wirt by Thomas Jefferson, who wrote: "He acted, as I have understood, as barkeeper in the tavern at Hanover Court House for some time. . . ." Colonel Meredith, who lived within four miles of the tavern, said, "the whole story of Patrick Henry keeping the bar of a tavern is utterly false," and declared that "There is no man to whom such an occupation would have been more abhorrent."[7] Mr. Henry's known temperance makes such an association doubtful. But even so, if the young lawyer did help his father-in-law in a pinch, what of it? And if perhaps once or twice during court week he answered a midnight rap on the tavern door with one shoe off and one on, did it give his critics something to chatter about and later to say he went barefoot?[8] Apparently it did!

That he had attained proficiency and was well known in his practice even in the adjacent counties is evinced in that he was engaged at this time as counsel for the defenders in the Parson's Cause. Tobacco was the issue in the Parson's Cause, which no doubt accounted for the historian's remarks that "a true history of tobacco would be the history of English and American Liberty."[9] It was the high value of tobacco that first brought the settlers to Virginia; unlike the New England colonists, they were distinguished as Plantation Gentry. Columbus first made mention of the Indian weed in his diary of November 20, 1492. Some years after that, the cultivation of tobacco was commenced in Spain, and by 1525 the Spaniards were operating tobacco plantations in Mexico and the West Indies. From Spain, tobacco was shipped to England and became the cause of much controversy. Tobacco was later carried into France by a Portuguese ambassador, Jean Nicot, whence derives the word nicotine. Tobacco cultivation was first started by the English settlers in

---

[7] Morgan, *Henry*, pp. 431–432.

[8] A County legend.

[9] Chandler & Thames, *Colonial Virginia*, p. 146–155. Mr. Moncure Conway, a Virginia writer.

Virginia in 1612 under John Rolfe, who imported the seed from Trinidad and Caracas. Its increase was rapid, and by the year 1619, 20,000 pounds were shipped to England.[10] Thirty years later the cultivation of tobacco increased to fifty million pounds. Tobacco in gold-leaf became the standard of value, as the colonies had not yet been permitted to coin money. There were some Spanish coin and British sterling exchanged among the colonists, but only in small quantities and tobacco became accepted as legal tender. Tobacco was money. In 1621, 120 pounds of best leaf tobacco was ordered as payment for a maiden brought to Virginia to become the wife of a bachelor of the colony.[11] In 1620, every planter and tradesman above sixteen years was ordered to pay ten pounds of tobacco and one bushel of corn to the Rev. Francis Bolton for his services. Mr. Bolton was the first rector from the Church of England on the Eastern Shore of Virginia.[12]

The widespread distress caused by the enforcement of the navigation laws was the cause of universal discontent that might easily have inflamed into most serious outbreaks but for the conservative spirit of loyalty to the old country. The first of these navigation acts was passed in 1651. It forbade the bringing of goods into England except in English ships or in ships built by the owners of the goods.[13] The application of the navigation act to the American colonists meant that the colonists could trade only with England and could use only English ships. . . . The result was that Englishmen bought tobacco on their own terms and sold their English goods at their own price, every sort of competition being eliminated by the operation of the navigation laws. Numerous and vigorous protests went up from many sources, but all were futile. The inevitable result was the depreciation in the price of tobacco.[14]

In 1664 the tobacco crop of Virginia was worth less than three pounds and fifteen shillings to each person. In 1667 the price of tobacco fell to one halfpenny per pound. Under such condition of things it was quite impossible for the colonists to maintain loyal and uncomplaining relations with the old country, and out of this universal discontent began those eruptions that

---

[10] *Ibid.*, p. 159.
[11] Chandler & Thames, *Colonial Virginia*, p. 167.
[12] *Ibid.*, p. 193.
[13] *Ibid.*, p. 153.
[14] *Ibid.*, pp. 154–155.

finally resulted in the War of Independence.[15] It was noted that there were "but three influences restraining the smaller land owners in Virginia from rising in rebellion, namely: faith in the mercy of God, loyalty to the King, and affection for the Government."[16]

In 1696, the salaries of the clergy of the Established Church were fixed by statute at 16,000 pounds of tobacco annually, to be levied by the vestries on the parishes. This did not include the use of the glebes nor the charge of marriage and burial fees. With a fifty percent increase in the staple in 1748, this law was revised and re-enacted by the approval of the King, stipulating that the levies for the clergy were to be "laid in net tobacco"—16,000 pounds for each.

In 1755 a long drought made a shortage in the tobacco crop. The House of Burgesses, observing that it would be impossible for the planters to pay their tobacco debts with tobacco, passed an act which for ten months made it lawful for debtors to pay all tobacco debts in money, at the rate of sixteen shillings and eight pence for every hundred pounds of tobacco.[17] Because of the two pence per pound rate, the act became known as "the two penny act"; this had been the established rate after a long period. In 1758, bad weather again cut the production of tobacco, which caused the Assembly to pass an act similar to that of 1755, to be continued in force for one year. The Governor had given his nod, but without permission, and the new law required the King's sanction before its enforcement. The Burgesses had asked permission from his Majesty to act on their own initiative in certain emergencies, in such cases as tobacco losses in warehouses from high water, etc., but their requests were disallowed.

The clergy of the Anglican (Episcopal) Church, whose salaries had been paid in tobacco, fumed over the new act. And although it affected all salaries, only the clergy seemed to wish to fight it.[18] They held a convention, at which time petitions were sent to the Bishop of London, and many speeches were made and pamphlets distributed. The Rev. John Camm, who had attacked the Virginia Assembly for its actions, was elected to go to London with a petition to have the act vetoed. He was suc-

---

[15] *Ibid.*, pp. 154–155.

[16] *Ibid.*, p. 155. Mr. Bruce quoting from Thomas Ludwell writing to Lord Berkeley in London.

[17] Henry, *Henry,* I, p. 31. Chandler & Thames, *Colonial Virginia*, pp. 150–151.

[18] Henry, *Henry,* I, p. 32.

cessful in obtaining an order from the Council which was expected to render the act void. Several clergymen immediately brought suit in the county courts to recover the difference due them in the value of tobacco.

Dr. Moses Coit Tyler, a student of the case, concluded: It was "a rough but obvious system of fair play. When the price of tobacco was down the parson was expected to suffer the loss; when the price of tobacco was up, he was allowed to enjoy the gains." But the act he considered "wrong both in law and in equity," noting, "it was the function of the vestrymen under law to hire the rectors and fix the amount of salary they were to receive, and it had been understood from early times that the amount agreed upon was not in money, but in tobacco. The clergy as a whole felt that 'the two penny act'[19] was a breach of contract, and one which would greatly reduce their standard of living. There were about sixty-five of these clerical gentlemen, and naturally enough they were thrown into a great state of agitation over the proposed enforcement of the law."[20]

Opinions varied throughout the colony as to the justice of the act. In some of the counties where there was little tobacco, the vestry for some time had desired to pay the clergy in currency.

William Wirt Henry, Patrick Henry's grandson and an authority on early Virginia history, noted:

> The act was general and relieved all debtors who owed tobacco; that it operated not to reduce the quantity, but to fix a fair value of the staple contracted for.

He stated further that the act,

> The necessity of which was so obvious, was very generally acquiesced in by creditors. As it was an effort to regulate a fluctuating currency by one acknowledged to be the standard, and only directed the value to be placed on that which had fluctuated which was in the minds of the parties to the contracts involved, and of the legislature when the public taxes were laid, it must be admitted to have been right and proper. The same principle was applied in settling debts in the United States, in France, and in the late Confederate States, upon the failure of their revolutionary currencies. Debtors were allowed to pay

---

[19] Tyler, *Henry, American Statesman,* p. 38.

[20] Chandler & Thames, p. 151.

> their debts contracted with reference to the collapsed paper money as a standard of value, in the equivalent value in specie.[21]

Hard times compounded the troubles of the colonists. The French War brought on high taxes, and the debtors were scarcely able to meet their tobacco dues. The long drought had also ruined the grain crops. "Our people are loaded with debt. Money is scarcer than it has been for years. . . ." wrote the Rev. James Maury of Fredericksville Parish in a letter to a friend. It might appear that Mr. Maury was in sympathy with the people in their distress, but this was apparently not the case. We find him later as the chief plaintiff in the Parson's Cause.

Beginning in 1651 with the first passage of the navigation acts, the seeds of the Revolution took root in the distress and discontent brought about from the vicious parliamentary acts and the resulting low prices of tobacco.[22] In the course of events it was tobacco that became the "entering wedge of the final and complete separation of church and state soon to take place, not only in Virginia, but throughout the United States."[23] Thus, from Patrick Henry's daring defense of one of the tobacco suits rose the hopes of religious liberty and the individual rights of man.

---

[21] Henry, *Henry*, I, pp. 31–32–33.

[22] Chandler & Thames, p. 155.

[23] *Ibid.*, p. 151.

V

THE PARSON'S CAUSE

THE FIRST OF DECEMBER, 1763, dawned bleak and cold. It was court week in Hanover County and the people began gathering at the courthouse from all sections of Hanover and adjacent counties. This was the day set for the trial by jury of the popular case known as the Parson's Cause.

A stiff wind was blowing and the parsons in the courtyard drew their great cloaks about them. In a cedar nearby, juncos lighted and feasted richly on the pale blue berries. Beyond, on the old brick wall, Virginia trumpet creeper flapped its long gold pods and freed its flat brown seed.

Presently, a young man rode up on horseback to the hitching post. This was Patrick Henry, then 27, tall, straight and rugged. Seeing his uncle and namesake, the clergyman, step from his carriage, he crossed the road and approached him. After greeting him respectfully, he asked him not to appear in the courtroom that day. "Why?" asked the old gentleman. "Because," replied his nephew, "I am engaged in opposition to the clergy, and your appearance there might strike me with such awe as to prevent me from doing justice to my clients." "Rather than that effect should be produced, Patrick," said his uncle, "I will not only absent myself from the courthouse, but will return home."[1]

The case had attracted countywide attention because of an article in the *Virginia Gazette* by the Rev. John Camm, who had attacked the General Assembly for its action in passing the "two penny act." Two prominent men in the colony, Col. Landon Carter and Col. Richard Bland, answered him. The debate grew bitter and the cause of the clergy became so unpopular that Mr. Camm had been obliged to go to Maryland to find someone

[1] Henry, *Henry*, I, pp. 36–37.

who would print his response, which was entitled "The Colonels Dismounted."[2]

The case had first been heard April 1, 1762, against the collectors of the parish levies, Major Thomas Johnson and Tarleton Brown, in the name of the vestry of the Fredericksville Parish in Louisa County. Peter Lyons, the King's Attorney, "who was well on his way to becoming president of the Virginia Court of Appeals," was the Rev. Mr. Maury's counsel.[3] John Lewis, another able lawyer, appeared for the defendants. He based his case on the act of September 14, 1758, with which the defendants had complied fully in collecting the revenue. The plaintiff demurred to the plea of the defendants, which put the validity of the act in issue. Arguments on the demurrer were heard November 5, 1763. The court sustained the demurrer, which resolved the issue of the validity of the act in favor of the plaintiff. Upon this decision remained only the amount of damages to be determined and fixed by a jury, which was to be based on the difference between the money actually paid the plaintiff and the market price of the tobacco to which he was entitled.

The trial was set for the December term of court. The clergy felt confident over the litigation. Mr. Lewis had considered his client's case hopeless, and it was then that Patrick Henry was engaged for the defense.

Among the observers were a large group of Dissenters from among the Presbyterians, Methodists and Baptists—"New Lights"—who, having been persecuted because of their religious beliefs, were at odds with the clergy of the Anglican Church and were eager that judgment be rendered in favor of the collectors.

The crowd had come on foot, on horse and in carriage, and pushed their way in the concourse. There were not enough benches for all. Some filed along the walls and into the doorway, and many stood outside the windows.[4] Patrick Henry edged his way into the crowded courtroom and met his clients, Messrs. Johnson and Brown. Col. John Henry, Patrick's father, presided. He was appointed a member of the County Court of Hanover on April 27, 1737,[5] and he was the presiding justice for 26 years.

---

[2] *Ibid.*, I, p. 32.

[3] *Ibid.*, p. 34.

[4] Wirt, *Henry*, p. 41, (1836 edition.) Mr. Wirt declared, "On Henry's arrival, he found in the courtyard such a concourse as would have appalled any other man in his situation."

[5] History of Hanover County Sheriffs, Honorable Leon M. Bazile.

Colonel Henry took his seat on the bench and beside him, right and left, sat the other justices. Mr. Maury sat with his counsel, and on a long bench sat the twenty parsons. They were joined by the Rev. Alexander White of King William County and the Rev. Thomas Warrington of York County. Both had lost similar cases in the courts of their respective counties and were solicitous of the rights of the clergy.

Court opened and the case of Maury against Johnson and Brown was called. The sheriff was summoned to select the jury. The list of the jurors taken from the records of the case follows: Benjamin Anderson, John Wingfield, George Dabney (grandfather of General J. E. B. Stuart), John Thornton, Samuel Morris, Brewster Sims, William Claybrook, Stephen Willis, Jacob Hundley, Roger Shackelford, John Blackwell "of Blackwell's Neck," and Benjamin Oliver "of Retreat farm on the Pamunkey."[6] Three of them, Dabney, Morris and Shackelford, were Dissenters, the last two having been prosecuted in 1745 for allowing the Rev. John Roane to preach in their homes.

We learn the line of argument in this celebrated case from a letter written by the plaintiff to the Rev. John Camm, and from Capt. Thomas Trevillian, one of the audience, who related passages from it.

Mr. Maury's counsel introduced the bond of the defendants as collectors, and also the order of the vestry, 1759, for a levy to be made for the salary of the plaintiff. Two large dealers in tobacco were questioned to determine the market price in the county in 1759, and Mr. Lyons rested his case. Mr. Maury's receipt for £144 for the sum paid was introduced, and the defense rested their evidence.

Mr. Lyons then arose and began explaining to the jury the issues involved, which, "when narrowed down to the application of the law," was merely the difference between the £144 actually paid the plaintiff and the value of 16,000 pounds of tobacco at 15 shillings per hundred; that, instead of receiving the full amount due, the plaintiff had actually received only a third of the amount. Then, before resting his case, he began eulogizing the clergy of the Anglican Church throughout the diocese and after a lengthy discussion on their benevolence, he took his seat.[7]

When Patrick Henry rose to reply to Mr. Lyons, he looked

---

[6] List of Jurors, Henry, *Henry*, I, p. 37.

[7] Henry, *Henry*, I, p. 38.

at his father seated in the high bench. He saw the long row of clergymen and the packed courtroom. His words came slowly. Wirt said he hesitated, looked abashed and somewhat awkward. The planters hung their heads at his poor beginning. The clergymen exchanged sly looks and Judge Henry sank back from his bench in confusion.[8] Then a stillness set in, but only momentarily. Suddenly, Henry's voice became lofty and challenging, and his face lighted up. There was a look of lean nobility about him and his blue eyes flashed. The people leaned forward in their seats as he explained the issues involved in the case: of the clergy bringing suit in opposition to an act that had been justly rendered. In a "voice and emphasis peculiarly charming," he discussed the mutual relationship and the reciprocal duties of the King and his subjects, declaring that government was an arbitrary agreement composed of mutual and dependent covenants, whereby the King is sworn to protect and the people to support and obey. He reminded them that in Colonial Virginia, the Burgesses was the House of Commons; the Council the House of Lords; the Governor the King. That the King had given the province of Virginia the right to make its own laws of taxation, therefore the act of 1758, which provided for the necessities of the people, having the approval of the Burgesses, the Council, and the Governor, was a good law—a valid law; and if disallowed by the King, it proved misrule and neglect, and that even a King had not the right to declare void a law made by the people. . . . In so doing, he was no longer worthy to rule them. "When a King degenerates into a tyrant," he cried, "he forfeits all right to obedience!" At this point, the King's Attorney cried out with warmth, "The gentleman has spoken treason, and I am astonished that your worships can hear it without emotion, or any mark of dissatisfaction." "Treason! Treason!" was the murmur from some gentlemen behind the bar.[9] But Patrick Henry disregarded the interruption. He doubtless noted the poor planters who had toiled hard, yet could afford only the bare necessities, while across from them sat the merchants and idle rich. In tones both passionate and overpowering he spoke of the oppressions and poverty of the people and the high taxation caused by the French War, and dwelt at length on the failure of the tobacco crops and the struggles of the poor planters to keep their families from starving.

---

[8] *Ibid.*, I, pp. 38–39.

[9] *Ibid.*, p. 40.

He then scanned the twenty parsons on the bench—wearing wigs, smug and secure, sitting together off to themselves. Patrick Henry warmed up. He spoke on the relationship of the clergy to the people, saying, "The purpose of the Established Church and clergy in society was to enforce obedience to civil sanctions, and the observance of those which are called duties of imperfect obligations; that when a clergy cease to answer these ends, the Community have no further need of the ministry, and may justly strip them of their appointments; that the clergy of Virginia, in this particular instance of their refusing to acquiesce in the law in question, so far from answering, had most notoriously counteracted those great ends of their institution; and therefore, instead of useful members of the State, they ought to be considered as enemies of the community; and that in the case now before them, Mr. Maury, instead of countenance and protection and damages, very justly deserved to be punished with a signal severity."[10] Patrick Henry's eloquence rose to the occasion:

> We have heard a great deal about the benevolence and holy zeal of our reverend clergy, but how is this manifested? Do they manifest their zeal in the cause of religion and humanity by practicing the mild and benevolent precepts of the Gospel of Jesus? Do they feed the hungry and clothe the naked? Oh, no, gentlemen! Instead of feeding the hungry and clothing the naked, these rapacious harpies would, were their powers equal to their will, snatch from the hearth of their honest parishioner his last hoe-cake, from the widow and her orphan children their last milch cow! the last bed, nay, the last blanket from the lying-in woman![11]

Judge Henry was in tears upon hearing the powerful words of his son, which "aroused in the audience an intense feeling against the clergy, which became so apparent as to cause the reverend gentlemen to leave their seats on the bench, and to quit the courthouse in dismay."

But Patrick Henry talked on. Those who heard him said "he made their blood to run cold, and their hair to rise on end."[12] With passionate momentum he continued his speech for nearly an hour, describing the bondage of a people who were not allowed to enact their own laws, and charged the jury that,

---

[10] *Ibid.*, I, p. 41.
[11] *Ibid.*, p. 41.
[12] *Ibid.*, p. 39, 41.

unless they would choose to "rivet the chains of bondage on their own necks," they should make an example of the plaintiff before his brethren which would thereafter be a warning to those who would dispute the validity of laws made by the government of the colony.[13] Before Patrick Henry took his seat he told the jury that they must find for the plaintiff, since it was the ruling of the court, but only one farthing—one farthing would be sufficient, he told them, and closed his speech. The people were in great excitement as they awaited the decision of the jury. In less than five minutes it returned with a verdict that fixed the damages for the plaintiff at only one penny. Mr. Lyons arose immediately and objected to the verdict, saying it was contrary to the evidence. He was promptly overruled by the court. He then requested a new trial, which was also refused, but his appeal to the General Court was granted. Court adjourned midst shouts of applause. There was a wild uproar as the crowd pushed their way to reach the young lawyer. Pressing forward, they lifted him on their shoulders and carried him into the courtyard.[14]

It was a triumph for Patrick Henry. Never before had anyone dared to denounce the tyranny in church and state. Colonel Henry, discussing his son's speech with Judge Winston, said Patrick spoke in a manner that surprised him, and showed himself well informed on a subject of which he did not know he had any knowledge. Some of Mr. Henry's critics cast doubt on the authenticity of this speech, but one may find similar expressions in his speeches on the Federal Constitution.[15]

The plaintiff, Mr. Maury, wrote the following letter to Mr. Camm, attempting to explain the purpose of Patrick Henry's actions:

> After the court was adjourned, he apologized to me for what he had said, alleging that his sole view in engaging in the

[13] *Ibid.*, p. 42.

[14] *Ibid.*, p. 43.

[15] Parson's Cause: "these rapacious harpies." Federal Constitution Convention, June 5, 1788: "When these harpies are aided by excisemen."*

**American Oratory, or Selections from the Speeches of Eminent Americans,* Edward C. Biddle (1836) p. 28.

Parson's Cause: "rivet the chains of bondage on their own necks"; Henry, *Henry,* III, p. 627, Speeches, "Tyranny has riveted its chains." Federal Constitution Convention, June 7, 1788: "riveted the fetters of bondage on themselves and their descendants."*

**American Oratory, or Selections from the Speeches of Eminent Americans,* Edward C. Biddle, (1836) p. 60.

> cause, and in saying what he did, was to render himself popular. You see, then, it is so clear a point in this person's opinion that the ready road to popularity here is to trample underfoot the interests of religion, the rights of the Church, and the prerogative of the Crown. If this be not pleading for the "assumption of power to bind the King's hands," if it be not asserting "such supremacy in provincial legislation" as is inconsistent with the dignity of the Church of England, and manifestly tends to draw the people of these plantations from their allegiance to the King, tell me, my dear sir, what is so, if you can.[16]

Patrick Henry's generosity of spirit and desire for good will caused him to search out Mr. Maury after the trial. After the defeat of the Parson's Cause, his popularity soared. He now added 164 new clients and charged 555 fees in the year afterward, as shown in his fee books.[17]

That same year Patrick Henry was called to Williamsburg as counsel for his friend, Capt. Nathaniel West Dandridge, to debate in the Assembly the seating of James Littlepage, a returned member, before the Committee of Privileges and Elections. "It was the week of the Assembly meeting and the town was a-stir with elegant society." Patrick Henry was little known among them, but he attracted attention in his country garb. He "quickly distinguished himself by a copious and brilliant display on the rights of suffrage. Such a burst of eloquence from a man so plainly dressed had never been heard before within those walls and struck the Committee with amazement, so that a deep and perfect silence took place during his speech, that not a sound, but from his lips was heard in the room."[18]

Patrick Henry "fired the colonial heart to a beginning of the struggle for religious liberty" which was to follow. "Official assertion and sanction"[19] of the doctrine under the last two—and most important—articles in the Declaration of Rights written by Patrick Henry, gave complete and final separation of church and state in Virginia, later taking place throughout the United States.

---

[16] Henry, *Henry*, I, pp. 43–44.
[17] *Ibid.*, I, p. 46.
[18] *Ibid.*, p. 47.
[19] Chandler & Thames, *Colonial Virginia*, p 352.

VI

STAMP ACT

Chief Justice John Marshall set down a couple of the great enduring truths of society—'that the power to tax involves the power to destroy, and that the power to destroy may defeat and render useless the power to create.'

—McCulloch v. Maryland

THE FAME OF Patrick Henry in the defeat of the parsons had now spread far and wide. In London the British Lion crouched, while the men in Parliament began asking questions about the defiant Henry.[1]

In Louisa, home county of the Rev. James Maury, the people faced grave times, and having perceived Mr. Henry's abilities, they wished him to represent them in the House of Burgesses to fill a vacancy which had occurred during the recess. That Major Thomas Johnson, the defendant in the Parson's Cause, should have preferred Patrick Henry to succeed his brother William in the House is understandable. And had he any inkling of the mischief in the plot for a loan "scheme," it could be understood why he wished to have Patrick Henry seated in the Assembly. With control in the hands of the so-called conservatives, he must have explained to Mr. Henry the constant vigil that would be required to keep up with the "old guards." The state of things in the Assembly regarding the proceedings during one of the previous sessions has been quoted in the following:

"You little know of the plots and schemes and contrivances

[1] The Rev. John Camm had appeared before the Lords of Trade and the Privy Council with an order to render the two penny act void. Henry, *Henry*, I, p. 33.

that are carried on there . . . one holds the lamb while the other skins. Many of the members are in places of trust and profit and others want to get in, and they are willing to assist one another in passing their accounts, and it would surprise any man to see how the Country's money is squandered away, which he had used his endeavors to prevent, and could never succeed but once, and that in a trifling amount."[2]

Mr. Henry took his seat in the House of Burgesses on May 20, 1765, and was placed on the Committee of the Courts of Justice. The second or third day a financial proposition was brought forward to establish a Loan Office to cover up the Treasurer's deficit, which called for quick thinking and sound sense on the part of Patrick Henry. It was proposed that the colony borrow £240,000, of which £140,000 would be lent out on "permanent security," and the remaining £100,000 be used to take up the paper money (which should have been burned)[3] from expenses of the French War. John Robinson, the Treasurer, was also Speaker, in which capacities he had held office for 30 years.

Mr. Jefferson wrote William Wirt that Robinson had "used freely" of the public money in the treasury to save his wealthy friends and "especially those who were of the assembly." Robinson had in fact shorted the funds of the colony in the amount of £138,708,[4] "relying on his own means and the securities on the loans for replacement."[5] Robinson realized that his deficit was so enormous that a discovery must soon take place, for as yet the public had no suspicion of it. Robinson "devised therefore, with his friends in the assembly, a plan for a public loan," and "had it succeeded, the debts due to Robinson on these loans would have been transferred to the public, and his deficit thus completely covered."[6] The proposition of the loan, its advantages and general plan were explained by a borrowing member in the *Gazette*, making it clear to the members of the assembly before the meeting. Jefferson related that "Henry attacked the scheme on other general grounds, in that style of bold, grand, and overwhelming eloquence, for which he became so celebrated afterwards." The expressions were indelibly impressed on his

[2] Meade, *Henry*, I, p. 156. Dr. Meade quoting Johnson.
[3] Henry, *Henry*, I p. 76; Mays, *Pendleton*, I, p. 186
[4] Mays, *Pendleton*, I, p. 186
[5] Henry, *Henry*, I, p. 76.
[6] *Ibid.*, pp. 76–77. Jefferson to William Wirt.

memory, he said when he quoted Henry: 'What sir, is it proposed, then, to reclaim the spendthrift from his dissipation and extravagance, by filling his pockets with money?' "He laid open with so much energy the spirit of favoritism, on which the proposition was founded, and the abuses to which it would lead, that it was crushed in its birth."[7]

Jefferson said the state of things was not yet known, but apparently Henry knew the group of men who would have benefited by such a deal. But Jefferson was in error in saying the scheme was defeated in the House. The proposition passed the House, but was disapproved by the Council. Edmund Pendleton, "apparently," was one of the leading advocates[8] of the scheme, in which it was "urged, that from certain unhappy circumstances of the colony, men of substantial property had contracted debts, which if extracted suddenly, must ruin them and their families, but with a little indulgence of time, might be paid with ease."[9] (Were not these the same times in which young Henry was criticized for failure in his store business? Yet he was not insolvent.)[10]

Pendleton's biographer thinks the scheme was not devised primarily to save Robinson,[11] even though previous historians have considered it all along to have been the purpose. Had it been of great advantage to the colony, would Patrick Henry, of all men, have fought it so bitterly? Pendleton, who had showed the treasurer's account in order in 1762[12] in his report to the House, had given it a coat of whitewash. He himself owed £1,020, but delayed payment for fifteen years.[13] Pendleton has been represented as one of the authors[14] of the loan office, and Edmund Randolph is quoted as saying that Pendleton prescribed "no bounds to his gratitude for his primary patron, Mr. Robinson," the nephew of his foster father.

---

[7] Wirt, *Henry*, pp. 69–71. Jefferson to William Wirt; as cited in Henry, *Henry*, I, p. 77.

[8] Henry, *Henry*, I, p. 78 Mays, *Pendleton*, I, p. 174.

[9] Henry, *Henry*, I, p. 77.

[10] *Ibid.*, p. 17.

[11] Mays, *Pendleton*, I, Robinson Affair, chapter 11, pp. 175–176.

[12] *Ibid.*, I, pp. 176–177.

[13] Mays, *Pendleton*, I, pp. 183–202.

[14] *Ibid.*, p, 210, As cited by Dr. Mays. Henry Tazewell, in criticizing Pendleton's efforts to protect his benefactor, recorded the following:

"In the year 1766 when the enormous fraud committed by Speaker Robinson was detected, Mr. Pendleton, whose patron and personal friend the

Students of history should study thoroughly the Robinson case if they are to discover the connecting link in colonial politics.[15] Only then can they fully understand the bitter factionalism behind Patrick Henry's turbulent fight to throw off the yoke of colonialism.

It is certain that the historian, William Wirt Henry, in his searching study of his grandfather's life, knew of the intrigue in the Virginia Assembly.[16] He is obliged to have recognized the politics behind the scenes, especially the design in making Robinson's protegé, Pendleton (his uncle's foster son), an executor of the Robinson estate. Pendleton, year after year, carried over the indebtedness of his party members to the colony, running to a quarter of a century;[17] while they in return sent him again and again back to his high post in the Assembly to uphold the hierarchy of the Robinson régime and carry on the "subterfuges of Toryism."[18] The historian, William W. Henry, must have

---

> Speaker was, exerted his power to ward off the blow which threatened him, but yet so conducted himself throughout the enquiry, that he was finally represented as one of its authors."

Mr. Tazewell's grandfather, Benjamin Waller, was the Clerk of General Court, and the exposure has been credited to the exertions of his grandfather, of whom it is stated:

> "his efforts upon this occasion drew upon himself for a time the resentment of many of the speaker's friends."

Mays, *Pendleton*, op. cit., P. 336, n.

[15] Note chapter, "Colonial Politics."

[16] Morgan, *Henry*, pp. 29–30 n.

[17] Mays, *Pendleton*, I, pp. 200–201–202.

[18] Patrick Henry wrote Richard Henry Lee:

> "May your powerful assistance be never wanted when the best interests of America are in danger. May the subterfuges of Toryism be continually exposed and counteracted by that zeal and ability you have so long displayed to the peculiar honor of your native country, and the advantages of all the United States." Grigsby, *The Virginia Convention of 1776,* p. 141–142 n.

Grigsby stated:

> 'Should the state of parties during the time specified (1776) ever be recorded with any fullness and by an impartial hand, it will make up one of the most unexpected and most thrilling chapters in our annals. And let me add, that unless the effort be made ere long to write that portion of our secret history, it will be lost to posterity." Grigsby, *The Virginia Convention of 1776*, p. 141.

The Robinsons were nephews, and great-nephews respectively, of the Bishop of London. "Colonial Politics," op. cit.

The Established Church "largely" controlled Colonial politics. Wirt asked Jefferson why there was no record made of this motion, (Loan Office) on the journals of the day. He replied, "Abortive motions are rarely entered.

"It is the modern introduction of yeas and nays which has given the

had his suspicions on many matters, particularly in the destruction of Henry's Copies of the Records and Proceedings in the Suits against the Robinson Estate, which are missing.[19] Here, as in many instances with Henry documents, history fakers apparently have ransacked the department of truth. In the case of the Loan Office plan, Jefferson, who heard the debate, sent the details to Wirt, but even here he was inaccurate and misleading as to its passage.

Later, when Patrick Henry was giving his views on important matters, he said: "Tell me no more of ideal wealth. Away with the schemes of paper money and loan offices, calculated to feed extravagance, and revive expiring luxury." These evils were still on his mind later on in expressing his views "as to the duty of his fellow-citizens in shaping the destinies of the colony."[20]

In his fight against the loan office we are able to see the moral excellence of Patrick Henry and his conformity to moral law. Now almost 29, he was from the first vigilant and alert to the best interest of the colonies and in the functioning of sound government. Thus in his wisdom, rigidity, and thrift, he endeared himself to the people. He courageously maintained his convictions of public duty against the strong aristocratic leaders of the Assembly. Wirt says, however: "From this moment, he had no friends on the aristocratic side of the house. They looked upon him with envy and with terror. They were forced at length to praise his genius; but that praise was wrung from them with painful reluctance. They would have denied it if they could." But, explained Mr. Wirt: "If, however, he had lost one side of the house by his undaunted manner of blowing up this aristocratic project, he had made the other side his fast friends."[21]

It was this scheming that caused Henry and Lee later to advocate the separation of the offices of Speaker and Treasurer, which was "stoutly opposed by Pendleton." The bill offered by Lee brought bitter debate, but Henry's argument for the division forced its passage.[22]

In all fairness to Edmund Pendleton, however, certain facts

---

means of placing a rejected motion on the journals: and it is likely that the speaker, who, as treasurer, was to be the loan officer, and had the direction of the journals, would choose to omit an entry of the motion in this case." Wirt, *Henry*, p. 71, n.

[19] Mays, *Pendleton*, I, p. 200.

[20] Henry, *Henry*, I, p. 116.

[21] Wirt, *Henry*, p. 73.

[22] Henry, *Henry*, I, p. 111. *Ibid.*, I, p. 52.

should be set down. He was a competent estate manager and knew the business practice of his time. He had the "highest executive genius and was skilled in figures." And "although there were several executors of the Speaker-Treasurer's great estate, with all its intricate and embarrassing accounts, the largest share of the burden fell on Edmund Pendleton. Always competent and painstaking, he now set forth on a task which would absorb the best years of his career and make him 'shoulder multiple burdens that no fiduciary had faced before in Virginia.' "[23] The report to the Assembly in March, 1768, showed the debt to the colony from the estate including interest, had increased to £109,335:9:2. The House called upon Pendleton to appoint commissioners to enforce collections against the estate. "The action of the Assembly compelled Pendleton to proceed at once with liquidation of the physical assets of the Estate, a step he had avoided for the most part for two years while seeking to liquidate the claims of the Estate against others."[24] The mansion house of the widow Robinson was spared until the Estate was compelled by the Assembly to put it up for sale.

"The course that he followed—to give the debtors every consideration in meeting their obligations—under the circumstances probably resulted in the recovery of as much for the Estate as immediate sales would have brought, but the process was much slower than he could have imagined, and it was not until fifteen years later (1781), and after a stroke of good fortune, that the indebtedness of the Estate to Virginia (more than £100,000, plus interest) was paid in full."[25] For his untiring efforts in settling the Robinson accounts, Virginia is greatly indebted to the name, Edmund Pendleton!

Scarcely had Patrick Henry ended his grapple with the loan scheme on the home front, when his attention was directed to the British scheme in Parliament known as the Stamp Act. For some time he had viewed with displeasure the unfair monopoly of the commerce of the colonies by the British. The bitter enforcement of the Navigation Act had been witnessed from his own Hanovertown, where he had seen as many as 1600 hogsheads of tobacco exported annually. But the only vessels that came and went were owned and manned by the British.[26]

---

[23] Meade, *Henry*, I, p. 213.
[24] Mays, *Pendleton*, I, p. 198.
[25] *Ibid.*, I, p. 186.
[26] Henry, *Henry*, I, p. 52.

The colonies were not left free to buy and sell to their own advantage and cultivate a profitable trade. The King's restricting their trade portended a gradual strangulation of the colonies' resources. Moreover, by another amendment, "the liberty of free traffic between the colonies was taken away, and a duty imposed on intercolonial trade equal to that required on exports to England." Such laws grew out of the avarice of British merchants; the revenue accruing to the state was trifling, while the profits to the English traders were enormous.[27] At the December session of the Assembly, a Committee of the House of Burgesses made an address to the King, and a memorial to the House of Lords, both by the pen of Mr. Lee, and a remonstrance to the House of Commons drawn by George Wythe.[28] All were in the form of remonstrances only, neither intending outright opposition. Edmund Pendleton wished only to make "a redress of grievances."

The obnoxious Navigation Act also disrupted the shipping industry of New England, then involving a thousand vessels, half that number being used in overseas trade. In attempting to enforce these laws, the King had given his officers "writs of assistance" by which they entered home and ship. James Otis of Boston, in February, 1761, lashed out at such enactments which gave to the officers of customs authority to search ships when and where they pleased. Otis argued that the writs were injurious to the rights of the people; that the law was opposite to the British Constitution, and that "an Act of Parliament against the Constitution is void."[29]

The Stamp Act passed the House of Commons on February 27, 1765, and was later agreed to by the Lords on March 8, without debate; without hearing the protests of the colonies. The circumstances of Virginians and their feelings over the tax had been expressed in a memorial to the House of Lords by the committee at a previous meeting of the Assembly, November 30, 1764. It stated:

> The late war made a debt of nearly one-half million dollars; this with the Indian wars, the low price of tobacco, lack of specie, and the late restrictions upon the trade of the colonies, rendered the circumstances of the people extremely distressful, and which, if taxes are accumulated upon them, by the British Parliament, will make them truly deplorable.

---

[27] *Ibid.*, I, p. 61.
[28] Henry, *Henry*, I, pp. 54–59.
[29] Henry, *Henry*, I, p. 63.

> Your memorialists cannot suggest to themselves any reason why they should not still be trusted with the property of their people, with whose abilities, and the least *burthensome* mode of taxing (with great deference to the superior wisdom of Parliament,) they must be best acquainted.
>
> If a sum of money must be raised in the colonies, why not in a constitutional way? And if a reasonable apportionmt be laid before the Legisl' of this country, their Past Compliance with his Majesty's several Requisitions during the late expensive War, leaves no room to doubt they will do everything that can reasonably be expected of them.

It was Grenville's purpose to assign 20,000 soldiers to America and by means of the Stamp Act to raise £300,000 for their support. Col. Isaac Barré, bearing a bullet wound in his cheek received while aiding General Wolfe at Quebec, arose in Parliament and opposed the taxation of the Americans, calling them "Sons of Liberty," and lashed out at Lord North's proposals. Camden in the House of Lords declared:

> My position is this—I repeat it, I will maintain it to my last hour—taxation and representation are inseparable; this position is founded on the laws of nature; it is more, it is itself an eternal law of nature; for whatever is a man's own is absolutely his own; no man hath a right to take it from him without his consent, either expressed by himself or representative; whoever attempts to do it attempts an injury; whoever does it commits a robbery; he throws down and destroys the distinction between liberty and slavery. Taxation and representation are coeval with, and essential to, this Constitution.

William Pitt, in the House of Commons, urged the repeal of the act, and said:

> I rejoice that America has resisted. Three millions of people so dead to all the feelings of liberty as voluntarily to submit to be slaves, would have been fit instruments to make slaves of the rest.

Benjamin Franklin, who had accepted the position of Agent for Massachusetts in London in order to secure the repeal of the Stamp Act, and had tried everything within his power to prevent its passage, wrote: "The tide was too strong against us. The nation was provoked by American claims of independence (of the Power of Parliament,) and all parties joined by resolving in this Act to settle the point. We might as well have hindered the sun's setting."[30]

The notice that the Stamp Act had become law "crept in" sometime during the last days of May before the meeting of the Assembly had adjourned. The Burgesses were notified of the bill passed in Parliament which proposed to lay stamp duty upon paper and leather, sheet, vellum, parchment, or skin—anything bearing printed or engrossed matter. This was to include all documents such as bonds, deeds, wills, marriage licenses, etc.; marriages so licensed would be null unless stamps were used.[31] Already sugar and molasses imported to the colony had been taxed. The law would place a stamp on all documents of a legal nature and was to go into effect on All Saints' Day, November 1, 1765. These extreme measures aroused all the colonies throughout America. Those who opposed the tax were called "Whigs" and "Patriots"; those supporting the administration were called "Loyalists" or "Tories."[32] Protests were made by nearly all the colonies against the raising of a tax without their consent and without representation in Parliament, but these were in the form of petitions only.

What, now, were the reactions of the leaders in the Colonies since the Stamp Act had become law? The historian William Wirt Henry says that it appears they had turned toward compliance:

Five weeks after news of the passage of the Act, the Chief Justice of the Colony of Massachusetts, Hutchinson, wrote the ministry: "The Stamp Act is received among us with as much decency as could be expected; it leaves no room for evasion, and will execute itself."[33] In Boston, James Otis, the member of the Assembly who had been the leading spirit behind the opposition in the northern colonies, now bowed to the decision of the Legislature saying, "We yield obedience to the Act granting duties."[34] Otis, however, influenced the Assembly in proposing to the colonies that a Stamp Act Congress be held in New York in October, "to consult together on the present circumstances of the colonies, and the difficulties to which they are and must be reduced, by the operation of the Acts of Parliament for levying

[30] *Ibid.*, pp. 59–63.
[31] *Ibid.*, I, p. 60.
[32] *Ibid.*, I, p. 60.
[33] *Ibid.*, I, p. 66.
[34] *Ibid.*, I, p. 64.

duties and taxes on the colonies; and to consider of a general and united, dutiful, loyal, and humble representation of their condition to His Majesty, and to the Parliament, and to implore relief."[35] This, the only action taken by the Massachusetts Legislature, observed William Wirt Henry, was aided by the royal Governor, Bernard, who thus gained control of the movement and managed to have two "government men," Oliver Partridge and Timothy Ruggles, associated with Otis on the delegation from that colony. A list of the colonies having a tendency toward submission to the Stamp Act is given in the following:

> So little did the legislature of New Hampshire care for the Act, that it adjourned without even accepting the invitation of Massachusetts. The Colony of Rhode Island appeared ready to submit to Parliament, as did Connecticut. From New York Lieutenant-Governor Colden wrote to the Ministry that the passage of the Act caused no disturbance in that colony. The legislature of New Jersey declined the invitation of Massachusetts to meet in a convention. The legislature of Pennsylvania was in session when intelligence of the Passage of the Act was received at Philadelphia but it adjourned without taking notice of it. The legislature of Delaware had no opportunity of taking action before the Congress met in New York on October 7, but no signs of resistance to the execution of the Act appeared in that colony. The Governor of Maryland reported that the Act would be carried into execution. In North Carolina the legislature, so far from resenting the passage of the Act, took steps, at the instance of Governor Tryon, to support the Church of England by a general tax, although many of the inhabitants were Dissenters. The legislature of South Carolina did not meet till July, and no sign of resistance was seen in that colony. Her legislature, however, was the first to respond favorably to the call of Massachusetts. In Georgia the Act was deemed an equal mode of taxation, and it had been defended by Knox, the Agent of the Colony. In Virginia the people prepared themselves to submit, but with despondent feelings. They determined, by frugality, and banishing articles of luxury of English manufacture, to cause the Act to recoil on England.[36]

Such were the conditions when the Burgesses assembled in Williamsburg May 1; none of the members proposed resistance or made further protests. "However much the matter may have been discussed in private and personal capacities, no one ventured

[35] *Ibid.*, I, p. 65.
[36] *Ibid.*, I, pp. 66–67.

to secure from the House of Burgesses any formal or official utterance on the subject."[37] Richard Lee, who had protested against the Act at the preceding session, was now absent. The majority of the people considered the Act oppressive and a violation of their rights, yet they knew no recourse to action.

Patrick Henry, seeing that the resources of the colonies which were the direct results of private enterprise were to be denied them, became provoked over the new tax, added now to the customs laws. It had been the exclusive right of Virginians for 157 years to levy their own taxes, none to be laid without consent of the parties to be taxed, as given by their respective representatives.

Henry, but nine days a member of the House, would not countenance submission. He was determined to lay bare the whole scheme of tax tyranny at the hands of the British ministry. He was thoroughly familiar with the earliest provisions contained in the charter granted by King James on April 10, 1606, to the London Company, which had declared the rights of the English colonies in America:

> Also we do, for us, our heirs, and successors, declare, by these presents, that all and every the persons, being our subjects, which shall dwell and inhabit within every or any of the said colonies and plantations, and every of their children, which shall happen to be born within any of the limits and precincts of the said several colonies and plantations, shall have and enjoy all liberties, franchises, and immunities, within any of our other dominions, to all intents and purposes as if they had been abiding and born within this our realm of England, or any other of our said dominions.[38]

The early acts of the Virginia Assembly of 1624 declared that the "Governor shall not lay any tax or impositions upon the Colony, their lands or commodities, other than by the authority of the General Assembly, to be levied and employed as the said Assembly shall appoint."[39]

With the Stamp Act now law, the people of the Virginia Colony awaited the decision of the Burgesses. Three days only remained before the House would adjourn; yet no one had come forward. It was May 29, Patrick Henry's 29th birthday. He had

---

[37] Chandler and Thames *Colonial Virginia*, p. 339.

[38] Henry, *Henry*, I, p. 50.

[39] Chandler and Thames, *Colonial Virginia*, pp. 143–144. Henry, *Henry*, I, p. 51.

waited, hoping that someone would venture forth to dispute the Act. "Finding the men of weight averse to opposition, and the commencement of the tax at hand, and that no person was likely to step forth," Mr. Henry "determined to venture, and alone, unadvised, and unassisted," wrote "on a blank leaf of an old law-book" his resolutions against the Stamp Act, which he showed to George Johnston of Fairfax, and John Fleming of Cumberland, who promised their support.[40]

Mr. Johnston took the floor and moved that the House go into the Committee of the Whole. Patrick Henry seconded the motion, which carried. Henry then arose and offered five resolutions; Johnston "seconded these resolutions successively."[41] They are given us with the preamble, the copy of which was in the hands of William Wirt Henry at the time he wrote the history:

> Whereas, The Honorable House of Commons, in England have of late drawn into question how far the General Assembly of this colony hath power to enact laws for laying of taxes and imposing duties payable by the people of this, his Majesty's most ancient colony; for settling and ascertaining the same to all future times, The House of Burgesses of this present General Assembly have come to the following resolves.
>
> Resolved, That the first adventurers and settlers of this his Majesty's colony and dominion brought with them, and transmitted to their posterity, and all other his Majesty's subjects since inhabiting in this his Majesty's said colony, all the privileges, franchises, and immunities that have at any time been held, enjoyed, and possessed by the people of Great Britain.
>
> Resolved, That by two royal charters, granted by King James the First, the colonists aforesaid are declared entitled to all the privileges, liberties, and immunities of denizens and natural-born subjects, to all intents and purposes as if they had been abiding and born within the realm of England.
>
> Resolved, That the taxation of the people by themselves, or by persons chosen by themselves to represent them, who can only know what taxes the people are able to bear, and the easiest mode of raising them, and are equally affected by such taxes themselves, is the distinguishing characteristick of British freedom, and without which the ancient Constitution cannot subsist.
>
> Resolved, That his Majesty's liege people of this most ancient

---

[40] Henry, *Henry,* I, pp. 81–82. In the words of Patrick Henry.

[41] *Ibid.,* I, p. 82. Wirt, *Henry,* 78–79. Jefferson to Wirt.

colony have uninterruptedly enjoyed the right of being thus governed by their own Assembly in the article of their taxes and internal police, and that the same hath never been forfeited or in any other way given up, but hath been constantly recognized by the Kings and people of Great Britain.

Resolved, therefore, That the General Assembly of this colony have the only and sole exclusive right and power to lay taxes and impositions upon the inhabitants of this colony, and that every attempt to vest such power in any person or persons whatsoever, other than the General Assembly aforesaid, has a manifest tendency to destroy British as well as American freedom.[42]

Two other resolutions written by Patrick Henry did not pass the House:[43]

Resolved, That his Majesty's liege people, the inhabitants of this colony, are not bound to yield obedience to any law or ordinance whatever, designed to impose any taxation whatsoever upon them, other than the laws or ordinances of the General Assembly aforesaid.

Resolved, That any person who shall, by speaking or writing, assert or maintain that any person or persons, other than the General Assembly of this Colony, have any right or power to impose or lay any taxation on the people here, shall be deemed an enemy of his Majesty's colony.[44]

The latter Dr. Tyler thinks should be numbered six and seven. He believes that all seven resolutions, with the Preamble, were introduced by Mr. Henry, that the last two were lost in the committee and the Preamble struck out. The resolutions were thrice read, according to the printed Journal. The four revised resolutions as written in the Journal, and the last two, appeared in the *Williamsburg Gazette*. But Dr. Tyler quotes William Gordon in his history of the American Revolution as saying: "A manuscript of the unrevised resolves soon reached Philadelphia, having been sent off immediately upon their passing, that the earliest information of what had been done might be obtained by the Sons of Liberty. . . . At New York the resolves were

---

[42] Henry, *Henry*, I, pp. 80–81. Tyler, *Henry*, pp. 69–70–71.

[43] *Ibid.*, I. p. 91. W. W. Henry quoted John Marshall, whose father was a member; also, Gordon's *History of the American Revolution* as saying they all passed the committee but the last two, which were lost.

[44] Morgan, *Henry*, p. 101. Morgan cited Dr. Tyler as saying the last two resolutions should be numbered six and seven. Henry, *Henry*, I, pp. 92–93.

handed about with great privacy: they were accounted so treasonable that the possessors of them declined printing them in that city." Dr. Tyler stated further that a copy of them was procured with much difficulty by an Irish gentleman from Connecticut, who "carried them to New England, where they were published and circulated far and wide in the newspapers without any reserve, and proved eventually the occasion of those disorders which afterwards broke out in the colonies. . . . The Virginia resolutions gave a spring to all the disgusted; and they began to adopt different measures."[45]

Mr. Henry's resolutions created a sensation. The people of Virginia have spoken "very sensibly," said the *Boston Gazette*, but Mr. Otis declared them treasonable, as did the leaders in government. Nevertheless, secret societies began to form under the name of The Sons of Liberty, promising by all lawful means to resist the Act.[46] In writing the resolutions, Patrick Henry expressed the first opposition to the Stamp Act, the first act of resistance after it had become law. In so doing, he affirmed the rights and liberties in the charters as had been understood by precedent. "The same principle was re-enacted in 1631, again in 1632, again in 1642, and still again in 1645, and again in the Articles of Agreement of 1652 between commissioners representing the Commonwealth of England and Cromwell and the 'Grand Assembly of the Governor, Council and Burgesses' of Virginia, in which articles are found these words: 'That Virginia shall be free from all taxes, customs and impositions whatsoever, and none to be imposed on them without the consent of the Grand Assembly.' "[47] Virginia's claim Patrick Henry would not see surrendered, and her position he was now reiterating.[48]

If Henry were only paraphrasing the previous memorials, and his resolves were merely a repetition of those of December 1764, why did the old guard attempt to rescind Henry's? Why did Henry's resolutions, if similar, throw them into such terror; cause such an uproar, and the debate become "most bloody"? Jefferson was wrong in giving reasons such as: Henry was opposed by the old members on the ground that the same sentiments had been expressed at their preceding session in a more concilia-

---

[45] Tyler, *Henry*, op. cited., p. 80.
[46] Henry, *Henry*, I, p. 94.
[47] Chandler and Thames, *Colonial Virginia*, p. 143.
[48] *Ibid.*, p. 143.

tory form, to which the answers were not yet received.[49] The answer *had* been received. A copy of the Stamp duties from the Agent of the Burgesses in Britain had been received "near the end of the session."[50] This had precipitated Henry's argument.

Edmund Pendleton, an ardent supporter of the administration's policies, wrote 25 years later that he was not present at the Stamp Act proceedings when Patrick Henry introduced his resolutions.[51] Of course, this was many years after the Revolution had been won. Dr. David John Mays is perhaps right in assuming that Pendleton did go home, and that Jefferson was mistaken in asserting that Pendleton was one of the leaders of the opposition to Henry's Stamp Act resolves. But was this not Pendleton's usual procedure—opposing every opposition to the Crown? Grigsby states that in regard to the great legislative measures which paved the way for the Revolution, he (Pendleton) was invariably found in the negative, and that he opposed the Stamp Act resolutions.[52] Governor Fauquier did not list Pendleton among those of the "most strenuous opposers of this rash heat,"[53] but neither did he name Robert Carter Nicholas, another staunch conservative who did oppose Henry's resolutions.

Mays stated, "After he (Pendleton) had driven his program through the House, only to see it (the loan-office scheme) beaten in the Council, he thought his work for that session was over, and thereafter his place in the House was empty." (Mays acknowledged that Pendleton was one of the leaders in the agitation of the loan-office scheme, and made examination of the Treasurer's accounts.) He left for home. This "mistake caused him to miss some of the stirring scenes, for the whole Stamp Act controversy was suddenly thrust upon the Burgesses."[54] "How was Pendleton to know, as he turned toward Caroline, that both Lords and Commons would pass the Stamp Act 'with less opposition than a turnpike bill. . . .' "[55] asked Mays. Pendleton must then have overlooked the letter from the Agent containing the copy of the Stamp Act duties that came in at the end of the

[49] Henry, *Henry*, I, p. 82; Jefferson to Wirt, *Wirt Henry*, pp. 78–79.

[50] Mays, *Pendleton*, I, p. 161, Pendleton to Madison: Henry, *Henry*, I, p. 88. Governor Fauquier to the Lords of Trade, explained that near the end of the session a copy of the Stamp Act crept into the House.

[51] *Ibid.*, I, p. 163.

[52] Grigsby, *The Virginia Convention of 1776*, p. 47.

[53] Henry, *Henry*, I, p. 89.

[54] Mays, *Pendleton*, I, p. 161.

[55] *Ibid.*, I, p. 159.

session,[56] of which he later wrote Madison.[57] If it were not overlooked, did Pendleton go home to evade the whole issue? One concludes that Mays regrets Pendleton's absence, if he was absent, when Henry's resolves were put over in the House; that he had to confess to Pendleton's missing out when "Liberty had found a tongue," particularly at this critical juncture.

In referring to the epochal events in the House at this period, Dr. Mays and Mr. Brant have both quoted from the *Journal of a French Traveler in the Colonies* regarding Henry's Stamp Act speech. From the report in this journal, one sees Mr. Henry in a different focus from that of former historians. The Frenchman quoted Patrick Henry as apologizing to the Speaker of the House at the shouts of "treason," and attributed what he had said to the interest of his country's dying liberty, which he had at heart.[58] Several discrepancies confuse the picture of Henry's action. One point in question is the Frenchman's statement that: "The whole house was for Entering resolves on the records but they Differed much with regard to the Contents or purpose thereof."[59] This is contrary to facts as shown by the margin of votes, and by the actions of the opposition themselves, who tried to strike the resolutions off the records. Had the whole House been for entering the resolves on the Journal, the debate would not have been "most bloody." As to Henry's alleged apologizing when the cry of "treason" was heard—this is a hitherto unheard statement. Neither Governor Fauquier, Judge Carrington, the Rev. William Robinson, nor Jefferson,[60] who gave eyewitness accounts, mentioned any compromise. Mays himself said, "Henry was loose and could not be stopped."[61] Had Henry recoiled at the sound of "treason," there would have been no occasion for the bitterness that ensued, neither would Henry have hurled back the words: "Make the most of it!" Patrick Henry did not recoil from his principles. He had not drawn back when the outbursts of "treason" were heard in the Parson's case, neither did he stop talking. Perhaps the Frenchman could not understand the "tor-

---

[56] Henry, *Henry*, I, p. 88. Fauquier to the Lords of Trade; Mays, *Pendleton*, I,

[57] Mays, *Pendleton*, I, p. 161. Pendleton, Col. James Madison, Feb. 15, 1766.

[58] Mays, *Pendleton*, I, p. 162, n. Brant, *Madison, The Virginia Revolutionist, 1751–1780*, pp. 185–186.

[59] *Ibid.*, I, p. 162; See Frenchman's praise, Brant, *Madison*, p. 421 n.

[60] *Ibid.*, I, p. 83. Jefferson stated, "that Burk's statement of Mr. Henry's consenting to withdraw two resolutions, by way of compromise with his opponents, is entirely erroneous."

[61] *Ibid.*, I, p. 162.

rents of sublime eloquence" from Patrick Henry. Ten years later, July 1775, Edmund Pendleton and his coterie of old guards, Randolph, Wythe, Bland and Nicholas, as well as Jefferson, Mason and others in the Convention, would still be declaring their faith and true allegiance to his Majesty, George the Third, their only lawful and rightful King, and promising to defend him to the utmost of their power.[62]

Brant, Madison's biographer, also referred to the quotations from the Frenchman's journal. Young Madison, then 14 years old, was enrolled at Robertson's Academy, under the instruction of Patrick Henry's great-uncle. He was not present for the Stamp Act drama. Brant said, "Henry's rule of conduct was simple: always to be on the popular side and never too far ahead."[63] Henry's biographer, William Wirt, had quite a different opinion of Henry's political intrepidity. He declared:

> . . . it has sometimes been objected to him, that he waited on every occasion, to see which way the popular current was sitting, when he would artfully throw himself into it, and seem to guide its course. Nothing can be more incorrect: it would be easy to multiply proofs to refute the charge;—but I shall content myself with a few which are of general notoriety.[64]

Mr. Wirt used five pages in proving his point, but the scope of this chapter will permit only a part of the facts to be given:

> The upper circle of society did not take its impulse from the people, Patrick Henry unquestionably gave the revolutionary impulse to this circle, as affirmed by Mr. Jefferson; demonstrated by the resistance given Mr. Henry's measures, by those who afterward became staunch advocates of the revolution; and by Franklin's sentiment, in which he considered resistance to the British power to be premature.
>
> In the resolutions (on the Stamp Act) ushered into the House by Patrick Henry: on this great occasion, it is manifest that he did not wait for the popular current; but on the contrary, he alone, by his single power, moved the mighty mass of stagnant waters, and changed the silent lake into a roaring torrent.
>
> In the Powder Affair: the upper circle were disposed to acquiesce in the plunder of the magazine; the people were composed, except in Henry's immediate sphere of influence; yet,

---

[62] Brenaman, *A History of Virginia Conventions,* p. 25. Grigsby, *The Virginia Convention of 1776,* p. 148

[63] Brant, *James Madison, The Virginia Revolutionist, 1751–1780,* p. 186.

[64] Wirt, *Henry,* p. 432. (1836 edition)

> in spite of the entreaties and supplications, and the threats of Dunmore, Henry pressed firmly and intrepidly on, until the object of his expedition was accomplished; in the second convention (his 'call to arms') Mr. Henry carried his bold measure in spite of the pacific counsels of Randolph, Pendleton, Nicholas and Wythe; in the Federal Constitution, with the majority in favor of its adoption, Patrick Henry was the chief leader of the opposition. . . .[65]

But to return to the Stamp Act; the Rev. James Maury, who had lost his suit in the Parson's Cause because of Patrick Henry, was now rejoicing over the turn of events in a letter to Mr. John Fountaine in London, December 31, 1765: "But what has given a most general alarm to all the colonists on this continent, and to most of those in the islands . . . is a late Act of the British Parliament, subjecting us to a heavy tax. . . . The execution of this Act . . . hath been, with unprecedented unanimity, opposed and prevented. . . . For this 'tis probable some may brand us with the odious name of rebels, and others may applaud us for that generous love of liberty which we inherit from our forefathers."[66]

Other contemporary evidence should be cited to clear up further questions. Governor Fauquier wrote on June 5 apologizing to the Lords of Trade for Mr. Henry's actions, which had caused him to dissolve the Assembly:

> On Wednesday, May 29, just at the end of the session, . . . there being but thirty-nine present, a motion was made to take into consideration the Stamp Act, a copy of which had crept into the House; and in a committee of the whole, five resolutions were proposed and agreed to, all by very small majorities. On Thursday, the 30th, they were reported and agreed to by the House . . . the greatest majority being twenty-two to seventeen; for the fifth resolution, twenty to nineteen. On Friday, the 31st, there having happened a small alteration in the House, there was an attempt to strike all the resolutions off the journals. The fifth, which was thought the most offensive, was accordingly struck off, but it did not succeed as to the other four. The most strenuous opposers of this rash heat were the late Speaker, the King's Attorney, and Mr. Wythe; but they were overpowered by the young, hot, and giddy members. In the course

[65] *Ibid.*, pp. 432–433–434–435–436. When Patrick Henry took the high road to independence, through revolution, could this be called the popular side? True, discontent was popular, but was not his prescience as to the outcome, doubtful?
[66] Henry, *Henry*, I, pp. 97–98.

of the debates I have heard that very indecent language was used by Mr. Henry, a young lawyer, who had not been above a month a member of the House, and who carried all the young members with him. . . . .[67]

The language of Mr. Henry referred to here was, no doubt, that spoken of in the letter of the Rev. William Robinson, Commissary for Virginia and a cousin of the Speaker of the House, John Robinson. Mr. Robinson appears to be sulking under his cousin's disgrace. Writing in a letter to his kinsman, the Bishop of London, on August 12, 1765, he referred to the Mr. Henry of the "Parson's Cause" and continued with the following:

He has since been chosen a representative of one of the counties, in which character he has lately distinguished himself in the House of Burgesses, on occasion of the arrival of an Act of Parliament for stamp duties while the Assembly was sitting. He blazed out in a violent speech against the authority of Parliament and the King, comparing his Majesty to a Tarquin, a Caesar, and a Charles the First, and not sparing insinuations that he wished another Cromwell would arise. He made a motion for several outrageous resolves, some of which passed, and were again erased as soon as his back was turned. Such was the behavior in the Lower House of Assembly, that the Governor could not save appearances without dissolving them. They were accordingly dissolved, and Mr. Henry, the hero of whom I have been writing, is gone quietly into the upper parts of the country, (Mr. Robinson is writing from King & Queen County) to recommend himself to his constituents by spreading treason, and enforcing firm resolution against the authority of the British Parliament. This is at least the common report. The concluding resolve which he offered to the House, and which fell among the rejected ones, was that any person who should write or speak in favor of the Act of Parliament for laying stamp duties, should be deemed an enemy to the colony of Virginia; such notions has he of liberty and property, as well as of authority.[68]

But here is Mr. Henry's own modest account, in his handwriting on the back of the paper containing his resolutions:

The within resolutions passed the House of Burgess in May, 1765. They formed the first opposition to the Stamp Act and the scheme of taxing America by the British Parliament.

---

[67] Henry, *Henry*, I, pp. 88–89

[68] *Ibid.*, I, pp. 89–90.

All the colonies, either through fear, or want of opportunity to form an opposition, or from influence of some kind or other, had remained silent. I had been for the first time elected a Burgess a few days before, was young, inexperienced, unacquainted with the forms of the House, and the members that composed it. Finding the men of weight averse to opposition, and the commencement of the tax at hand, and that no person was likely to step forth, I determined to venture, and alone, unadvised, and unassisted, on a blank leaf of an old law-book, wrote the within. Upon offering them to the House violent debates ensued. Many threats were uttered, and much abuse cast on me by the party for submission. After a long and warm contest the resolutions passed by a very small majority, perhaps of one or two only. The alarm spread throughout America with astonishing quickness, and the Ministeral party were overwhelmed. The great point of resistance to British taxation was universally established in the colonies. This brought on the war which finally separated the two countries and gave independence to ours. Whether this will prove a blessing or a curse, will depend upon the use our people make of the blessings which a gracious God hath bestowed on us. If they are wise, they will be great and happy. If they are of a contrary character, they will be miserable. Righteousness alone can exalt them as a nation. Reader! Whoever thou art, remember this: and in thy sphere practice virtue thyself, and encourage it in others.

P. Henry.[69]

The original, priceless manuscript of Patrick Henry's Stamp Act Resolves, including the above explanatory statement, was sold in 1910 in Philadelphia, by the S. V. Henkel's auction house, for $1,400.

Thomas Jefferson bears witness to the genius of Patrick Henry in his autobiography, written in later life:

I attended the debate at the door of the lobby of the House of Burgesses, and heard the splendid display of Mr. Henry's talents as a popular orator. They were great indeed; such as I have never heard from any other man. He appeared to me to speak as Homer wrote.[70]

Mr. Jefferson thus salutes Mr. Henry's oratory. But what was this Revolutionary hero doing at this zero hour—the hero of "The Common Glory" of present-day historians? Where lay

---

[69] *Ibid.*, I, pp. 81–82.
[70] *Ibid.*, I, p. 83.

Jefferson's pen when America's destiny was being determined, which enabled him later to draft the Declaration of Independence? Then, but a law student, Jefferson was standing spellbound against the doorpost in the old capitol at Williamsburg, listening to Patrick Henry. As recalled by Jefferson many years later, here is the account which he sent to Wirt:

> Mr. Henry moved and Mr. Johnson seconded these resolutions successively. They were opposed by Messrs. Randolph, Bland, Pendleton, Wythe and all the old members, whose influence in the House had, till then, been unbroken. They did it not from any question of our rights, but on the ground that the same sentiments had been, at their preceding session, expressed in a more conciliatory form, to which the answers were not yet received. But torrents of sublime eloquence from Henry, backed by the solid reasoning of Johnston, prevailed. The last, however, and strongest resolution was carried but by a single vote. The debate on it was most bloody. I was then but a student, and stood at the door of communication between the House and the lobby(for as yet there was no gallery) during the whole debate and vote; and I well remember that, after the members on the division were told and declared from the chair, Peyton Randolph (the Attorney General) came out at the door where I was standing and said, as he entered the lobby: "By God, I would have given 500 guineas for a single vote"; for one would have divided the House, and Robinson was in the chair, who he knew would have negatived the resolution. Mr. Henry left town that evening, and the next morning, before the meeting of the House, Colonel Peter Randolph, then of the Council, came to the Hall of Burgesses, and sat at the clerk's table till the House-bell rang, thumbing over the volumes of journals, to find a precedent for expunging a vote of the House, which, he said, had taken place while he was a member or clerk of the House, I do not know which. I stood by him at the end of the table a considerable part of the time, looking on, as he turned over the leaves, but I do not recollect whether he found the erasure. In the meantime, some of the timid members, who had voted for the strongest resolution, had become alarmed; and as soon as the House met, a motion was made and carried to expunge it from the journal. There being at that day but one printer, and he entirely under control of the Governor, I do not know that the resolution ever appeared in print. I write this from memory, but the impression made on me at that time was such as to fix the facts indelibly in my mind. I suppose the original journal was among those destroyed by the British

> or its obliterated face might be appealed to. And here I will state that Burk's statement of Mr. Henry's consenting to withdraw two resolutions by way of compromise with his opponents, is entirely erroneous.[71]

In the above, Jefferson supposes that perhaps the original journal was among those destroyed by the British. But Judge Paul Carrington, a member of the House, stated that on May 30, the day after Mr. Henry left for home, on motion of the Attorney General, the fifth resolution was erased from the record, and adds that the journal was missing soon afterward.[72] Judge Carrington explained to Wirt that the manuscript journal was missing ten years before hostilities between the two countries and could not have been destroyed as Jefferson supposed.[73] From Jefferson's statement and Governor Fauquier's letter to the Lords of Trade, we ascertain that the first four resolutions, which were carried by a majority of 22 to 17, alone remained on the journal as the final official utterance of Mr. Henry. The fifth and the most important of the resolutions, giving impetus to the rest, was expunged from the journal after Mr. Henry was well out of town.

Had the Stamp Act gone into effect, it would have cost the sum of £50,000 sterling to the Virginia Colony alone. Today, in the sixth decade of the twentieth century, with an American tax system involving a debt of 1.25 trillion,[74] little sympathy may be given the colonies over their objection to the Stamp Act. By comparison, it was a mere pittance. Their debt from the French War was only two and a half million. There was no high cost of living in those Revolutionary days, except for salt. Extracted from sea water, this commodity sold for $10 a bushel. In 1776,[75] a lady's velvet bonnet could be bought for $2; a hind of veal weighing 23 pounds cost only $5.50; a 16-pound side of lamb—$3.00. But the amount of the tax was not the issue. It was those early agreements; those claims to self-government; those rights

---

[71] *Ibid.*, I, pp. 82–83.

[72] *Ibid.*, I, p. 84. Campbell, *Ancient Dominion of Virginia*, p. 543.

[73] Wirt, *Henry*, p. 80 (1836 ed.) The journal containing Henry's resolutions were in all probability destroyed by the Tory officebearers who were guardians for the king.

[74] Senator Harry F. Byrd (D-Va), said the total debt and other commitments of the United States Government are approaching 1.25 trillion, May 31, 1962.

[75] The Letters of a merchant and his family, in the Estate of Bayard Blackwell Rodman, New York Public Library, shows the high cost of living in 1776.

so dear to the people, that were involved, and which Patrick Henry had no idea of surrendering.

With the history of England Mr. Henry was thoroughly familiar. Magna Charta was a symbol before him. He knew that tyranny and oppression could not be borne if the colonies were to remain free and independent. He was willing to risk his life and his property for principles of government. He knew that once the Stamp Act was submitted to, it would be fully established and he tolerated not a thought of submission. With eloquence beyond all power of description, Patrick Henry boldly and courageously assailed the wicked practices of the Crown. Gripping his resolves in his hand, his eyes flashing, he cried: "Caesar had his Brutus, Charles the First his Cromwell, and George the Third"—"Treason," shouted Speaker Robinson, "Treason, Treason!" exclaimed some of the older members. "And George the Third," he repeated, "may profit by their example—if this be treason make the most of it."

In this his first sitting in the House, with his words ringing in every ear, Patrick Henry had now become a leader.

On the evening of May 30, after the adoption of the resolutions,[76] Mr. Henry rode homeward, leaving the cares of Williamsburg behind him for a time. He had now to turn some attention to his frail wife and young children. Judge Carrington, who walked a pace at his side, patted his horse as he extended congratulations and reassuring farewells.[77]

Back in Hanover, he would be asked how he could, so soon after his arraignment of the King in the Parson's Cause, have the courage to become the champion of the Stamp Act Resolutions. According to his own words to Judge Tyler:

"He was convinced of the rectitude of the cause and his own views, and that although he well knew that many a just cause had been lost, and for wise purposes Providence might not interfere for its safety, yet he was well acquainted with the great extent of our back country, which would always afford him a safe retreat," he declared. Moreover, "he was always satisfied that a united sentiment, and sound patriotism, would carry us safely to the wished for port, and if the people would not die or be free, it was of no consequence what sort of government they lived under."[78]

---

[76] Henry, *Henry*, I, p. 84.

[77] *Ibid.*, I, p. 84, n.

[78] Judge Tyler's MS. to William Wirt; Henry, *Henry*, I, p. 109.

Governor Fauquier, finding he could not enforce the stamp duties, wrote the ministry 14 days later: "Government is set at defiance, not having strength enough in her hands to enforce obedience to the laws of the Community."[79] Henry's Stamp Act Resolutions, flashed from the pages of the *Williamsburg Gazette*, "rolled back the opening scene to the Revolution and established full resistance throughout the colonies." His opposition to the Stamp Act was to lead directly to the establishment of American independence.

In Patrick Henry's calling the King's hand and revivifying the colonies' covenants was "inaugurated the beginning of ostensible opposition to British government. . . ."[80] The passage of his resolutions "was the first great blow which British supremacy received on this side of the Atlantic."[81]

---

[79] Henry, *Henry*, I, p. 95.
[80] Chandler & Thames, *Colonial Virginia*, p. 356.
[81] Grigsby, The Virginia Convention of 1776, p. 7

VII

ORATOR OF NATURE AND REVOLUTIONARY CAUSES

The ancient Anglo-Saxon foundation of all our criminal justice is trial by jury. . . . We regard it as a fundamental safeguard of our democratic liberties and life, and a principle which has been woven into the whole history of our judicial system that the supreme question, "Guilty or Not Guilty" shall be decided by ordinary folk.
—Winston Churchill, House of Commons, 1948

AFTER THE REPEAL of the Stamp Act, the name of Patrick Henry was on every tongue. Wherever men gathered, at taverns, on stagecoaches and at every meeting of importance, Henry, and the Stamp Act virtually nullified, were discussed by Whigs and Tories alike. At the time of his famous resolutions, he was representing Louisa County in the Assembly, but it is doubtful that he had removed his family to the Roundabout Plantation until the fall of 1765. It has been pointed out that his carpenter was employed from March 1, 1765,[1] evidently to construct the Louisa home, which could hardly have been completed by the last of May. "Tradition says that Mr. Henry settled in this county in 1764, and left here in 1767."[2] But it is also pointed out that there was a conveyance of land in 1770 as well as in 1764, and that his name is seen frequently in the records of Louisa County.[3] His accounts show that he sold his home, Piney

[1] Meade, *Henry*, I, p. 155. Henry, *Henry*, I, p. 70. "A bond executed in August, 1765, describes him as a resident of Hanover County."

[2] Morgan, *Henry*, p. 113.

[3] *Ibid.*, pp. 113–114. Morgan cites the letter of Captain W. T. Meade of Louisa.

Slash, in the lower end of Hanover, in 1764, for £350.[4] It is possible that the Henrys remained at Piney Slash cottage until 1765 before moving to Louisa, even though the property had been sold. Where the Henry family made their home on their return to Hanover has not been ascertained. Patrick Henry did not purchase Scotchtown until 1771.[5] But one question presents itself: Could the Henry family have shared half of the large Scotchtown manor house with their cousin, Mary Coles and her husband John Payne, until the Payne home on a part of the Coles Hill tract was completed?

In Henry's move to the Roundabout Valley in Louisa, some of his critics, ignorant of the terrain, have taken the word to mean that Patrick Henry was always moving "roundabout." Such was not the case. Mr. Henry doubtless hated to leave his many relatives and friends in Hanover, but duty called him and the path was opened up leading to the Virginia Assembly, although it would be only a short period before he would be called back to Hanover to represent his longtime neighbors. Moreover, he must better his opportunities. The Roundabout Valley was "just between two great thoroughfares that led from the mountains to the seaboard; and tradition says that the location was then considered one of the best in this region."[6] Patrick Henry knew what he was doing. His fee books mark his "success and industry" as a lawyer. "In 1764 he charged five hundred and fifty-five fees; in 1765, five-hundred and fifty-seven; in 1766, when the colony was under great political excitement, his fees fell off to one hundred and fourteen; in 1767 they reached five hundred and fifty-four, and then the renewal of the trouble with England reduced his business, until finally, in 1774, the courts were closed. Thus he charged in 1769 one hundred and thirty-two fees; in 1770, ninety-four; in 1771, one hundred and two; in 1772, forty-three; in 1773, seven; and 1774, none."[7] This does not include the fees in criminal cases. Regarding Mr. Henry's disposition and abilities as a lawyer, Thomas Jefferson wrote William Wirt:

> I think he was the best humored man in society I almost ever knew and the greatest orator that ever lived; he had a consummate

[4] Henry, *Henry,* I, pp. 121–122.

[5] *Ibid.,* I, p. 149. Colonel Samuel Meredith stated that Mr. Henry returned to Hanover in '67 or '68 when he purchased Scotchtown. Morgan, *Henry,* p. 433.

[6] Morgan, *Henry,* p. 114.

[7] Henry, *Henry,* I, pp. 119–120.

knowledge of the human heart, which directing the efforts of his eloquence enabled him to attain a degree of popularity with the people at large never perhaps equalled, his judgement on other matters was inaccurate, and in matters of law it was not worth a copper; he was avaricious and rotten hearted; his two great passions were the love of money and of fame; but when these two came into competition the former predominated.[8]

Jefferson also stated:

He turned his views to the law, for the acquisition or practice of which he was too lazy. His powers over a jury were so irresistible, that he received great fees for his services and had the reputation of being insatiable in money. He was totally unqualified for anything but mere jury cases, he devoted himself to these, and chiefly to the criminal business. From these poor devils, it was always understood that he squeezed exorbitant fees of 50, 100, and 200 £.[9]

Two collaborating historians have observed in this connection: "For misinformation and misunderstanding of Mr. Henry's career as a lawyer, Thomas Jefferson is supposed to be largely responsible. Fortunately in more recent years certain documents have been brought to light which prove that Mr. Henry was an unusually successful lawyer from the beginning, and that many of the impressions hitherto had concerning his capacity and fitness for the practice of law were entirely erroneous."[10] But Mr. Jefferson added this to his estimate of Patrick Henry, the lawyer, in a letter to Mr. Wirt:

He never undertook to draw pleadings if he could avoid it, or to manage that part of the cause, and very unwillingly engaged but as an assistant to speak in the cause, and the fee was an indispensable preliminary, observing to the applicant that he kept no accounts, never putting them to paper, which was true.[11]

Jefferson's statements here are not factual. Mr. Henry's rates were considered moderate for the times, and this is borne out in the case of the Parson's Cause, one of the most important legal cases in American history, in which he charged Thomas

[8] Stan V. Henkels, p. 1. Introduction to the letters of Thomas Jefferson to William Wirt. First appeared in the Historical Society of Pennsylvania, October, 1910. Later issued privately by Mr. John Gribbel, of Philadelphia. Virginia State Library.

[9] Letters of Thomas Jefferson to William Wirt, Gribbel Collection, pp. 9–10.

[10] Chandler & Thames, *Colonial Virginia*, pp. 336–337.

[11] Letters of Thos. Jefferson to Wm. Wirt, p. 10.

Johnson the modest sum of fifteen shillings as attorney for the defendants.[12]

At such rates, he must have been an excellent businessman in order to provide for his fast-growing family. "This he did, and in addition was able to lay the foundation of a comfortable estate. Such a practice demonstrates his industry, business capacity, and legal acquirement."[13] But Patrick Henry believed in "frugal living" and he used great economy and careful management in his affairs. In this way, he was able by 1764 to lend money to his father, and in 1767 to his father-in-law. His plantation in Louisa was bought with funds lent his father, and with the loans he had made to Mr. Shelton he was able to buy from him 1,400 acres on Mockison Creek, and one tract of 940 acres on the Holston River, and still another tract on the same river of 995 acres.[14] Thus, at the age of 32, Patrick Henry owned more than 3,335 acres, and he was soon to purchase the Scotchtown property.

It was about this time, 1767, that Mr. Henry took William Christian into his office as a law student. Christian later won the hand of Henry's sister, and under Governor Henry's dispatch, would daringly defend the frontiers from the Indians.

Two years later Patrick Henry would find himself face-to-face with the ablest men in the profession by coming to the bar of the General Court. Here he would contend with all comers and never be found wanting in legal knowledge. Before the General Court as counsel for the captain of a Spanish vessel in a case in Admiralty involving libel of a cargo under the Navigation Act, Mr. Henry's argument and eloquence made him "greatly superior" to Pendleton or any of the other counsel, according to William Nelson, a member of the court. Later, Carter Nicholas, the treasurer, "who had enjoyed the first practice at the bar," would turn over his unfinished business to Mr. Henry, recognizing his fidelity and fine attainments.[15]

In the court, Patrick Henry wore a black suit and tie wig. A Roman cast was noted in his profile. His nose was long, and his forehead high and straight. His eyes—described as the finest feature in his face—have been called blue, and a deep gray, with eyelashes long and black, and dark eyebrows that made his eyes appear black and penetrating. His cheekbones were said to

[12] Meade, *Henry,* I, p. 126.
[13] Henry, *Henry,* I, p. 120.
[14] *Ibid.*
[15] Henry, *Henry,* I, p. 124.

be rather high and thin; he had a well-rounded chin. "His countenance was grave, penetrating, and marked with the strong lineaments of deep reflection," and his manner was solemn and impressive.[16] He is said to have had "a perfect command of a strong and musical voice, which he raised or lowered at pleasure, and modulated so as to fall in with any given chord of the human heart."[17]

In reviewing Patrick Henry's sudden rise to fame in the revolution, and his powerful effect as an orator, the question naturally arises: Was he "the first orator in America," or simply a mere declaimer and demagogue as branded? His biographer, William Wirt, answers the question:

"A mere declaimer and demagogue could never have gained, much less have kept for more than thirty years, that ground which Mr. Henry held with the people." He imputed such statements to "obviously the effect of envy and mortified pride" by those "whose ranks he had scattered, and whom he had thrown into the shade. . . ."[18]

What, then, were the awakening excellencies of his genius—that magic touch with which he drew men to him? What were his essential qualities as an orator?

John Randolph of Roanoke is quoted as saying:

"The united powers of painting and eloquence could, alone, give a faint idea of what he was. . . ." that "he was a Shakespeare and Garrick combined." He said that "when Henry was speaking one felt like whispering to his neighbor, 'hush, don't stir, don't speak, don't breathe!'"[19] It was said also that "Patrick Henry was not less admirable as a man than as an orator; for his religious convictions were even profounder than his political, and he was irreproachably faithful, besides, to every obligation of civic, social and domestic life."[20]

Elaborating further, the same speaker stated:

"Of Henry, it may be safely said that he belongs to the same category of supreme orators as Demosthenes, Cicero, Chatham and Mirabeau."

---

[16] Wirt, *Henry*, p. 427 (1836 ed.)

[17] Morgan, Henry, pp. 447–454, According to Judge Spencer Roane.

[18] Wirt, *Henry*, p. 84 (1836 ed.)

[19] Address on Patrick Henry and John Randolph of Roanoke, as Orators. Delivered by Wm. Cabell Bruce, (Father of the present Ambassador to Great Britain) At Charlotte Court House, Virginia, on November 4, 1935. p. 2.

[20] *Ibid.*

Dr. Tyler declared: "The genius of Patrick Henry was powerful, intuitive, swift; by a glance of the eye he could take in what an ordinary man might spend hours in toiling for; his memory held whatever was once committed to it; all his resources were at instant command; his faculty for debate, his imagination, humor, tact, diction, elocution, were rich and exquisite; he was also a man of human and friendly ways, whom all men loved, and whom all men wanted to help; and it would not have been strange if he actually fitted himself for the successful practice of such law business as was then to be had in Virginia, and actually entered upon its successful practice with a quickness the exact processes of which were unperceived even by his nearest neighbors."[21] In criminal cases he was said to be the "arch magician" who "by a few master-strokes upon the evidence, could in general stamp upon the cause whatever image or character he pleased and convert it into tragedy or comedy, and with a power which no efforts of his adversary could counteract."[22] In describing Mr. Henry as an orator, Mr. Wirt made the following observations:

> His delivery was perfectly natural and well timed. He had the habit of thinking for himself, and looking directly at every subject, with the natural eyes of his understanding . . . this habit of relying more on his own meditations than on books, was perhaps of service to him as an orator, for by this course, he avoided the beaten paths and roads of thought. . . . Some ascribe his excellence wholly to his manner, others, in great part, to the originality and soundness of his reasoning . . . many to his aphorisms; his wit; his pathos; the intrinsic beauty of his imagination, etc. . . . but it was not in any single charm, but the joint force and full result of all.
>
> The basis of Mr. Henry's intellectual character was *strong natural sense.* He had not the 'high polish' of the orators of England; nor the exuberant imagery which distinguishes those of Ireland . . . he was loose, irregular, desultory—sometimes rough and abrupt—careless in connecting the parts of his discourse, but grasping whatever he touched with gigantic strength. In short, he was the Orator of Nature. . . .[23]

From the November, 1766, session, till March 31, 1768, Governor Fauquier had been proroguing the Assembly from time

---

[21] Tyler, *Henry*, pp. 34–35.
[22] Wirt, *Henry*, p. 93. (1836 edition)
[23] *Ibid.*, pp. 439–440–442.

to time, but it had not slowed the spirit of resistance. Petitions were received by the Council, pointing to the dangers fatal to the liberties of a free people in the late *Acts of Parliament* from the Counties of Amelia, Chesterfield, Dinwiddie, Henrico, Prince William, and Westmoreland.[24]

The House of Burgesses was now called together in March 1768 to pacify the Indian frontier. Mr. Henry was appointed a member of a committee on Indian affairs, in which murders of friendly Indians were discussed. The committee agreed to strengthen the treaties with the Indians and to maintain a broader view of their relations to the colony, and to the laws against crime. In the November session, the committee stated "that all treaties with the Indians ought to be made by or under the authority of Government only, and that for any private person or persons to enter into negotiations with them, or to invite them into the colony for such treaty, is a great misdemeanor, and may be attended with the most dangerous consequences."[25] The Board of Trade had proposed as the western boundary with the Indians a line extending from the point where the extension north of the North Carolina line would strike the Holston River, to the mouth of the Great Kanawha on the Ohio. Mr. Henry was familiar with the Holston, having journeyed the year before to the western frontier, and he knew the value of this section and of the Mississippi to our commerce. He considered this matter of grave importance, since it would cut off some of Virginia's settlements and give to the Indians the large territory later known as Kentucky, and the greater part of what is now known as West Virginia, which would have exposed the settlers on the western frontiers to Indian attacks. In committee, Patrick Henry insisted upon a new line that would begin at the western end of the North Carolina line and run due west to the Ohio, taking in Kentucky.[26] Lord Hillsborough, the committee noted, had tried to divert settlement from this section, and immigration had instead been encouraged where he considered it to be more profitable and more easily controlled toward the seacoast. Through a treaty with the Six Nations of Indians at Fort Stanwix in November, 1768, Hillsborough had attempted to prevent the cession of this territory to the colonies. But then William Johnson and Thomas Walker, the former being in charge of the northern district and

[24] Henry, *Henry*, I, p. 133.
[25] *Ibid.*, I, p. 145; Journal of the House of Burgesses, 1769, pp. 137–138.
[26] *Ibid.*, I, pp. 145–146.

the latter representing Virginia, succeeded in having the Indian Nations cede the territory south of the Ohio as far as the Cherokee or Cumberland River. Mr. Henry was unwilling to abandon the claim and worked unceasingly for possession of the entire territory for the colonies, feeling that it belonged to Virginia through her chartered rights.[27]

Within the colonies there was now great rejoicing over the repeal of the Stamp Act; however, their joy was not to be for long. The King at once regretted his actions and decided on alternate measures of taxation equally burdensome. The Governors were instructed to recommend to the legislators the support of British soldiers who would soon be quartered among the colonies. This became known as the Billeting Act.

With the repeal of the Stamp Act came the collapse of the Rockingham Ministry. William Pitt, the Earl of Chatham and friend of the colonies, formed a new cabinet in which he hoped to help the cause, but before the end of the year his health worsened and he was obliged to leave London. Charles Townshend, Chancellor of the Exchequer, taking advantage of Pitt's absence, laughed at the colonies in their differences over internal and external taxes and called it "nonsense." Speaking loud enough for the merchants and colonial agents in the gallery to hear him, he said, "the distinction is ridiculous; if we have a right to impose the one, we have a right to impose the other," adding, "England is undone if this taxation is given up."[28] In May he proposed in the House of Commons that the legislature of New York, in British headquarters, be closed until the lawmakers met with the demands of the Billeting Act. Added to this was the Duty Act—port duty to be laid and collected in America on all articles such as oil, wine, fruits, glass, paper, lead, painters' colors, and tea. These measures were adopted and were to have taken effect November 20, 1767. The King, favoring the Act, was to enforce it through a board of trade of his own choosing, to be stationed in the colonies and directed under his authority.[29] Under the new Act the King's commission was given power to search and seize at will, and where assistance was necessary to call on the military and naval forces in the colonies.

The subtlety in juggling the Duty Act did not deceive Mr. Henry. The distinction between "internal" and "external" taxes

[27] *Ibid.*, I, pp. 146–147.
[28] *Ibid.*, I, p. 130.
[29] *Ibid.*, I, p. 131.

did not affect the nature of the Act. In this regulation of commerce, he saw plainly the intention to raise a revenue, and the question was still: Could Parliament "take money out of our pockets without our consent" by any tax whatsoever? The Burgesses had been prorogued at this time and Henry was now back in Hanover. Such news exasperated him. Losing no time, he quickly read the dispatch, wrestled into his coat, retied his wig, and immediately mounting his horse, rode away. Stopping off in Hanovertown, in upper Hanover, in Louisa; at taverns, stores and everywhere he went, Patrick Henry talked, calling at plantations along the countryside. When he pointed to the evils in the new Act, the people believed in him and trusted his leadership. As Jefferson told Daniel Webster, it was to Patrick Henry that we were indebted for the unanimity that prevailed among us. There were able writers also during this period. Richard Bland of Virginia penned an article entitled "An Enquiry into the Rights of the British Colonies." Samuel Adams, the spiritual patriot from Massachusetts, wrote many articles, as did also Daniel Dulany of Maryland and John Dickinson of Pennsylvania.

When the Massachusetts Assembly met in December, Samuel Adams persuaded the legislature to petition the King in behalf of the rights of the colonies, pointing to the injustice and oppression of the new acts of Parliament, and asking for their repeal. He also drafted a circular letter to be sent to all the colonies, urging their cooperation and efforts in obtaining a repeal and welcoming any suggestions they deemed wise.[30]

By the March session of the Virginia Assembly, Governor Fauquier had died, and John Blair was acting temporarily as president of the Council. Adams's letter was brought to the attention of the Assembly at this meeting. Petitions from many counties in Virginia had also been dispatched to the Burgesses, all protesting the injustice of the Act. After careful consideration, the Virginians replied to the Assembly of Massachusetts congratulating them on their stand for American liberty, and urged a united, firm, but decent oppostion to every measure affecting their rights, requesting that their decisions be made known to all the colonial assemblies.[31] Such a spirit of resistance prevailed at this time in the Virginia Assembly that a petition, boldly worded, was sent to the King, also a memorial to the House of Lords, and a remonstrance to the House of Commons.

[30] *Ibid.*, I, p. 138.

[31] *Ibid.*, I, p. 134.

Governor Bernard of Massachusetts, looking upon the circular letter of that Assembly as paving the way for a Confederacy, sent a copy to the British ministry. At this time, it seems, the people of England were heaping abuses on Governor Bernard as well as on the Americans. General Oglethorpe, seeing Bernard in a coffee shop, called him "a dirty, factious, scoundrel, and smelled strong of the hangman; that he had better leave the room, as unworthy to mix with gentlemen of character, but that he would give him the satisfaction of following him to the door, had he anything to reply. The Governor left the house like a guilty coward."[32] In the meantime, Charles Townshend had died before the Act took effect. He was replaced by Lord Hillsborough, who brought the Massachusetts letter to the attention of the Cabinet on April 15. It was considered as an incentive to rebellion. The King was enraged over the colonies' resistance, and regardless of the law involved, issued two royal orders: First, that the Assembly of Massachusetts rescind their circular letter, and second, that the assemblies of the other colonies treat it with contempt and further disregard. Should the King's orders be not complied with, their assemblies were to be immediately dissolved.[33]

Richard Henry Lee, writing to a gentleman of influence in England, March 27, 1768, concerning the oppressive measures—the Billeting Act, the act for suspending the Legislature, the duties on paints and glass, etc.—said of the latter, that inasmuch as the connection between us and the mother country rendered it necessary that we exclude all other nations, and take manufacture only from her, the imposition became arbitrary, unjust and destructive of that mutually beneficial connection which every good subject would wish to see preserved.[34]

At the next meeting of the Massachusetts Assembly in June, 1768, British ships stood in the harbor and a regiment of British troops was stationed in the town of Boston. Regardless of Governor Bernard's actions, the Assembly met as usual, and by a vote of 92 to 17 refused to rescind its letter. The Governor therefore immediately dissolved that Assembly. In London in November, before a meeting of Parliament, Massachusetts was singled out for her actions. Addresses were made in both Houses asking the King to have the offenders brought to England to be tried by a special commission, under punishment of treason. Such

[32] Wirt, *Henry*, p. 99 (1836 ed.) *Pennsylvania Gazette*, August 30, 1770.
[33] Henry, *Henry*, I, p. 135.
[34] Ballagh, *The Letters of Richard Henry Lee*, I, p. 27.

a procedure, which began with Henry the Eighth, before England had her colonies, was no longer in use in Britain, and the effort to revive and enforce it throughout America was cause for greater alarm.[35]

Immediately Virginia, with the other colonies, sent expressions of sympathy to Massachusetts. Baron de Botetourt was appointed the next Governor of the Virginia Colony, taking up his office in November, 1768. He was chosen for his attractive and friendly manner, in hopes that he might be able to sway the Virginians from their existing state of mind. In a speech before the new Assembly he told of the King's great esteem for the people of the colony and promised to use every effort to bring about good relations between his Majesty and his subjects, even refusing to issue writs of assistance to enforce the Revenue Act. Yet he made it a point to let the Assembly know that he would not tolerate their support of the actions taken by Massachusetts. But Governor Botetourt had not calculated the temper and firmness of the Virginians, nor had he yet heard the voice of Patrick Henry. In the new Assembly of May 11, 1769, Patrick Henry was present as a delegate from his own county of Hanover, and was pehaps living at Scotchtown, sharing the manor house with his cousins, the Paynes, until Scotchtown could be purchased in 1771. At this session, he was working steadily upon the Committees of Privileges and Elections, on Propositions and Grievances, and Religion—a position of power in which his services, so greatly valued, had now placed him.[36]

The House of Burgesses had now to decide what course to pursue. "It was a critical moment. Had Massachusetts been deserted, even the steady hand of Samuel Adams might not have been able to keep her in her course, for a desertion by Virginia would have caused most certainly a desertion by the other colonies, which looked for the action of Virginia with the greatest anxiety. In fact, the desertion of Massachusetts now would have stranded the bark of the Revolution."[37]

The Burgesses at once began deliberating the matter fully, having before them the late tyrannical actions of Parliament. In a committee of the whole on May 16, 1769, the following resolutions were adopted:

---

[35] Henry, *Henry,* I, p. 135.
[36] *Ibid.,* I, pp. 136–137.
[37] *Ibid.,* I, p. 137.

> Resolved, nemine contradicente [unanimously], That the sole right of imposing taxes on the inhabitants of this his majesty's colony and dominion of Virginia, is now, and ever has been, legally and constitutionally vested in the House of Burgesses, lawfully convened according to the ancient and established practice, with the consent of the Council, and of his Majesty the King of Britain, or his Governor for the time being.
>
> Resolved, That it is the undoubted privilege of the inhabitants of this colony, to petition their sovereign for redress of grievances, and that it is lawful and expedient to procure the concurrence of his Majesty's other colonies, in dutiful addresses, praying the royal interposition in favor of the violated rights of America.
>
> Resolved, That all trials for treason, misprision of treason, or for any felony or crime whatsoever, committed or done in this His Majesty's said colony and dominion, by any person or persons residing therein, ought of right to be had and conducted in and before His Majesty's courts held within his said colony, according to the fixed and known course of proceeding; and that the seizing of any person or persons residing in this colony, suspected of any crimes whatsoever committed therein, and sending such person or persons to places beyond the sea to be tried, is highly derogatory of the rights of British subjects, as thereby the inestimable privilege of being tried by a jury from their vicinage, as well as the liberty of summoning and producing witnesses in such trial, will be taken away from the party accused.
>
> Resolved, That an humble dutiful and loyal address, be presented to His Majesty, to assure him of our inviolable attachment to his sacred person and government, and to beseech his royal interposition, as the father of his people however remote from the seat of his empire, to quiet the minds of his loyal subjects of this colony, and to avert from them those dangers and miseries which will ensue, from the seizing and carrying beyond sea any person residing in America suspected of any crime whatsoever, to be tried in any other manner than by the ancient and long established course of proceeding.[38]

It was further "ordered that the Speaker of this House do transmit, without delay, to the Speakers of the several Houses of Assembly on this continent, a copy of the resolutions now agreed to by this Virginia House of Burgesses, requesting their concurrence therein," and also, "that the resolutions of the Lords, and the address of the Lords and Commons to the King, and the resolutions of this House reported and agreed to, be printed

[38] *Ibid.*, I, pp. 138–139.

in the *Virginia Gazette*." Nor did the Burgesses stop with these resolutions. An address was sent the King pointing to the violated rights as against the charters, and begging redress. Those chosen to outwit his Majesty were: Patrick Henry, John Blair, Richard Henry Lee, Carter Nicholas, Thompson Mason and Benjamin Harrison. Thomas Jefferson had now for the first time become a member of the House of Burgesses. The address to the King was turned over to the agent of the colony to be delivered to his Majesty, and copies were ordered published in the British papers.

These actions taken by the Burgesses were in full knowledge that the Assembly would be dissolved if discovered, and although the meeting was held behind closed doors, the ink was hardly dry on the pages of the Journal before they were called to appear before the governor and were accordingly dissolved. This was not the first time such actions had taken place, but the Burgesses were not now to be intimidated. Instead of returning to their homes as usual, the Virginians met quietly in the Apollo Room of the Raleigh Tavern at Williamsburg. Once seated around the long table, they pledged themselves against importing anything further from England which would be taxed. All the other colonies made similar agreements. Homespun suits would be the rage. At last Mr. Henry would be in style! The women of the colonies at once resolved to use every effort to supply their needs. Spinning wheels would hum and knitting needles fly. Through frugal living they would no longer need to rely on Great Britain for their necessities. Since tea would also be taxed, there would be no more tea parties among the colonial dames. Catnip, sage and raspberry would sustain them for a time.

When the news reached Parliament of the Non-Importation agreement in the colonies, a great cry arose from the merchants and manufacturers, who decided to petition the Prime Minister in their behalf. But in April, 1770, on a motion by Lord North, the duty on all articles except tea was repealed, the King contending that "there must always be one tax to keep up the right."[39] To the colonies there was no difference between taxed paper and taxed tea. In the meantime they had learned of the attack March 5 upon the people of Boston by British soldiers stationed in the streets of the town with fixed bayonets. Five citizens were killed and eight wounded.[40] This anxiety was

[39] *Ibid.*, I, p. 147.
[40] *Ibid.*, I, p. 148.

eased when the guilty soldiers were brought to trial in civil court and the troops moved temporarily from the town.

In the fall of 1770 Governor Botetourt died. The Virginia colony felt that he had earnestly solicited in their behalf, and they lamented his passing. He was succeeded by a Scotchman of Tory principles, John Murray, the Earl of Dunmore. Edmund Randolph said of the new governor that his manners and sentiments did not surpass barbarism, nor was he regulated by an ingredient of religion. Such were the descriptions of the new Governor sent to hold the whip over the "hot-headed" Virginians, as was the custom whenever there was open rebellion. Dishonest and arbitrary agents were put in power over the colonies in defiance of the British Constitution, assemblies were dismissed, laws were disregarded and changed. British ships were stationed at all important harbors with orders to obstruct commerce. Since January, "business had been dull beyond all precedent—scarcely a ship moving; debts not to be collected; money hardly to be had at any price; and the poorer sort of people in dire need for want of employment."[41] The sort of treatment accorded vessels belonging to the colonies is shown in the actions of the British ship, *Gaspee*, in the harbor of Providence, Rhode Island; it had used that harbor for the obstruction of commerce by stopping and searching vessels in an unlawful manner, seizing their cargoes.[42] These methods of piracy were covered by an act of Parliament passed in 1772, decreeing the death penalty for the least destruction to the British Fleet, with all offenders to be sent to England for trial.

Richard Henry Lee described conditions in the House of Burgesses in March, 1772, when he wrote Landon Carter thus: "I cannot give you a better account of this Session than by saying it began idly, proceeded busily, and is likely to end with having done nothing. The great bills were all drop't, either by the Council or in the House."[43]

Such were the prevailing conditions among the colonies when the Virginia Burgesses, having been prorogued by the Governor, held their meetings in secret in the Apollo Room, March 12, 1773. Mr. Henry and other members, realizing that urgent steps must be taken if they were to become a free and independent people, noted that what had happened in Narragansett

[41] Becker, *The Spirit of '76*, p. 33.
[42] Henry, *Henry*, I, pp. 155–156.
[43] Ballagh, *The Letters of Richard Henry Lee*, I, p. 63.

Bay could easily happen in Virginia. In the secret of the Raleigh Tavern, they consulted together on the state of affairs and determined upon a course of action. Resolutions were drawn up to be laid before the respective assemblies of the colonies. They condemned the court of inquiry lately held in Rhode Island in which power was given to transport persons accused of offences committed in America to places beyond the seas to be tried. A standing Committee of Correspondence was organized, composed of eleven members, of which Mr. Henry was one. Their business was to obtain and disseminate all information of acts and resolutions of the British Parliament to the sister colonies, which were requested to form similar committees to communicate from time to time with each other.[44]

Jefferson, in writing of this in his memoir, stated:

> Not thinking our old and leading members up to the point of forwardness and zeal which the times required, Mr. Henry, Richard Henry Lee, Francis L. Lee, Mr. Carr and myself agreed to meet in the evening, in a private room of the Raleigh, to consult on the state of things. There may have been a member or two more whom I do not recollect. We were all sensible that the most urgent of all measures was that of coming to an understanding with all the colonies, to consider the British claims as a common cause to all, and to produce a unity of action; and for this purpose that a committee of correspondence in each colony would be the best instrument for intercommunication; and that their first measure would probably be, to propose a meeting of deputies from each colony, at some central place who should be charged with the direction of the measures to be taken by all. We therefore drew up the resolutions which may be seen in Wirt, page 87. The consulting members proposed to me to move them, but I urged that it should be done by Mr. (Dabney) Carr, my friend and brother-in-law, then a new member, to whom I wished an opportunity should be given of making known to the house his great worth and talents. It was so agreed; he moved them; they were agreed to *nem.*con., and a committee of correspondence appointed of whom Peyton Randolph, the speaker, was chairman.[45]

Concerning the Committee of Correspondence, Richard Henry Lee wrote John Dickinson on April 4, 1773: "They have now adopted a measure, which from the beginning they should have fixed on, as leading to that union and perfect understanding

[44] Henry, *Henry*, I, pp. 159–160.

[45] *Ibid.*, I, pp. 160–161; *Wirt*, Henry, pp. 107–108.

with each other, on which the political salvation of America depends . . ."[46]

This union of counsel proved to be very important. It was the preliminary to the Continental Congress and American Union, according to the historian, W. W. Henry. Patrick Henry made an urgent and pressing plea in March, 1773, advocating the appointment of such a committee. Judge St. George Tucker (though not yet a judge), "had attached to the idea he had formed of an orator all the advantages of voice which delighted him so much in the speeches of Mr. Lee—" (though he had never heard a speech in public except from the pulpit—being then between nineteen and twenty)—"the fine polish of his (Mr. Lee's) language which that gentleman united with that harmonious voice, so as to make him sometimes fancy that he was listening to some being inspired with more than mortal powers of embellishment—and all the advantages of gesture which the celebrated Demosthenes considered as the first, second, and third qualifications of an orator." Mr. Tucker, though "not present when Mr. Henry spoke on this question," was told by some of his fellow-collegians that Mr. Henry far exceeded Mr. Lee, whose speech succeeded the next day. Mr. Tucker said, "Never before had I heard what I thought oratory; and if his speech was excelled by Mr. Henry's, the latter must have been excellent indeed."[47]

In writing to Mr. Wirt concerning the appointment of the standing Committee of Correspondence, Jefferson made no reference to the speeches of Patrick Henry or Richard Lee, the advocates of the committee. Jefferson, then 26, was elected a Burgess in 1769. He was named a member to the first general Committee of Correspondence, but "he was not a member of what now would be called the Executive Committee of that body of 11."[48] He named some of the members of the committee and placed Patrick Henry at the head of the list of those of forwardness and zeal, who were sensible that the most urgent measures were necessary in coming to an understanding with all the other colonies. Mr. Henry had become weary of the slow-moving compromises and the tepid resolutions at the hands of such men as Peyton Randolph and Edmund Pendleton. It was during this

---

[46] Henry, *Henry,* I, p. 162.

[47] *Ibid.*, I, pp. 164–165. Wirt, *Henry,* p. 109.

[48] The Historian, Dr. Douglas S. Freeman, *Revision of the 'Common Glory,'* Richmond News Leader, December 13, 1948.

critical time that he assailed the King with such fiery words that all at once the spectators in the gallery rushed out, believing the house to be on fire, which was not so. An onlooker, incited by Mr. Henry's speech, had lighted a torch to the royal flag as it hung suspended outside the building. Some of the Tidewater Tories, hearing the cry, rushed up to the cupola and doused the flag with a bucket of water.[49]

The Burgesses' proposals for a Committee of Correspondence and Inquiry were joyfully received among the colonies. The long-desired union was at last established and the people were greatly heartened. Honor was due in large measure to Patrick Henry and Richard Henry Lee. It was on July 25, 1768, that Mr. Lee first suggested the appointment of such a committee, and he and his close associate, Mr. Henry, usually seeing eye to eye on most views pertaining to the colony, had probably discussed the necessity for such a committee early that year and were perhaps only awaiting the country's readiness. This method of political correspondence was used in the days of the Stuart Kings. It seemed the answer now.

Among those responding to the actions taken by the Virginia Burgesses was the sister colony, Massachusetts. She wrote on May 27, 1773, saying: "This house has a very grateful sense of the obligations they are under to the House of Burgesses in Virginia, for their vigilance, firmness and wisdom, which they have discovered at all times in support of the rights and liberties of the American colonies, and do heartily concur with them in their said judicious and spirited resolves."[50]

Similar letters were received from the assemblies in the other colonies. In the meantime, the vessel *Gaspee*, which had caused so much concern, was seized by a group of armed patriots and burned. The people of Massachusetts, in the spring of 1773, petitioned the King for permission to support the colonial governor and judges out of their own coffers instead of having them paid by the royal treasury. This his Majesty refused, and being greatly angered, he set upon a new scheme of taxation. The news of the united resistance in the colonies having already reached London, threatened panic to the Ministry. The Non-Importation agreement between the colonies was having a serious and embarrassing effect upon the business of the kingdom and upon the

[49] Judge Roane's Ms. Letter to William Wirt.

[50] Henry, *Henry*, I, pp. 165–166.

Notable guests at unveiling of Patrick Henry bust in Richmond. Governor John Garland Pollard, center, with Wirt Henry Dabney, 5-year-old great-great-great grandson of Henry, and son of Mr. and Mrs. Fred A. Dabney of Richmond, right. F. William Sievers, Richmond sculptor of bust, at extreme right, front row, with State Senator Henry T. Wickham. Others in the group are related to the Henry family.

Courtesy Virginia State Library

Fork Church

Courtesy Virginia State Library

Rural Plains

Courtesy Virginia Cavalcade Magazine

Scotchtown today

Courtesy New York Public Library

Courtesy New York Public Library

Above:
Patrick Henry, from an early engraving

Left:
Dorothea Spotswood Henry, daughter of Patrick Henry, at 18. Portrait by Sharples

Courtesy Virginia State Library

Hanover Courthouse

Bust by F. William Sievers in Capitol at Richmond

East India Company, the latter having now accumulated 17,000,000 pounds of tea stored in warehouses in England without market. Being in financial difficulties, the company decided to ask for a loan, for which they applied to Parliament. It was proposed by Lord North in April that in order to relieve their distress, they be permitted to export their tea to America free of British duty, but that the colonies be required to pay a duty of three pence per pound.

When this news was learned, anger and indignation arose throughout the American colonies, and they determined to resist the Tea Act. Apprehension grew in the four important harbors from Boston to Charleston. The Massachusetts committee on October 21, 1773, wrote urging prompt action to meet this new threat. They insisted upon alertness and vigilance, with a readiness to come to the aid of any who might be singled out for oppression, as was "the true design of the establishment of our committee of correspondence." They suggested that the wise heads of the committees should consult to decide upon a right, agreeable to all, which they would not surrender. The one that all the colonies had emphasized read, "the sole and inalienable right to give and grant their own money, and to appropriate it to such purposes as they judge proper. . ." Adding, "we are far from desiring the connection between Great Britain and America should be broken. Esto perpetua is our most ardent wish; but upon the terms only of equal liberty." Reference was made to the shipments of tea, urging that each colony "take effectual methods to prevent this measure from having its designed effect."[51]

So stirred were the people of Philadelphia that the citizens in a meeting on October 18, 1773, demanded that the consignees resign the commission giving them the right to receive the tea. They at once complied. Likewise in Charleston the consignees resigned. At a gathering of the patrons in the City Hall in New York, resolutions were made prohibiting tea from being landed in that harbor. Boston made the same demands as Philadelphia, but was promptly refused. A vessel tied up at that port on November 28, 1773, and was followed in a few days by two other vessels, all loaded with tea. They were intercepted, however, by a group of citizens chosen as guards, who prevented their landing. Every effort was made to induce them to return their unloaded cargoes to London. When they refused, a band

---

[51] *Ibid.*, I, pp. 170–171.

of brave men in the guise of Indians boarded the vessels on the night of December 16, and cutting open the tea chests, dumped the entire lot overboard.[52] The vessels directed to New York and Philadelphia were prohibited from unloading and were forced to return to England. In Charleston, the tea landed there was chucked into cellars, where it remained. Maryland's "tea party," later in 1774, ended in the burning of the brig *Peggy Stewart*, containing 17 chests of tea. Virginia also was the scene of a "tea party." A group of citizens of Yorktown, in 1774, boarded a ship in the harbor and threw into the river tea consigned to a firm in Williamsburg.[53]

When the news was known, shouts and hurrahs resounded throughout the colonies. Dispatches of praise were sent to the guardsmen and townspeople in the ports for their firmness and bravery. In London, fury seized the British government. The King charged the colonies with subverting the Constitution, and advised punishment for their open rebellion. Upon request of the King, Lord North asked Parliament for permission to issue a bill to close the port of Boston until reparations were made for the tea and the colonies obeyed the Acts of Parliament. The bills, which proposed five measures in all, were denounced by the colonists as Intolerable Acts. The first and most irritating to the people was the Port Bill. The next, known as the Regulating Act, disregarded the rights in the charters as understood and exercised by the people of Massachusetts. Under the new act, freedom of suffrage would be greatly limited. The third act, intended to quell rioting and insurrections, called for the offenders to be sent to other localities, or to England, for trial. Another repressive measure, called the Quartering Act, provided for quartering troops upon the inhabitants of the colonies. The fifth, known as the Quebec Act, called for regulating the government of that province, and directed that all the French settlement between the Ohio and Mississippi Rivers, later known as the Northwest Territory, be annexed to the Province of Quebec.[54] This Patrick Henry surveyed with unusual suspicion. Later, as governor, he would exert himself strenuously to averting this expansion.

In Parliament, conciliatory debate by Burke, Dowdeswell and Sawbridge went unheeded. Little opposition to the measures

---

[52] *Ibid.*, I, p. 172.

[53] Allen, *Old Dominion Oddities*.

[54] Henry, *Henry*, I, pp. 189–190; Hicks, *The Federal Union*, p. 122.

was heard in the House of Lords, and the bill passed on March 30. From his sick bed the Earl of Chatham called it a "mad and cruel measure." He said, "Reparations ought first to be demanded in a solemn manner, and refused by the town and magistracy of Boston, before such a bill of pains and penalties can be called just."

In Virginia, conditions grew ominous. The Burgesses met May 24, 1774, but as yet no mention had been made of the Tea Act, discussion of which was postponed, through fear of dissolution of the House at the hands of the Governor. The Port Bill, which had now arrived in America via His Majesty's ships, was to become law on June first. In order to call attention to the seriousness of the times and to come to some agreement as to their stand with Massachusetts, the leaders in the House—Mr. Henry, Richard Henry Lee, Francis L. Lee, Thomas Jefferson and others—decided to draw up some resolutions as used by the Puritans of that day, proclaiming the first of June, the day the Port Bill would take effect, as a day of fasting and prayer.[55] On the 24th of May, 1774, the House adopted the following resolutions:

> This House . . . deem it highly necessary that the said first day of June be set apart, by the members of this House, as a day of Fasting, Humiliation, and Prayer, devoutly to implore the Divine interposition, for averting the heavy Calamity which threatens destruction to our Civil Rights, and the Evils of civil war; to give us one heart and one mind firmly to oppose, by all just and proper means, every injury to American rights.
>
> They petitioned also that the mind of his Majesty and his Parliament be inspired from above with wisdom and justice.[56]

Two days later, on May 26, between 3 and 4 o'clock in the afternoon, Governor Dunmore called the Assembly together and dissolved them.

The next day, May 27, the 25 members of the House met in the Raleigh Tavern to draw up the plan which had already been agreed upon by the Committee of Correspondence. The measures taken were signed by the Speaker, the members of the House of Burgesses, clergymen, and many of the inhabitants of the colony. They indicated that since the executive part of their government was no longer permitted to function, they were using the only method they had left to point out to their country-

---

[55] *Ibid.*, I, pp. 176–177.

[56] Brenaman, *A History of Virginia Conventions*, p. 7.

men such measures as seemed best fitted to preserve their dearest rights and liberties. They noted with grief that Great Britain had not only disregarded their petitions and remonstrances but that the British Parliament had determined to reduce the inhabitants of these colonies to slavery, as shown by their latest acts and in closing the harbor of their sister colony, Massachusetts Bay, until such taxes had been met. These they considered arbitrary and a dangerous attempt to destroy the constitutional rights and liberty of British America. They urged their sister colonies not to purchase any commodities whatsoever from the East India Company except saltpetre and spices until their grievances were redressed. They considered an attack made upon one of the colonies as an attack upon all British America. In that spirit they recommended that the Committees of Correspondence consider the expediency of appointing deputies from the several colonies of British America to meet annually in general Congress in a convenient place, there to deliberate on those general measures which the united interests of America might from time to time require.[57]

A sub-committee composed of Peyton Randolph, Robert C. Nicholas and Dudley Digges was selected to write the twelve colonies, notifying them of the recommendations made by the Virginia committee for a perpetual congress to meet annually and urging that their sentiments on the matter be furnished them. Patrick Henry's grandson, in elaborating on these recommendations, commented: "The measures proposed, as a last resort, to effect the repeal of the obnoxious Acts of Parliament, was a discontinuance of all commercial intercourse with England. Thus Virginia held her position in the front of the Revolutionary movement, conspicuous for her wisdom, firmness and conservatism." He stated further that "the action of the House of Burgesses was the first call for a Continental Congress by any Colonial Assembly, after the Tea Act."[58]

The last of May the Burgesses, twenty-five in all, wrote to their counties, requesting them to appoint delegates from each county to meet at a convention to be held in Williamsburg on August 1, to discuss the seriousness of affairs and elect representatives to Congress.

Samuel Adams sent out resolutions on May 13 from the Committee of Correspondence of Massachusetts, requesting that "the colonies stop all importations from Great Britain, exporta-

---

[57] Henry, *Henry*, I, p. 180.

[58] *Ibid.*, I, pp. 182–184.

tions to Great Britain, and every port of the West Indies, till the act for blocking up this harbor be repealed."[59]

Following the lead of Virginia, the assemblies of the other colonies took similar measures. On June 13 the Connecticut committee praised the proceedings of the Virginia Burgesses and made grateful reference to the contributions of Virginia counties, chiefly of corn, wheat and sheep, for the relief of the people of Boston. The City of Williamsburg and the County of James City sent 358 pounds ten shillings and four pence Pennsylvania currency, being the produce of two sterling bills of exchange delivered to Peyton Randolph, Esquire, as their donation for Boston. The County of Hanover donated 150 pounds Pennsylvania currency, being the produce of a bill of exchange for £100 sterling which Patrick Henry would later deliver to Samuel Adams on reaching Philadelphia to attend the Continental Congress.[60]

Proposals similar to Virginia's were taken on May 21 by the Providence, Rhode Island, Committee, and on May 23 at town meetings in New York and Philadelphia. Suggestions for a general congress were also received on May 26 by the Delaware committee. But Virginia had already taken definite steps determining such action on May 24, following her proposals of prayer and fasting, which were devised principally by Patrick Henry. Other colonies which chose delegates were: Massachusetts, Maryland, Pennsylvania, New Hampshire, New Jersey, Delaware, North Carolina and South Carolina. In New York—British Headquarters—deputies had to be chosen from the districts.

Information sent by Governor Dunmore to the British ministry telling of events shaping in the Virginia colony, brought quite a different response from that of the Connecticut letter. Lord Dartmouth, after mentioning the grave concern caused him by the actions of Parliament respecting the town of Boston, added:

> There was reason to hope, from appearances in the other colonies, that the extravagant proposition of the people of Boston would have been everywhere disregarded. But it may now be well doubted, whether the extraordinary conduct of the Burgesses of Virginia, both before and after their dissolution as a House, may

---

[59] *Ibid.*, I, p. 185.

[60] *The Writings of Samuel Adams*, collected and edited by Harry Alonzo Cushing, New York, G. P. Putnam's Sons, 1908, vol. 3. p. 224. Courtesy of the Boston Public Library, Richard G. Hensley, Chief Librarian, Division of Reference and Research Services; also Henry, *Henry*, I, pp. 195–250.

> not become (as it has already in other instances) an example to the other colonies.[61]

Lord Dartmouth, in pointing to the "other instances," no doubt had in mind the actions of that singular intellect in the case of the Parsons, and in the Stamp Act proceedings.

In Boston, the Port Bill was not the only cause for alarm. The other acts passed by Parliament had been given to the government of Massachusetts Bay. Town meetings were disallowed except to elect town officers and only then upon permission of the governor. No longer could the assembly appoint the council. The governor would appoint the sheriffs, who in turn would appoint the juries. These acts, including the one for quartering troops anywhere in the colonies, only tended to stiffen the resistance of the colonists.

The people in every county in Virginia met to elect their delegates for the convention to be held August 1. At a meeting of the Freeholders of Hanover County, at the Court House, on Wednesday, July 20, 1774, the following address was agreed to:

> To John Syme and Patrick Henry, junior, Esquires.
>
> Gentlemen:
>
> You have our thanks for your patriotic, faithful and spirited conduct, in the part you acted in the late assembly as our burgesses. . . .
>
> We are free men; we have a right to be so; and to enjoy all the privileges and immunities of our fellow subjects in England; and while we retain a just sense of that freedom, and those rights and privileges necessary for its safety and security, we shall never give up the right of taxation. Let it suffice to say, once and for all, we will never be taxed but by our own representatives; this is the great badge of freedom. . . .
>
> United We Stand, Divided We Fall.
>
> (They also instructed their deputies against importing any goods from Britain except articles most needed and which could not be had in America.)
>
> The African trade for slaves we consider as most dangerous to the virtue and welfare of this country; we therefore most earnestly wish to see it totally discouraged.[62]

John Syme and Patrick Henry, sons of the same Dissenter-mother, were not novices in the legislature. From the year 1726,

---

[61] Henry, *Henry*, I, p. 188.

[62] *Ibid.*, I, pp. 191–192.

when Hanover County was first formed from New Kent, there had been, except for a few intermittent years, a John Syme-Burgess member.

The delegates assembled the first day of August, 1774, and sat for six days. On every tongue were the happenings in Boston—General Thomas Gage was now Governor and his four regiments of troops were patrolling her streets, her harbors seized.[63] Defiance was in the air. Colonel Washington spoke his mind in the convention: "I will raise one thousand men, subsist them at my own expense, and march myself at their head for the relief of Boston."[64] Jefferson could not be present, because of illness en route. However, he drafted two copies of suggestions, one to Patrick Henry and one to his kinsman, the speaker of the House, Peyton Randolph. But Mr. Jefferson's ideas, "A Summary View of the Rights of British America," did "not appear to have influenced materially the action of the brief Convention."[65] In writing of this in later life, Jefferson said that "Mr. Henry probably thought it too bold as a first measure, as the majority of the members did. . . ." Jefferson is speaking for Henry, but such were hardly his views. No doubt the "ejaculative" Mr. Peyton Randolph may have had such ideas, but not Patrick Henry. His earliest attacks, his every challenge, had been those of defiance.

The instructions which were accepted and "wisely preferred" were prepared with a great deal of privacy, and by very few members. The paper was headed: "Instructions for the Deputies appointed to meet in General Congress on the part of this Colony," in which it is certain Henry had a hand. It explained that since the unhappy disputes between Great Britain and her colonies were continually increasing, they were in danger of being deprived of their chartered rights, which aroused their most serious consideration. It condemned the power exercised by Great Britain over the lives, the property and the liberty of American subjects, who were not, and from their local circumstances, could not be there represented. British subjects in America, it stated, were entitled to the same rights and privileges that their fellow subjects possessed in Britain; and therefore the power assumed by the British Parliament to bind America by their statutes, in all cases whatsoever, was unconstitutional and the

[63] *Ibid.*, I, p. 190.
[64] *Ibid.*, I, p. 198.
[65] Dr. Douglas S. Freeman, *Revision of the 'Common Glory,'* Richmond News Leader, December 13, 1948.

source of those unhappy differences . . . Especially observed were the several Acts of Parliament for raising a revenue in America; for extending the jurisdiction of the Courts of Admiralty; for seizing American subjects and transporting them to Britain to be tried for crimes committed in America; and the several late oppressive Acts respecting the town of Boston and province of Massachusetts Bay. All these they considered of a nature destructive to their rights as contained in the original constitution, investing the assemblies with the sole right of directing their internal policy.[66]

General Gage's proclamation, declaring it treasonable for the inhabitants of the Province of Massachusetts Bay to assemble themselves to consider their grievances and form associations for their common conduct, and requiring the civil magistrates to apprehend all such persons to be tried for their offenses, were considered the most alarming process that ever appeared in a British government. "That if the said General Gage conceives he is empowered to act in this manner, as the commander-in-chief of His Majesty's forces in America, this odious and illegal Proclamation must be considered as a full declaration, that this despotick viceroy will be bound by no law, nor regard the constitutional rights of His Majesty's subjects whenever they interfere with the plan he has formed for oppressing the good people of Massachusetts Bay; and, therefore, that the executing, or attempting to execute, such a Proclamation, will justify resistance and reprisal."[67] The people of the colony, thus circumstanced, "being deprived of their usual mode of making known their grievances, have appointed us their Representatives, to consider what is proper to be done in this dangerous crisis of American affairs."

"It being our opinion that the united wisdom of North America should be collected in a general Congress of all the colonies, we have appointed the Honourable Peyton Randolph, Esquire, Richard Henry Lee, George Washington, Patrick Henry, Richard Bland, Benjamin Harrison, and Edmund Pendleton, Esquires, Deputies to represent this Colony in the Said Congress, to be held at Philadelphia, on the first Monday in September next. . . ."[68]

---

[66] Henry, *Henry,* I, pp. 198–199.
[67] *Ibid.,* I, p. 202.
[68] *Ibid.,* I, p. 199.

VIII

SCOTCHTOWN: ITS SPHERE OF IMPORTANCE IN THE POLITICAL SCENE

BEFORE THE NEW delegate-elect to the First Continental Congress leaves his home, Scotchtown, for Philadelphia, something should be known of this ancient landmark where he lived during the foremost years of his service to the colony and the nation.

Here, in the redlands of upper Hanover, the county of the mighty Powhatan, Meechumps, Totopotomoi, and of the hot-headed Scotsman who willed his son a rib of James the Fifth stands Scotchtown, the home of Patrick Henry, and of Dolley (Payne) Madison, the wife of President James Madison. The mansion is built on a high elevation, and in the days of open fields it was possible on a clear day to see, from the attic ballroom or roof top, Carter's Mountain and the foothills around Charlottesville. It has been described in Waterman's *Mansions of Virginia, 1706–1766*, as probably the oldest of the Virginia plantation houses.

There is much about Scotchtown that engages, and distinguishes it from other old houses in the country. Of rectangular shape, it is an immense story-and-a-half frame structure, with eight rooms and a great hall on the first floor, a huge attic and a full-height brick basement of arresting proportions. The house, 85 feet long by 36 feet wide, has a jerkin-head roof covering the building, and a modillioned cornice runs the entire length of the house, front and back. Shingled of cypress, the manor house was originally placed to form one side of a courtyard. Around it were grouped smaller houses which were used to quarter the young men of the household, and for the schoolhouse, office, kitchen, warehouse, washhouse, ashhouse and blacksmith shop.

There were 30 cabins and a mill on New Found River. At the rear of the house to the left is the bricked-up dry well, one of the few of its kind in existence. Long before the ice house, this colonial deep freeze, approximately eight by ten feet with a depth of twenty-five feet, was used to store foods.

There are two massive chimneys, each serving four rooms with corner fireplaces. The mantels in the front rooms were originally of the finest marble, but during the nineteenth century the chimneys were changed and some of the interior trim and paneling were removed. Restoration, however, has been accomplished, and the mantels have been replaced and the chimneys reconstructed to their original lines. Notable are the three long flights of exterior steps of paneled stone, framed by mouldings. A 12-foot hall from front to rear of the house has heavy wainscoting of heart pine, four feet high, running full length on both sides. The floors throughout the house are of heavy ten-inch heart pine, laid on four-by-twelve hand-hewn sills; the huge cross-beams and studding are held together by wooden pins. The doors are beautiful, of four, six, and eight-panel cross-type grain walnut, with heavy original wrought-iron H & L hinges. The basement rooms are separated by a dark cellar directly under the hall which has been referred to as a "dungeon." But as there were once wine vaults along both sides, it was actually a wine cellar.

It is tradition that Scotchtown was once raided by the Indians; later that a duel was fought in the hall, accounting for the bloodstains on the floor. The raider, Banister Tarleton, is said to have ridden his horse up the stone steps of the south portico, into the wide hall, and out the opposite doorway. Lafayette, retreating northward before Cornwallis, was here in May, 1781, and Cornwallis himself stopped here in June of the same year.

Baron Ludwig Von Closen visited Scotchtown in February, 1782, and gave the following description:

> This plantation, which is called *Scotchtown*, is charmingly situated in the midst of a plain 6 leagues from Porter. The house is spacious and handsome, extremely well furnished, and delightfully well ordered. In a word, it is one of the most pleasing establishments in America. An English garden below adds a great deal of charm to this estate.

On July 9, Von Closen again visited Scotchtown and noted:

> The grounds around *Scotchtown* are very pretty, and there are little woods in the shade of which we took some country

> walks. The garden is an attractive sight. There are several rather pretty flower-beds although these are still neglected in this country.[1]

Scotchtown was built by Col. Charles Chiswell of Williamsburg. The Scotchtown property, consisting of 9,976 acres, was patented by Chiswell, July 15, 1717, when Spotswood was governor. The law at that time required that all property be seated within two years, so it is thought that the house was started in 1719.[2] Chiswell, no doubt, selected this site for his country home in order to be near his iron foundries. In recent years, bars of pig iron have been discovered here with the initials CC 1737—(Crown Colony) or (Charles Chiswell)?

Col. Chiswell was residing at Scotchtown when, in 1732, William Byrd of Westover stopped here while prospecting for minerals on New Found River. He recorded:

> I arrived about two o'clock and saved my dinner. I was very handsomely entertained, finding everything very clean, and very good . . . . I retired to a very clean lodging in another house, and took my bark. . . .[3]

Charles Chiswell came from Scotland to the colony sometime during the late seventeenth century. He brought a colony of Scots and Scottish builders to Virginia, who came inland to upper Hanover County and cleared land for the purpose of establishing a township. They at once began to build the large dwelling, which they called Scotch Town, to house some of the settlers. After the completion of the house and the necessary outbuildings, they started laying a large stone and brick foundation about half a mile northwest of Scotchtown for the erection of a castle. The land was divided into ten-acre tracts separated by straight roads, which were intended for streets. Before the building got under way, however, two or three of the carpenters contracted fever and died. Fearing an epidemic, most of the men became discouraged and returned to Scotland, leaving only a small number behind.[4]

---

[1] Acomb. *The Revolutionary Journal of Baron Ludwig Von Closen, 1780–1783.* pp. 181–209.

[2] Register of Land Office New Kent County, Book 10, p. 323.

[3] *Virginia, A Guide to the Old Dominion,* pp. 353–354.

[4] History of the settlers, as told by the Sheppard family, who moved to Scotchtown 22 years after the Henry family had moved away.

Soon after Col. Chiswell's arrival in the colony he made influential connections, and by 1706, if not earlier, he served as clerk of the General Court,[5] and later became a member of the King's Council. In addition to his Williamsburg property, he was the owner of Chiswell's Ordinary, which was between Green Spring, Governor Berkley's home, and Williamsburg.[6] In a position of power, he began in 1722 to make further successful petitions for grants of land in the counties of Henrico, Spotsylvania, Goochland and Amelia. The owner of 24,500 acres already from grants, he was further authorized in 1735 to make a survey of land in what was then Albemarle County, of 30,000 acres on Rockfish River. Still later he acquired, through grants, a share (with four other gentlemen) of a 30,000-acre tract in the region south of the James.[7]

His huge land holdings gave Chiswell (pronounced "Chizzel") social and political prestige. But for the great landlords among the aristocracy, to be a gentleman did not necessarily indicate financial security.[8] At Charles Chiswell's death in April, 1737, Scotchtown, with its large tract of land on the South Anna River, and other estate in land, was deeded to his son John.

John Chiswell was married to Elizabeth Randolph, the daughter of Col. William Randolph of Turkey Island. He represented Hanover County in the House of Burgesses for thirteen years and later sat as a Burgess from the city of Williamsburg for two years. His eldest daughter, Susannah, married John Robinson, the Speaker of the House of Burgesses and Treasurer of the Colony, a man of great wealth who largely controlled the politics of Virginia. Turning his attention to agriculture, John Chiswell became interested in raising tobacco and cleared large acres for the cultivation of the weed. In 1754, he exchanged a "fine parcel" of Scotchtown tobacco for "European Goods" valued at £1,500 sterling.[9] However, his speculation in the tobacco business did not augment his fortune, and his new enterprise found him "chronically short of cash and land poor."[10]

---

[5] *Bridenbaugh, Violence and Virtue in Virginia, 1766: or, The Importance of the Trivial,* Massachusetts Historical Society. Proceedings, p. 10, vol. 76 (1964).

[6] On authority of J. Francis Speight, Member, Antiquarian Society.

[7] Bridenbaugh, *Violence and Virtue in Virginia, 1766: or, The Importance of the Trivial,* Massachusetts Historical Society Proceedings, p. 10 vol. 76 (1964).

[8] *Ibid.,* pp. 10–12.

[9] *Ibid.,* p. 12.

[10] *Ibid.*

He was able to relieve his situation with borrowed money and later invested in "The Lead Mining Company" in partnership with two others. The mine works became known as "Chiswell's Mine" with Chiswell superintendent, and with John Robinson advancing "nearly all the funds invested," which was discovered at Robinson's death to be the enormous sum of £8,085 12s. 5d. owed to the Robinson estate by the mine company.[11] Thus, Scotchtown on May 31, 1760, with certain other properties, was sold to John Robinson to help Chiswell meet his obligations.[12]

Chiswell, ironically, faced a real calamity six years later in the shocking indebtedness of his son-in-law to the colony, which was not known until Robinson's sudden death, May, 1766.[13] The next month, on June 3, Chiswell, "a testy and choleric man," killed his friend, Robert Routledge, by running him through with a sword in a "drunken brawl" at Ben Mosby's Tavern at Cumberland Court House. In an unapologetic outburst he declared: "He deserves his fate, damn him; I aimed at his heart and I have hit it."[14]

After being denied bail and spending seven days in the county gaol, he was taken under the custody of Sheriff Jesse Thomas, with the warrant of the Examining Courts, to Williamsburg. Before the sheriff and his prisoner reached the public prison near the Capitol, they were stopped and Chiswell was released upon admission to bail on the orders of three judges of the General Court "out of sessions," and "without seeing the record of his examination in the County or examining any of the witnesses against him," who were sworn to appear at the trial in Williamsburg.[15] The action of the judges was based upon the legal advice of three "eminent Lawyers," among whom was George Wythe, Esq.[16]

Thus the case stood until the middle of June when the controversy over the murder of Robert Routledge and the astonishing release of Charles Chiswell was carried by a free press. The details of the murder and of the sophistry and chicanery involved in the case were uncovered by Rind's and Purdie & Dixon's, two *Virginia Gazettes*, each completely reversing its former policy of

[11] *Ibid.*, p. 14, op. cit., Mays, *Edmund Pendleton*, I, 203–364.
[12] *Ibid.*, p. 13.
[13] *Ibid.*, p. 9.
[14] *Ibid.*, p. 6.
[15] *Ibid.*
[16] *Ibid.*

complacency since the Stamp Act.[17] Articles appeared over such anonymous names as, "Metriotes," "Dikephilos," "Marcus Fabius," "Marcus Curtius," and others.

The Rev. Jonathan Boucher, the most prolific contributor in the "party disputes," compared the murder to the Stamp Act, in which many gentlemen stood ready to give their lives to keep away oppression and secure their liberties, but in this partiality they apprehended "more dreadful consequences than even that detestable act of power could have been, because this must effect our lives, while that could only effect our estates."[18] It was feared by many persons, knowing the relationship of the King's Attorney, Peyton Randolph, to Col. Chiswell's wife, that he would "occasion the prosecution for the King to be carried on in a different manner from what it ought to be."[19] His "going out of the county the very morning of the day when the (Examining) Court was held and leaving no one to officiate for him, must, in the eyes of all men who are not blind, look extremely dark."[20] One writer expressed the people's "amazement" when informed "that three Judges of the General Court have dared to do a most flagrant injury, both to Prince and people, by presuming to rescue a person, charged with the murder of his fellow subject, from the custody of a sheriff, who by an order of an examining court, was conveying him to public prison. . . . .[21] In such actions, a "pernicious precedent" had been established by this "power of licensing homocides," at the discretion of the General Court.[22]

The effect, or the result of the proceedings uncovered that summer by the press, has been described by a present-day historian in these words: "The more that serious men read and thought about the deficiencies in the legal system and the breaches of public trust in the House of Burgesses, the more some of them began to question the governing of Virginia in the interests of a class by a small faction of that class. These patriots understood very well the danger for the Old Dominion that lay in the perpetuation of a corrupt aristocracy like the one in England they censured."[23]

---

[17] *Ibid.*, pp. 15–16.
[18] *Ibid.*, p. 20.
[19] *Ibid.*
[20] *Ibid.*, p. 22n.
[21] *Ibid.*, p. 17.
[22] *Ibid.*, p. 18.
[23] *Ibid.*, p. 29.

Such was the condition of affairs in the government of Virginia when Patrick Henry entered the political scene. What is important, and what has been overlooked, is the connection between the Robinson scandal affecting the colony's treasury and the wealthy Tidewater gentry, and the exposé of colonial politics in the Routledge-Chiswell murder case.[24] The corruption in politics under Treasurer Robinson, and the evasion of justice in the murder case, aroused the populace to indignation and apprehension of greater loss to liberty. They found in the young orator, Patrick Henry—a new Burgess member—an exceeding amount of political courage.

John Chiswell left for his mines soon after giving his bail; however, he returned on September 11, in time to make plans for his trial. But before his case came up, he died, on October 17, 1766, from what his physician described as "nervous fits," owing to constant uneasiness of mind.[25] When his body was brought to Scotchtown for burial, Routledge's friends followed behind and demanded that the coffin be opened in order to ascertain if the corpse was that of Chiswell, which it was recognized to be.[26] Because of Robinson's indebtedness to the colony, his estates were seized to defray his debts. Scotchtown was sold at auction at Hanover Court House the first Thursday next in September, 1770. The report made by Pendleton and Lyons and filed on November 22, 1769, shows that Scotchtown contained 3,866 acres of land, 56 slaves, 140 head of cattle, 180 hogs, 54 sheep and 7 horses.[27]

Many questions have arisen over the different owners of Scotchtown and it may be interesting to point to the several transfers. John and Mary (Coles) Payne, the parents of Dolley Payne Madison, were the next owners of Scotchtown. In order to determine the date on which the Paynes purchased Scotchtown, it is necessary to refer to the church records: John and Mary Payne requested admittance to the Cedar Creek Meeting, the Quaker Church in the vicinity of Scotchtown, on September 8, 1764, and were received May 11, 1765. They were granted a certificate from the Cedar Creek Meeting to the New Garden

---

[24] *Ibid.*, p. 10. Not overlooked by the historian, Carl Bridenbaugh.

[25] *Ibid.*, p. 23.

[26] *Ibid.*, p. 24n. op. cit., a copy of the original papers, loaned to Colonial Williamsburg Research Library; Boucher, *Reminiscences of a Loyalist.* The body was identified by Col. William Dabney.

[27] *Journal of the House of Burgesses,* 1766–1769 p. 281.

Quaker Meeting in Guilford County, North Carolina, on October 12, 1765. They returned to Hanover County and, with a certificate from the New Garden Meeting dated February 25, 1769, they were received into the Cedar Creek Meeting April 8, 1769.[27] Dolley was nine months old when her parents returned to Hanover County.[28] Scotchtown was sold in September, 1770,[29] and as Patrick Henry bought it in 1771, Dolley Payne apparently lived at Scotchtown only a little more than a year, unless, as has been suggested, the Paynes remained on, sharing the large, rambling Scotchtown house with their kinsmen, the Henrys, until the completion of the Payne home on the Coles Hill tract. John Payne moved from Scotchtown to Coles Hill, ten miles away, which was the home of Dolley's maternal grandparents.[30] Her grandmother, Lucy Winston Coles, was the aunt of Patrick Henry and the sister of his mother.

Patrick Henry was the next owner of Scotchtown. Here he lived with his first wife, Sarah Shelton, and here ended their 21 years together.[31] Sarah was the patient of Dr. Thomas Hinde, Patrick Henry's personal physician. Dr. Hinde's account of Patrick Henry's bereavement is given by the doctor's son:

> Here (at Scotchtown) resided the illustrious patriot and statesman at the breaking out of the American Revolution. Here his family resided, whilst Henry had to encounter many mental and personal afflictions known only to his family physician. Whilst his towering and master-spirit was arousing a nation to arms, his soul was bowed down and bleeding under the heaviest sorrows and personal distresses. . . . I cannot reflect on my venerable deceased father's rehearsal of the particulars, without feeling myself almost a bleeding heart. It was such men that Almighty God raised up to assert and maintain our rights.[32]

Dr. Hinde, an eminent surgeon in the Revolution, was with

---

[28] Hinshaw & Marshall, *Encyclopedia of American Quaker Genealogy*, v. 6. p. 262; John and Mary Payne granted a certificate to Philadelphia, 4–12–1783.

[29] Ella Kent Barnard, *Dorothy Payne Quakeress*. p. 28; Meade Minnegerode, *Dolly Madison, An Informal Biography*, p. 3, *The Saturday Evening Post*, November 29, 1924. *Virginia Gazette*, July 26, 1770. Scotchtown was sold in September, 1770.

[30] William Coles of St. Martin's Parish to his daughter Mary Payne, 176 acres. Sept. 5, 1771. Purchased from Wm. Winston, Jr. deceased. Hanover County Court Records 1783–1792. p. 110. Sept. 5, 1771.

[31] Henry, *Henry*, I, p. 318; Index p. 670.

[32] Meade, *Patrick Henry Patriot in the Making*, I, p. 281.

General Wolfe in Quebec. He later moved to Hanover County and was the close friend of the patriot.

The children of Patrick Henry, by Sarah Shelton, were six: three boys and three girls. Martha, the eldest daughter, married Col. John Fontaine. Anne, the next daughter, became the wife of Judge Spencer Roane, Justice of the Supreme Court of Appeals of Virginia. Their son was the brilliant young United States Senator, William Henry Roane. Elizabeth, the youngest of the girls, married Philip Aylett and became the mistress of Fontainebleau, the Aylett estate in King William County. They were the parents of the young orator, Patrick Henry Aylett, who lost his life in the Richmond Theatre fire.[33] Of Patrick Henry's three sons by Sarah Shelton, only John married. With his wife, Sally Jones, he moved to Sevier County, Tennessee. William died unmarried, as did Edward, the "Neddy" of his father's affection, who died in young manhood.

From Scotchtown Patrick Henry often rattled down the Williamsburg road to the House of Burgesses. From here he journeyed by horseback to the First and Second Continental Congresses, and afterward organized the First Independent Company of Volunteers in Virginia. Also from here, he attended the First Virginia Convention held in Williamsburg; the Second Revolutionary Convention which met in St. John's Church, when he moved to arm the colony and gave his great "Liberty or Death" speech. Later he left on his march down the peninsula to retrieve the gunpowder removed from the Powder Horn by Governor Dunmore. Returning from the Second Congress in time for the Third Revoluntionary Convention assembled in Richmond, he was appointed Commander-in-Chief of all the Virginia forces.

On duty with the Army, he was absent at the Fourth Virginia Convention, but he was returned later as a delegate to the Fifth, and final, Virginia Revolutionary Convention, held May 6, 1776, when his resolutions, calling upon Congress to make a Declaration of Independence,[34] cast off the yoke, and he was elected the first governor of an independent state in the annals of the world.[35] In

---

[33] Morgan, *Henry*, p. 238.

[34] Henry, *Henry*, I, pp. 395–397. Henry's Resolution No. I, alone of the three resolutions, called upon Congress to make a full Declaration of Independence. Pendleton's, No. 3, did not mention the word, Independence, and it was not supported. See Brant, *James Madison, The Virginia Revolutionist, 1751–1780*, pp. 223–425. See note, 14.

[35] Brenaman, *Virginia Conventions*. See Constitutional Convention, 1776.

the great hall at Scotchtown, Governor Henry received George Rogers Clark and discussed with him the serious situation in Kentucky, resulting from the British emissaries inciting the Cherokees to attack. Governor Henry gave Colonel Clark an order for £500 of gunpowder and sent him on his way to save the Kentucky Colony. Later, we shall see him dispatch Clark with a contingent of troops to save the great Northwest.

His election as Governor necessitated his removal to Williamsburg. He had been traveling to and from Scotchtown while the Governor's Palace was being renovated for the Henry family. On October 8, 1777, His Excellency, Patrick Henry, married Dorothea Dandridge, the daughter of Nathaniel West Dandridge, and grand-daughter of Governor Alexander Spotswood.

Governor Henry had his half-brother, Col. John Syme, advertise Scotchtown on March 6, 1778. (See Purdie: *Virginia Gazette*, March 6, 1778, p. 4, col. 2.):

> For sale, the pleasant and healthy seat called Scotchtown, in Hanover County, 23 miles above Hanover town and 27 miles above Richmond. The quantity of land is 1000 acres, 400 of which are cleared, and under proper enclosure for farming. The soil is very good, and there is very fine meadow cleared and to clear in sufficient quantity. The best white marl is found there in abundance. The dwelling house is about 88 feet long and 36 feet wide, very commodious, with a garden. Negroes or money will be accepted in payment. For further particulars apply to Col. Syme in Hanover, or the printer of this Gazette.

Soon thereafter, Scotchtown was sold to Col. Wilson Miles Cary, whose home near the bay was taken over and used by the Virginia troops for a smallpox camp.[36] At the end of his third term as Governor it was the patriot's desire to return to his beloved Hanover, but his negotiations for land from General Nelson failed.[37]

On June 19, 1787, there was filed in Hanover County a deed from Wilson Miles Cary and Sarah, his wife, of Elizabeth City County, to Benjamin Forsythe, for the tract known as Scotchtown. The sale consisted of 960 acres.[38]

This property was next conveyed to Capt. John Mosby

---

[36] Henry, *Henry*, I, p. 618; Morgan, *Henry*, p. 250n.

[37] Morgan, *Henry*, p. 323.

[38] Hanover County Court Records, 1783–1792.

Sheppard in 1802. The Sheppards resided at Scotchtown until the owner's death in 1824, when it was sold to Capt. John J. Taylor. It remained in the hands of the descendants of Captain Taylor until June 26, 1958, when Scotchtown was acquired by the Association for the Preservation of Virginia Antiquities.

The historical eminence of this ancient house began with Patrick Henry's epochal entry across its threshold. Here he pondered the crucial questions of the pre-war years. This was familiar territory, for he had traveled the Scotchtown road with his mother to and from the upper Fork Church. This location divided in half the distance between the Louisa, Goochland, and Hanover Courts and brought him into close proximity with the counties of Caroline, King William, and New Kent where he held many important court cases.

At the death of the first Mrs. Henry, the responsibility and management of the children devolved upon Mr. Henry. A letter he wrote to one of his daughters shows his devotion to them. It is addressed to Annie, whose husband, seven years after their marriage, was appointed a judge of the Supreme Court of Appeals. It should be ranked with the finest of eighteenth-century belles-lettres:

> My Dear Daughter:
>
> You have just entered into that state which is replete with happiness or misery. The issue depends upon that prudent, amiable, uniform conduct which wisdom and virtue so strongly recommend on the one hand, or on that imprudence which a want of reflection or passion may prompt on the other.
>
> You are allied to a man of honor, of talents, and of an open, generous disposition. You have, therefore, in your power all the essential ingredients of that system of conduct which you ought invariably to pursue—if you will now see clearly the path from which you will resolve never to deviate. Our conduct is often the result of whim or caprice—often such as will give us many a pang, unless we see beforehand what is always the most praiseworthy, and the most essential to happiness.
>
> The first maxim which you should impress upon your mind is never to attempt to control your husband, by opposition, by displeasure, or any other work of anger. A man of sense, of prudence, of warm feelings, cannot, and will not, bear an opposition of any kind which is attended with an angry look or expression. The current of his affections is suddenly stopped; his attachment is weakened; he begins to feel a mortification the most pungent; he is belittled in his own eyes; and be assured that the wife who

once excites those sentiments in the breast of a husband will never regain the high ground which she might and ought to have retained. When he marries her, if he be a good man, he expects from her smiles, not frowns; he expects to find her one who is not to control him—not to take from him the freedom of acting as his own judgment shall direct, but one who will place such confidence in him as to believe that his prudence is his best guide. Little things that in reality are mere trifles in themselves, often produce bickerings and even quarrels. Never permit them to be a subject of dispute; yield them with pleasure, with a smile of affection. Be assured, one difference outweighs them all a thousand, or ten thousand, times. A difference with your husband ought to be considered as the greatest calamity—as one that is to be studiously guarded against; it is a demon which must never be permitted to enter a habitation where all should be peace, unimpaired confidence, and heartfelt affection. Besides what can a woman gain by her opposition or her indifference? Nothing. But she loses everything; she loses her husband's repect for her virtues, she loses his love, and with that, all prospect of future happiness. She creates her own misery, and then utters idle and silly complaints, but utters them in vain.

The love of a husband can be retained only by the high opinion which he entertains of his wife's goodness of heart, of her amiable disposition, of the sweetness of her temper, of her prudence, of her devotion to him. Let nothing upon any occasion ever lessen that opinion. On the contrary, it should augment every day; he should have much more reason to admire her for those excellent qualities which will cast a lustre over a virtuous woman whose personal attractions are no more . . .

Cultivate your mind by the perusal of those books which instruct while they amuse. Do not devote much of your time to novels. . . . History, geography, poetry, moral essays, biography, travels, sermons, and other well-written religious productions will not fail to enlarge your understanding, to render you a more agreeable companion, and to exalt your virtue.

Mutual politeness between the most intimate friends is essential to that harmony which should never be broken or interrupted. How important, then, it is between man and wife! . . . I will add that matrimonial happiness does not depend on wealth; no, it is not to be found in wealth, but in minds properly tempered and united to our respective situations. Competency is necessary. All beyond that is ideal. . .

In the management of your domestic concerns let prudence and wise economy prevail. Let neatness, order, and judgment be seen in all your different deportments. Unite liberality with a just frugality; always reserve something for the hand of charity; and never let your door be closed to the voice of suffering humanity. Your servants especially will have the strongest claim upon your charity; let them be well fed, well clothed, nursed in sickness, and let them never be unjustly treated.[39]

He desired for his daughters the attainment of all womanly graces; and he pleaded for the freedom and independence of his son-in-law and wished these not to be denied him. He had a heart, too, for suffering humanity. It was this human understanding and consideration that endeared him to his servants.

The slave question gravely distressed Patrick Henry. He abhorred the slave trade and tried to put a stop to it, but all efforts had been ignored by the King of England, who was receiving large revenues from the traffic.[40] Patrick Henry saw the Negroes alien to the New World and to its customs, and he felt that it would be prudent to help them to help themselves; but first, he should help to free the white man from his shackles.

Patrick Henry fed and clothed his slaves and ministered to their ills. In a letter written at Scotchtown in 1773 to Robert Pleasants, thanking him for the Frenchman Benezet's book on the subject, Mr. Henry discussed his opinions on slavery:

Hanover, Jany 18th, 1773.

Dear Sir,

I take this opportunity to acknowledge the receit of Anthony Benezet's Book against the slave trade. I thank you for it. It is not a little surprising that the professors of Christianity, whose chief excellence consists in softening the human heart, and in cherishing and improving its finer feelings, should encourage a practice so totally repugnant to the first impressions of right and wrong. What adds to the wonder is that this abominable practice has been introduced in the most enlightened ages. Times, that seem to have pretentions to boast of high improvements in the arts, and sciences, and refined morality, have brought into general use and guarded by many laws, a species of violence and tyranny, which our more rude and barbarous, but more honest ancestors detested. Is it not amazing, that at a time when the rights of Humanity are defined and understood with precision in a country above all others fond of liberty, that in such an age and in such a country, we find men professing a religion the most humane, mild, meek, gentle and generous, adopting a Principle as repug-

[39] Morgan, *Henry*, pp. 243–244.
[40] Henry, *Henry*, I, p. 151.

> nant to humanity, as it is inconsistent with the Bible and destructive to liberty? Every thinking honest man rejects it in speculation, how few in practice from conscientious motives.
>
> Would any one believe that I am master of slaves of my own purchase! I am drawn along by the general inconvenience of living without them. I will not, I cannot justify it. However culpable my conduct, I will so far pay my devoir to virtue, as to own the excellence and rectitude of her precepts and to lament my want of conformity to them.
>
> I believe a time will come when an opportunity will be offered to abolish this lamentable evil. Everything we can do, is to improve it if it happens in our day; if not, let us transmit to our descendants, together with our slaves, a pity for their unhappy lot, and an abhorrence of slavery. If we cannot reduce this wished-for reformation to practice, let us treat the unhappy victims with lenity, it is the furthest advance we can make toward justice. It is a debt we owe to the purity of our Religion to show that it is at variance with that law which warrants slavery.
>
> I know not when to stop. I would say many things on this subject, a serious review of which gives gloomy perspective to future times.[41]

Patrick Henry's retained his slaves. Jefferson did also. Following Patrick Henry's pattern of opposition to slavery, he wrote later: "All men are created free and equal. I have sworn upon the altar of God eternal hostility against every form of tyranny over the mind of man." Yet at the same time Jefferson was the owner of a large number of slaves, which he kept until his death. How deep-rooted the slavery question had become was evident in Jefferson's proposals to Congress that the children of slaves be declared free, and the enslaved remain so until death. His recommendation did not pass.

The Toleration Act also was a source of agitation to the mind of Mr. Henry. He had no patience with the favored position of the Anglican Church, which prohibited the free exercise of worship to other faiths. Particularly was he in sympathy with the Presbyterians, Methodists, Baptists, and Lutherans, many of whom had been jailed for preaching their beliefs throughout the colony. Henry traveled many weary miles, riding from courthouse to courthouse, through rain and snow, denouncing all such practices of the established church. "He often listened to the Dissenters, while they were waging their steady and finally effectual war

---

[41] Henry, *Henry*, I, pp. 152–153.

against the burthenes of the established church and from a repetition of his sympathy with the history of their sufferings, he unlocked the human heart, and transferred into civil discussions many of the bold licenses which prevailed in the religious." Mr. Henry also solicited the cause of the Quakers, as is shown in the diary of Rachel Wilson, the grandmother of the noted John Bright, who toured Virginia in 1769. Dating her letter March 31, Williamsburg, Virginia, she recorded: "We returned that night to Francis Clark's. Called by the way to see one of the Assemblymen, who was a man of great moderation, and had appeared in Friend's favor; his name was Patrick Henry. He received us with great civility and made some sensible remarks. We had an open time in the family."[42] Patrick Henry was opposed by many of the old leaders who were hostile to his views, but he was convinced nevertheless, of the earnestness and zeal of those wishing to proclaim the gospel as they understood it. He vigorously protested in the courts of Caroline, where Edmund Pendleton was presiding and active in the persecution of non-conformists.[43] Semple's history of the *Baptists in Virginia*, discussing their attempts to obtain liberty of speech from the courts, relates: "It was in making these attempts that they were so fortunate as to interest in their behalf the celebrated Patrick Henry; being always a friend of liberty, he only needed to be informed of their oppression; without hestitation he stepped forward to their relief. From that time until the day of their complete emancipation from the shackles of tyranny, the Baptists found in Patrick Henry an unwavering friend. May his name descend to posterity with unsullied honor!"[44] James Madison, writing to a friend in 1774, spoke of "That diabolical hell-conceived principle of persecution," adding: "There are at this time in the adjacent county not less than five or six well meaning men in close jail for proclaiming their religious sentiments, which are in the main quite orthodox."[45]

Twenty pounds was the amount of bond the Dissenting ministers were required to pay, and ten pounds was the amount of security for good behavior. Those who were imprisoned for

---

[42] *Ibid.*, I, p. 117.

[43] *Ibid.*, I, pp. 117–119. "The Bishop of London had always had the supervision of the clergy of Virginia, this colony being a part of the London diocese, . . ." (Chandler & Thames, *Colonial Virginia*, p. 206). Judge Pendleton in Caroline Court, ignored the freedom of conscience and persecuted the Dissenters in their right to worship. (Chandler & Thames, *Colonial Virginia*, pp. 361-362).

[44] Henry, *Henry*, I, pp. 117–118.

[45] Chandler & Thames, *Colonial Virginia*, p. 203.

preaching in unlicensed places complained that there were not enough licensed houses. The Act of Toleration called for Dissenting ministers to be licensed to preach and to have Episcopal ordination. One Lewis Craig was brought before the Courts of His Majesty's Justice, Edmund Pendleton presiding, for having a license to preach, but lacking the oath of ordination. He was ordered to the gaol of the County of Caroline, "there to remain til he give security himself in the sum of twenty pounds & two securities in the sum of ten pounds each for his good behavior a year and a daye."[46]

Among the Baptist ministers imprisoned in Caroline County for preaching the gospel was the Rev. John Waller. Judge Spencer Roane, in writing to the biographer, Mr. Wirt, stated: "Mr. Pendleton, on the bench of Caroline Court, justified the imprisonment of several Baptist preachers, who were defended by Mr. Henry, on the heinous charge of worshipping God according to the dictates of their own consciences."[47] Another victim was the Rev. John Weatherford, jailed for five months in the County of Chesterfield, whose court was presided over by Col. Archibald Cary; the charge, that of creating a disturbance by preaching. He also obtained the services of Mr. Henry, who ordered his release, but it was refused him until his jail fees over the long period were first paid. As the sum was much more than the minister was able to pay, he had to remain in prison. Later he was freed, some friend who wished his name to be kept secret having paid the charges. Twenty years later when Mr. Weatherford became a minister in Charlotte County, and the neighbor of Patrick Henry, he learned while discussing his struggle for religious liberty that it was Mr. Henry who had been his benefactor, paying his fine to the jailer in Chesterfield.[48]

The privileges of the Anglican Church which other churches did not have, brought on increased resentment among the Dissenting bodies. The increasing persecutions of religious Dissenters in the mother country had been made known from father to son, and it was in their descendants that the principles of popular liberty were to be found.

It was Patrick Henry's influence in the Assembly that brought

---

[46] Lewis Peyton Little, *Imprisoned Preachers and Religious Liberty, Caroline County Order Book for 1770–1772*, pp. 247–248.

[47] Morgan, *Henry*, Appendix B. p. 440. Judge Spencer Roane's Memorandum, See also, page 247.

[48] Henry, *Henry*, I, pp. 118–119.

about additional tax on the importation of slaves and the exemption of Quakers from military service. Later he would write into the original draft of the sixteenth article of the Virginia Bill of Rights "the first formal and official assertion and sanction of the doctrine of religious liberty that had ever been given in Virginia."[49]

Virginia's fight against oppression had begun more than a century before the great events of 1776. In 1676 there died Nathaniel Bacon, Jr., who had led a successful rebellion against Sir William Berkeley's autocratic government. His few volunteers beat back the Indians whose depredations had been left unpunished by the Governor, then defeated Berkeley's troops and burned Jamestown. Their point made, they went back to their frontier homes, only to be hunted down like animals by the government troops. Bacon's Rebellion was not forgotten.

[49] Chandler & Thames, *Colonial Virginia*, p. 352.

IX

THE CONTINENTAL CONGRESS

The law of nature is simple and rational, as opposed to that which is artificial and arbitrary . . . It is superior to all other law . . . because it is the expression of the purpose of the Deity or of the highest reason of man.[1]
Lord Kilmuir, quoting the late Lord Bryce.

ON THE EARLY MORNING of August 29, 1774, the delegate from Hanover County, Patrick Henry, left his home to attend the First Continental Congress. The vicissitudes of the times can be seen in a letter written by Patrick's mother to the wife of Col. William Fleming. Her daughter, Anne, was on a visit to her mother at this time while her husband, Colonel Christian, was away fighting the Indians. She wrote:

15 October, 1774.

Dear Madam:

Kind Providence preserved me and all with me (Mrs. Annie Christian and her little ones) safe to our home in Hanover. Here people have been very sickly, but hope the sickly season is nigh over. My dear Annie has been ailing two or three days with a fever. The dear children are very well. My son Patrick has gone to Philadelphia near seven weeks. The affairs are kept with great secrecy, nobody being allowed to be present. I assure you we have our lowland fears and troubles with respect to Great Britain. Perhaps our good God may bring us out of these many troubles which threaten us not only from the mountains but the seas. I can not forget to thank my dear Mrs Fleming for the great kind-

[1] Lord Kilmuir, speaking of the "law of nature," quoting the late Lord Bryce.

ness that you showed us in Botetourt, and assure you that I remember Colonel Fleming and you with much esteem and best wishes, and shall take it very kind if you will let me hear from you.

My daughter Betty joins me in kind love to yourself and Miss Rosie, and especially to your dear good mother when you see her.

I am, dear madam, your humble servant.

Sarah Henry.[2]

It was two days' journey on horseback from Hanover to Mount Vernon. As Patrick Henry rode along with the morning mist in his face the countryside about him lay asleep. Alone with his thoughts, the events of the past year probably unfolded before him: The February past, he had lost his aged father, whom he had honored and esteemed. Turning aside from thoughts of his family, he no doubt recalled Dunmore's mischief in causing new outbreaks between the warlike Indians on the Ohio and the colonists.[3] Among Dunmore's latest designs was the attempt to divide the Colony of Pennsylvania from the Virginia Colony.[4] There was no denying Dunmore's shrewdness in commissioning the unprincipled John Connolly to gather forces to hold the territory around Fort Pitt, disputed by the Pennsylvania authorities. In his purpose to provoke civil strife and an Indian war, Connolly had committed violence upon persons supporting Pennsylvania and had murdered several friendly Indians. But the Governor's scheme had been thwarted. The Burgesses had refused him troops, and the squabble over the boundary of Fort Pitt had been left to his Majesty's decision. This, Henry saw as a temporary settlement only.[5]

The real deviltry of Dunmore was seen in the Lewis expedition of July 12, 1774, in which reportedly the Governor intended to let Andrew Lewis and his men be sacrified at Point Pleasant in order to divert public attention from politics. It was charged that Dunmore had a private understanding with the Indians to attack and thus put an end to Lewis and his men and thereby break the colony's military resistance to England.[6]

Disturbing Patrick Henry further was the information that

---

[2] Henry, *Henry*, I, p. 249.
[3] *Ibid.*, I, p. 174.
[4] *Ibid.*, I, p. 175.
[5] *Ibid.*, I, p. 176.
[6] *Ibid.*, I, pp. 203–204–205.

Gen. Thomas Gage, the new commander-in-chief of North America, and his ten regiments,[7] were stationed at Boston. The question was: how long before troops would be assigned to subdue Virginia?

Reaching Caroline County, Patrick Henry was soon joined by Edmund Pendleton, another delegate, and the two rode on—on horseback, taking a bridle path through the forest, swimming the streams. Stopping only to rest, the two men reached Mount Vernon, where they had been invited by Washington to pass the night. Patrick Henry must have found the home on the Potomac interesting, and particularly the hostess; for he surely remembered with pleasure that Christmas of 1759 in the home of Martha's uncle, Col. Nathaniel West Dandridge, the brother of her father.[8] It was not known then, of course, that Patrick Henry's daughter, Betsy, would later marry into the same family as Martha's sister, Mrs. John Aylett. Neither could it have been imagined that Patrick Henry, then married to Sarah Shelton, would later marry Dorothea Dandridge, the cousin of Martha, and of Sarah.

The two gentlemen spent a day and night at Mount Vernon, and on August 31, joined by Washington, set out on horseback. As they were leaving, Mrs. Washington said, "I hope you will all stand firm; I know George will."

There was no question concerning the firmness of the delegate from Hanover. For nine years his convictions had never wavered. The three statesmen took the path leading from Mt. Vernon to the Falls, where they crossed the Potomac and rode on toward Baltimore, finally reaching Philadelphia.

Benjamin Harrison, Richard Bland and Peyton Randolph had gone on ahead. Richard Henry Lee was delayed. Most of the delegates had already arrived when the Henry party reached Philadelphia. They went first to the City Tavern, and later walked to Carpenter's Hall, the meeting place. There were present, including the seven Virginians, 55 delegates, representing the eleven Colonies. New York as a whole, and Georgia, were not represented. At the beginning, politics seem to have been rampant. Philip Vickers Fithian noted in 1774, "the universal topic is politics."

Concerning the Virginia delegates, Madison wrote: "This

---

[7] *Ibid.*, I, p. 190; *Ibid.*, I, p. 224. The regiments were raised from four to ten on September 1st; *Ibid.*, I, p. 201. General Gage had proclaimed it treasonable for the inhabitants to assemble to discuss their grievances, or to form Associations.

[8] Morgan, *Henry*, p. 318.

Colony has appointed seven delegates to represent it on this grand occasion; most of them glowing patriots and men of learning and penetration. It is however the opinion of some good judges that one or two might be exchanged for the better."[9]

The two delegates from the province of Philadelphia were "known to be inimical to the Liberties of America . . . Galloway the author of the detestable piece signed Americanus in the time of the Stamp Act; and one Humphries, an obscure assembly-man who but the moment before he was appointed, voted against the having a congress at all."[10]

From the start there was division among the members: those who wished only to meet in council, or make redress of grievances, of whom Galloway and Humphries of Pennsylvania, John Jay and James Duane of New York were the leaders; and those rash and impatient for action, led by the Adams-Henry group. Several of the delegates had met previous to the meeting. Some exchanged bows and few touched elbows. All now sat, answering to the roll-call.

Election of officers was in order. The South Carolina delegate, Mr. Lynch, arose and nominated Peyton Randolph of Virginia for president. Mr. Charles Thompson, a popular man in the cause of liberty around Philadelphia, but not a delegate, was proposed and sent for and was elected secretary. Randolph, elected president of the convention on August 1, gave the delegates to the Congress "instructions very temperately" both as to style and matter.[11]

The delegates from the different colonies were called upon to indicate their instructions, whereupon grievances and recommendations were heard. A motion was made by Duane of New York for appointing a committee to determine the regulations of the Congress. There were some objections, and John Adams inquired what particular rules Mr. Duane had in mind, to which was referred the method of voting, whether it should be by colonies, by poll, or by interest. A dull stillness ensued. None seemed willing to break the eventful silence, until a grave looking member in a plain dark suit of minister's gray, and unpowdered wig, arose. All became fixed in attention on him.

"Conticuere omnes, intentique ora tenebant."[12]

"Then," the secretary, Mr. Thompson, said, he "felt a sense of

---

[9] Brant, James Madison. *The Virginia Revolutionist, 1751–1780*, p. 142.

[10] *Ibid.*, Bradford to Madison.

[11] Brenaman, *Virginia Convention*, p. 15.

[12] "All grew still and intently maintained silence."

regret that the seeming country parson should so far have mistaken his talents, and the theatre for their display. But as he proceeded, he evinced such unusual force of argument, and such novel and impassioned eloquence, as soon electrified the house. Then the excited inquiry passed from man to man, Who is it? Who is it? The answer from the few who knew him was, 'It is Patrick Henry!' "

"Ille regit dictis animos et pectora mulcet."[13]

From memory, the secretary in later life[14] further described the scene:

> . . . After a short silence, Patrick Henry arose to speak. I did not then know him; he was dressed in a suit of parson's gray and from his appearance, I took him for a Presbyterian clergyman, used to haranguing the people. He observed that we were here met in a time and on an occasion of great difficulty and distress; that our public circumstances were like those of a man in deep embarrassment and trouble, who had called his friends together to devise what was best to be done for his relief;–one would propose one thing, and another a different one, whilst perhaps a third would think of something better suited to his unhappy circumstances, which he would embrace, and think no more of the rejected schemes with which he would have nothing to do. I thought that this was very good instruction to me, with respect to the taking the minutes. What Congress adopted, I committed to writing; with what they rejected I had nothing farther to do; and even then this method led to some squabbles with the members who were desirous of having their speeches and resolutions, however put to rest by the majority, still preserved upon the minutes!

John Adams recorded in his diary a brief summary of Patrick Henry's answer to Mr. Duane's regulations for Congress:

> Mr. Henry then arose, and said this was the first General Congress which had ever happened; that no former congress could be a precedent; that we should have occasion for more general congresses, and therefore that a precedent ought to be

[13] "With his words he rules their minds and soothes their hearts."

[14] Henry, *Henry*, I, p. 220, Quoting *American Quarterly Review*, I, 30, whence it is quoted in the works of John Adams, III, 29, 30, n. Tyler, *Patrick Henry*, pp. 109–110, n. states: "As regards the value of this testimony of Charles Thomson, we should note that it is something alleged to have been said by him at the age of ninety, in a conversation with a friend, and by the latter reported to the author of the article above cited in the *American Quarterly Review*."

established now; that it would be great injustice if a little colony should have the same weight in the councils of America as a great one, and therefore he was for a committee.[15]

The discussions on regulations were resumed the next day, midst cries in the street of "War! War!" based on rumors from Boston. Henry and Lee took the lead in the discussions of the "weight" of each colony in the voting. Patrick Henry for his part was willing that the relative weights be determined on the basis of populations, with the exclusion of slaves. Richard Lee, who had not been seated until the second day, objected, with some of the others, noting that they had not the material to estimate the weight of the colonies. Patrick Henry replied:

> I agree that authentic accounts cannot be had, if by authenticity is meant attestations of officers of the Crown. I go upon the supposition that government is at an end. All distinctions are thrown down. All America is thrown into one mass. We must aim at the minutiae of rectitude.[16]

Calling their attention to the precedent that was set in this their first meeting of Congress, Patrick Henry went on to show the critical conditions facing the country. He pointed to the dissolution of all authority, courts of justice suspended with no means for regulating civil police; no government sufficient to the exigencies of their affairs and the people in a state of nature.[17] With "novel and impassioned eloquence," he declared:

> Government is dissolved. Fleets and armies and the present state of things show that government is dissolved. Where are your landmarks, your boundaries of colonies? We are in a state of nature, sir. I did propose that a scale should be laid down; that part of North America which was once Massachusetts Bay, and that part which was once Virginia, ought to be considered as having weight. Will not people complain? Ten thousand Virginians have not outweighed one thousand others.
>
> I will submit, however; I am determined to submit, if I am overruled . . . I hope future ages will quote our proceedings with applause. It is one of the great duties of the democratical part of the constitution to keep itself pure. It is known in my Province

---

[15] Henry, *Henry*, I, p. 221, citing *Life and Works of John Adams*, II, p. 365.
[16] *Ibid.*, I, p. 222.
[17] Brenaman, *Virginia Conventions*, p. 19. Henry showed the "state of our laws . . . some of which are already expired, and others will shortly do so." The Courts were also closed.

that some other Colonies are not so numerous or rich as they are. I am for giving all the satisfaction in my power.

"A worthy gentleman near me," Henry noted, "seemed to admit the necessity of obtaining a more adequate representation." Could it have been John Jay of whom Henry was speaking? Jay would fight Henry later, but as for the relative population or wealth of the colonies, Jay said:

> To the virtue, spirit, and abilities of Virginia we owe much. I should always, therefore, from inclination as well as justice, be for giving Virginia its full weights.[18]

Then, Patrick Henry, wishing to pin importance to confederation or union, and to show the common purpose, declared those great words that gave meaning to the United States of America:

> The distinctions between Virginians, Pennsylvanians, New Yorkers, and New Englanders, are no more. I am not a Virginian, but an American!

Thus, "that patriotic utterance was in truth a prophesy of the United States of America."[19] Patrick Henry not only opened Congress, he gave impulse to the later action of Congress to change the name from United Colonies to the United States.

Henry's speech was given only in part, taken out of context. Speeches and resolutions "put to rest by the majority" were not recorded in the minutes.

Henry pointed to "the fleets and armies and *nature* of things"—the vessels in the harbor; General Gage and his ten regiments crouched over Boston, erecting fortifications and ready to strike.[20] He urged Congress to provide for the exigencies by establishing government at once.

But where, now, were all Henry's Virginia colleagues? Those "epochal revolutionists"; those patriots portrayed in the "The Common Glory"; those leaders celebrated by present-day historians? Jefferson was not among the members at the first Congress who were supposed to be contending for civil liberty and setting a design for the fabric of freedom. But what of Randolph, Bland, Pendleton and Harrison?

Where were they in this crisis hour? Where were they later on when the wretched politicians, those crafty proprietary men,

---

[18] Henry, *Henry*, I, pp. 221–223.

[19] *Ibid.*, I, p. 223.

[20] *Ibid.*, I, pp. 224–225.

tried to slip the vicious Galloway Plan past Henry? What did Patrick Henry's contemporaries do at this stage of America's destiny? Lee and Washington would show their colors later, as we shall see; but what of the other four horsemen of Virginia?

As none of Patrick Henry's associates supported him in his quest for government, John Jay of New York arose and replied:

> . . . The measure of arbitrary power is not full; and I think it must run over, before we undertake to frame a new constitution.[21]

Thus did John Jay answer Patrick Henry's crisis speech, and nothing further was done about it. John Adams wrote Jefferson:

> In the Congress of 1774, there was not one member, except Patrick Henry, who appeared to me sensible of the precipice, or rather, the pinnacle on which he stood, and had candor and courage enough to acknowledge it.[22]

The delegate from Connecticut, Silas Deane, wrote his wife:

> Mr. Henry . . . is the completest speaker I ever heard. If his future speeches are equal to the small samples he has hitherto given us, they will be worth preserving; but in a letter I can give you no idea of the music of his voice, or the high wrought yet natural elegance of his style and manner. Col. Lee is said to be his rival in eloquence, and in Virginia and to the Southward they are styled the Demosthenes and Cicero of America. God grant they may not, like them, plead in vain for the liberties of their country! These last gentlemen are now in full life, perhaps near fifty, and have made the constitution of Great Britain and America their capital study ever since the late troubles between them have arisen.[23]

The debates continued behind closed doors in Congress, and the next day, since it was impossible to determine the relative weights of the colonies by population or wealth, the following resolution was adopted:

> Resolved, That in determining questions in this Congress, each colony or province shall have one vote. The Congress not being possessed of, or at present able to procure proper materials for ascertaining the importance of each colony.[24]

---

[21] Tyler, *Henry*, pp. 112–113.

[22] John Adams to Thomas Jefferson, November 12, 1813; *Life and Works of John Adams*, X, p. 78.

[23] Morgan, *Henry*, pp. 167–168.

[24] Henry, *Henry*, I, p. 223.

Appointment of committees were the next duties of Congress. First was appointed a committee for declaring the rights of the colonies, to show the infringements upon them, and of obtaining, if possible, their restoration. A second committee was instructed to examine the British statutes affecting colonial trade and the manufactures of the colonies. Patrick Henry was placed on this important committee with Mr. Cushing and Mr. Mifflin. Since their report was related to the Committee on Rights, etc., Mr. Cushing, Mr. Henry and Mr. Mifflin were also assigned to this committee.[25] Concerning the Committee on Rights, an agreement was reached and reported, to found the rights of the colonies on the *laws of nature*, the principles of the English Constitution, and the American charters.

Another committee to which Patrick Henry was appointed in Congress was the one to petition the King.[26] Mr. Henry had been a member of a committee in the Virginia Assembly, May 11, 1769, to draw up a similar address.[27] In Congress the petition to his Majesty was debated three days, causing the greatest concern.[28] "John Adams spent the evening with Mr. Henry at his lodgings consulting about a petition to the King."[29] A committee to draft the address was composed of Richard Henry Lee, John Adams, Thomas Johnson, Patrick Henry and John Rutledge. Later John Dickinson was added to this group. The first draft was recommitted. In Dickinson's words, the original draft "was written in a language of asperity, very little according with the conciliatory disposition of Congress."[30] Henry's ideas of the grievances were perhaps too vehement for the moderate members, and Dickinson was called in to soften the sentiments. His proposal, which John Adams called an "olive branch," was adopted by the Congress on July 6th. Both Lee and Dickinson are said to have written the address to the King. They were also on a committee to prepare memorials to the people of Great Britain, British America, and later to Quebec.

---

[25] *Ibid.*, I, p. 226.

[26] Morgan, *Henry*, p. 170.

[27] Henry, *Henry*, I, pp. 139–140.

[28] Henry, *Henry*, I, p. 235.

[29] *Ibid.*, I, p. 237; Morgan, *Henry*, p. 175; Tyler *Henry*, p. 118n.

[30] Henry, *Henry*, I, p. 245. The matter of who wrote the address to the King seems not to be settled. *Ibid.*, I, p. 245. A very "imperfect copy" of a petition to the King, containing none of the matters inserted as directed by Congress appeared in the Southern Literary Messenger of March, 1860, claimed to be in the handwriting of Lee, according to his biographer.

Patrick Henry was keenly aware of the need for immediate action determining the future policy of the nation which would declare absolute their rights and liberties. Fully conscious "of the perilous position of the Colonies, and the necessity of energetic counsels, yet he saw the greater necessity of a united people, and he forbore to drive off men of influence by attacking with his powers of invective their half-hearted measures. The wisdom of this course was fully demonstrated, by the final alignment of the true but halting Whigs with the front ranks of the patriots."[31]

"Precisely what part Patrick Henry took in the preparation of this address is not now known; but there is no evidence whatever for the assertion that the first drafts which, when submitted to Congress, proved to be unsatisfactory, were the work of Patrick Henry. This draft, as is now abundantly proved, was prepared by the chairman of the Committee, Richard Henry Lee, but after full instructions from Congress and from the committee itself. In its final form, the address was largely moulded by the expert and gentle hand of John Dickinson. No one can doubt, however, that even though Patrick Henry may have contributed nothing to the literary execution of this fine address, he was not inactive in its construction, and that he was not likely to have suggested any abatement from its free and manly spirit."[32]

Early in the first Congress, an attempt was made to drive a wedge into the united effort of the colonies. Joseph Galloway, a "Tory in disguise,"[33] who later "fled the Province under cover of Howe's army" and embraced the British cause, rose up with "A plan of proposed Union between Great Britain and the Colonies": "A British and American legislature, for regulating the administration of the general affairs of America," in which each of the individual colonies would be permitted to "retain its present constitution, and powers of regulating and governing its own internal police, in all cases whatsoever."[34] The proposal called for a President-General to be appointed by the King and a Grand Council to be elected by the colonies for a three-year term, which would exercise the same rights, liberties and privileges as the House of Commons. It would require the nod of the President-General in all acts, becoming "an inferior and distinct branch of the British legislature, united and incorporated with it" for the

---

[31] Henry, *Henry*, I, pp. 237–238.
[32] Tyler, *Henry*, pp. 117–118.
[33] Morgan, *Henry*, pp. 169–170; Henry, *Henry*, I, pp. 230–233.
[34] *Ibid.*, I, pp. 230–231–232–233; American Archives, 4th series, I, 905.

general purposes of the colonies; the regulations of which might originate, "be formed and digested," "either in the Parliament of Great Britain or the Grand Council" to be "transmitted to the other for their approbation or dissent," requiring that the assent of both should be requisite to their validity.

Such a plan did not appeal to Patrick Henry. On the same day of its proposal, he assailed it, saying: "The original constitution of the colonies was founded on the broadest and most generous base. The regulation of our trade was compensation enough for all the protection we ever experienced from her (England). We shall liberate our constituents from a corrupt House of Commons, but throw them into the arms of an American legislature that may be bribed by that nation which avows, in the face of the world, that bribery is a part of her system of government.

"Before we are obliged to pay taxes as they do, let us be as free as they; let us have our trade open with all the world.

"We are not to consent by the representatives of representatives.

"I am inclined to think the present measures lead to war."[35]

The above is only an outline of Patrick Henry's speech as recalled by John Adams. Patrick Henry alone is said to have opposed Galloway in debate. Lee, or Henry, was always placed on the important committees. On the Galloway plan, Lee seemed undecided. Content with the colonial government prior to 1763, he now said, "This plan would make such changes in the legislature of the colonies, that I could not now agree to it without consulting my constituents."[36] Patrick Henry at once saw the plan as a disaster to the colonies if passed. He said the Galloway system would ruin the cause of America.[37] It was defeated by only one vote. No record was made of the votes cast. But Lee and Henry are given the credit for its defeat. Henry's grandson, William Wirt Henry, said, "The action of Congress on it constitutes a crisis in the history of America."[38] As another biographer, George Morgan, declared, "Galloway very near smothered the Republic at its birth."[39]

The two delegates from New York, Jay and Duane, and Edward Rutledge of South Carolina, supported the Galloway

[35] Tyler, *Henry*, p. 116; *Work of John Adams*, II, p. 390.

[36] Henry, *Henry*, I, p. 233.

[37] *Ibid.*, I, p. 237, Adams stated, that Henry "has a horrid opinion of Galloway, Jay, and the Rutledges. Their system, he says, would ruin the cause of America."

[38] *Ibid.*, I, p. 234.

[39] Morgan, *Henry*, p. 170.

proposals. But the Henry and Adams group held to the purpose of the Congress, contending that "the Delegates did not come with authority to consent to a political union between the two countries." Galloway's plan was looked upon as a surrender of many of the colonial rights.

Dr. Tyler declared: "Could it have been adopted, the disruption of the British empire would certainly have been averted for that epoch, and, as an act of violence and of unkindness, would perhaps have been averted forever; while the thirteen English colonies would have remained English colonies, without ceasing to be free."[40]

Other resolutions drawn up called for supplying the necessities, and alleviating the distresses, of "our brethren at Boston." These "generous, noble sentiments, and manly eloquence," caused Adams to write in his diary: "This was one of the happiest days of my life." He would even wager "that America will make a point of supporting Boston to the utmost."[41]

Congress took further steps to "deliberate on the means most proper to be pursued for a restoration of our rights." Suspension of commercial intercourse with Great Britain as a proper and effective means to procure redress from arbitrary taxes was recommended. Several days were spent in debate on measures of non-exportation, non-importation and non-consumption. At the mention of non-exportation, a cry arose from the delegates representing the merchants and exporters in whose respective colonies harbors would be affected. Virginia had no main harbor in 1774 and was partially exempt. The South Carolina delegates, Middleton, Rutledge and Lynch, but not Gadsden, objected to the measure, feeling that it would be ruinous to their markets, perceiving that their warehouses would be overflowing with rice and their vats with indigo.[42] In this dilemma, they issued an ultimatum, which was later withdrawn, after a compromise granting shipments of rice to Europe.

Congress having set up the above agreements—known as the plan of the association, which they considered might force Britain's hand to respect American rights—the date, November 1, 1774, was suggested for the stopping of all imports, and August 10, 1775, for putting an end to all exports. Mr. Henry, humanitarian that he was, felt that time for a little more warning to the merchants

---

[40] Tyler, *Henry*, pp. 115–116.
[41] Henry, *Henry*, I, pp. 225–226.
[42] *Ibid.*, pp. 228–229.

should be given, saying, "We don't mean to hurt even our rascals, if we have any. I move that December may be inserted instead of November."[43] His motion carried; December 1, 1774, was fixed for non-importation, and September 10, 1775, for non-exportation, if in the meantime the acts had not been repealed.

The first Congress was a busy assemblage. Methods had to be pursued with greatest tact and caution. Declared Adams: "We have a delicate course to steer. Tedious, indeed is our business—slow as snails. I am wearied to death. . . ." Starting at nine, lasting till three, "they most earnestly engaged in debates upon the most abstruse mysteries of state." Nor did Adams fail to set down the interesting: the feast of ten thousand delicacies—Madeira, Claret, and Burgundy. Dinner of turtle, and every other thing, flummery, jellies, sweetmeats of twenty sorts, trifles, whipped sillabubs, floating islands, etc., etc.[44] Coaxed by such dainties, the delegates held on, tussling with the problems.

The Adams-Henry group was now holding the lead, and on October 14 a "Declaration of Rights" was adopted which was the prelude to the Declaration of Independence. It was in the form of ten resolutions, founded on "the immutable laws of nature, the principles of the English constitution, and the several charters or compacts."[45]

An address was sent to the people of Quebec, Nova Scotia, Georgia, and East and West Florida, who were not represented in the Congress.[46] To make the measures of Congress effective, it was necessary that they be observed throughout the colonies. It was urged that a committee for this purpose be appointed in every county, city, and town in America.

Congress was now ready for adjournment. It was recommended that there should be a second Congress on May 10, unless in the meantime there should be a redress of grievances from Britain.

Henry and Adams anticipated no such beneficence on the part of the British ministry, and similar views were held by their group. The majority of the members, however, felt that their actions would result in a redress of grievances. John Adams's letter to William Wirt, dated January 23, 1818, shows Patrick Henry's feelings in the matter:

---

[43] *Ibid.*, I, p. 229.
[44] Morgan, *Henry*, pp. 168–175.
[45] Burnett, *Continental Congress*, p. 53.
[46] Henry, *Henry*, I, p. 238.

When Congress had finished their business, as they thought, in the autumn of 1774, I had with Mr. Henry, before we took leave of each other, some familiar conversation, in which I expressed a full conviction that our resolves, declaration of rights, enumeration of wrongs, petitions, remonstrances, and addresses, associations, and non-importation agreements, however they might be expected by the people in America, and however necessary to cement the union of the colonies, would be but waste paper in England. Mr. Henry said they might make some impression among the people of England, but agreed with me that they would be totally lost upon the government. I had but just received a short and hasty letter, written to me by Major Joseph Hawley, of Northampton, containing "a few broken hints" as he called them, of what he thought was proper to be done, and concluding with these words: "After all we must fight." This letter I read to Mr. Henry, who listened with great attention; and as soon as I had pronounced the words, "After all we must fight," he raised his head, and with an energy and vehemence that I can never forget, broke out with, "By G–d, I am of that man's mind". . . . The other delegates from Virginia returned to their state, in full confidence that all our grievances would be redressed. The last words that Richard Henry Lee said to me, when we parted, were, "We shall infallibly carry all our points, you will be completely relieved; all the offensive acts will be repealed; the army and fleet will be recalled, and Britain will give up her foolish project."

Washington only was in doubt. He never spoke in public. In private he joined with those who advocated a non-exportation, as well as a non-importation agreement. With both he thought we should prevail; without either he thought it doubtful. Henry was clear in one opinion, Richard Henry Lee in an opposite opinion, and Washington doubted between the two. Henry however appeared in the end to be exactly right.[47]

Thomas Jefferson was not at the first Congress; yet he wrote Wirt that Patrick Henry's work at the first Congress was a minor matter, that he was incapable of composition. Jefferson stated that "the superior powers of Patrick Henry were manifest only in debate, and that he and Richard Lee took the undisputed lead in the Assembly during the first days of the session while general grievances[48] were the topic, and that both of them were completely thrown in the shade when called down from the heights of declamation to that severer test of intelligent excellence, the details of

[47] Henry, *Henry*, I, p. 239; Tyler, *Henry*, p. 125.
[48] Tyler, *Henry*, p. 122.

business." Wirt considered the above to be the true estimate of the delegate's capacity, since with Wirt nothing became authentic history that did not first have Jefferson's stamp of approval. But such statements by Thomas Jefferson, made in the shades of life, are unfounded. As has been pointed out, grievances were not taken up during the first days of the session. Patrick Henry took a most active part in all pertinent aspects of the convention. The delegate from Hanover is defended from this disparagement in the following words: "Mr. Jefferson throughout seems to have been at special pains to make the impression that Mr. Henry's ability consisted only and solely in his power of declamation, when the real truth is that in all the different conventions in which he met, and in all the conferences held during these exciting times his services as a wise and far-seeing stateman were called more into requisition than the use of his gifts as a speaker and orator. The fact that in all the committees into whose hands were committed matters of most practical importance, Mr. Henry was a member, is a very clear indication of the esteem in which he was held by those bodies."[49]

Jefferson and Wirt both had been better informed about Patrick Henry. Adams's letter to Jefferson has already been given. To William Wirt, January 23, 1818, Adams also wrote: "I esteem the character of Mr. Henry an honor to our country. . . . From personal acquaintance, perhaps I might say a friendship, with Mr. Henry of more than thirty years, and from all that I have heard or read of him I have always considered him as a gentleman of deep reflection, keen sagacity, clear foresight, daring enterprise, inflexible intrepidity and untainted integrity, with an ardent zeal for the liberties, the honor, and the felicity of his country and his species."[50]

Adams had not forgotten: It was the effect of Patrick Henry's Stamp Act resolves that had brought them together in Congress in the first place. If, in the first Congress, Patrick Henry had done nothing more than thwart the dismal Galloway Plan of Union, that alone would have marked his abilities and distinguished him as a member.

The Congress adjourned on October 26. Most of the Virginia delegates, because of matters demanding the attention of the Burgesses, had left for their homes on October 23. Only Lee and Washington remained to finish up the business, and were re-

[49] Chandler and Thames, *Colonial Virginia*, pp. 345–346.

[50] *Works of John Adams*, X, p. 277; Tyler, *Henry*, p. 124.

quested to sign the names of the Virginia delegates on the petition to the King. Washington wrote the signatures of Pendleton, Harrison and Bland. Lee added Patrick Henry's and his own name to the list. Peyton Randolph's name was missing; nobody signed for him. Perhaps it was just as well not to have had the name of the King's Attorney on the petition. As to the name of Patrick Henry, it had been a familiar, though bad, omen, to the eyes of Parliament and the King since 1765.

Patrick Henry had now started home. The events of the past weeks in Congress had taxed his energies. The long ride was coming to an end as he crossed the North Anna and the New Found Rivers in Hanover. The grim forebodings he had held for his country's future were brushed aside, temporarily, as the great roof of his manor house came into view.

X

ST. JOHN'S CHURCH, ALERTING THE COLONY—"WE MUST FIGHT!"

> *"They tell us, sir, that we are weak—unable to cope with so formidable an adversary. But when shall we become stronger? Will it be when we are totally disarmed, and when a British guard shall be stationed in every house? Shall we gather strength by irresolution and inaction? . . . Sir, we are not weak, if we make a proper use of those means which the God of nature hath placed in our power. Three millions of people, armed in the holy cause of liberty, and in such a country as that which we possess, are invincible by any force which our enemy can send against us. . . . The battle, sir, is not to the strong alone; it is to the vigilant, the active, the brave. . . ."*
>
> —Patrick Henry in the second Virginia Convention, March 23, 1775.

THE FIRST OF NOVEMBER, 1774, found Patrick Henry back at Scotchtown, resting from the rigors of the past weeks. The instructions of Congress were still fresh in his mind as he turned his attention to carrying out the plans for organizing the association and for appointing the Hanover Committee,[1] later to be known as the "Committee of Safety," to assume the functions of government in the county.

[1] Henry, *Henry,* I, p. 250. The Association was appointed under the direction of Patrick Henry early in November.

On November 9, he called together the "younger part" of the militia and asked them to meet him at Smith's Tavern, now Merry Oaks, where he addressed them with a spirited speech, pointing to the necessity to arm in the defense of their rights and urging that they form themselves into a volunteer company to be "prepared for every emergency." With Patrick Henry as their captain, they were enrolled at once, each armed with only a short carbine and a tomahawk, and wearing hunting shirts; they became the first independent military company in Virginia to be enlisted after the adjournment of Congress, and were known as the Hanover Volunteers.[2]

Prior to, or during this time, "before one drop of blood was shed in our contest with Great Britain," Mr. Henry was visiting at "Plain Dealing,"[3] in company with Colonel Morris, John Hawkins and the owner of the home, Colonel Samuel Overton, when he was asked by the latter whether he supposed Great Britain would drive her colonies to extremities? And if she should, what he thought would be the issue of the war? After looking around to see who was present, he replied confidentially: "She will drive us to extremities—no accommodation will take place—hostilities will soon commence—and a desperate and bloody touch it will be." Then asked Colonel Samuel Overton, "Do you think, Mr. Henry, that an infant nation as we are, without discipline, arms, ammunition, ships of war, or money to procure them—do you think it possible, thus circumstanced, to oppose successfully the fleets and armies of Great Britain?" "I will be candid with you," replied Mr. Henry. "I doubt whether we shall be able, alone, to cope with so powerful a nation. But," he continued (rising from his chair, with great animation), "Where is France? Where is Spain? Where is Holland?—the natural enemies of Great Britain—where will they be all this while? Do you suppose they will stand by, idle and indifferent spectators to the contest? Will Louis XVI be asleep all this time? Believe me, no! When Louis XVI shall be satisfied by our serious opposition, and our *Declaration of Independence*, that all prospect of reconciliation is gone, then, and not till then, will he furnish us with arms, ammunition, and clothing; and not with these only, but he will send his fleet and armies to fight our battles for us; he will form with us a treaty offensive and

[2] Henry, *Henry*, I, p. 251. No doubt some of these were the sons of Col. John Henry's militia-men.

[3] "Plain Dealing" was the home of Colonel Samuel Overton, according to Judge Leon M. Bazile, Hanover County Historian.

defensive against our unnatural mother. Spain and Holland will join the confederation! Our independence will be established, and we shall take our stand among the nations of the earth!" Here he ceased; and Colonel John Overton says, "at the word *independence*, the company appeared to be startled; for they had never heard before anything of the kind even suggested."[4]

Mr. Henry's belief in the aid of our allies was so firm, he reiterated it in his St. John's Church speech.[5]

Moreover, independence was to him the only conceivable strategy by which the colonies could proceed to a glorious victory and the attainment of freedom. Although he was heartened by his volunteers and freeholders of the Hanover "backwoods," and was encouraged as well by the actions of the Sons of Liberty; by the "minute-men, raised in a minute," and by the zeal of the people at large, it must have been impossible for him to understand the untoward and dilatory attitude of some of the men of weighty influence. Of grave concern to the patriot, no doubt, was the fact that Virginia had not as yet taken any general steps toward a state of war. Public men, to his chagrin, were unwilling to admit that the chance for reconciliation had passed.[6] Imperiled as the nation was, he must have viewed with alarm the insufficient number of troops—only seven independent volunteer companies had been organized within the Virginia Colony. From what had already happened in Massachusetts Bay, at any hour a fresh wind might speed his Majesty's sails toward the Virginia Peninsula.[7]

Also of great anxiety to him at this time was the condition of Mrs. Henry's health, which was steadily worsening. Her subsequent death was "a loss which had forced him to abandon all things which recalled her to him."[8] Dying early in the year, she left behind six children, all under twenty-one. Martha (Patsy), the eldest, who later married Col. John Fontaine, took over the care of the younger children. Through the solicitude and loyalty of

---

[4] Henry, *Henry*, I, pp. 207–208; Wirt, *Henry*, pp. 111–112. (1836)

[5] Campbell, *Ancient Dominion*, p. 751. The truth of Henry's prediction at "Plain Dealing" in Hanover, is borne out by Washington's acknowledgement of the 20th October, 1781. In congratulating the army on their glorious victory, he declared that it was owing to the assistance of the French allies.

[6] Henry, *Henry*, I, pp. 238–239–240.

[7] *Ibid.*, I, p. 266. St. John's Church speech: "The next gale that sweeps from the North . . ."

[8] Sarah Shelton Henry died in the Spring of 1775. *Memoirs of the Life of Philip Mazzei*, p. 276.

this daughter, Mr. Henry was permitted to render the services to his country that were afterward required of him.

It was in such a calamitous spring that the scene is shifted to the living room at Scotchtown, where one might imagine Mr. Henry on the evening of March 19, 1775.

On the morrow, Monday, he would be going down to Richmond as the delegate from Hanover County to attend the Second Virginia Convention, held in St. John's Church, out of reach of Governor Dunmore's army at Williamsburg. Mr. Henry was sitting alone by his fire. In the quietness, his thoughts must have turned to the convention. He knew that tomorrow he must face an irresolute body; that he would be opposed by the powerful, wealthy, Tory element among the members. He realized that the Loyalists were insidiously entrenched and the outcome was uncertain.[9] Patrick Henry's risk was tremendous—one that could easily bring him to the block. At the Continental Congress, "he saw with great clarity that the Declaration of Rights and Grievances, and the further agreements of non-importation were not sufficient weapons for the disarmed colonies."[10]

The next morning a light March snow was falling as he left the stone steps of Scotchtown. Drawing his great cloak about him, he rode off to Richmond. . . .

The day had cleared when Mr. Henry reached St. John's Church. Horses were hitched everywhere and many gigs and carriages could be seen. The delegates scurried to their seats. They represented in all 61 counties. A howling March wind sweeping the Church Hill added further depressive notes. Patrick Henry sat in the third pew.

The Convention opened with Peyton Randolph, the Speaker of the House, elected president as usual. With Randolph in the chair now, as in Congress, it must from the beginning have seemed to Patrick Henry a hopeless situation. The former King's Attorney, now the Speaker, was always in the chair to checkmate him. Randolph recommended to the Convention that they proceed

---

[9] Tyler, *Henry*, pp. 147–150; Henry, *Henry*, I, p. 269. Fontaine Manuscript, Cornell University, as quoted by Dr. Tyler for Mr. Wirt, taken from John Roane whose father, Colonel William Roane, was a member of the old House of Burgesses. John Roane described the closing sentences of Henry's St. John's Church speech: " 'Forbid it, Almighty God!' He then turned toward the timid loyalists of the House, who were quaking with terror . . ."

[10] Dr. James P. Lucier, Associate Editor, Richmond *News Leader*, July 4, 1964.

in the "deliberations and discussions with prudence, decency and order. . . ."[11]

The proceedings of the Continental Congress were discussed and approved, and the delegates were thanked for discharging their duties. Looking toward the second meeting of Congress to be held in Philadelphia in May, Mr. Henry and the other delegates were reappointed by ballot. On Thursday, the third day of the convention, after much of the preliminaries had been dispensed with, the important matter of arming the colony was to be taken up. This, Mr. Henry probably awaited with impatience, feeling the keen necessity for an efficient, well-organized army, financed and controlled by the colony. In the meantime, however, Speaker Randolph pushed forward a petition and memorial from the Island of Jamaica, addressed to the King three months before, on December 28, 1774. In this was seen a "bold" vindication of the colonies' rights, except for two misleading positions: "It traced the grant of colonial rights to the King, and claimed that the royal prerogative annexed to the Crown was totally independent of the people, who could not invade, add to, or diminish it. This extreme Tory doctrine was not to the liking of the advanced patriots, nor necessary for the vindication of American rights, which were not dependent on royal grants alone.[12] Moreover, there were other disturbing or objectionable matters contained in the declaration from the Jamaica Assembly. It noted that 'owing to their weak condition, caused by slavery, it could not be supposed they intended, or ever could have intended, resistance to Great Britain.' " The balance of the paper, however, was a "severe rebuke to the British Government, and an able defense of America. This last pleased many members of the Convention and led them to overlook what was deemed objectionable."[13] But not Patrick Henry! His mind was intent upon the complete statement.

"The too abject tone of these resolutions aroused the patriotic indignation of Patrick Henry."[14] He arose and proposed the following resolutions:

> Resolved, That a well-regulated militia, composed of gentlemen and yeomen, is the natural strength and only security of a free government; that such a militia in this colony would forever render it unnecessary for the mother country to keep among us,

---

[11] Brenaman, *A History of Virginia Conventions*, p. 18.

[12] Henry, *Henry*, I, p. 255; *American Archives*, 4th Series, I, pp. 1072–1074.

[13] *Ibid.*, I, pp. 255–256.

[14] Brenaman, *A History of Virginia Conventions*, p. 18.

for the purpose of our defense, any standing army of mercenary soldiers, always subversive of the quiet, and dangerous to the liberties of the people, and would obviate the pretext of taxing us for their support.

That the establishment of such a militia is, at this time, peculiarly necessary, by the state of our laws for the protection and defense of the country, some of which have already expired, and others will shortly do so; and that the known remissness of government, in calling us togther in legislative capacity, renders it too insecure, in this time of danger and distress, to rely, that opportunity will be given of renewing them in General Assembly, or making any provision to secure our inestimable rights and liberties from those farther violations with which they are threatened.

Resolved therefore, That this colony be immediately put into a posture of defense, and that . . . be a committee to prepare a plan for the embodying, arming and disciplining such a number of men as may be sufficient for that purpose.[15]

The first of these resolutions had been used before in the Maryland convention of Dec. 8; by the Delaware committee, December 21; by the Fairfax County committee on January 17, and in other bodies among the colonies which were arming and drilling their militia. "But the second resolution of Mr. Henry looked to an immediate preparation for a conflict of arms; not simply to the drilling of the militia, but to the embodying of an army for the defense of the Colony. The resolution itself clearly disclosed its object, and Mr. Henry, in his speech enforcing it, left no doubt of his purpose. He would have the Convention, with him, give up all hope of a peaceful settlement, and recognize the fact that they were virtually at war with Great Britain."[16] The King's decision of January 12 in a cabinet council made it clear that he would yield "nothing to the colonies, and it was determined to interdict all commerce with them, to protect the loyal Colonists, and to declare all others traitors and rebels."[17] The opposition of his colleagues in the Congress was repeated here. According to the records, Pendleton, Bland, Harrison, Nicholas and Wythe opposed Henry's resolution, conceiving it to be prema-

[15] Brenaman, *A History of Virginia Conventions,* p. 19; Henry, *Henry,* I, pp. 257–258.

[16] Henry, *Henry,* I, pp. 258; Tyler, *Henry,* p. 133; *Ibid.,* p. 142. Henry asked; What means this martial array, if its purpose be not to force us to submission?

[17] Bancroft, VII, p. 193; Henry, *Henry,* I, p. 254. Southern Literary Messenger November 1859. Richard H. Lee's letter of February 24, 1775, to his brother Arthur in London, declared that there was astonishment and concern by the people of America over the King's speech to Parliament.

ture,[18] and this produced an animated debate. "But in themselves his resolutions, so far from being premature, were rather tardy; they lagged weeks and even months behind many of the best counties in Virginia itself, as well as behind those other colonies to which in political feeling Virginia was always most nearly akin."[19]

Dr. Tyler pointed out that "all who are familiar with the politics of Virginia at that period will see in the cluster of names some clue to the secret of their opposition. It was an opposition to Patrick Henry himself, and as far as possible to any measure of which he should be the leading champion." But Dr. Tyler pointed out that even this was not enough. He noted that "Others had said, 'The war must come and will come,—unless certain things are done.' " "Patrick Henry brushing away every prefix or suffix of uncertainty, every half despairing 'if,' every fragile and pathetic 'unless,' exclaimed, in the hearing of all men: Why talk of things being now done which can avert the war? Such things will not be done. The war is coming: it has come already." "Patrick Henry would have this Convention, by adopting his resolutions, virtually declare war itself." It was in this alone that Dr. Tyler thought Henry's resolutions "premature"; that the very men who opposed them would have favored them had Mr. Henry "left that door open, or even ajar" instead of closing it "against the possibility of peace."[20]

Jefferson declared: "Subsequent events favored the bolder spirits of Henry, Lee, Page, Mason, etc., with whom I went in all points."

Memoirs of the scene and of Henry's speech in support of his resolutions at St. John's Church have been left by Edmund Randolph, Judge John Tyler and Judge St. George Tucker, who sat in the audience.[21] Mr. Wirt's version is said to have given the substance of Henry's speech.[22]

---

[18] Brenaman, *A History of Virginia Conventions*, p. 19; Henry, *Henry*, I, p. 258. St. George Tucker, who was present, but not a member, (thirty years later) recalled the names of the same men (except Wythe) who were among the opposition to Henry's resolutions after which followed the animated debate.

[19] Tyler, *Henry*, p. 138; *Ibid.*, p. 133. Tyler quotes Governor Dunmore's letter to the Earl of Dartmouth, Dec. 24, 1774, saying "Every county is now arming a company of men . . ." But this is in error. See Henry, *Henry*, I, p. 252.

[20] *Ibid.*, pp. 137–138–139.

[21] Edmund Randolph, MS. in possession of the Virginia Historical Society; Henry, *Henry*, I, p. 261.

[22] Henry, *Henry*, I, pp. 261–262–263–264; Tyler, *Henry*, p. 133.

Before the multitude who had gathered for the Convention, Patrick Henry is said to have evoked St. Paul while preaching at Athens, and to have spoken as man was never known to speak before. In his utterances, "he solicited no admiring look from those who surrounded him. If he had, he must have been abashed by meeting every eye fixed upon him. Henry was his natural self." "He paused, but he paused full of some rising eruption of eloquence. When he sat down, his sounds vibrated so loudly if not in the ears, at least in the memory of his audience, that no other member, not even his friend who was to second him was yet adventurous enough to interfere with that voice which had so recently subdued and captivated." "After every illusion had vanished, a prodigy yet remained."[23]

Another hearer, who on this "occasion felt a first full impression of Mr. Henry's powers," said, "In vain should I attempt to give you any idea of his speech. He touched upon the origin and progress of the dispute between Great Britain, and the colonies —the various conciliatory measures adopted by the latter, and the uniformly increasing tone of violence and arrogance on the part of the former."[24]

Continuing his description, Judge Tucker compares Patrick Henry with the orators of Old Rome:

"Imagine to yourself this speech delivered with all the calm dignity of Cato of Utica; imagine to yourself the Roman Senate assembled in the capital when it was entered by the profane Gauls, who at first were awed by their presence as if they had entered an assembly of the gods. Imagine that you had heard that Cato addressing such a Senate. Imagine that you saw the handwriting on the wall of Belshazzar's palace. Imagine that you had heard a voice as from heaven uttering the words, 'We must fight,' as the doom of Fate, and you may have some idea of the speaker, the assembly to whom he addressed himself, and the auditory, of which I was one."[25]

Another spectator declared that the orator's "voice, countenance and gestures gave irresistible force to his words, which no description could make intelligible to one who had never seen him or heard him speak. . . . When Patrick Henry pled, 'Forbid

---

[23] Edmund Randolph, MS. in possession of Virginia Historical Society

[24] Henry, *Henry*, I, p. 264.

[25] *Ibid.*, p. 265.

it, Almighty God,' his arms were extended aloft; his body was thrown back, his coat flung right and left. The tendons of his neck stood out white and rigid like whipcords. His brow was knit, every feature marked with the resolute purpose of his soul. . . . The sound of his voice was like that of a Spartan paean on the field of Plataea. . . . 'Liberty' he spoke with an emphasis never given it before. His countenance was radiant; he stood erect and defiant; while the sound of his voice and the sublimity of his attitude made him appear a magnificent incarnation of Freedom, and expressed all that can be acquired or enjoyed by nations and individuals invincible and free."[26]

Patrick Henry magnificently answered the mandates of a corrupt Ministry with his call to arms:

> Mr. President, no man thinks more highly than I do of the patriotism, as well as abilities, of the very worthy gentlemen who have just addressed the house. But different men often see the same subject in different lights; and, therefore, I hope it will not be thought disrespectful to those gentlemen, if entertaining, as I do, opinions of a character very opposite to theirs, I shall speak forth *my* sentiments freely, and without reserve. This is no time for ceremony. The question before the house is one of awful moment to this country. For my own part, I consider it as nothing less than a question of freedom or slavery. And in proportion to the magnitude of the subject, ought to be the freedom of debate. It is only in this way that we can hope to arrive at truth and fulfill the great responsibility which we hold to God and our country. Should I keep back my opinions at such a time, through fear of giving offense, I should consider myself guilty of treason toward my country, and of an act of disloyality toward the majesty of Heaven, which I revere above all earthly kings.
>
> Mr. President, it is natural for a man to indulge in the illusions of hope. We are apt to shut our eyes against a painful truth—and listen to the song of that siren till she transforms us into beasts. Is this the part of wise men, engaged in a great and arduous struggle for liberty? Are we disposed to be of the number of those who, having eyes, see not, and having ears, hear not, the things which so nearly concern their temporal salvation. For my part, whatever anguish of spirit it might cost, I am willing to know the whole truth; to know the worst and to provide for it.

---

[26] *Ibid.*, pp. 269–270; Tyler, *Henry*, p. 150, Quoting John Roane from the Manuscript of the Rev. Edward Fontaine, Cornell University, as given by Dr. Tyler.

I have but one lamp by which my feet are guided; and that is the lamp of experience. I know of no way of judging the future but by the past. And judging by the past, I wish to know what there has been in the conduct of the British ministry for the last ten years to justify those hopes with which gentlemen have been pleased to solace themselves and the house? Is it that insidious smile with which our petition has been lately received? Trust it not, sir; it will prove a snare to your feet. Suffer not yourselves to be betrayed with a kiss. Ask yourselves how this gracious reception of our petition comports with those warlike preparations which cover our waters and darken our land. Are fleets and armies necessary to a work of love and reconciliation? Have we shown ourselves so unwilling to be reconciled that force must be called in to win back our love? Let us not deceive ourselves, sir. These are the implements of war and subjugation—the last arguments to which kings resort. I ask gentlemen, sir, what means this martial array, if its purpose be not to force us to submission? Can gentlemen assign any other possible motive for it? Has Great Britain any enemy in this quarter of the world to call for all this accumulation of navies and armies? No, sir, she has none. They are meant for us: they can be meant for no other. They are sent over to bind and rivet upon us those chains which the British ministry have been so long forging. And what have we to oppose to them? Shall we try argument? Sir, we have been trying that for the last ten years. Have we anything new to offer upon the subject? Nothing. We have held the subject up in every light of which it is capable; but it has been all in vain. Shall we resort to entreaty and humble supplication? What terms shall we find which have not been already exhausted? Let us not, I beseech you, sir, deceive ourselves longer. Sir, we have done everything that could be done to avert the storm which is now coming on. We have petitioned—we have remonstrated—we have supplicated—we have prostrated ourselves before the throne, and have implored its interposition to arrest the tyrannical hands of the ministry and Parliament. Our petitions have been slighted; our remonstrances have produced additional violence and insult; our supplications have been disregarded; and we have been spurned, with contempt, from the foot of the throne. In vain, after these things, may we indulge the fond hope of peace and reconciliation. *There is no longer any room for hope.* If we wish to be free—if we mean to preserve inviolate those inestimable privileges for which we have been so long contending—if we mean not basely to abandon the noble struggle in which we have been so long engaged, and which we have pledged ourselves never to abandon until the glorious object of our contest shall be obtained—we must fight! I repeat it, sir, we must fight!! An appeal to arms and to the God of Hosts is all that is left us!

They tell us, sir, that we are weak—unable to cope with so formidable an adversary. But when shall we be stronger? Will it be the next week, or the next year? Will it be when we are totally disarmed, and when a British guard shall be stationed in every house? Shall we gather strength by irresolution and inaction? Shall we acquire the means of effectual resistance by lying supinely on our backs, and hugging the delusive phantom of hope, until our enemies shall have bound us hand and foot? Sir, we are not weak, if we make a proper use of those means which the God of nature hath placed in our power. Three millions of people, armed in the holy cause of liberty, and in such a country as that which we possess, are invincible by any force which our enemy can send against us. Besides, sir, we shall not fight our battles alone. There is a just God who presides over the destinies of nations, and who will raise up friends to fight our battles for us. The battle, sir, is not to the strong alone; it is to the vigilant, the active, the brave. Besides, sir, we have no election. If we were base enough to desire it, it is now too late to retire from the contest. There is no retreat, but in submission and slavery! Our chains are forged, their clanking may be heard on the plains of Boston! The war is inevitable—and let it come!! I repeat it, sir, let it come!!!

It is in vain, sir, to extenuate the matter. Gentlemen may cry, peace, peace—but there is no peace. The war is actually begun. The next gale that sweeps from the North will bring to our ears the clash of resounding arms! Our brethren are already in the field! Why stand we here idle? What is it that gentlemen wish? What would they have? Is life so dear, or peace so sweet, as to be purchased at the price of chains and slavery? Forbid it, Almighty God! I know not what course others may take; but as for me, give me liberty or give me death![27]

"This electrifying declaration, which shattered the complacency of the delegates, was no mere criticism of British misrule as had been the outcry in 1770 by Samuel Adams after the Boston Massacre, or John Hancock's speech in 1774 in Boston memorializing that tragedy of colonial misrule. This was a trumpet voice, uttered during a time of confused thinking and timid indecision. This was an outright defiance of British might, an appeal directed to the hearts of men who loved Liberty. This was the spark needed to fire into action the plans for freedom and independence already

[27] Tyler, *Henry,* pp. 140–141–142–143.

formed by the Continental Congress. This, truly, was a proud moment in our American heritage.

"Remember, as Patrick Henry's immortal words were being spoken, British forces were being constantly reinforced: toward Boston, where four regiments of British troops already encamped in that city; toward New York and the nearer Chesapeake Bay, where squadrons of British vessels from the world's mightiest navy were ready for action.

"For Patrick Henry the die was cast. There was no turning back. He had spoken up—his stand was crystal clear."[28]

A soldier, Col. Edward Carrington, listening from a window in the east end of the church, was so moved by Henry's eloquence that he exclaimed, "Let me be buried on this spot." His request was respected 35 years later.[29]

In the audience sat Mason, Jefferson and Washington exposed to Henry's great contagion of liberty. Washington's "looks bespoke a mind absorbed in meditation on his country's fate: When Patrick Henry with indignation ridiculed the idea of peace 'when there was no peace,' a positive concert between Washington and Henry was exhibited . . . "[30] His shout of 'Liberty or Death' must have echoed and re-echoed in the ears of Washington until that final victory at Yorktown. From Church Hill, Patrick Henry's speech traveled to colonial empires around the world.

In Richmond, St. John's Church is still standing, a living memorial to the patriot. Here, in the year 1959, 51,000 people came to pay their respects to a great patriot and to see the very enclosure where he sat, and to have pointed out to them where he stood when he delivered those immortal words that "turned a world upside down."

Immediately following Mr. Henry's bold and vehement call to arms a committee was appointed, in spite of those opposing the resolutions. Making up the committee, with Mr. Henry as chairman, were the following members: Richard Henry Lee, Robert Carter Nicholas, Benjamin Harrison, Lemuel Riddick,

[28] *Patrick Henry "American Credo"* Stamp Ceremony. From the speech given by Mr. L. Rohe Walter, Special Assistant to the Postmaster General, St. John's Church, Richmond, Virginia, January 11, 1961. The historian, Mr. Henry, declared that General Gage took steps in September, 1774 to concentrate all the British soldiers in America, *ten* regiments, at Boston and wrote to England for more reinforcements. Henry, *Henry,* I, p. 224. See also p. 190.

[29] Henry, *Henry,* I, p. 270.

[30] Edmund Randolph's MS. in possession of the Virginia Historical Society; Henry, *Henry,* op. cit. I, p. 260.

George Washington, Adam Stephen, Andrew Lewis, William Christian, Edmund Pendleton, Thomas Jefferson and Isaac Lane.[31] Here we see some of the old members who were formerly Mr. Henry's principal opponents now working side by side with him. Thus did he "consolidate the phalanx which breasted the powers of Great Britain."[32] Among those influenced by Patrick Henry's power of persuasion was "the generous and noble-minded Thomas Nelson, who now for the first time took a more than common part in a great discussion, convulsed the moderate by an ardent exclamation, in which he called God to witness, that if any British troops should be landed within the county of which he was the lieutenant, he would wait for no orders, and would obey none which would forbid him to summon his militia and repel the invaders at the water's edge. His temper, though it was sanguine, and had been manifested in less scenes of opposition, seemed to be more than ordinarily excited. His example told those who were happy in ease and wealth that to shrink was dishonorable."[33] Later, it was this same patriot, Gen. Thomas Nelson, Jr., who supplied a thousand horses for Washington's army and gave $200,000 to the cause, for which he was never reimbursed.[34]

The effectiveness of the committee under its chairman, Patrick Henry, is evidenced in that "it took them only one day to prepare its plan for enlisting, arming and disciplining the militia . . . "[35] Mr. Henry must have given much thought to the subject in advance.

What can be said of Patrick Henry's anticipation of British reaction to his resolutions and to his speech? No conciliatory offers were made to the colonies. Lord Chatham's motion to withdraw the troops from Boston was voted down by the House of Lords in January, a fact as yet unknown to Mr. Henry and America. Chatham's other bill, offered in February for an effectual settlement of the colonies' troubles, called for repeal of the Acts of Parliament and a free grant of revenue. This likewise was debated and dismissed.[36] Lord North on February 20 introduced

---

[31] Henry, *Henry*, I, p. 271.

[32] Wirt, *Henry*, pp. 143–144, Jefferson to William Wirt.

[33] Morgan, *Henry*, p. 197 n.

[34] Morgan, *Henry*, p. 198; Chandler and Thames, *Colonial Virginia*, p. 367. It is pointed out also that "Mann Page fed Washington's whole army for a week from his own plantation," Mansfield.

[35] Chandler & Thames, *Colonial Virginia*, p. 347.

[36] Henry, *Henry*, I, p. 272.

a scheme which he thought, if not effectual, might divide the colonies and unite England. His bill would permit the colonies to raise the revenue required by the King and Parliament as they deemed best, but all the claims of Parliament and the hurtful Acts would be continued.[37] These proposals were denounced by some of the outstanding speakers in Parliament. Edmund Burke declared the measures not at all conciliatory. In his speech on *Conciliation with America,* he said: "The temper and character which prevail in our colonies are, I am afraid, unalterable by any human art. We cannot, I fear, falsify the Pedigree of this fierce people, and persuade them that they are not sprung from a nation in whose veins the blood of freedom circulates. The language in which they would hear you tell them this tale would detect the disposition; your speech would betray you. An Englishman is the unfittest person on earth to argue another Englishman into slavery. . . . Slavery they can have anywhere. It is a weed that grows in every soil. . . ."[38] Fox said, "The Americans will reject it with disdain." Chatham called North's proposals "mere verbiage, a most puerile mockery." The day before Mr. Henry's speech at St. John's Church, Burke offered his resolutions for repealing the hurtful acts imposed on the colonies. His great speech, however, went unheeded. The bill of February 10, calling for the restraint of the trade and commerce of the colonies of New England, as well as the measures by the Committee of Supply for the augmentation of his Majesty's army and navy, were both adopted in the House.[39]

Through Patrick Henry's keen perception and timing, the colony was now a step in advance of British decision.

Notwithstanding the fact that this great speech has been credited to Patrick Henry for almost two centuries, it has been the purpose of some present-day writers to question its authenticity and even shroud it in mystery.

Much of the misinformation and malignity stems from the pen of Thomas Jefferson.

A professor of history, Dr. Mayo, recently stated that "students interested in the myths of history and how they develop find Patrick Henry a favorite subject because his career is still

---

[37] *Ibid.*, I, p. 273.

[38] Chambers *Cyclopaedia of English Literature,* IV, p. 382. Edmund Burke, From the "Speech on Conciliation with America, 1775."

[39] Henry, *Henry,* I, p. 273.

a great enigma." He stated further that Washington, Jefferson and Henry are all "heavily myth-encrusted, but of the trio Patrick Henry is by far the most perplexing for those scholars who would separate history from myth."[40]

One reason given for Dr. Mayo's statement is that 39 volumes of Washington's writings and a possible 50 to 60 volumes of Jefferson's edited letters and papers help solidify their places in history, but Henry's preserved writings fill only one volume.

This is true, but it is also a natural consequence, considering that Washington and Jefferson were both Presidents and Henry was not; although he was urged to run for this office and might well have been elected.[41]

Henry's extant letters and speeches fill many pages. His most important ones are those written while Governor of Virginia, to the President of Congress; to Virginia's delegation in Congress; to the Board of War, and to General Washington. No doubt many of the latter written to the General in the field were lost. It is regrettable at this writing that his services in aiding General Washington are not fully known. Unlike Jefferson, Mr. Henry did not write his memoirs.

The great work of Patrick Henry's grandson, entitled *Patrick Henry, Life, Correspondence and Speeches*, should be read by every student of American history. True, his remaining letters comprised only one volume in 1891, but since then, many of his letters have come to light and much historical data has been unearthed which should place him again where he belongs: "in the first rank and file of the Nation." His great fame is evidenced by the many books bearing his name, and the numerous histories of the Revolution wherein his name appears throughout.

Another problem about Patrick Henry which Professor Mayo cites is that "there is no accurate contemporary record of his Richmond speech in St. John's Church remembered by the phrase, 'Give me liberty or give me death.' "[42]

This is true. There is no complete record of the speech supported by contemporary evidence. But the language and line of reasoning is certainly Henry's. One finds similar expressions in

---

[40] Dr. Bernard Mayo, professor of History, University of Virginia. Special to the *News Leader*, Charlottesville, November 20, 1960.

[41] Morgan, *Henry*, p. 453.

[42] Dr. Bernard Mayo, Professor of History, University of Virginia.

his arraignment in the Parson's Cause.[43] His arguments against the Federal Constitution were along the same general lines: Freedom, as against "chains and scourges."

To those who know the politics of Henry's day, it is not surprising to find the records incomplete. It should be remembered that Henry's "trumpet-voice" was heard at a time of "confused thinking and timid indecision." Henry's harangues were downright defiance of British misrule and were frowned upon by the Speaker and the steady adherents, who veiled all such opposition in secrecy to "save appearances." All of Henry's actions involving the rights and liberties of the people had to be "conducted with a great deal of privacy."[44] The "conservative" and Tory members would hardly have recorded or made public any of Henry's prolonged outbursts of denunciation for Governor Dunmore's watchful eye. It is shown that the Governor had prorogued the Assembly, and in March had issued a proclamation forbidding the appointment of delegates to the next Congress.[45] Proof of the Crown agents' dilemma is seen in the *Stamp Act* procedure.[46] If a copy of Mr. Henry's St. John's Church Speech was put in the record, it probably received the same treatment, or was destroyed, since it wore the aspect of treason and "its features could not be smoothed."

To reiterate:

The volume of Mr. Henry's Executive Journal for the year 1779, and his letter-book for the first three years as Governor, are missing. Mr. Jefferson, who followed Governor Henry into

---

[43] Henry, *Henry*, op. cit., p. 39 n. Henry, *Henry*. I, p. 42. In a letter written a few days after the Parson's case to the Rev. John Camm, and as related by Captain Thomas Trevilian. "Parson's Cause": ". . . unless they were disposed to rivet the chains of bondage on their necks, . . ." Henry, *Henry*, I, p. 263. St. John's Church speech: "They are sent over to bind and rivet upon us those chains, . . ." In Federal Constitution, June 7, 1788.

[44] Henry, *Henry*, I, p. 249. Sarah Henry to Mrs. Fleming: "My son Patrick has gone to Philadelphia near seven weeks. The affairs are kept with great secrecy, nobody being allowed to be present." *Ibid.*, I, p. 183. George Mason declared all measures involving the rights and liberties were conducted with a great deal of privacy.

[45] *Ibid.*, I, p. 275.

[46] *Ibid.*, I, p. 83–84. Peyton Randolph, who was at that time King's Attorney, was warmly attached to the royal government and was averse to taking any step which would be censured by the Ministry. He had Patrick Henry's fifth resolution (Stamp Act) expunged from the journal the day after the patriot had left for home, May 31. Judge Paul Carrington pointed out that the journal of the House was missing soon afterward.

office, stated that the above were probably destroyed by the British, but this is doubtful.[47]

At the first Congress the Secretary, Mr. Thomson, recorded only "that which was adopted" and gave only short sketches from Mr. Henry's speeches. He made only bare reference to Patrick Henry's concern over the condition of the boundaries, fraught with danger and disunion.[48]

There was no full and accurate record of Henry's Brutus-Caesar speech, but Jefferson had an unforgettable impression of this as well as of the Stamp Act speech, which shows that neither speech was apocryphal. He wrote Wirt:

"I well remember the cry of treason, the pause of Mr. Henry at the name of George the III and the presence of mind with which he closed his sentence, and baffled the charge vociferated."[49]

Judge St. George Tucker "felt a full impression of Mr. Henry's powers in his St. John's Church speech." The very judicious and careful writer, Dr. Moses Coit Tyler, after examining the evidence, concluded that Wirt's version "certainly gives the substance of the speech as actually made by Patrick Henry; and for the form of it . . . it is probably far more accurate and authentic than are most of the famous speeches attributed to public characters before reporters' galleries were opened, and before the art of reporting was brought to its present perfection."[50]

The Hon. John Roane, son of Col. William Roane, a member of the House of Burgesses, witnessed the Henry speech at St. John's Church, and in 1834 verified the language and correctness of the speech as given, and gave assurance that Mr. Wirt's account was not exaggerated.[51]

Chief Justice Marshall's father, Thomas Marshall, described

---

[47] *Ibid.*, I, p. 458 n.

[48] *Ibid.*, I, p. 220.

[49] *The Confidential Letters of Thomas Jefferson to William Wirt,* p. 16. Purchased by Mr. John Gribbel, Philadelphia, 1910.

[50] Tyler, *Henry*, pp. 150–151.

[51] The Rev. Edward Fontaine's Manuscript: "Patrick Henry, corrections of biographical mistakes and popular errors in regard to his character . . . 1872." Cornell University. A document written by a great-grandson of Patrick Henry. From a sort of preface in Fontaine's manuscript:

> "The admirable Biography of Patrick Henry written by the amiable and eloquent William Wirt, in 1817 had passed through fifteen editions; & it will doubtless continue to hold its place for many generations . . . But it abounds in mistakes; and a sense of duty prompts me to correct some of them in this essay, which is only intended as a contribution to some future

it "as one of the most bold, vehement, and animated pieces of eloquence that had ever been delivered."[52]

The speech given at St. John's Church was written, published and accepted as Patrick Henry's for 195 years. It should not be questioned now. There has been no ghost writer brought forward to claim this masterpiece, therefore it must be assumed to be Henry's own. Jefferson, who was present when the speech was delivered, and revised Mr. Wirt's manuscript, advised its publication.[53]

The "enigma" critics can continue to downgrade Patrick Henry, Jefferson-style, and chapters in history can be falsely headed, but the facts scarcely are debatable. *The Enigma of Patrick Henry*, the article written by Dr. Bernard Mayo for *The Virginia Quarterly Review*, was based on three lectures he gave which were collected in the book, *Myths and Men: Patrick Henry, George Washington, Thomas Jefferson.* Later Dr. Mayo attempted to separate the myth—which, he said, grew from the overstatement of Henry's *virtues* (italics mine) in William Wirt's biography and the resulting attacks based on comments of contemporary political adversaries—from the man who actually existed.[54]

---

edition of that elegantly written & deservedly popular work."

From p. 30 ff.

"It is with regret that I shall have to close this humble contribution of a few new facts . . . without satisfying the curiosity which every admirer of eloquence must feel to know in what the charm of his oratory consisted. The only contribution I can give in the form of a fact to aid your conceptions of his manner while speaking, I will present, as it was related to me by the venerable John Roane of King William Co. Va., who heard his famous speech on his resolutions for arming the Virginia Militia made in St. John's Church Richmond in March, 1775.

"In 1834 I visited the Honorable John Roane of King William County Virginia, then the last surviving elector of the first President of the United States. He had represented his district in Congress 40 years, & was more than ninety years old; but his mind was very little impaired by age, & his memory perfect in retaining past events. He told me many anecdotes about Patrick Henry, interested me greatly by describing the scene which he witnessed in the House of Burgesses when he made the speech with which every college youth is familiar. He verified the correctness of the language of the speech as it was written by Judge Tyler for Mr. Wirt. I remarked that I could not understand how that speech, eloquent as it was, could have produced the effect described by Mr. Wirt, & I supposed his account of it must have been somewhat exaggerated. He assured me that it was not . . ."

[52] Wirt, *Henry*, p. 142.

[53] Kennedy's *Life of William Wirt*, I, p. 413.

[54] Dr. Bernard Mayo, Professor of History, University of Virginia, *The Roanoke Times, November* 22, 1960.

Dr. Mayo declared Jefferson wrote his criticism of Patrick Henry when there "were many rumors that Henry planned to make himself a dictator with absolute power."

This statement should also be corrected. Mr. Jefferson did not write his confidential letters to William Wirt until after Mr. Henry's death; the cry of dictator was credited to one man only (Archibald Cary) and the statement was presumably made upon Mr. Henry's becoming first Governor.[55]

Dr. Mayo further stated: In the struggle between those defending Henry from every attack and those who attacked him to defend their own heroes, Henry's true accomplishments were lost.

Through Dr. Mayo's attempts to separate the myth from the facts, he has given some interesting points in Henry's favor which appeared in the November issue (1960) of *Best Articles and Stories*:

Patrick Henry was more than a firebrand orator, he pointed out. Along with his gifted oratory and "common touch," Henry had ability and a sense of political timing which made him the most popular and powerful figure in Virginia politics until his retirement in 1790. Those whose views differed alternately attacked him or tried to woo his support, for that support meant life or death for proposed legislation.

Thomas Jefferson, who had broken with Henry in 1781, looked back as he neared his own death to those days when they had been the Pen and the Trumpet of the Revolution, and delivered the final view of Henry as quoted in Dr. Mayo's article: Not only was Henry's eloquence "sublime," but as "our leader" he "was far above all . . . in the Revolution." Indeed, said the Master of Monticello, "It is not now easy to say what we should have done without Patrick Henry."[56]

[55] *Sketches of the Life and Character of Patrick Henry*, Revised Edition, pp. 149–150, published by Andrus, Gauntlett, & Co. Ithaca, New York, 1818. William Wirt stated in his book that he had met with no one who will venture to affirm that the project of dictator was suggested by Mr. Henry or received his countenance. He called the Cary rumor "tradition." He said "the charge, moreover, seems preposterous. Neither General Washington himself, nor any other patriot, had maintained the principles of the revolution with more consistency and uniformity than Patrick Henry . . . ." He pointed out that "it is impossible to believe that the legislature themselves could have entertained a doubt of Mr. Henry's innocence; since at the next annual election for governor . . . he was re-elected unanimously; the house being composed of nearly the same members, and the same Colonel Cary being Speaker of the Senate."

[56] Dr. Bernard Mayo, Professor of History, University of Virginia, *The Roanoke Times*, November 22, 1960.

XI

THE POWDER AFFAIR

Let Britons now sunk into tyrants and slaves
Submit to be govern'd by fools and by knaves;
Not so will their kindred on this side the sea:
American Britons will ever be FREE.
(*Virginia Gazette,* Dixon & Hunter, May 27, 1775.)

For, so just is our cause, and so valiant our men, . . .
We'll fight for our freedom again and again.
(*Virginia Gazette,* Dixon & Hunter, July 29, 1775.)

THE SPIRIT and influence of Patrick Henry's speech was felt throughout the colony, and before long his words were put to verse and song. The direct result is shown in the close of one verse, ending with these words: "Each free-born Briton's song should be, Or give me DEATH or LIBERTY."[1]

The day after the convention ended in St. John's Church, and five days after Mr. Henry's speech, a proclamation was issued by Governor Dunmore forbidding the appointments of delegates to Congress. In the meantime all gunpowder shipments from Britain had been stopped upon orders of the King. Not only were the colonies prohibited from purchasing necessary ammunition, the governors were instructed to seize and take away all gunpowder which had been stored throughout the colonies for their protection. On April 18, Gen. Thomas Gage, who was also governor, ordered his troops to Concord to destroy the military supplies which the people of Massachusetts had stored there for the protection of the colony. These actions precipitated the battle of Lexington.[2]

---

[1] Mays, *Pendleton,* op. cit., II, p. 358.
[2] Henry, *Henry,* I, p. 277.

Governor Dunmore, who had "recently returned from the great Indian campaign on the Ohio . . . had put a debt of a hundred thousand pounds upon the distressed colony, and yet failed to release any of the vast tracts of land west of the Alleghenies to speculators or settlers."[3] At this time he had for his protection such vessels as the *Fowey* stationed in the York River, and the *Magdalen*, a very formidable ship lying in the James at Burwell's Ferry. "On the twentieth of April, his lordship learning that the New Englanders were on the verge of war with the British soldiers in Boston, seized a part of the colonial powder in the arsenal at Williamsburg, and had it placed safely in the hold of the *Magdalen*. The fat was in the fire."[4]

The powder magazine had been erected by Alexander Spotswood in 1716.[5] It was the depository for the powder and arms supply for the colony. Carrying out the Governor's orders at midnight, his men removed 20 barrels of gunpowder stored in the powder horn for the colony's safety and took it upon the vessel. When the people of Williamsburg learned of these happenings, they became upset, having great anxiety for their security —not alone from Britain, but from insurrection by the slaves. Taking up arms, the irate citizens determined to force the return of the powder. They at once called upon the Council and, on behalf of the safety of the colonists, urged its immediate restoration. This brought the response from the Governor that he had removed the powder from the magazine to a place of perfect safety, and that upon his word and honor, whenever it was needed for insurrection it would be delivered in half an hour. He showed surprise that the people were up in arms over the incident and declared he did not think it wise to place the powder in their hands at such a moment. He further declared, the next day, that if any injury or insult was meted out to himself, to his secretary Captain Foy, or to Captain Collins, he would free and arm the slaves and burn Williamsburg to the ground. Governor Dunmore's reply, though cleverly worded, did not allay the fears of the people. However, Peyton Randolph and other members of the Council tried to quiet them for the moment with the promise of compliance.[6]

[3] William E. Dodd, *The Spirit of '76*, "Virginia Takes the Road to Revolution," p. 104.

[4] *Ibid.*, p. 105.

[5] William & Mary College Quarterly, *Historical Magazine*, October 5, 1896–1897, p. 213.

[6] Henry, *Henry*, I, pp. 277–278–279.

Patrick Henry, who was watching the events from his home, Scotchtown, and knew Dunmore, was assured that this was no vain threat. He considered that the powder belonged to the people and not to the government. On the third night after the incident, which was also the third day after the battle of Lexington, Mr. Henry hurried down the stone steps at Scotchtown and mounted his horse. He and the freeholders of Hanover, whom he had already informed of the happenings at Williamsburg, were incensed. At New Castle he talked with the Hanover Volunteers and the County Committee. Decisions were reached to send messengers at once to Williamsburg and offer assistance. Other groups throughout the colony were also in readiness. Four days after the powder incident, Washington's company at Fredericksburg, with other companies, sent word to Colonel Washington offering to defend the honor of Virginia. The messengers from the different assemblies were sent to Williamsburg, reaching there on the 26th, offering their services. They were told by Peyton Randolph that everything had quieted down and that the Governor had assured the return of the gunpowder, though no date had been set. Randolph sent letters back advising "that matters be quieted for the present."

In Fredericksburg three days later, the 102 gentlemen representing the 14 companies met to hold a conference before their march to Williamsburg, which was to take place the same day. However, upon reading Peyton Randolph's letter assuring them that the gunpowder would be returned satisfactorily, and having the advice of Colonel Washington not to march, they returned peaceably to their homes. Resolutions were drawn up pledging themselves "to be in readiness to reassemble and by force of arms to defend the law, the liberty and the rights of this or any other sister colony from unjust and wicked invasion."[7]

The matter appeared to be settled and the crisis past. "Randolph made ready his toilet and cleaned his wig to start north, expecting to stop a day with Edmund Pendleton at Bowling Green, fifty miles away."[8] He "journeyed leisurely, as became the eighteenth century, to the home of his friend Pendleton, and the two took up their journey toward Philadelphia. They had hardly started when another messenger brought the most exciting news that had yet come; the British soldiers at Boston had tried to take

[7] Tyler, *Henry*, pp. 157–158.

[8] William E. Dodd, *The Spirit of '76* "Virginia Takes the Road to Revolution," p. 105.

Massachusetts's powder at Lexington, and at once the long-dreaded issue was joined. At Lexington and all along the winding road that led back to Boston the enraged farmers had fought as freemen ought to fight. Northern and western Virginians were in wild excitement again. At such moments military men make statesmen obsolete."[9]

At this point it has been observed that "no biographer has explained why Patrick Henry was lingering at his rambling *Scotchtown* home after Randolph and Pendleton had departed for the great convention."[10]

But Henry, hearing of the outcome of the conference, felt keen disappointment and regret that the companies had dispersed. He had hoped that immediate aggressive steps would be taken—delay, he felt, would be fateful. News that war had already commenced with the battles of Lexington and Concord, resulting from a similar seizure of powder by Governor-General Gage, must have set him seething, although "his was a mind that watched events with the coolness and sagacity of a veteran statesman."[11] He decided that he himself would strike an immediate blow. Back in the direction of Hanover he hurriedly turned his horse. Calling upon the County Committee for approval, he requested the Hanover Volunteers to meet him in arms at New Castle on May 2 on a matter of greatest importance to American liberty. On that date he addressed the volunteers and citizens in a fiery speech. He showed the purpose of the British ministry to subjugate the colonies by seizing their only means of defense, pointing to similar attacks on the military stores at Cambridge and at Charlestown. He declared:

> . . . that the moment was now come in which they were called upon to decide, whether they chose to live free, and hand down the noble inheritance to their children, or to become hewers of wood, and drawers of water to those lordlings, who were themselves the tools of a corrupt and tyrannical ministry—he painted the country in a state of subjugation, and drew such pictures of wretched debasement and abject vassalage, as filled their souls with horror and indignation—on the other hand . . . he showed them the land of promise, which was to be won by their valor, under the support and guidance of heaven, and sketched a vision of America enjoying the smiles of liberty and peace, the rich

---

[9] *Ibid.*, p. 106.

[10] *Ibid.*, pp. 106–107.

[11] Wirt, *Henry*, Revised Edition 1836, p. 154.

> productions of her agriculture waving on every field, her commerce whitening every sea, in tints so bright, so strong, so glowing, as set the souls of his hearers on fire . . . It was for them now to determine . . . whether they would accept the high boon now held out to them by heaven—that if they would, though it might lead them through a sea of blood . . . the same God still reigned, unchanged and unchangeable—was still the enemy of the oppressor, and the friend of the oppressed . . . no time was to be lost—that while their enemies in this colony were now few and weak—that it would be easy for them, by a rapid and vigorous movement, to compel the restoration of the powder which had been carried off, or to make a reprisal on the King's revenues in the hands of the receiver general, which would fairly balance the account—that the Hanover volunteers would thus have an opportunity of striking the first blow in this colony, in the great cause of American liberty, and would cover themselves with never-fading laurels.[12]

Inflamed by Patrick Henry's speech, the men acclaimed him their Captain and declared themselves ready to follow. The officer in command resigned in Henry's favor and Patrick Henry took over leadership.[13] Peyton Randolph, Carter Nicholas and other conservatives considered this as a precipitation of war and sent messages urging Mr. Henry to return home. But Patrick Henry, spirited to action by his convictions of right, heeded not. Dispatching Ensign Parke Goodall with 16 men in the direction of Laneville, King William County, he gave them instructions to go directly to the home of the King's Receiver-General, Col. Richard Corbin, and demand from him £330 as payment for the gunpowder. They were ordered, in case he refused, to take him prisoner and report to Doncastle Ordinary.[14] Captain Henry, with Samuel Meredith and 150 men, started their march to Williamsburg, taking a near cut from New Castle along the course of Famous Creek between Atlee and Polly Hundley's corner to recover the gunpowder.[15] When news spread of his bold stand, crowds cheered him along the way. So stirred were the people that volunteers in arms lined up along his route, eager to join in retaking the powder. Companies on horse and foot flocked to his

---

[12] Henry, *Henry*, I, pp. 280–281; Wirt, *Henry*, Revised Edition 1836, pp. 156–157.
[13] Wirt, *Henry*, p. 158. Captain Samuel Meredith, Henry's brother-in-law, resigned in Mr. Henry's favor.
[14] William E. Dodd, *Spirit of '76*, "Virginia Takes the Road to Revolution," p. 107.
[15] Henry, *Henry*, I, pp. 281–282.

assistance. His name aroused such enthusiasm throughout the colony that 5000 men rallied to join him in his march to Williamsburg.[16]

On the same day, May 2, Governor Dunmore requested the Council to meet at the palace to explain to them his conduct in taking the powder. He charged that the excitement was due to "headstrong and designing people, by whom plans and schemes are unquestionably meditated in this colony for subverting the present, and erecting a new form of government." His proclamation, issued the next day and opposed only by John Page, the youngest member, was said to have been aimed at Captain Henry, whom he credited with the disturbance, calling him a coward in not setting out for the Continental Congress with Randolph and Pendleton. It was circulated that Dunmore had planned to arrest the three delegates on their way to Congress and hold Henry, whom he considered the rebel and trouble-maker, for punishment.[17]

When news reached Dunmore that Patrick Henry was headed for Williamsburg with an army, he became terrified. He appealed to Captain Montague of the English ship *Fowey* in the York River for a detachment of Marines to be stationed in the town to protect the palace. He also armed his slaves and Indian hostages and concealed a cannon at the palace entrance. His family was sent aboard the *Fowey* for safety, where, it is said, Dunmore later went himself. Calling upon some of the men of influence in Williamsburg, he asked them to send dispatches to Henry begging him to check his march. Mr. Henry, instead, held the men and kept a steady advance until he reached Doncastle, 16 miles from Williamsburg, where he was to await word from Ensign Goodall. The officer, however, had failed to see the Receiver-General, Colonel Corbin being at that time in Williamsburg.

Meantime, "hundreds of volunteers a-foot, in hunting shirts with guns on their shoulders or on horseback with pistols or swords at their sides, crowded to the camp of Patrick Henry. Robert Carter Nicholas and Thomas Nelson, who had made the arrangement with the Governor a week before, were anxious. Dunmore was excited, frightened; all Williamsburg was in an uproar, expecting 'five thousand' armed men to appear at the door of the palace at any moment. Everyone knew something of Patrick Henry; and none doubted that, once in town, there would be

[16] Wirt, *Henry*, Revised Edition 1836, p. 159.
[17] Henry, *Henry*, I, pp. 282–283.

trouble."[18] The citizenry armed themselves, determined to have the powder restored.

The town council and some of the "graver inhabitants," fearing Dunmore's threat to burn the town if he were molested, considered measures that could be used to have the powder returned without bloodshed. The conservatives, Nicholas, Braxton and others, used every method possible to prevent a clash between the colonies and Dunmore. But the Governor, having no word from Patrick Henry, and fearing his attack, sent Colonel Corbin's son-in-law, Carter Braxton, with the offer to compensate for the powder, since it had been carried aboard the schooner and "could not be come at."[19]

Braxton appeared on the scene May 4, offering indemnity and having with him Corbin's bond to pay for the powder. "Henry refused the bond of a Tory. Braxton, a man of wealth, offered to endorse for Corbin, but the leader of the people refused to take the endorsement of the son of a Tory." On the same day, "Thomas Nelson offered to endorse Corbin's bond. Henry could not refuse a man who was wealthy enough to entertain regiments of troops for weeks and hardly feel the loss. He took the promise to pay three hundred and thirty pounds for the powder, twice as much as it was worth, and agreed to advise his men to return to their homes. The Governor was greatly relieved."[20]

Before the men disbanded, Patrick Henry offered the assistance of guards to protect the treasury of the colony in case there was danger. "The Treasurer replied—what was untrue—that there was not the remotest danger of disturbance or danger at the capital."[21]

Accounts describing Captain Henry's march down the peninsula record that only with the "greatest difficulty" was the patriot dissuaded from entering Williamsburg, it being feared by the conservative leaders that he might seize the Governor.

From this probably arises a belated attempt by a twentieth century historian to misinterpret historic truth. Dr. Eckenrode called Henry's march a scheme to seize control of the Virginia

[18] William E. Dodd, *Spirit of '76*, "Virginia Takes the Road to Revolution," p. 108.

[19] Brant, *Madison, The Virginia Revolutionist*, pp. 181–182. James Madison to Bradford, May 9, 1775, delivered to him in Philadelphia by Patrick Henry: "the powder could not be come at."

[20] William E. Dodd, *Spirit of '76*, "Virginia Takes the Road to Revolution," p. 108. See Henry, *Henry*, I. p. 283; Morgan, *Henry*, p. 204.

[21] *Ibid.*, p. 109.

government by force of arms. Henry's change of face, Eckenrode believed, came about when the Conservative leaders in the capital "brought such strong pressure to bear on him that he abandoned his plan in the interests of harmony."[22]

This statement by Dr. Eckenrode is contrary to facts. Nothing could have been further from Patrick Henry's mind than such a maneuver, though none can doubt that it would have been a good thing had he pressed on to the capital, seized the Governor and put him in irons. Certainly it would have saved the people much suffering later from Dunmore's many ravages and harassments. And no doubt Mr. Henry would have considered taking him, had the Council not intervened with the offer of compensation. But further than that he would have had no part. However, it is significant that he did later succeed Dunmore in office, his bravery placing him at the head of an independent government even before the Revolution was won. Had Mr. Henry entertained any such idea in his march, as suggested by Eckenrode, it is hardly possible that the patriot would have changed his mind. Of course it cannot be denied that Peyton Randolph, Edmund Pendleton, and Treasurer Nicholas put "pressure" on him to get him to turn back. Carter Nicholas, in a "terrible panic," wrote letters all over the country trying to prevent the military companies from meeting.[23] But Patrick Henry was not to be intimidated, neither was he a man to lose his nerve.

Freedom, alone, spurred Henry's movements: The powder had been paid for by the people, placed in the magazine for their protection, and he was determined to retrieve it, or the equivalent of it, which he did. Any other suggestion is sheer nonsense. Had Colonel Washington and the "600 armed men from the counties surrounding Fredericksburg" decided to march on Williamsburg against Peyton Randolph's advice, would such charges have been brought against Washington? Certainly not. We are told that Captain Henry's advance was conducted in the most perfect order, and with the most scrupulous respect to the country through which he passed.[24] Unlike the usurper, he moved deliberately and orderly, but sure of purpose. Moreover, in his first having the sanction of the Hanover Committee, and the backing of the people

[22] Brant, *Madison, The Virginia Revolutionist,* 1751–1780, op. cit., p. 182; See Wirt, *Henry,* p. 200 (1836 edition). Eckenrode, *The Revolution in Virginia,* p. 51.
[23] *Magazine of History,* II, p. 159; Brant, *Madison, The Virginia Revolutionist, 1751–1780,* op. cit., p. 419 n.
[24] Wirt, *Henry,* p. 159, Revised Edition, p. 159.

themselves, he is absolved from such criticism. Henry had always to be within the bounds of delegated authority, and he was particular to do things lawfully. Madison affirms Henry's actions as having been carried out in the strictest regularity, and he has fully vindicated him here from Eckenrode's belated charges.[25] Before Henry left for Congress, he wrote a letter to Francis Lightfoot Lee explaining his actions.[26] His purpose, and justification of his march, were written five days before he left Scotchtown.

Declaring that he chose to be active in making the reprisal for the sake of the public tranquillity, as well as of justice, he pointed out that his attendance at Congress would prevent him from being present at the Convention. Answering the conservatives who opposed his march on the same ground as the Governor —claiming that the powder belonged to the King—he showed all such pretense to be a quibble. He pointed to the address of the City of Williamsburg, and the Governor's reply to it, to prove the contrary:

> Why does he promise to return it in half an hour? And again what powder was he to return, or did he take? I answer the powder . . . that which was provided for the safety of the Colony, and for the loss of which Williamsburg was so much alarmed. But I ask, suppose it was the King's, what right had any one to deposit it in the magazine, built expressly for the purpose of receiving such ammunition as was at any time necessary for our safety? His Majesty can have no right to convert the houses, or other conveniences necessary for our defense, into repositories for engines of our destruction. So that the presumption is, that the powder being there it was ours . . . You will readily perceive the absurdity of the pretense, that the King can have a property in anything distinct from his people, and how dangerous is the position that his protection (for which we have already paid him) may be withdrawn at pleasure . . .

Henry declared also that "the hostilities to the Northward would have justified much greater reprisals, which I chose to decline as the Convention might probably so soon meet." Wishing Lee to understand the facts in the case, should the matter be brought up in the Convention while he was in attendance at Congress, Mr. Henry purposely

> referred to the Convention whether any of the money ought to be returned, lest presuming too much might be alleged against me,

[25] Brant, *Madison, The Virginia Revolutionist, 1751–1780,* p. 183.
[26] Henry, *Henry,* I, pp. 287-288-289.

I trouble you, sir, with this to be an advocate for the measure if you think it right . . . To the collective body of my country I chose to commit my conduct . . . that you may not be surprised at some objections against my proceedings, which I fear will be made by some gentlemen from below (i.e. the tidewater). If any doubt remains as to the fitness of the step I have taken, can it lay over until I am heard? I can mention many *facts* which I am sure will abundantly warrant what is done.[27]

A letter written at this time by James Madison, Sr., concerning the powder episode, far from looking upon Henry's actions with disfavor, tells us that Henry's march "gained him great honor in the most spirited parts of the country." The letter, published for the first time by the biographer of James Madison, is said by him to have been carried to Henry's home (Scotchtown) by Madison himself or dispatched to Patrick Henry by the County Committee's messenger, to be delivered to William Bradford on Henry's arrival in Philadelphia. Dated May 9, 1775, Madison's letter stated:

We have lately had a great alarm here about the Governor's removing a large quantity of powder from our magazine and conveying it on board a ship of war. Not less than 600 men well armed and mounted assembled at Fredericksburg on this occasion with a view to proceed to Williamsburg (to) recover the powder and revenge the insult. The propriety of such a step was warmly agitated and weighty arguments adduced both for and against it: at length the advice of Peyton Randolph, Edmund Pendleton, Richard H. Lee and George Washington Esqrs delegates for the Congress, to return home was complied with.

The reasons however that induced these gentlemen to give this advice did not appear satisfactory to P. Henry Esq another of our delegates, whose sentiments were not known at Fredericksburg. This gentleman after the dispersion of the troops at the above named place, under the authority of the committee of his county and at the head of an Independent Company, undertook to procure redress, which he resolutely accomplished by taking of the King's quitrents as much money as would replace the powder, which had been removed so far that it could not be come at. This affair has prevented his appearing at the Congress as early as his colleagues, and has afforded me this opportunity of sending you a few lines.

I expect his conduct as contrary to the opinion of the other delegates will be disapproved of by them, but it has gained him great

[27] Henry, to Lee, as cited.

> honor in the most spirited parts of the country and addresses of thanks are already presenting to him from different quarters. The gentlemen below (i.e., at tidewater) whose property will be exposed in case of a civil war in this Colony were extremely alarmed lest Government should be provoked to make reprisals. Indeed some of them discovered a pusillanimity little comporting with their professions or the name of Virginia.[28]

Madison himself declared his contempt for timid and cowardly delegates—such men as Peyton Randolph, Edmund Pendleton, Treasurer Nicholas, Richard Bland, and others among the Tidewater gentry. Satisfied with the ease and wealth that a brisk trade had brought them, their actions in pulling back were not in keeping with their profession as representatives of the people, sworn to preserve civil liberties.

Mr. Henry lived many miles from Fredericksburg, yet the vigilant Henry knew what was going on. In less than three days after Colonel Washington's decision not to march, and in the same number of days after news was published in a supplement to the *Gazette* telling of the British attack on Concord, Patrick Henry and his men were already headed on their expedition. His move could hardly be considered precipitous, for in less than a month after he drew reins in Philadelphia May 18, to attend the Second Congress, Bunker Hill had been lost. Yet, in the lower counties and in Williamsburg, some among the loyalists and conservatives considered his march ill-timed, and a step which could easily precipitate war. The "clash of resounding arms" at Concord and Lexington they refused to hear. The Council also condemned Mr. Henry's bold move, with the exception of Mr. John Page of Rosewell, who took sides with the populace; this caused Governor Dunmore to smash his fist down on the table, crying: "Mr. Page, I am surprised at you!"[29] The other members of the Council aside from John Page were: Thomas Nelson, Richard Corbin, William Byrd, Ralph Wormley, Jr., and the Rev. John Camm (the suit-bringing parson). The Council issued a proclamation on May 15 expressing "abhorrence and detestation of that licentious and ungovernable spirit that is gone forth, and misleads the once happy people of this country." But "the people generally looked upon the whole Council with suspicion, and held them with the Governor, as enemies of Virginia, a feeling which was greatly intensified by

[28] Brant, *Madison, The Virginia Revolutionist, 1751–1780,* pp. 181–182.
[29] Morgan, *Henry,* p. 200.

the proclamation."[30] Some of the members were known loyalists, who openly approved of royal authority.[31]

The name of Patrick Henry had now become widely respected. Letters of grateful appreciation were extended the patriot from near and far. Still extant are warm messages praising his course of action from the Counties of Louisa, Orange, Spottsylvania, Prince William, Loudoun, Lancaster, Prince Edward, and Fincastle.[32]

Pendleton's biographer, in speaking of Henry's march to recapture the powder, stated that ". . . Henry never went counter to a popular trend; he always capitalized it."[33] But was the march popular before Henry started on his way? It appeared to have been a most unpopular step, since Pendleton called it off in Bowling Green and refused to let the troops go.[34] The situation was so tense that Pendleton and Randolph composed a letter urging the Fredericksburg troops under Washington to return home,[35] and Washington, and Lee also, discouraged the march. When the two palace guards had averted the march, Pendleton's biographer stated, "Randolph and Pendleton—both good judges of the fragrance and mellowness of old Madeira—probably drew a long breath and opened a fresh bottle to steady their nerves."[36]

"As Henry turned his horse homeward, messengers came from many directions, telling of other meetings and other volunteer companies. Everywhere people shouted hurrah for Patrick Henry; no wise man could have doubted who was the real master of Virginia, though the Governor, not content to leave matters to Nelson and Nicholas, issued the following proclamation:

> Whereas I have been informed that a certain Patrick Henry and his deluded followers have taken up arms, excited the people and committed acts of violence, I have thought proper, with the advice of His Majesty's council and in His Majesty's name, to issue this proclamation charging all persons not to aid, abet or give counte-

---

[30] Henry, *Henry*, I, pp. 286–287, op. cit., *American Archives*, 4th Series, ii., p. 587.

[31] Boyd, *Jefferson, The Papers of Thomas Jefferson*, I, pp. 475–476 R. C. Fleming to Jefferson.

[32] Henry, *Henry*, I, p. 289 n. op. cit., for proceedings: See *American Archives*, 4th Series, ii., p. 529, at seq. also, Tyler, *Henry*, pp. 164–65.

[33] Mays, *Pendleton*, II, p. 16.

[34] *Ibid.*, II, p. 14.

[35] Burk's *History of Virginia*, III, p. 411; Charles Campbell, *History of Virginia*, p. 609.

[36] Mays, *Pendleton*, II, p. 15.

> nance to the said Patrick Henry, else the whole county must be involved in the most direful calamity. God save the King.[37]

But "the most direful calamity" was yet to be seen—in the attack on and burning of Norfolk, during which the very powder "that Dunmore stole from the Powder Horn Magazine" was used in burning that city.[38]

---

[37] William E. Dodd, *The Spirit of '76*, "Virginia Takes the Road to Revolution," pp. 109–110.

[38] Chandler & Thames, *Colonial Virginia*, p. 252.

XII

THE SECOND CONTINENTAL CONGRESS

AFTER PATRICK HENRY settled the powder affair, he left for Philadelphia.[1] Governor Dunmore's implied desire for his arrest caused the volunteers of Hanover, King William, and Caroline Counties to honor him with a military escort across the Potomac to safety. En route, Patrick Henry rode by the side of Ensign Parke Goodall.

The delegates to the second Continental Congress began assembling May 10. There were 78 members in all. Here, as in the first Congress, Peyton Randolph was seated in the chair as speaker. Later the president's chair was filled by John Hancock, when Peyton Randolph stepped down to preside over the Virginia Assembly.

The first matter of business concerned the letter from the colonial agents in London, showing the lack of interest with which the petition to the King was received and rejected, and the general situation in the tyrannical affairs of Parliament. The important matter of the moment, and one causing the most alarm, was the stirring events in Concord and Lexington. This communication explaining the unprovoked hostilities came from the Provincial Congress of Massachusetts. After its reading, a decision was reached to go into committee of the whole on the following Monday, for the consideration of the state of America. Congress had been in session for a week when Patrick Henry arrived. Mr. Henry took his seat on Thursday, May 18, having missed little more than the preliminaries.[2]

What must have proved heartening to him the day he took his seat was the news of the capture of Ticonderoga on Lake

[1] Cushing, *The Writings of Samuel Adams*, III, p. 224.
[2] Burnett, *The Continental Congress*, p. 62.

Champlain and the quantity of arms and ammunition stored there. This daring attack was led by Col. Ethan Allen in the early morning of May 10, and had followed upon the heels of the similar movement by Mr. Henry on May 2. Yet, despite the importance of this achievement, which helped clear the way into Canada and furnished the supplies so greatly needed for the colonies, it seems to have been a headache to the delegates in the face of the other momentous news from New York, informing Congress of the expected arrival of British troops there. Despite the prize and the need—which no doubt brought joy to a good many of the delegates—the aggressiveness by which the military stores had fallen into the colonies' hands was treated by Congress with utmost tact. It instructed that an exact inventory be made of all the supplies for the purpose of a safe return when harmony was restored between Great Britain and the Colonies.

Mr. Henry early recognized that Congress had no power. The delegates' hands were tied by their former instructions, given before hostilities, and they found themselves without power to steer the crisis. These instructions, in the main, called for the redress of grievances, the restoration of American rights and liberties, and the restoring of the general harmony between the two countries.[3] The Virginians laid no specific instructions on the table of Congress. The reactions at St. John's Church spoke for them. Patrick Henry considered the above objectives inadequate and unavailing. The attitude of the Congress raised the ire of John Adams, who condemned simultaneously holding the sword in one hand and the olive branch in the other. The cancer, he said, was too deeply rooted and too far spread to be cured by anything other than cutting it out entirely.[4] Adams declared that "The delegates from Virginia had never been entirely united in their policy, one portion of them always holding back against energetic measures." In Adams's view, "the middle way" was none at all. Adams named Patrick Henry, the Lees and George Wythe as among the most decided advocates of independence who "felt the necessity of commencing a reform by going at once to the root of government itself."[5] Seeing the emergency that had arisen, and necessity demanding it, Adams called for an army and navy to be raised at once, for all loyalists or friends of British Government to be held as hostages for the people of Boston, and for the arrangement

[3] Henry, *Henry*, I, pp. 293–294.

[4] Burnett, *The Continental Congress*, p. 74.

[5] Charles Francis Adams, *Life and Works of John Adams, p.* 207.

of negotiations for peace.[6] Jay and Dickinson and the passive party, as in the first Congress, held to their efforts at reconciliation, with only such defensive measures as might be necessary for the colonies' safety. Their party in debate was much in the lead, to the chagrin of Adams and Henry. The delegates held no fear of the British troops daily expected to land in New York. Instead, they instructed the citizens not to resist their landing, to act strictly on the defensive, but to be prepared to protect themselves. They urged another petition to the King as a means of reconciliation.[7] Patrick Henry did not approve of a second petition from Congress to the King, considering it useless. Yet we find his name heading the list of the Virginia delegates on the petition of July 8, 1775.

For eleven days—from the 15th to the 26th—the Congress sat deliberating the state of America. Added to these considerations was the application laid on the desk on the 26th from the Assembly of New Jersey, asking counsel in dealing with the proposals of Lord North. In the effort to solve the crisis, the tyrannical acts of Parliament and the recent outbreak of hostilities in Concord and Lexington were debated by Congress and were the center of the discussions. Finally, after thrashing over and over their hurts and objectives, the Committee of the Whole resolved in effect, that because of the oppressive acts of Great Britain against the colonies, they had been "reduced to a dangerous and critical situation"; second, that "for the purpose of securing and defending these colonies, and preserving them in safety against all attempts to carry the said Acts into execution by force of arms, these Colonies be immediately put into a state of defense"; third, that there should be "a restoration of the harmony formerly subsisting between our Mother Country and these colonies," and, in order to obtain that end, "an humble and dutiful petition be presented to His Majesty"; and fourth, that they resolved "to enter into negotiations to that end."[8] Here, in the second resolution, Congress is seen echoing the exact cry of Patrick Henry from St. John's Church.

Two more months were to pass with the delegates entertaining thoughts chiefly on a posture of defense. The Committee of the Whole recommended to New York that a post at Kingsbridge

---

[6] Henry, *Henry,* op. cit., I, p. 293; *Life and Works of John Adams,* II, p. 411. Adams to James Warren, July 24, 1775.

[7] Henry, *Henry,* op. cit., I, p. 293; *Life of John Jay,* I, p. 36.

[8] Burnett, *The Continental Congress,* p. 71; *Henry,* I, p. 295–296.

be fortified to protect the city, and that another commanding the navigation of the Hudson be established at Highlands, later known as West Point, and at Lake George. Three thousand troops were recommended for the command. Recommendations also called for arming and training the New York militia, and for dispatching troops for New York City's protection.[9]

Colonel Washington, recognized for his abilities in the French and Indian War as well as in the Virginia Assembly, was at the outset made chairman of a committee to study the strategic posts in the state of New York for the purpose of occupying them. Requests were directed to Connecticut and New York to have the Champlain forts manned. The New York Congressmen were advised "to persevere the more vigorously in preparing for their defence, as it is very uncertain whether the earnest endeavors of the Congress to accommodate the unhappy differences between Great Britain and the colonies by conciliatory measures, will be successful." It is pointed out that in the above resolutions is seen "a rejection of Lord North's proposals for accommodation, and a determination to enter at once upon the war which might be the consequence, but at the same time an offer to treat for peace on condition of the recognition of their liberties—a condition they had but little hope of securing."[10]

On June 15, Washington was unanimously elected Commander-in-Chief of the forces defending American liberty. Afterwards he turned to Patrick Henry and remarked, "This day will be the commencement of the decline of my reputation."[11] In George Washington, Mr. Henry had placed his trust. It was Washington whom he had singled out in the First Congress as the "man of most judgment and information." His election as Commander of all the Continental forces, with the country now put into a state of defense, was cause for exultation among the colonies. Charles Lee was notified of his appointment as second Major-General by a committee of which Mr. Henry was chairman. An entry in the Journal of June 21 shows that "Mr. Henry informed the Congress that General Washington had put into his hands sundry queries to which he desired the Congress would give an answer." Patrick Henry was one of a committee of five to report the proper answers.[12]

---

[9] Burnett, *The Continental Congress,* p. 71.

[10] Henry, *Henry,* I, pp. 295–296.

[11] *Ibid.,* I, p. 298.

[12] *Ibid.,* I, p. 300.

The continuation of the boundary dispute between Virginia and Pennsylvania, which had been agitated by Governor Dunmore, was referred to the Congress. It fell to Mr. Henry and his colleagues to find a peaceful solution, and they accordingly dispatched a letter to the inhabitants of the two colonies in an attempt to effect tranquillity. Here again the name P. Henry, Jr., heads the list of the delegates from Virginia. Mr. Henry was greatly concerned over the actions of the notorious John Connolly to divide the colonies.[13] "The troubles which grew out of the disputed boundary between Virginia and Pennsylvania continued to increase under the violence of John Connolly, the unprincipled agent of Lord Dunmore, who was anxious to embroil the two colonies in civil strife. To prevent this, and to unite the people on the border in the struggle between the colonies and Great Britain, was the ardent wish of Mr. Henry and his associates in Congress from the two colonies."[14] They requested that all animosities among the distinct colonies give place to generous and concurring efforts for the preservation of the general interest of their country. It was recommended that all bodies of armed men be dismissed; that all in confinement, or under bail, be discharged and that every person be permitted to retain his possessions unmolested until the dispute be decided.[15] Here again, as in the resolutions calling for a Committee of Correspondence designed to unite all the colonies, Mr. Henry's zeal to insure united action in every step of the controversy is seen.[16]

Benjamin Franklin, the newly appointed first Postmaster-General, drafted a proposal for consideration which he called "Articles of Confederation and Perpetual Union." But this measure was laid aside for the time by those members hoping for reconciliation.

In the address "To the President of the Virginia Convention," the name P. Henry, Jr., headed the list of the Virginia delegates, and in the letter "From the Virginia Delegates in Congress to George Washington" are the names Richard Henry Lee, P. Henry

---

[13] Henry, *Henry,* I, pp. 174–176–206. The student of history should pursue these pages to understand the crux of the disputes.

[14] *Ibid.,* I, p. 302.

[15] *Ibid.,* I, pp. 302–303.

[16] Wirt, *Henry,* (1836) edition, p. 106; Henry, *Henry,* I, p. 160; Mr. Henry, early in the conflict, had been appointed to meet with commissioners from the Colonies of Quebec, New York, New Jersey, Maryland, Pennsylvania and Delaware for the purpose of a plan to regulate Indian trade; Henry, *Henry,* I, p. 148.

and TH: Jefferson. Mr. Henry also wrote a personal letter to General Washington on the day before Congress adjourned.[17]

These many duties and appointments which demanded Patrick Henry's attention bespeak his judgment, efficiency and reputation. We have a clear picture of his activities in all the practical affairs of the Congress. Jefferson, however, attempted to detract from Patrick Henry's accomplishments with such slighting words as he wrote to Wirt forty years afterward:

> I found Hr. Henry to be a silent, and almost unmeddling member in Congress. On the original opening of that body, while general grievances were the topic, he was in his element, and captivated all with his bold and splendid eloquence. But as soon as they came to specific matters, to sober reasoning and solid argumentation, he had the good sense to perceive that his declamation, however excellent in its proper place, had no weight at all in such an assembly as that, of cool-headed, reflecting, judicious men. He ceased therefore in a great measure to take any part in the business. He seemed indeed very tired of the place, and wonderfully relieved when, by appointment of the Virginia Convention to be Colonel of their 1st regiment, he was permitted to leave Congress about the last of July."[18]

Such denigration shows an ungenerous side in Mr. Jefferson. It is impossible to envision Patrick Henry at any time as lacking "sober reasoning" and "solid argument." In fact, the Congressional debates calling for safety measures and particularly the declaration setting forth the causes and necessity of their taking up arms, was the direct result of, and response to, Patrick Henry's "call to arms" in Richmond in March. In the second Congress, as in the first, "Mr. Henry seems to have been most active in all the practical work of the body. In the accounts of this convention there exists a wide discrepancy between the representations made by Mr. Jefferson, as he recalled them forty years afterward, and the real facts of the case." Nevertheless, Mr. Jefferson "persisted in the view that as a practical man Mr. Henry was of very little account in the convention."[19]

The student of history may gather the salient facts of Mr. Henry's activities in the second Congress from Dr. Tyler:

---

[17] Henry, *Henry*, I, p. 305.

[18] Thomas Jefferson's *Letters to William Wirt*. Jefferson's *Recollections of Patrick Henry*. Issued by Mr. John Gribbel of Philadelphia, with an Introduction by Stan V. Henkels, p. 9.

[19] Chandler and Thames, *Colonial Virginia*, p. 349.

On June 16, he was placed with General Schuyler, James Duane, James Wilson and Philip Livingston on a committee; on June 19, he served with John Adams and Thomas Lynch on a committee; on June 21 . . . Washington put into Henry's hand sundry queries, to which he desired the Congress would give an answer, and it is pointed out that these queries involved subjects of serious concern to the cause and would certainly require for their consideration "cool-headed, reflecting, and judicious men." On the committee were Silas Deane, Patrick Henry, John Rutledge, Samuel Adams and Richard Henry Lee; on July 10 a committee was composed of Philip Livingston, Patrick Henry and John Alsop; on July 13 the commissioners for the management of the middle department for Indian affairs were elected, namely, Franklin, Patrick Henry and James Wilson; on July 17 a committee consisting of Thomas Cushing, Patrick Henry and Silas Deane was appointed to negotiate with the Indian missionary respecting his past and future services among the Six Nations, to secure their friendship and continue them in a state of neutrality in the controversy between Great Britain and the colonies. On July 31, next to the last day, Patrick Henry served on a committee headed by Washington and made up of one member for each colony "for the very practical and urgent purpose of inquiring after virgin lead and leaden ore, and the best methods of collecting, smelting, and refinishing it"; also after "the cheapest and easiest methods of making salt in the colonies."[20] Dr. Tyler pointed out that this was not a committee on which any man could be useful who had only "declamation" to contribute to its work. Furthermore, "the organization of some kind of national government for thirteen colonies precipitated into a state of war; the creation of a national army; the selection of a commander-in-chief, and of the officers to serve under him; the hurried fortification of coasts, harbors, cities; the supply of the troops with clothes, tents, weapons, ammunition, food, medicine; protection against the Indian tribes along the frontier of nearly every colony; the goodwill of the people of Canada, and of Jamaica; a solemn, final appeal to the King and to the people of England; an appeal to the people of Ireland; finally, a grave statement to all mankind of 'the cause and necessity of their taking up arms,'—these were among the weighty and soul-stirring matters which the second Continental Congress had to consider and to decide upon. For any man to say, forty years afterward, even though he say it with

[20] Tyler, *Henry*, pp. 172–173–174–175. As pointed out by Dr. Tyler.

all the authority of the renown of Thomas Jefferson, that, in the presence of such questions, the spirit of Patrick Henry was dull or unconcerned, and that, in a Congress which had to deal with such questions, he was 'a silent and almost unmeddling member,' is to put a strain upon human confidence which it is unable to bear."[21]

Perhaps the principal value of Mr. Jefferson's testimony to Mr. Wirt is "to serve as an illustration of the extreme fragility of any man's memory respecting events long past, even in his own experience. Thus, Jefferson here remembers how 'wonderfully relieved' Patrick Henry was at being 'permitted to leave Congress' on account of his appointment by the Virginia Convention 'to be colonel of their first regiment.' But from the official records of the time, it can now be shown that neither of the things which Jefferson thus remembers, ever had any existence in fact. In the first place, the journal of the Virginia Convention indicates that Patrick Henry's appointment as colonel could not have been the occasion of any such relief from congressional duties as Jefferson speaks of, for that appointment was not made until five days after Congress itself had adjourned, when, of course, Patrick Henry and his fellow delegates, including Jefferson, were already far advanced on their journey back to Virginia. In the second place, the journal of Congress indicates that Patrick Henry had no such relief from Congressional duties, on any account, but was bearing his full share in its business, even in the plainest and most practical details, down to the very end of the session."[22]

Six weeks had passed before Mr. Jefferson made his appearance at the second Congress—a substitute for Peyton Randolph, who, being also the Speaker of the House of Burgesses, had to withdraw temporarily from Congress.

During the absence of Mr. Henry and the other delegates at Congress, Governor Dunmore in Virginia had set to work to strengthen his hand. He called the Assembly together on the first of June for a showdown—to feel them out on the "olive branch" proposals of Lord North. Peyton Randolph, the Speaker of the House, had left Congress in the latter part of May to preside over the meeting. There had not been a session of the Burgesses in ten years, nor a revolutionary convention, over which he had

---

[21] *Ibid.*, pp. 170–171.

[22] *Ibid.*, pp. 169–170; op. cit., 4 American Arch. III, p. 375; 4 American Arch. II, p. 1902.

not presided.[23] In this session "Carter Braxton, son-in-law of Corbin was there, and Dudley Digges, Thomas Nelson, Jr., and the other great planters or scions of planter families, distressed at these uneasy times, wondering whether all the issues might not easily be adjusted if only the control of affairs might be left where control ought always to lodge, in the hands of men of property—the wise and the good. There were other Virginians; Thomas Ludwell Lee, brother of Richard Henry Lee, deserter of his class, and Thomas Johnson . . . from Louisa, William Christian, the Indian fighter from Fincastle, Adam Stephen from Frederick, William Fleming, Jefferson's friend from Cumberland, and a score of others like these—talking *liberty* and *equality*, manhood suffrage and equal representation, their long trusty rifles standing in the corners of the room; tall, sinewy, weather-beaten, hard-handed men ready for arduous adventures; the men who within the year had fought desperately at Point Pleasant and beaten twice their own number of Indians, were without wigs. More than half Virginia spoke through these representatives in hunting shirts and feathered caps, all that wide region that lay along the eastern foothills of the Blue Ridge, the populous counties between Staunton and the Potomac, and the great wild mountain fastness that lay toward the Ohio. It was certain to be a troublesome session."[24]

Randolph took his seat and the members sat through the Governor's address, in which he told them England was ready with her proposals of peace. But before taking up these proposals, the false and malicious letters of Dunmore to the Earl of Dartmouth of May 29 and December 24, 1774, were discussed by the Burgesses, who called for an explanation from the Governor.[25] The charge that there were independent companies in every county was also declared false when the facts showed that there were not more than six or seven companies throughout the whole 61 counties. The Governor's conduct was questioned on several issues, including the expenses incurred and number of militia lately called up. An investigation disclosed his effort to embroil the Indians against some of the colonies. A committee was appointed to investigate the stores remaining in the magazine. Upon examination it was discovered that the locks to the arsenal containing the arms for the colony had been taken. Investigation proved a

---

[23] William E. Dodd, *The Spirit of '76, Virginia Takes the Road to Revolution,* pp. 111–112.

[24] *Ibid.*, pp. 112–113.

[25] Force, 4th series, II, pp. 1222–1231.

trap had been set with spring guns, which inflicted serious injury to the shoulder of one of the men and to the wrist and hand of another.[26] Several barrels of powder were also found concealed under the floor of the magazine, intended to do further damage. The people, hearing of the Governor's actions, became enraged, and the next day Dunmore fled with his family on a man-of-war, saying that he no longer felt safe in Williamsburg. The Burgesses, having received his message, made known their willingness to assure his lordship's security. Dunmore's reply ordered them to disarm the independent companies, accept the conciliatory proposals of Parliament and adjourn to meet aboard his vessel for future consultations.[27] After several unsuccessful negotiations with the Governor, the Assembly turned its attentions to the public duties, taking up first the consideration of both addresses in Parliament and the resolution of the House of Commons. When the members had "viewed it in every point of light," the committee on June 12 made its report. Setting down the many reasons the terms of that resolution were unacceptable, the report declared that it only changed the form of oppression without lightening its burden.[28] This was the response of the House of Burgesses of Virginia to Lord North's proposals. After all the important matters were completed, the Assembly adjourned on June 24, and never being able to obtain a quorum again, the House of Burgesses ceased to be an active body. The Governor, in abandoning his legislative duties, had put an end to colonial government in Virginia.

Hardly had the House adjourned, however, before some of its members were getting ready to attend the third Virginia Convention. This important meeting followed on July 17 in Richmond. The unhappy differences in the colony brought the members together to deliberate on the situation of the country and to provide in a constitutional way for the exigencies of government. The *Declaration of the Delegates* in this convention sets forth the causes leading to dissolution.[29] Already instructions from Congress for the protection of the colony were being carried out. Two companies of riflemen were equipped and in camp by mid-August. Among those assembled for the Convention was the

---

[26] Wirt, *Henry,* (1836) edition, pp. 168–169.

[27] Henry, *Henry,* I, pp. 308–309; Wirt, *Henry,* p. 171.

[28] Burnett, *The Continental Congress,* p. 95.

[29] Brenaman, *History of Virginia Conventions,* pp. 24–25; Henry, *Henry,* I, p. 309; Henry, *Henry,* III, p. 631, "America went into a state of nature."

new member, George Mason, who was elected from Fairfax to replace George Washington. He was described by Thomas Jefferson as "a man of the first order of wisdom among those who acted on the theatre of the Revolution, of expansive mind, profound judgment, cogent in argument . . . and earnest for the republican change on democratic principles."[30] George Mason earnestly engaged in the cause and became the loyal friend of Patrick Henry. Here in the revolutionary convention, as well as in the House of Burgesses, Peyton Randolph, the Speaker, presided. "Thomas Johnson and his colleague of Louisa, Thomas Walker, were already known by their works; John Talbot of Bedford, John Bowyer of Botetourt, and Robert Rutherford of Berkeley of the up-country party, were ready for independence or war, or both. Paul Carrington of Charlotte, William Fleming of Cumberland, William Christian of Fincastle, and Samuel McDowell of Augusta, partisans of Henry, were on the ground to press the cause of their leader not yet returned from Philadelphia. The absence of Henry was countered by the absence of his rival, Pendleton; nor may we doubt that Robert Carter Nicholas, Carter Braxton, William Robinson, Joseph Hutchins, and others from the river counties were ready for still another contest on behalf of sanity and deliberation."[31]

Aboard his vessel, Dunmore was now plotting to make war against the colonies.[32] Despite the mounting danger, many matters had to await the arrival of the delegates from Congress. "On the second day of the convention a great committee was ordered to prepare a comprehensive scheme for doing what was voted the preceding March, arming the colony. Isaac Zane, George Mason, William Christian and others from the warlike sections of the dominion united with their low-country brethren to recommend a plan by which two regiments of regulars were to assemble at Williamsburg and two battalions were to be organized and scattered at strategic points on the eastern shore of the Chesapeake Bay and along the gaps of the Allegheny Mountains. All the counties were to have a more active militia than ever before, and in addition some six thousand minute men were to assemble frequently, drill intensively, and hold themselves in readiness to move at a moment's notice. Arms and ammunition were to be

---

[30] *Ibid.*, p. 311.

[31] William E. Dodd, *The Spirit of '76, Virginia Takes the Road to Revolution*, pp. 114–115.

[32] Henry, *Henry*, I, p. 311.

bought wherever they could be found. A powder mill was to be set up at Fredericksburg, and lead was to be mined and smeltered in the Fincastle district, probably at Wytheville of our day. Every man who had a rifle, gun-powder, or gun was asked to sell or loan the same to the colony."[33]

Officers to command the regiments were elected on August 5. Feelers had been sent to Patrick Henry at Congress by some of his friends, and his name was now offered for colonel of the first regiment. Opposition to Patrick Henry arose from some of the divisive members who argued that he was not an experienced military man. Nevertheless, Patrick had had some military training under his father. His rearing was strongly influenced by his father's strict, methodical training as a regimental commander. He had watched the march and drill movements, witnessed the carrying of arms and the handling of muskets. These early instructions at the hands of his father qualified him later to organize and train the Hanover Volunteers. In his march to Williamsburg he had exhibited gallantry and leadership. When the first ballot was cast, Patrick Henry received 40 votes, Hugh Mercer 41. For Thomas Nelson there was the count of 8 votes and for Woodford, 1. In the second ballot between Mercer and Henry, Mr. Henry was elected. Thus, we see him chosen to the high office of Commander-in-Chief of all the forces for the protection of the Virginia Colony and Colonel of the First Regiment of Regulars.

On August 9, four days after the election of officers, Patrick Henry, Edmund Pendleton, Benjamin Harrison and Thomas Jefferson arrived at the convention from Congress and took their seats. Richard Henry Lee made his appearance two days later. The thanks of the convention were expressed to the delegates for their faithful discharge of their duties in Congress, and it was resolved that "the powder purchased by Patrick Henry, Esquire, for the use of this colony be immediately sent for."[34]

The colony, now left without a Governor, had reached that impasse which was to close royal rule. The Convention had become an executive as well as a legislative body. Faced with continuous demands, the body adopted the recommendations of Congress and appointed a Committee of Safety. Its purpose was "for the more effectual carrying into execution the several rules and regulations established by this Convention for the protection of this

---

[33] William E. Dodd, *The Spirit of '76, Virginia Takes the Road to Revolution*, p. 115. Henry, *Henry*, I, p. 312.

[34] 4 American Archives, III, pp. 377–378; Henry, *Henry*, I, p. 316.

Colony."[35] Those selected to serve on this committee were Edmund Pendleton, George Mason, John Page, Richard Bland, Thomas Ludwell Lee, Paul Carrington, Dudley Digges, William Cabell, Carter Braxton, James Mercer and John Tabb. "Whether Henry asked his lieutenants to yield one cannot say. But when the great committee was elected Edmund Pendleton was chairman. Carter Braxton, the 'Tory' of the gunpowder episode, was a member; and young William Cabell of the upper James River country, no advocate of foolish radicalism, was likewise a member. The majority of the committee was composed of Henry's enemies. Government by deadlock, the American method, for Henry as commander-in-chief would have to cooperate with Pendleton, head of the Committee of Safety."[36] Here in the third Virginia Convention, as in Congress, party feeling and factionalism ran high.[37] "There was, in truth, something extremely singular and embarrassing in the situation of the parties in regard for each other. It was not war, nor was it peace. The very ordinance by which these troops were raised, was filled with professions of allegiance and fidelity to George III . . . 'professions confined to the exercise of his constitutional powers,' yet they were connected with the expression 'of their firm determination to resist any attempts on the liberties of the country.' " It is pointed out that the " 'only intelligible purpose, therefore, for which these troops were raised, was a preparation for defense; and for defense against an attempt to enforce the parliamentary taxes upon the colony. With respect to Lord Dunmore, he was indeed considered as having abandoned the duties of his office: yet still he was regarded as the governor of Virginia; and there seems to have been no

---

[35] Henry, *Henry*, I, p. 315.

[36] William E. Dodd, *The Spirit of '76, Virginia Takes the Road to Revolution*, pp. 119–120.

[37] Henry, *Henry*, op. cit., I, p. 314. George Mason wrote General Washington October 14 following the Convention:

> "I hinted to you in my last the parties and factions which prevailed at Richmond. I never was in so disagreeable a situation, and almost despaired of a cause which I saw so ill conducted. During the first part of the Convention, parties ran so high that we had frequently no other way of preventing improper measures, than by procrastination, urging the previous question and giving men time to reflect. However, after some weeks, the babblers were pretty well silenced, a few weighty members began to take the lead, several wholesome regulations were made, and if the Convention had continued to sit a few days longer, I think the public safety would have been as well provided for, as our present circumstances permit."

Writing of Washington, III, p. 152.

disposition to offer violence to his person.' "[38] Moreover, according to the terms of Colonel Henry's commission, he was obliged to obey all orders and instructions from the Convention and the Committee of Safety.[39] Faced with a strictly defensive policy, Patrick Henry must have had a disciplined spirit indeed, particularly in the difficulties of restraining a tumultuous people.

The Convention heard on August 14 of Dunmore's plans for an attack, and orders were issued to the volunteers and militia to be ready to repel any invasion of Williamsburg. Enlistments were ordered for 8,180 militiamen to be equipped and trained as minutemen in addition to the regiments and battalions already in service. The Convention also ordered a munitions factory to be established at Fredericksburg and called for extensive manufacture of arms and supplies. The nonexportation of tobacco had stopped all sales and depleted the value of currency. Paper money was to be issued to meet the expenses of the war and a tax imposed.[40] Mr. Henry, responding to a request, made a motion that permission be given all dissenting clergymen to preach in camp to the troops holding to their respective faiths. This liberty was granted. At the close of the Convention on August 26, with his commission signed by the Committee of Safety, Colonel Henry left for his home at Scotchtown.

Mr. Henry had been absent from his home at this time for over three months, devoting his full time to the affairs of his country. Many of his domestic problems had to be worked out before he could take command, and he was doubtless glad for this opportunity to be with his children, who had been looked after in his absence by his mother and his sister, Elizabeth.[41]

On September 20, after his business had been put in order and he had received his instructions, Colonel Henry was ready to leave for the field of duty. Surrounded by his affectionate children, he took up his orders and headed his horse in the direction of Williamsburg to the rendezvous of his troops.

At the capitol also was the headquarters of the Committee of Safety presided over by Pendleton. Because of ill health, George Mason sat but little in this important body. Neither was he able

---

[38] Wirt, *Henry*, (1836 edition), pp. 177–178; See the conclusion of the address, Henry, *Henry*, I, p. 318.

[39] Tyler, *Henry*, p. 177; Wirt, *Henry*, (1836 edition), p. 185 n.

[40] Henry, *Henry*, I, p. 317; William E. Dodd, *The Spirit of '76, Virginia Takes the Road to Revolution*, p. 115.

[41] Preston, *Paths of Glory*, p. 94–97–101–102; Henry, *Henry*, I, p. 318. See also pages 329–330.

to be present at the fourth Virginia Convention the same year, December 1775. Pendleton reputedly had his way in most matters during Mason's absence.[42] Regrettably, Mason soon resigned from the Committee.

In Williamsburg, Colonel Henry was warmly received by his troops. His arrival was announced in the *Gazette*, September 23, 1775, thus:

> Thursday last arrived here Patrick Henry Esq. Commander-in-Chief of the Virginia forces. He was met and escorted to town by the whole body of volunteers, who paid him every mark of respect and distinction in their power, in testimony of their approbation of so worthy a gentleman to the appointment of that important trust, which the convention has been pleased to repose in him.[43]

The knowledge of Patrick Henry's appointment accounted for a large body of volunteers. There had been no difficulty in filling the two regiments.[44] He pointed out the field that he had chosen for his encampment and the troops escorted him to the grounds west of the college. William Christian, Patrick Henry's brother-in-law, was appointed lieutenant-colonel, and Francis Eppes, major, to the first regiment; Charles Scott, lieutenant-colonel, and Alexander Spotswood, major, to the second regiment—all appointed by the Convention. John Green was the captain in the Culpeper company and the "stripling" John Marshall, lieutenant in the company from Fauquier.[45] Men gathered in various military outfits; some were without uniforms. Troops of the First Regiment were equipped with hunting shirts and leggings of buckskin. The Culpeper company was the most noticeable. They wore green shirts emblazoned with "Liberty or Death" in white letters on their breasts, flaunting bucktail hats, tomahawks and scalping knives.[46] This exhibit of Patrick Henry's motto would have brought a chuckle from the colonel, perhaps, had he not been too concerned over the lack of arms. So scarce were these that many of the men had to carry their own fowling-pieces. The troops were organized and assigned to the two regiments, after which they commenced drilling and other military tactics.

---

[42] Morgan, *Henry*, p. 219; Henry, *Henry*, op. cit., I, pp. 333, Mason's letter to Washington, April 2, 1776, American Archives, 4th Series, V, p. 760.

[43] 4 American Archives, III p. 776.

[44] Henry, *Henry*, I, p. 319.

[45] *Ibid.*, I, p. 320.

[46] Morgan, *Henry*, p. 220.

This routine continued through October as more regulars kept pouring in. There were now nine companies in all and tents were spreading. It was Colonel Henry's leadership, without doubt, that was responsible for the good spirit and appearance of the troops so much praised in the *Gazette*, "and had the purpose been offensive war, Colonel Henry was soon in a situation to have annihilated any force that Lord Dunmore could at that time have arrayed against him."[47]

"But while the commander-in-chief set his school of war in order, Edmund Pendleton, the foil of Henry in every great political conflict since the first scandalous day when the gentleman from Hanover uncovered the financial corruption of the Robinson régime; Edmund Pendleton, wary, shrewd, skeptical of democracy in all its ways, was now the autocrat of the commonwealth, chairman of the Committee of Safety in perpetual session there in the palace recently vacated by the Earl of Dunmore. Henry was master of all the little army, the planner of campaigns, leader in battle itself; but Pendleton and his quorum of the committee was also master of the army, legal planner of campaigns, although as a committee it could hardly lead a charge against the British 'tyrant.' Here was a situation."[48]

The Governor in the meantime had removed himself from Colonel Henry's haunts, and sailed to safer waters at Norfolk. Mr. Wirt describes the circumstances of his departure: "no commotion . . . had ensued to justify his retreat. The people, indeed, were highly indignant, but they were silent and quiet. The suggestions of his lordship's conscience had alone produced his flight."[49] Fear stands out as the cause of his sudden departure. This is evident in the Assembly's promise of a safe return for his lordship, when he ascribed his movement to "apprehensions for his personal safety . . . that the disorders in Williamsburg and in other parts of the country, had driven him from the palace," and also in his accusation charging the Assembly with "giving countenance to the violent and disorderly proceedings of the people. . . ."[50] From these quotations, it appears Mr. Wirt has understated the disposition of the people, who were everything but "silent and quiet." Governor Dunmore's proclamation of May

---

[47] Wirt, *Henry*, (1836 edition), p. 177.

[48] William E. Dodd, *The Spirit of '76, Virginia Takes the Road to Revolution*, p. 123.

[49] Wirt, *Henry*, (1836 edition), p. 169.

[50] *Ibid*, p. 173.

singled out "a certain Patrick Henry of the county of Hanover, and a number of deluded followers," who were "the great terror of all His Majesty's faithful subjects."[51] Patrick Henry, then, was the fear of Governor Dunmore.

The King's proclamation replying to the second petition of Congress was received on October 31; in it the colonies were denounced and charged with open rebellion. It carried instructions to all loyal subjects to use their efforts to suppress the rebellion, giving the promise that 10,000 additional troops would be sent to aid the British forces in America.[52]

Already aboard the *Fowey*, Dunmore had become a threat to the peace along the Chesapeake. "The rivers of Virginia fall into the Chesapeake Bay, and they were navigable at that time to Georgetown, Fredericksburg, and Richmond for sea-going vessels; thus all over the low-country formidable war craft might easily enter the rivers, creeks, and bays and terrorize the plantations, carrying off negroes and supplies at will. The colony of Virginia had only one ship that might be called a war vessel and few others of any kind."[53]

Dunmore, having the control of the shoreline, moved up and down, carrying on a savage and piratical war of plunder and murder. He seized and incited slaves as well as Indians for the purpose of attack, using every method possible to distract the colonists from their defense efforts. Sent to his aid were three vessels—"the *Mercury*, a warship of twenty-four guns, the *Kingfisher*, sixteen, and the *Otter*, fourteen, and a number of sloops and supply craft."[54] Capt. Matthew Squire of the sloop *Otter* embarked upon a similar system of piracy—cruising along the James and York on illegal excursions of plunder in which he carried off slaves, cattle, and everything that came to hand. Vessels were intercepted, passengers and private property were seized in a continuous harassment along the coast. The people in the territory of Norfolk, Newport News and Hampton began to feel the effects of the shipping hazard and held constant fear of attack. Captain Squire with his sloop, a schooner, and three tenders made ready his plans to land and burn Hampton, which he

---

[51] *Ibid.*, p. 164.

[52] Henry, *Henry*, I, p. 321.

[53] William E. Dodd, *The Spirit of '76*, "*Virginia Takes the Road to Revolution,*" p. 121.

[54] *Ibid.*, p. 120.

attempted on October 26.[55] He was repulsed by a company of regulars and minute-men in the town. However, a second attack was expected on the next day and Colonel Woodford was dispatched to the scene with Captain Green's company from Culpeper. They arrived in time to take a part in this repulse. It was the first conflict and the first victory on Virginia soil in the Revolution.[56] There were no casualties among the Virginians, but the British suffered some losses.

Governor Dunmore was angered over the outcome, and still claiming to govern the colony, was more than ever determined in his plans for its destruction. On board the ship *William*, he issued a proclamation, November 7, declaring martial law and calling upon all loyal subjects to join His Majesty's troops. He promised freedom to all indentured servants, Negroes, and rebels. Those not bearing arms and declaring allegiance to the King would be forced to leave their homes and property under threat of forfeiture. Disregarding treaties, he sent the notorious John Connolly to incite the Indians to an attack upon the western frontier, and to cut off all "communication between the northern and southern colonies."[57] In the meantime, Dunmore had gathered to his standard a body of Tories and Negroes with two companies from the 14th Regiment of regulars from St. Augustine and moved into a position on the Elizabeth River at Kemp's Landing. He made a surprise attack on Colonel Hutchings' company, capturing a group of Princess Anne minute-men, placing Suffolk in danger. From here, on the east branch of the Elizabeth River, he moved his forces to a stronghold on the south branch known as Great Bridge, thus threatening Norfolk, about 12 miles away.[58]

Patrick Henry saw the war effort imperilled should Lord Dunmore obtain control of this strategic area. In the Tory merchants he recognized a direct threat to the shipping industry.

---

[55] Henry, *Henry,* I, pp. 322–323–324–326; See also Mr. John Page's letter to Jefferson recounting the Affairs at Hampton. Boyd, *The Papers of Thomas Jefferson,* I, p. 256; Note also the Resolution of the Committee of Safety, Henry, *Henry,* I, p. 323; See the Declaration against Dunmore in the Virginia Convention on the 13th and 14th of December, Brenaman, *Virginia Convention,* p. 30.

[56] *Ibid.,* I, p. 324.

[57] *Ibid.,* I, pp. 325–326; Brenaman, *Virginia Conventions,* p. 25. The Convention of July, 1775, notes the insidious and cruel attempts to stir up the barbarous savages against the inhabitants on the frontiers of the different colonies.

[58] *Ibid.,* I, pp. 326–327. See Mr. John Page's letter to Mr. Jefferson concerning the Affairs of Princess Ann. Boyd, *The Papers of Thomas Jefferson,* I, p. 265.

Norfolk, he must have felt, should be held at all cost. The capital must also be protected, and this required a large concentration of troops. The lack of supplies presented another grave problem. Sensing the imminent dangers, Colonel Henry discussed the matter with Colonel Woodford, whereupon it was decided to urge the Committee of Safety to dispatch troops at once to the scene of trouble.[59] Mr. Henry's desire to hasten to the field had been made known and he impatiently awaited orders to strap on his knapsack and march against the enemy. Contrary to his wishes, however, the committee under Pendleton's direction ordered Colonel Woodford early in November to the troubled area. The decision to place so important a duty in the hands of his subordinate injured Patrick Henry considerably. But the sensible warrior stood back in the interest of unity, giving every assistance possible, furnishing first-rate troops and the best supplies he could muster. He took keen delight in the march of Captain Green's Culpeper Company, knowing the expert marksmanship of these riflemen.

A letter to Edmund Pendleton, the chairman of the committee, from Colonel Henry, written December 19, 1775, from Williamsburg, shows his alertness as commander-in-chief, and also presents the disadvantage under which he labored as well as the futility of trying to conduct a war, or steps necessary to war, by a committee or a convention:

> . . . Understanding that a large Ship & Sloop were in the Bay abt. 15 miles below, I thought it advisable to order out a party of Soldiers to make Discovery, & bring them in if possible.
>
> Capt. Barron accordingly set out with 20 men in a swift sailing Vessel & has brot in a Sloop from Turks Island having on board 900 Bushels Salt, a piece or two of Popns & Irish Linens, & a few other articles. The Sloop is just now brot within the Bar, and her Cargo waits the Disposition of the Convention. . . . I should be exceedingly glad if the Convention would please to determine what is to be done with the several Vessels now in this port. The near Neighbourhood of the Enemy makes it almost certain, that every one of them that go out from hence will fall into their hands. . . .

Further information was sent the chairman of the committee in a letter of December 23, telling of other vessels seized. Among them, he mentioned the agreeable news in the taking of the vessel

[59] *Ibid.*, I, p. 322.

of the British government bound to the Eastern shore for provisions, commanded by Capt. Collett & manned with 16 Negroes:

> Another Vessel of the same sort was Yesterday pursued by our people, & little doubt remained of taking her also. A third Vessel with 2,400 Bushels Salt is also taken, but not quite brot into the Harbor, the Tide falling.
>
> The Captives inform Col. Ellet, the Liverpool is laden with Guns, but the Brig with military stores. Both together have 400 men & have been 3 months & 3 days at Sea.
>
> Collett the Capt. . . . who is from every Circumstance a great Villain is closely confin'd & and seems a dangerous person. He says 57 men only were killed, wounded & taken at great Bridge . . .
>
> Any Commands you may please to have shall be instantly comply'd with.
>
> I hope the Vessel I order'd into the service may be order'd to continue, she being found so successful. I beg a line for that purpose.[60]

Patrick Henry's competence in the performance of duty is evident in his letters. Salt, the most needed commodity, was held up, awaiting the disposition of Pendleton. And "salt became so rare an article that men began to hoarde; there was not a cannon in the colony to answer the big guns that roared from the decks of the *Mercury* and the *Kingfisher*. Times were critical." Colonel Woodford "had seven hundred men, some of them the best marksmen in the world. But his bullet moulds did not match his rifles; his powder was scarce; and lead for the moulding of bullets was equally scarce. His men were none too well clad in their sleazy, nutbrown hunting shirts; their bare feet were upon the ground, and winter was approaching."[61]

Governor Dunmore with his motley crew of some 300 entrenched in the vicinity of Great Bridge, was holding his log fort

---

[60] Henry, *Henry*, III, pp. 3–4–5.

[61] William E. Dodd, *The Spirit of '76, Virginia Takes the Road to Revolution*, pp. 121–124–128; The Honorable John Page wrote Thomas Jefferson from Williamsburg, November 11, 1775:

> "If we had but Salt enough to satisfy our Country Men who begin to complain for want of it, and Arms and Ammunition, we should be able to make a very good Stand against all the Forces that can be sent to Virginia, for I can assure you nothwithstanding the Affair of Norfolk and Kemp's Landing, Your Country Men are brave and hearty in the Cause."

Boyd, *The Papers of Thomas Jefferson*, I, p. 259; See also George Gilmer's letter to Jefferson concerning the scarcity of Powder and salt. Boyd, *The Papers of Thomas Jefferson*, I, p. 237.

known as the "hog pen," preparing to stop Woodford. The immediate charge was in command of a brave officer, Captain Fordyce.[62]

Adding further to the tension was the news received by Washington telling of the Earl of Dartmouth's instructions to Dunmore:

> We intend to send twenty thousand men next spring. You should be able to collect from the Indians, negroes and other persons a force sufficient to subdue rebellion. If you can not subdue them come home and give the enclosed commission to Colonel Richard Corbin.[63]

Information was further made known of a great expeditionary force in a letter to the governor of North Carolina from Lord George Germain. It told of the armament now ready to send to the aid of British forces in America: seven regiments of infantry from Ireland, three artillery companies under command of Cornwallis; and such great war vessels as the *Bristol*, the *Acteon*, the *Boreas*, the *Soletay*, the *Syren*, the *Sphynx*, the *Deal Castle* and the *Hawk*.[64]

The fourth Revolutionary Convention of December 1, 1775, which had met in Richmond, adjourned to Williamsburg, nearer the theater of operations. The delegates for the first time were beginning to feel the grim hand of war. Seeing the further need of troops, the Convention ordered seven new regiments to be raised and equipped, 500 riflemen being dispatched to the area of Chesapeake Bay. Vessels were also ordered to be armed and provided.[65] Seeing the value of the currency affected by the nonexportation on tobacco, the matter was taken up in the Convention calling upon the Virginia delegates in Congress "to urge the opening of American ports to the trade of the world, except that of Great Britain, Ireland, and the West Indies."[66] Other ordinances adopted besides the raising of additional forces for the defense and protection of the colony called for appointing sheriffs; for providing arms and ammunition; for reviving and amending the ordinance appointing the Committee of Safety; for establishing tobacco payments during the discontinuance of the inspection

---

[62] *Ibid.*, p. 127.
[63] *Ibid.*, p. 125–126.
[64] *Ibid.*
[65] Henry, *Henry*, I, p. 331.
[66] *Ibid.*, I, p. 332.

law; for regulating the election of delegates and ascertaining their allowances.[67]

In this convention Patrick Henry did not sit as a member. "More than half his troops were off at Suffolk or pushed forward on the road to Great Bridge, their tents set near the bridge in a bog, their ammunition still scarce and their foodstuff running low. The remainder of the troops were without arms or undrilled about Williamsburg, at Richmond, or Hampton, doing guard duty, trying to thwart Dunmore's marauding parties."[68]

Mr. John Page wrote Mr. Jefferson, November 24, 1775:

> I think if we had but Powder enough some good Cannon and a few Privateers we might do very well. We have 3–18 Pounders some 12s, 9s and 4s but we have no Powder even to prove them, and I know not who will venture to import more since Gatrick and his Sons are Prisoners. For God's Sake endeavour to procure us Arms and Ammunitions and if our King is so determined a Tyrant as not to listen to your Petition, crave Assistance from any and every Power that can afford it. Our Committee had adjourned before the News of Ld. D______s Success reached Wmsburg which may be an unlucky Circumstance, if Woodford should be defeated, or should there be an Insurrection of the Negroes, since Col. Henry is not empowered to call in any Assistance but such as the neighbouring Minute and Militia Companies may afford, which is at present in Fact none at all.[69]

"John Page was trying to get a flotilla of gunboats upon the bay in the hope of checking the operations of His Majesty's governor and vice admiral. But there was Patrick Henry, still powerful, snubbed and insulted by Edmund Pendleton and his committee; angered by Colonel Woodford, who refused to report to or communicate with him at all—Henry, the voice of the people. The up-country members were enraged; members of Congress, even Washington himself offering advice, lamenting the foolish decision of Henry in abandoning 'the senate for the field,' forgetting that in the senate it had always been the one great task of the selfsame men to thwart the same Henry. As the month of December wore on something must be done."[70]

---

[67] Brenaman, *Virginia Conventions, p.* 31.

[68] William E. Dodd, *The Spirit of '76, Virginia Takes the Road to Revolution,* p. 128.

[69] Boyd, *The Papers of Thomas Jefferson,* I, pp. 265–266.

[70] William E. Dodd, *The Spirit of '76, Virginia Takes the Road to Revolution,* pp. 129–130.

All prospects now seemed to indicate that the commander-in-chief would be stationed permanently in Williamsburg. This was confirmed by an order requesting him to prepare winter quarters there for his regiment. Nothing in the way of plans tended to show that Colonel Henry would have an actual hand in the fighting. Furthermore, no word had been received from Colonel Woodford since his sojourn to Norfolk. Colonel Henry's anxiety over the situation, and his eagerness to hear how Woodford was getting on, prompted him to write the following letter:

On Virginia Service.
To William Woodford, Esq., colonel of the second regiment of the Virginia forces.

Headquarters, Dec. 6, 1775

Sir:
Not Hearing of any dispatch from you for a long time, I can no longer forbear sending to know your situation, and what has occurred. Every one, as well as myself, is vastly anxious to hear how all stands with you. In case you think any thing could be done to aid and forward the enterprise you have in hand, please to write it. But I wish to know your situation particularly, with that of the enemy, that the whole may be laid before the convention now here. The number and designs of the enemy, as you have collected it, might open some prospects to us, that might enable us to form some diversion in your favor. The bearer has orders to lose no time, and return with all possible haste.
I am sir,

Your most humble servant,
P. Henry, jun.

P.S. Capt. Alexander's company is not yet come.[71]

Replying to Colonel Henry's letter, Colonel Woodford wrote from Great Bridge, Dec. 7, 1775, dispatching the requested information, and added:

> When joined, I shall always esteem myself immediately under your command, and will obey accordingly; but when sent to command a separate and distinct body of troops, under the immediate instructions of the committee of safety—whenever that body or the honourable convention is sitting, I look upon it as my indispensable duty to address my intelligence to them, as the supreme power in this colony.[72]

From the above, Colonel Woodford's assumption seems to

[71] Wirt, *Henry*, p. 186.
[72] *Ibid.*, p. 187.

rest solely upon the clause in the ordinance which gave to the Committee of Safety the authority of regulating and controlling the officers and troops. The committee was invested with supreme authority when the convention was not in session, but communications with the military forces were to pass through the commander-in-chief, to whom all the officers should report, as was shown by the resolution. This raises a question: From whom had Colonel Woodford been receiving instructions since the adjournment of the committee in November, before the meeting of the convention in December? Was it not from Pendleton, instead of his nominal commander-in-chief? After Colonel Henry's letter, information was received at the convention telling of Woodford's victory at Great Bridge on December 9. However, before any message had come, Patrick Henry was well within his rights, and his duty, according to the terms of his commission, to require intelligence from his officers.

It was only through a ruse that Colonel Woodford won the battle of Great Bridge.[73] The feigned desertion by the servant of Major Marshall (father of Lieut. Marshall—both were in the battle) who in deceiving Dunmore as to the strength of Woodford's men, brought about his defeat: "On the eighth of December, nearly five hundred men in his (Woodford's) camp just south of Great Bridge, he hit upon a ruse, as I think, to deceive Captain Fordyce out of his 'hog pen.' A negro boy hurried to the British side of the river and told a tale of American distress and fear: There were only two or three hundred men; they were without proper ammunition, half-naked and in danger of starvation. Dunmore, who was himself present, believed the story, ordered Fordyce to attack next morning at sunrise. The brave leader obeyed, marched his men along the narrow causeway and over the bridge to the very border of Woodford's camp. Captain Bullitt, Indian fighter, first gave the alarm, and Captain Adam Stephens joined him in hasty measures of defense. Fordyce and his picked men advanced within twenty feet of Woodford's defenses when a deadly volley of rifle shot mowed down his men, the British captain being the first to fall. It proved a bitter and a costly attack. In two hours it was all over; a hundred of Dunmore's men lay dead or were unable to leave the muddy field. Woodford had lost one man; the hunting shirts (trained by Colonel Henry) had done the work. It was a godsend to the revolutionists of Vir-

[73] Henry, *Henry*, I, p. 327.

ginia; it stirred drooping spirits as they had not been stirred since the news of Lexington."[74]

Governor Dunmore retreated to Norfolk and once again took up his post aboard his war vessel. Col. Robert Howe in the meantime was dispatched from North Carolina to aid the Virginians and took command. Dunmore, desperately in need of provisions, called upon the merchants and planters to sell him supplies. This they were unable to do. He warned that if his needs were not met, and Colonel Howe continued to fire upon his vessels from the shore, he would bombard the town. Colonel Howe resisted his demand and Dunmore carried out his threat, opening a "heavy cannonade" upon Norfolk. "The warehouses were filled with combustibles, including many barrels of tar, pitch, and turpentine. At three o-clock on January 1, the British Navy began to bombard the town. Under cover of the guns men were sent ashore to fire the warehouses. Clouds of smoke and lurid flames arose. The wind set in strong from the sea. The town was quickly on fire. It was the work of the last British governor, an act that once more fulfilled all the prophesies of Patrick Henry." And "before the sun disappeared that cold, winter night, Norfolk was a heap of smouldering ashes, and thousands of poor folk were cast upon the mercies of the neighboring farmers or the generosity of the fourth Revolutionary Convention."[75]

Dunmore was severely rebuked for his inhuman acts by the convention. "Three times the representative of the royal authority had furnished fuel for the revolutionary fire in Virginia: by the seizure of the ammunition in the arsenal in April, which resulted finally in Henry's spectacular march upon the little capital; by the proclamation of November 7, whereby the servants and slaves of Virginia were declared to be free and promised arms to fight their former masters, which solidified the revolutionary party and brought from Washington a violent denunciation; and finally by the ultimatum which led to the utter destruction of Norfolk the first day of January, 1776. The powerful Edmund Pendleton and his many low-country supporters, themselves still in control of the Committee of Safety, hopeful even then of a reconciliation with the British government, were rendered helpless. Until lately Washington had declared that he had no thought of independence, and

---

[74] William E. Dodd, *The Spirit of '76, Virginia Takes the Road to Revolution*, pp. 130–131.
[75] *Ibid.*, p. 133.

Jefferson was writing: no man in America wishes to live under any other sovereignty than that of Great Britain."[76]

The victory at Great Bridge brought cheer to the patriots; however, there was a "rising murmur of protests from Colonel Henry's followers" over his treatment by the Committee of Safety. That his situation was a most embarrassing one there can be no question. "Colonel Henry's influence in the colony was very great and his soldiers were devoted to him, so that it would be dangerous to put an open indignity upon him."[77] The "public agitation" resulting from the alleged wrongs tendered him as the head of the military mounted throughout the colony and "the blame was openly and bluntly laid upon the Committee of Safety, who, on account of envy it was said, had tried to bury in obscurity his martial talents."[78] The convention apparently did not approve the chairman's actions. "One of the first things the Convention did was to reorganize the Committee of Safety,"[79] and in so doing, Pendleton fell from first place to fourth, but it is said that he was still strong enough to maintain his hold on affairs. His biographer noted, "There was no change in the leadership of the Committee, for Pendleton, politically speaking could always land on his feet."[80]

When Colonel Henry requested to know his status in this matter, it was shown that all orders were supposed to pass through his hands.[81] John Page, one of the members of the committee, recognized this when he wrote to Richard Henry Lee in February, 1776:

> I have been always of your opinion with respect to our present commander-in-chief. All orders do pass through him, and we really wish to be in perfect harmony with him.[82]

---

[76] *Ibid.*, pp. 133–134. Note, that Jefferson in writing to his distant kinsman Tory John Randolph on August 25, 1775, speaking of reunion with their parent country, declared:

> "I am sincerely one of those, and would rather be in dependence on Great Britain, proper limited, than on any nation upon earth, or than on no nation." Boyd, *The Papers of Thomas Jefferson*, I, p. 242.

[77] Henry, *Henry*, I, p. 340.

[78] Tyler, Henry, p. 184; Wirt, Henry, p. 196; Henry, Henry, I, p. 340.

[79] Brenaman, *Virginia Conventions*, p. 29.

[80] Mays, *Pendleton*, II, p. 76. Pendleton had enemies even in his own county of Caroline. One Brother lamented that the misfortune to his hip had not been transferred to his neck. Pendleton to Woodford, p. 145.

[81] Wirt, *Henry*, (1836) edition, p. 189.

[82] Henry, *Henry*, I, p. 345.

Pendleton, like Carter Braxton, possessed all the qualities of political finesse. Both men were perhaps responsible for fixing the arbitrary decisions so embarrassing to Colonel Henry. Here in part is a letter from Edmund Pendleton to Colonel Woodford:

> The field officers to each regiment will be named here, and recommended to Congress; in case our army is taken into continental pay, they will send commissions. A general officer will be chosen there, I doubt not, and sent us; *with that matter, I hope we shall not intermeddle, lest it should be thought propriety requires our calling, or rather recommending, our present first officer to that station.* Believe me, sir, the unlucky step of calling that gentleman from our councils, where he was useful, into the field, in an important station, the duties of which he must, in the nature of things, be an entire stranger to, has given me many an anxious and uneasy moment. In consequence of this mistaken step, which cannot now be retracted or remedied for he has done nothing worthy of degradation, and must keep his rank, we must be deprived of the service of some able officers, whose honor and former ranks will not suffer them to act under him in this juncture when we so much need their services.[83]

Further indignities were in store for the commander-in-chief. Col. Robert Howe of North Carolina was dispatched to Colonel Woodford's aid and, with the latter's approval, was placed in command of the joint forces. He addressed his communications also to the Committee of Safety and the convention, ignoring Colonel Henry's authority. Henry seemed doomed to continuous frustration.

Yet, the most harassing experience of all was still in the making—a cunningly devised plan to supersede Colonel Henry altogether. It was suggested to Congress by some of Patrick Henry's adversaries—Archibald Cary being one—that the six additional battalions to be raised should be put on Continental pay, plans being to exclude the first and second regiments. Furthermore, that the list of field officers picked in the convention and submitted to Congress for approval would, if commissioned by Congress, be placed over the heads of those officers commissioned by the colony. Colonel Henry would thus be outranked. "Congress expressed a willingness to comply with this request, but when it came to the knowledge of the Convention they saw the impropriety of this step" and to save face, urged Congress to include

[83] Wirt, *Henry*, (1836) edition, p. 193.

the two Virginia regiments in the six. This Congress determined upon February 13, adding the first and second regiments to the six battalions taken into Continental service. Congress also appointed the field officers selected by the convention, setting aside the former commissions of the colony. Patrick Henry's commission was now made to read colonel of only the first battalion of Virginia forces. The office of brigadier-general was likewise appointed over Patrick Henry's head, instead of following the regular order of promotions. Upon being notified of this, Colonel Henry promptly resigned his command and retired from military life.[84]

The student at once inquires the reasons for this first and only humiliation in Mr. Henry's long career. What could have been the motive behind it? We search for some flaw in the commander-in-chief that might account for Pendleton's actions; for certainly the accusing finger points to Pendleton. Pendleton had seized the opportunity to advance the reputation of a neighbor with whom he was well acquainted; Major Ben Robinson, Pendleton's one-time master, and Major William Woodford were close friends. But what right had Pendleton to abrogate the authority of the commander-in-chief which had been invested in Colonel Henry by the representatives of the people? Neither Edmund Pendleton, nor Woodford, complained of any laxity within the regiments, nor was there any remissness charged against the commander-in-chief. It has not been shown that Colonel Henry committed any blunders; none of his orders was countermanded. Had there been incompetency, we would have heard of it, not second-hand, but from Pendleton himself and from Colonel Woodford. Why, then, was Colonel Henry held inactive at Williamsburg and not permitted to have a hand in the actual fighting? The theater of war had switched to Norfolk since his entrenchment, though none could tell when Dunmore might return. Williamsburg of course was important. It was the seat of the conventions. Here also sat the Committee of Safety and here stood the capital of the colony. No red coat would be able to wrest the capital from Patrick Henry. Knowing these facts, it would seem wise strategy on the part of the chairman of the committee to hold Henry here, to tender advice, for which he was eminently qualified. But no such idea had been advanced and cannot in any sense account for his demotion or the bitter malice of the older members who had followed him after he took up the flickering torch.

[84] Henry, *Henry*, I, pp. 346–347; Tyler, *Henry*, p. 181.

Anyone familiar with the political scene in the Assembly of Virginia at the beginning of the struggle knows the complicated answer: He sees Edmund Pendleton influenced by a lifelong intimacy with Benjamin Robinson, in whose home Pendleton had lived as an indentured apprentice. Benjamin, an uncle of the Speaker and Treasurer of the House of Burgesses, was the son of a member of the Council and of a Secretary of the Colony. He was also a nephew of the Bishop of London. Besides, his brother held important offices, being President of the Council and later deputy governor. These ties made Benjamin Robinson politically powerful. This influence from the beginning (13 years before the "Robinson Affair"), placed Edmund Pendleton in good standing in the Assembly and helped to form his opinions. He headed the "conservative" party, comprising the "less ardent colleagues" Wythe, Bland, Randolph and Nicholas—who "consolidated the Phalanx which breasted the power of Britain." Patrick Henry, however, in one bold move, left them all behind. He became the leader of the younger and more spirited members, the Lees, Pages, Jefferson and Mason, representing the great body of the people who favored Henry's views as against the other party's, which had wielded such influence for their own advantage. Mr. Henry's influence eclipsed Pendleton and all the other members. Pendleton's treatment of Colonel Henry, then, stemmed not from any distrust of the latter's ability. It was that deeper wound, harder to heal, that had opened. All evidence points to Pendleton's guilt. His letter to Colonel Woodford showed him chafing under the accusations heaped upon him when he wrote:

> What does it signify that he resigned without any such cause, or assigning any reason at all? It is not without example that others should be censured for what he is applauded for.[85]

Jefferson, in his confidential letters to Wirt concerning Henry's military career, stated that it was the general belief of Henry's acquaintances that he (Henry) wanted personal courage, strengthened, he says, perhaps by inference from the fact that his brother William, and half brother Syme, were notorious cowards. Where Jefferson got such an idea concerning Patrick Henry is not known; Jefferson himself, as Governor, later suffered disgrace from charges of cowardice in retreating before Arnold.[86]

---

[85] Wirt, *Henry*, p. 206.

[86] Henry, *Henry*, II, p. 144.

Jefferson declared further:

> It is true indeed that Mr. Henry and Mr. Pendleton each, thought they saw in the character of the other something which they condemned . . . they were polite to each other, but nothing affectionate, possibly some of this grudge might have incorporated itself with Mr. Pendleton's judgments on the military merit of Mr. Henry: but since this trait in Mr. Henry's character has at least been believed, and no fact has been produced to prove it ill-founded (for his march to Williamsburg proved civil courage only, but not military, as he knew there was no enemy to meet him) why bring it into view at all? Mr. Henry's transcendent eminence as an Orator & Statesman, and especially his unquestioned primacy in bringing on the revolution gives him a mass of fame sufficient to satisfy any ambition, to claim for him questionable merits detracts more than it adds in the estimate of his character. Demosthenes like Henry was unquestioned as an Orator & Statesman, but doubted as a soldier.[87]

Mr. Wirt had up until now perhaps accepted certain erroneous ideas concerning Patrick Henry through the misinformation of Thomas Jefferson. But only up to a point were Jefferson's ideas plausible. The military part of Jefferson's story Wirt refused to accept.

Whether a fighter or not, Patrick Henry nevertheless "evinced a determined resolution to stake his reputation and his life on the issue of arms, and that he resigned his commission when the post of imminent danger was refused him, exhibits lucid proof that, whatever may have been his ultimate fortune, he was not deficient in two great elements of military success; personal enterprize and unquestioned courage."[88] Wirt knew this, and disregarding Jefferson's advice, he aired the full story about Henry and Pendleton. Wirt wrote that the chairman "came in at the time for his full proportion of this censure and that he smarted severely from it." He added that, "the Committee were severely spoken of at the day, and that the people as well as the soldiery, did not hesitate openly to impute their conduct toward Mr. Henry to personal envy."[89] Woodford's contempt seems to have extended even to Colonel Henry's troops. When the convention

---

[87] Thomas Jefferson's *Letters to William Wirt*, Jefferson's *Recollections of Patrick Henry*, issued by Mr. John Gribbel of Philadelphia with an Introduction by Stan V. Henkels, Introduction, iii-iv, pp. 28–29.

[88] Grigsby, *The Virginia Convention of 1776*, pp. 151–152.

[89] Wirt, *Henry*, (1836) edition, p. 196.

ordered a part of his first regiment to join Colonel Woodford, Captain Ballard, who was in charge, wrote Colonel Henry on December 20, 1775:

> Our reception at the Great Bridge was to the last degree cool, and absolutely disagreeable. We arrived there fatigued, dry and hungry, we were neither welcomed, invited to eat or drink, or shown a place to rest our wearied bones, but I thank my stars camp duty has taught us how to provide for ourselves when none will.[90]

The above shows the attitude of Woodford under Pendleton. Colonel Woodford, himself, would resign his post in the fall, after his honor had been wounded because he was not promoted when the next appointments were made. Pendleton wrote Woodford:

> They were picking up anything North or South to shun you. I cannot but approve your Resolution of visiting the Camp, as it will silence Insinuations which some people might make, however groundless, that the want of courage had produced your Resignation at this critical time.[91]

As to Colonel Henry's resentment over the indignity offered him, history is replete with many such examples of cabal. Washington, as well as Henry, was faced with individual jealousies and political intrigue. Early in the French and Indian War young Washington resigned rather than be outranked by officers holding royal commissions.[92] He was also to know the intrigues of a faction formed against him in the wretched Conway cabal. He would later have a "fierce squabble" over the question of rank amongst the general officers of his army.[93]

With characteristic dignity Patrick Henry resigned his command on February 28, 1776, but not without much resentment by the troops, which "threatened serious consequences" from

---

[90] Henry, *Henry*, I, p. 337 n. It was such treatment as this toward Colonel Henry's troops that no doubt accounted for Pendleton's comments that the 1st Regiment lacked discipline in Norfolk. Pendleton wrote Woodford he was sorry to hear that want of Spirit was amongst some, and, Your casting a Vail on this & concealing it from the Public Eye, was wise & consistent with your usual prudence. Mays, Pendleton, II, p. 81.

[91] Edmund Pendleton to Colonel William Woodford, Oct. 11, 1776. From Edmund Pendleton Papers in Southern Historical Collection, U. N. C. Library, Chapel Hill, N. C. Sept., 1955.

[92] Henry, *Henry*, I, p. 357.

[93] Burnett, *Continental Congress*, p. 98.

the commotion in camp. The *Gazette*, in publishing an account of it, said that when the troops in Williamsburg were informed of the resignation of their commander-in-chief, "the whole went into mourning, and under arms, waited on him at his lodgings, when they addressed him in the following manner:

> Deeply impressed, with a grateful sense of the obligations we lie under to you, for the polite, humane and tender treatment manifested to us throughout the whole of your conduct, while we had the honor of being under your command, permit us to offer you our sincere thanks, as the only tribute we have in our power to pay to your real merits.
>
> Notwithstanding your withdrawing yourself from the service fills us with the most poignant sorrow, as it at once deprives us our father and General, *yet, as gentlemen, we are compelled to applaud your spirited resentment to the most glaring indignity.* May your merit shine as conspicuous to the world in general as it hath done to us; and may Heaven shower its choicest blessing upon you.
>
> Williamsburgh, February 29, 1776.[94]

"Mr. Henry responded with the following:

> Gentlemen:
>
> I am extremely obliged to you for your approbation of my conduct. Your address does me the highest honor. This kind of testimony of your regard to me would have been an ample reward for services much greater than I have had the power to perform. I return you and each of you, gentlemen, my best acknowledgments, for the spirit, alacrity, and zeal, you have constantly shewn in your several stations. I am unhappy to part with you. I leave the service, but I leave my heart with you. May God bless you, and give you success and safety, and make you the glorious instruments of saving our country."[95]

When the officers received Colonel Henry's answer, they urged him to dine with them at the Raleigh Tavern, proposing afterward that they escort him out of town. This latter Mr. Henry had to decline, "some uneasiness getting among the soldiery, who assembled in a tumultuous manner and demanded their discharge, and declaring their unwillingness to serve under any other commander. Upon which Colonel Henry found it necessary to stay a night longer in town, which he spent in visiting the several

[94] Henry, *Henry*, I, pp. 348–349; Wirt, *Henry*, p. 199.
[95] *Ibid.*, I, p. 349; Wirt, *Henry*, p. 199.

barracks, and used every argument in his power with the soldiery to lay aside their imprudent resolution, and to continue in the service, which he had quitted from motives in which his honour, alone, was concerned, and that, although he was prevented from serving his country in a military capacity, yet his utmost abilities should ever be exerted for the real interest of the *United Colonies*, in support of the glorious cause in which they had engaged."[96] This produced the desired effect, the public being assured by the officers, "that those brave fellows are now pretty well reconciled, and will spend the last drop of their blood in their country's defense."[97]

Mr. Henry's resignation caused much concern among the citizenry. John Page, writing to Richard Henry Lee in April, noted, "Our people in some places disconcerted about Henry's resignation."[98]

An article appearing in the *Gazette* in defense of the committee by "A Friend to Truth" was answered by the officers, and by "An Honest Farmer" who came to Mr. Henry's defense in the next issue of the *Gazette*, declaring, in part:

> Envy strove to bury in obscurity his martial talents. Fettered and confined, with only an empty title, the mere echo of authority, his superior abilities lay inactive, nor could be exerted for his honour or his country's good. . . . Clad with innocence, as in a coat of mail, he is proof against every serpentile whisper. . . .[99]

A reply to this was published under the name of "Cato," and from its familiarity with the proceedings of the committee, was thought to have been written by one of its members. This was said to be no more satisfactory than the first. The resentment of the indignities to Colonel Henry shown by his troops, and also by the soldiers under Colonel Woodford's own command—more than 90 officers in all—proves Mr. Henry's popularity, declares his ability, and defends his honor:

> Address to Patrick Henry, Jun. Esq.,
> Late Commander-in-Chief of the Virginia Forces.
> Sir:
>
> Deeply concerned for the good of our country, we sincerely lament the unhappy necessity of your resignation, and with all

[96] *Ibid.*, I, p. 350; Wirt, *Henry*, pp. 199–200.
[97] *Ibid.*, I, p. 350.
[98] *Ibid.*, I, p. 356.
[99] Wirt, *Henry*, pp. 205–206.

the warmth of affection assure you, that whatever may have given rise to the indignity lately offered to you, we join with the general voice of the people, and think it our duty to make this publick declaration of our high respect for your distinguished merit. To your vigilance and judgment, as a Senator, this United Continent bears ample testimony, while she prosecutes her steady opposition to those destructive Ministerial measures which your eloquence first pointed out and taught to resent, and your resolution led forward to resist. To your extensive popularity the service, also, is greatly indebted for the expedition with which the troops were raised; and while they were continued, the firmness, candour, and politeness, which formed the complexion of your conduct towards them, obtained the signal approbation of the wise and virtuous, and will leave upon our minds the most grateful impression.

Although retired from the immediate concerns of war, we solicit the continuance of your kindly attention. We know your attachment to the best of causes; we have the fullest confidence in your abilities, and in the rectitude of your views, and, however willing the envious may be to undermine an established reputation, we trust the day will come when justice shall prevail, and thereby secure an honourable and happy return to the glorious employment of conducting our councils, and hazarding your life in the defense of Your country.

With the most grateful sentiments of regard and esteem, we are, sir, very respectfully your most obliged and obedient, humble servants.

Signed by upwards of ninety Officers, at Kemp's Landing, Suffolk, and Williamsburgh.[100]

Such was the devotion shown by the military under his command. Significant also is the fact that most of the old histories stressed only the importance of Mr. Henry's return to the Senate. And surely the great mind of the man was needed in setting up the republic. Washington noted this when he wrote: "I think my countrymen made a capital mistake, when they took Henry out of the Senate to place him in the field. . . ." Jefferson's letter to Mr. Wirt concerning Colonel Henry's retirement from the army stated:

He thus got back to that ground on which nature had formed him to command. He returned to our civic councils which were

[100] *Ibid.*, pp. 201–202.

his natural element, and in which his eminence at once placed him at their head.[101]

Be that as it may, the close of Mr. Henry's military life came only as the result of political intrigue and artful arrangement. It was not the will of the people who elected him to command, and except for the devotion of the military, his resignation might have had a disastrous effect upon the outcome of the Revolution. The hearts of the soldiers were with him. In him they had placed their trust, and he was the "idol of his country beyond any one that ever lived."

"But Patrick Henry, isolated, browbeaten, sore, and resentful there at Williamsburg, drilling his admiring recruits, meant more to the cause which was driving ancient Viriginia into the great, radical movement than the Committee of Safety with all its powers, more even than the rash and foolish governor whom a reactionary British ministry had put upon the greatest of the American colonies. Whatever the orator-colonel thought of his enemies and his jealous rivals, the old Dominion had taken the road to revolution, and her leaders must soon avow their purposes before the world—take their chances, very narrow chances, of becoming founders of the greatest nation in the world, or of adorning with their fine, powdered heads the gallows on Tower Hill, London."[102]

---

[101] Thomas Jefferson's Letters to William Wirt, Jefferson's Recollections of Patrick Henry. Issued by Mr. John Gribbel of Philadelphia, with an Introduction by Stan V. Henkels, p. 30.

[102] William E. Dodd, *The Spirit of '76, Virginia Takes the Road to Revolution*, pp. 134–135.

XIII

POLICIES AND PATRIOTS

THE REVOLUTIONARY PARTY in Virginia was largely composed of the Dissenter .population in the colony. "The defection from the established church was so great, and the growth of dissenting bodies so rapid, that at the time of the Revolution two-thirds of the populations were members of the dissenting churches, mainly of the Presbyterian, Baptist and Quaker denominations."[1] From among this group were the descendants of the Scotch who settled the North of Ireland. Presbyterians in their religion and church government, they became restless after the intolerable "Test Act" of 1705, requiring the Scotch in Northern Ireland to swear allegiance to the Church of England. Strongly opposing the persecutions under the reign of Queen Anne, the Scotch-Irish began a great immigration to America in the eighteenth century. Obtaining permission from Governor Gooch to settle the Valley of Virginia, they came to the colony in 1738, offering to guard the western frontier against the Indians. In other sections of the colony the Scotch-Irish could also be found in large numbers, but they were more thickly settled in the valley, where they were the controlling element. Making up this westward population in the piedmont and mountainous regions were the English, French Huguenots, Scotch and Germans. An admixture of these races was likewise scattered throughout the Virginia Colony, including the Tidewater. At first, however, the Tidewater was almost wholly settled by the English. "Entailed estates, and large property in slaves, had developed a decided aristocracy, which vied with the vice-regal court of the Governor at Williamsburg in their manner of living. They prided themselves on being loyal to the King and the Established Church."[2]

"Far different were the people who settled to the westward, and who, or whose immediate ancestors, had to subdue the

[1] Chandler and Thames, *Colonial Virginia*, p. 205.

[2] Henry, *Henry*, Vol. I, pp. 74–75.

forest and its savage inhabitants."[3] The Scotch-Irish and Germans took the major role in bringing civilization to the frontiers. Longing for freedom from corrupt rule, "they had left the Old World for motives of religion—to be free from persecutions and the burdens of taxation, thereby fullfilling a desire to be insulated from their European masters." The virile blood of the Scotch-Irish and Germans enriched the stock of the Valley of Virginia.

In 1730, Governor Gooch had granted to two Pennsylvania brothers, John and Isaac Van Meter, a tract of 40,000 acres in what is now known as Winchester. From them, Joyst Hite, also from Pennsylvania, purchased land and settled south of Winchester.[4] Governor Spotswood, 16 years before, in 1714, had brought a group of German settlers to guard the frontiers and establish an iron industry. Skilled in their trade, these master craftsmen, making up "twelve Protestant German families," settled in Spotsylvania County, and built a town they called Germanna, named for their homeland and in honor of Good Queen Anne. We are told that from their pastor, the Rev. Henry Haeger, were descended five statesmen who, in the nineteenth century, became Governors of their respective states. One of these was Governor James Lawson Kemper of Virginia.[5] Later, wishing to expand and claim land of their own, they moved to Fauquier County and established Germantown. We find among some of the early leaders in the immigration sponsored by Queen Anne such names as Baron Christopher Von Graffenried and Franz Ludwig Michel. The skill of these early Germans is pointed out in the records of *The German in Fredericksburg's History 1669–1702–1776*. Besides farming and mining, they were engaged in many types of trade and workmanship and held responsible positions. Jacob Holtzclaw is listed among the outstanding men early recognized by Governor Spotswood.

Other German settlers followed. Their loyalty and vigilance as they early took their stand alongside the patriots in the Revolution is shown in history.

The first to declare *outward* opposition were the valley Germans. At a meeting in Woodstock, Virginia, June 16, 1774, led by the Rev. Peter Muhlenberg, who later became distinguished

[3] *Ibid.*, I, pp. 74–75.

[4] Chandler and Thames, *Colonial Virginia*, p. 303.

[5] Charles Herbert Huffman, The Richmond *Times-Dispatch*, April 19, 1953. The Huguenot, John Fontaine, visited Germanna in 1715 and left an interesting account of the town.

as General Muhlenberg, the descendants of these early Germans were the first to make known their intentions to be free men, having "neither fear nor dread for His Majesty." Their resolutions, written a year before the celebrated Mecklenburg resolutions of North Carolina, and two years before the Constitutional Convention of Virginia, embodied the spirit of Luther and Calvin. They declared:

> "We will pay due submission to such acts of government as His Majesty *has a right by law to exercise over his subjects, and to such only*, (and) We will most heartily and unanimously concur with our suffering brethren of Boston, and every other part of North America, who are the immediate victims of tyranny, in promoting all proper measures to avert such dreadful calamities, to procure a redress of our grievances, *and to secure our common liberties.*[6]

From such patriots as these, whole German regiments were raised and shouldered their muskets in the Revolution.[7] An officer who early identified himself with the Germans was the fiery patriot of Fredericksburg who fought in the French and Indian campaigns as well as in the Revolution, Gerhard Von der Wieden (Weedon). He had served in the German army and was a native of Hanover, Germany.[8] He later became a Brigadier General in the Revolution. Another whose services were invaluable was Baron Frederick William Von Steuben. As Inspector General he was responsible for the training and discipline of Washington's troops. Von Steuben had been trained under the military art of Frederick the Great, and his genius was held in high esteem by the British officer, Simcoe,[9] and by Washington.

Christopher Gist (Geist or Guest), a descendant of the early German settlers, was selected by Colonel Washington to accompany him on his dangerous mission to deliver a message from Governor Dinwiddie to the French Commander on the Ohio, protesting the encroachment on Virginia Territory. Washington's choice and respect for the German patriots commenced with their loyalty, no doubt, in the French and Indian War. Making up a company, they met at Harper's Ferry and joined Washington in his advance westward. At Great Meadow in 1754, two Germans

[6] Embrey, *History of Fredericksburg, Virginia,* pp. 26–27.

[7] Henry, *Henry,* I, p. 344. Acomb, *The Revolutionary Journal of Baron Ludwig von Closen,* 1780–1783.

[8] Embrey, *History of Fredericksburg, Virginia, pp.* 134–135.

[9] Campbell, *History of Virginia,* p. 731.

mentioned in his report as serving under him were Ensign Carl Gustav von Splitdorf, and Lieutenant Edmund Wagner, who was killed in battle. "It was a longing for liberty and freedom which brought them to Virginia when even up to a time after the Revolution they knew they could not find that liberty and freedom in Germany. During the Revolution they saw men of their own country from Hesse fighting in the English Army against the Colonial Army, but these Virginia Germans knew, as all the world later knew, that the Hessian troops were the involuntary and unfortunate victims of a bargain and sale, worse than slavery, which the English King had arranged with covetous German Princes."[10] It has been pointed out that when these Hessian troops were captured by Washington at Trenton, he requested that they be well treated and given suitable quarters. Some of the officers asked permission to be moved from Winchester to Fredericksburg, a wish that was granted. It was their admiration for Washington, no doubt, and Von Steuben's and Weedon's association with him, that made them ask to be transferred to Washington's home town.

Next among the patriots in declaring *outward* opposition to corrupt rule were the Scotch-Irish. These Scots were "loyal to the conceded authority of the King, but held him to be bound, as well as themselves, by 'the solemn League and Covenant' made in 1643, by which the throne was pledged of the reformation, and of the liberties of the Kingdoms; they claimed the right of a free church; they practiced strict discipline in morals, and rigidly trained their youths in secular and religious learning; and as a race they combined, as perhaps no other did, acuteness of intellect, firmness of purpose, and conscientious devotion to duty."[11]

In offering to come and guard the frontiers, the Scotch-Irish requested only of Governor Gooch "that they be allowed the liberty of their consciences, and of worshipping God in a way agreeable to the principles of their education."[12] These freedoms being later jeopardized, the spirit of the Scotch-Irish settlers, like the Germans, can be seen in the early assertion of their rights, known as the Declaration of Augusta, which was adopted February 22, 1775. They declared:

> Many of us and our forefathers left our native land and explored this once savage wilderness to enjoy the free exercise of

[10] Embrey, *History of Fredericksburg,* pp. 23–24.
[11] Henry, *Henry,* I, p. 75.
[12] Henry, *Henry,* I, pp. 74–75.

> the rights of conscience and of human nature. These rights we are fully resolved with our lives and fortunes, inviolably to preserve; nor will we surrender such inestimable blessings, the purchase of toil and danger, to any ministry, to any Parliament, or to any body of men on earth, by whom we are not represented, and in whose decisions, therefore, we have no voice.

The intentions of these settlers were declared 16 months before the Declaration of Independence. Regarding this people, Jefferson wrote Wirt that the wild Irish had gotten possession of the valley . . . forming a barrier over which none ventured to leap and would still less venture to settle among.[13] Thomas Jefferson chose to plagiarize the word "inviolably" from the Augusta Declarations of these "wild Irish," finding it appropriate for use in the Declaration of Independence.

Later, we find that some of the Scotch-Irish settlers moved from Botetourt, Augusta and Frederick to settle on the Holston River. They were mostly Presbyterians and were a remarkable race of people, known for their "intelligence, enterprise and happy adventure." Many of these Southwest Virginia sons served in the Colonial and Continental armies and were almost constantly in military service. They volunteered for the battle of 1776 on the Long Island Flats of the Holston, in which they were victorious over the Indians. Some were members of William Campbell's company and Colonel Christian's regiment in the expedition against the Cherokees. Later they served under Gen. William Campbell, the hero of King's Mountain.

These patriots, from Protestant families, formed the group of people known as the Dissenters. Concerning this body, Dr. David Mays has observed that the Dissenters were for the most part to be found among the settlers along the frontiers. He stated that they were among the unlettered people generally, and were the same people who formed the backbone of the radical element in political matters.[14] But an accurate gage of the quality of the men behind the Revolution, whether educated or not, can be determined by their manner of thinking on government and in their readiness to act in the defense of their rights. The people of the western counties were more determined in their fight for independence than were their eastern counterparts. The vote of the west decided the two great issues of the war: opposition to

---

[13] *The Confidential Letters of Thomas Jefferson to William Wirt,* p. 21.
[14] Mays, *Pendleton,* Vol. II, p. 133.

the Stamp Act and the scheme of embodying the militia. In answering Dr. Mays' statement as to those forming "the backbone of the radical element in political matters," it might be interesting to note the kind of men behind the disturbance outside the coffee shop in Williamsburg the day after Patrick Henry's Stamp Act Resolutions when the crowd turned on Colonel Mercer, the Stamp Officer. Referring to this group, Governor Fauquier wrote that he would call them a mob, did he not know that it was chiefly if not altogether composed of Gentlemen . . . whether English, Scots, or Virginians.[15] Among these patriots described by Fauquier could doubtless be found such men as Adam Stephens, John Talbot, Robert Rutherford, Thomas Johnson, Thomas Walker, Robert Munford, John and William Fleming, Paul Carrington, William Christian and Samuel McDowell. Also in this group were Thomas Lewis and some of his brothers, who were four in number, from Augusta, who fought the battles of the Revolution, and the Bowyers of Fincastle, later from Botetourt and Rockbridge, prominent pioneer families during the Revolution. They were all excellent men, possessing the spirit of Patrick Henry, longing for freedom of thought and the right to mold their own lives. It is interesting to note that four of Mr. Henry's sisters chose husbands from among these Southwest Virginia pioneers.[16] His relatives formed a long line in the colony's defenses. Besides his brothers-in-law, his brother, William Henry, was major of militia; his daughter, Martha, married Col. John Fontaine. Another daughter, Elizabeth, was wed to Col. Philip Aylett, who was assistant commissary of Virginia.

The spirit of patriotism as seen in these Southwest Virginians is evinced by the daring of a soldier from Fincastle, Col. Henry Bowyer:

Later on in the Revolution being "present at 'Buford's De-

---

[15] Fauquier to the Lords of Trade. Mays, *Pendleton,* I, p. 165.

[16] Elizabeth Henry married Colonel William Campbell, later General Campbell, hero of Kings Mountain. He was from the Holston settlement in Fincastle County. Ann Henry married Colonel William Christian of Botetourt and Fincastle. Susanna Henry married Colonel Thomas Madison of Augusta. Jane Henry married Colonel Samuel Meredith of Hanover County. Lucy Henry married Colonel Valentine Wood of Goochland. Sarah Henry married Thomas Thomas of England. Mary Henry married Luke Bowyer of Augusta. Their relatives, the Flemings, were also from Botetourt. In Henry's second marriage to Dorothea Dandridge, daughter of Colonel Nathaniel West Dandridge, is seen a connection with General Washington. Her uncle, John Dandridge, was Washington's father-in-law.

feat' in South Carolina, when Tarleton refused quarter and butchered all the defeated patriot troopers his dragoons could overtake," Colonel Bowyer was sent into the enemy lines with a flag of truce, but Tarleton ordered his men to cut him down. The young colonel found himself surrounded by British horsemen. But Colonel Bowyer "defended himself by good sword play and horsemanship, until fire from his own men caused an opening in the circle of his opponents, through which he dashed, hotly pursued by antagonists, until he jumped his horse over a high fence they would not attempt to take and escaped." At another time, while stationed at Petersburg, it is reported that this same Col. Bowyer jumped his horse over a covered wagon, leaving hoof prints that were visible for years afterward.[17] This gallant horseman of the Revolution married Patrick Henry's niece, Agatha Madison.

The spirit of the pioneer women can also be seen in an article concerning the mother of Gen. William Campbell. His father, Charles Campbell, "had occasion to go to Orange Court House and while there was arrested for nonpayment of taxes, and kept in prison bounds until they were paid. He wrote to his wife and requested her to sell the Salt Lick tract and ransom him. She replied: 'Remain where you are and I will pay the taxes.' It was autumn and the flax was prepared for spinning, and she spun many hanks of beautiful, smooth thread, and, mounting her horse, took it to market and sold it for more than the amount of the taxes and brought her husband home."[18]

The frontiersmen, particularly, were skilled in the art of Indian warfare, in which they exhibited a spirit of daring and adventure. The strength of the colony, as William Bradford noted in a letter to James Madison, lay chiefly in the riflemen of the upland counties. Madison's biographer declared that, according to Richard Lee, six frontier counties could produce 6,000 men of amazing hardihood, whose skill with the rifle was so great that "not one of these men . . . wish a distance less than 200 yards

---

[17] Goodridge Wilson, *Botetourt Pioneers.* Roanoke *Times* March 25, 1956. In his article Mr. Wilson pointed out that Patrick Henry's sister, Mary Henry, married Luke Bowyer, and his other sister, Susannah Henry, married Thomas Madison. Their daughter, Agatha Madison, married Colonel Henry Bowyer. Agatha and Henry Bowyer's son, John, married Lucy Lewis, daughter of General Andrew Lewis: no issue. See Henry, *Henry*, II, p. 640.

[18] *Ibid.*, The Ancient Salt Works. The Roanoke *Times*, October 9, 1955. Mr. Wilson, op. cit., the great-grandson of Charles Campbell, Col. Thomas Lewis Preston.

or a larger object than an orange—every shot is fatal."[19] Brave men could be found scattered throughout the colony.

From Charlotte County—the county where Patrick Henry later made his residence—came the earliest published instructions for independence, which were given to the representatives, Paul Carrington and Thomas Read, Esq's., April 23, 1776.

Stating in the preamble their quarrel with the British Ministry, the people of Charlotte further pointed out the despotic plan to enslave America, . . . in which "our savage neighbors" and "more savage domestics" have been encouraged "to spill the blood of our wives and children . . . adding insult to their injustice by repeatedly pretending to hold out the olive branch of peace in such a way as teacheth us that they are determined to persist in their hellish designs, and that nothing is intended for us but the most abject slavery" . . . pointing to this proof in "a late letter from the Secretary of State to Governor Eden, and the late act of Parliament for seizing and confiscating all our ships and property that may fall into their hands.

"Therefore despairing of any redress of our grievances from King and Parliament of Great Britain, and all hope of a reconciliation between her and the United Colonies being now at an end . . . We are determined not to submit . . . we advise and instruct you cheerfully to concur and give your best assistance in our Convention, to push to the utmost a war offensive and defensive until you are certified that such proposals of peace are made to our General Congress as shall by them be judged just and friendly. And because the advantage of a trade will better enable us to pay the taxes, and procure the necessaries for carrying on a war, and in our present circumstances this cannot be had without a Declaration of Independence; therefore if no such proposals of peace shall be made, we judge it to be a dictate of the first law of nature, to continue to oppose every attempt on our lives and properties; and we give it you in charge to use your best endeavours that the Delegates which are sent to the General Congress be instructed immediately to cast off the British yoke, and to enter into a commercial alliance with any nation or nations friendly to our cause. And as King George the Third of Great Britain &c., has manifested deliberate enmity toward us, and under the character of a parent persists in behaving as a tyrant, that they, in our behalf, renounce allegiance to him forever; and that, taking the God of Heaven to be our King, and depending

[19] Brant, James Madison, *The Virginia Revolutionist*, p. 157.

upon his protection and assistance, they plan out that form of Government which may the more effectually secure to us the enjoyment of our civil and religious rights and privileges, to the latest posterity.

"In all other things, gentlemen that may come before you in Convention, we rely upon your known fidelity and zeal; resolving and giving you our faith, that we will at the risk of our lives and fortunes to the utmost of our abilities, support and defend you, our country and our sister Colonies, in the glorious cause in which we are now engaged."

XIV

HENRY'S INSTRUCTIONS—INDEPENDENCE

NEWS THAT Colonel Henry had left the army and was back in Hanover aroused in the freeholders, and in the Hanover Committee, the determination to return him as their delegate to the next convention.

Spring was in full bloom when in early May Patrick Henry and his half brother John Syme started out for Williamsburg.[1] This delegate, Syme, and Henry's older brother, William, were the men Jefferson later termed "cowards" to Mr. Wirt. But the people of Hanover County held no such views as those of the gentleman from Albemarle. In the hour of crisis, they had sent John Syme to the assembly as they had sent his father before him. William—later Col. William Henry—likewise was sent to represent the people from Fluvanna County. Three sons, then, of this Dissenter-mother had been made members of the Virginia legislature.

At the time of the convention, Mr. Henry was nearing his fortieth birthday. Mr. Syme was somewhat older, possibly by four or five years. On their way to the convention, John Syme must have noted that his brother's face seldom changed: his expression was that of the Stoic. Anyone passing the two brothers on the Williamsburg road that morning, and seeing Henry's serious, resolved face, would have thought him older. He rode his horse stooped forward, his clothes hanging loosely about him. On this important journey, Henry discussed with John the critical condition of affairs and the state of the nation; uppermost in his mind must have been the action of the King in January in declaring his determination "at every hazard and at the risk of every conse-

[1] Patrick Henry and his half brother, John Syme, were elected in April as delegates for the new Convention, set for the first Monday in May, 1776.

quence, to compel the colonies to absolute submission." Information told of his Majesty's measures to increase his naval powers and augment his land forces, and of his employment of foreign troops. In December Parliament had declared all trade with the colonies at an end; protection of the Crown removed, and orders were sent out to seize and confiscate American ships. Also in December, news had reached Congress of the critical condition of Arnold's and Montgomery's troops in Canada. It told of their "pitifully insufficient forces," their lack of provisions, and of their great sufferings from cold—"some of them being half naked." Then, January 17, came the shocking word of General Montgomery's death on December 13 in his attempt to storm Quebec. Besides, Colonel Arnold had been carried off the field wounded and their forces made to retreat.[2] It was a gloomy picture, and one that no doubt brought the question as to why the mission to Canada had not been handled more efficiently. In January it was reported further that a fleet with 5,000 men was heading toward the American coast. The same year, 1776, at this critical beginning of the Revolution, British forces in New York alone numbered 32,000 soldiers, 10,000 sailors, 10 line-of-battle ships and 20 frigates. And even after the evacuation of Howe's army in March, a portion of the British fleet consisting of five vessels, with seven transports of Highlanders, lingered in Boston harbor until the middle of June.[3] But what Henry probably feared more than fleets and armies was all the talk about commissioners. Since February, Congress had been looking for these agents—twenty in all—to "treat for peace," if not directly with Congress, to treat separately with the colonies. Weeks and months had passed and still no commissioners. Men were asking in Congress, "If they are

[2] Burnett, *The Continental Congress,* p. 112.

[3] The Boston Public Library noted: that after the evacuation of Boston by Gen. Howe on March 17, 1776 that "a portion of the British fleet consisting of five vessels, still lingered in the harbor, and was subsequently joined by seven transports filled with Highlanders. . . . The British finally left Boston harbor during the middle of June, leaving Boston and vicinity entirely free from an enemy, except in the few dissimulating Tories who lurked in secret places." Frothingham's *History of the Siege of Boston,* p. 312, lists the fleet as follows, "a fifty gun ship, Commodore Banks, the Milford, the Yankee Hero (captured by the Milford), an armed brig, and two schooners." *The Narrative and Critical History of America* by Justin Winsor, Boston, Houghton, Mifflin, 1889, vol. 8, note on p. 502, lists 31,626 British troops (including Hessians) as being in New York in 1776. Francis V. Greene in his work, *Revolutionary War,* New York, Scribners, 1911, p. 33, states that the British and Hessians in New York in 1776 numbered 32,000 soldiers, 10,000 sailors, 10 line-of-battle ships and 20 frigates.

to come, what is it that detains them?"[4] General Washington was concerned over the matter and had written Congress on March 24, 1776, to find out what course he should take in case the commissioners landed in Boston. He had been told in effect, that the colonies would cross that bridge when they came to it.[5] Politics ran high in Congress, as Adams noted. Some of the delegates, Henry knew, were advancing their own prejudices, which were in many instances contrary to the expressed will of the electorate. Those of the middle colonies—five in number—were in the main still holding out for "connexion" with Great Britain. New Jersey and New York were known to be Tory-ridden. Many delegates, especially those of the proprietary colonies, would have to be replaced by other representatives, Patrick Henry knew, before they could go forward towards independence. Fearful of every design of King George, Patrick Henry must have scorned any mention of the word "commissioners" as he rode along with his brother to the convention, seeing in the artful offer of conciliation a device to divide the colonies.[6] In February, Wythe of Virginia and John Penn had suggested forming an alliance, but were criticized for aiming at independence. No change in policy had taken place. After three months of discussion, however, it was finally decided on April 6 to open American ports to all countries except Great Britain.

Another bit of encouragement, certainly to Patrick Henry, was Thomas Paine's pamphlet, "Common Sense," published January 8, 1776. Men in public as well as in all walks of life were reading and writing about it. Proof of its popularity was in the 120,000 copies sold, and in the call for reprints within three months after its first publication. Thomas Paine declared: "The so much boasted Constitution of England . . . was noble for the dark and slavish times in which it was erected. . . . But that it is imperfect, subject to convulsions, and incapable of producing what it seems to promise, is easily demonstrated."[7]

Without doubt Paine's appeal went far in steering the colonies in the direction of independence, and there were many converts. On January 24 Gen. Charles Lee was already writing General Washington of its "masterly, irresistible performance."

---

[4] Burnett, *The Continental Congress,* p. 149.

[5] *Ibid.*, p. 149.

[6] Gov. Henry to Lee June 18, 1788 upon the arrival of the commissioners; Lee. *Life of Richard Henry Lee,* I, pp. 195–196.

[7] Burnett, *The Continental Congress,* p. 134.

And Washington on January 31 wrote Joseph Reed of "the sound doctrine and unanswerable reasoning" in Paine's words.[8]

Certainly it was convincing enough; yet, in this early May, as Henry and his half-brother rode down to the convention at Williamsburg, there still remained some among the old members who were holding out for reconciliation and had not been converted to Paine's sense. "All his (Henry's) contemporaries without exception not only did not desire independence but eagerly sought an honorable reconciliation with the mother country."

Jefferson, himself, on August 25, 1775, wrote his kinsman, Tory John Randolph, who then had been banished to England, that, "Looking with fondness toward a reconciliation with Great Britain, I cannot help hoping you may be able to contribute towards expediting this good work." In the same letter Thomas Jefferson declared that he was "sincerely one of those . . . who still wish for reunion with the parent country and would rather be in dependence on Great Britain, properly limited, than on any nation upon earth, or than on no nation."[9]

From the beginning Patrick Henry desired independence, but he understood the importance of unity. Patience he had learned long before; however, by now, he had become weary of waiting. And although the patriots had been slow in their decision to strike the blow, the events of the past winter in the disastrous reverses at Quebec,[10] besides the intercepted letter of Germaine in which it was revealed the ministry was determined to make war on the colonies,[11] all had left the freeholders, or freemen, with only one choice: independence or subjugation. Patrick Henry no doubt pointed out to John Syme the further urgency at hand in the destruction of Norfolk, which, in the eyes of many, was "inexcusable." It showed the ineptitude of the Committee of Safety under Pendleton's direction. In the Virginia colony, Pendleton and his committee were the chief obstructionists. John Page wrote Thomas Jefferson at Congress, July 15, "I hope every one here especially of our late Committee will remember how often I insisted on erecting Batters, and attacking this Fleet." (Dunmore's) "If I could have been listened to, I would have agreed to be hanged if I would not have saved Norfolk and destroyed the

---

[8] *Ibid.*, p. 132. Grigsby, *The Virginia Convention of 1776*, p. 148. Burnett, *The Continental Congress*, p. 151.

[9] Boyd, *The Papers of Thomas Jefferson*, I, pp. 241–242–243 n.

[10] Henry, *Henry*, I, p. 372.

[11] *Ibid.*, I, p. 371; Germaine to Governor Eden of Maryland. *Ibid.*, I, pp. 371–372.

Fleet before it—4—18's and as many 9 pounders would have done their Business." On July 20, Mr. Page again wrote Mr. Jefferson: "If half these Guns had been mounted in October as I advised, Norfolk would not have been burnt."[12] Col. Adam Stephen likewise wrote Jefferson on July 29, "Norfolk might have been easily saved. We feel the loss of it daily."[13] One of the members of the Committee of Safety was now writing: "God preserve the United States. We know the race is not to the swift nor the Battle to the Strong. Do you not think an Angel rides in the whirlwind and directs the Storm?"[14]

On May 6, 1776, the little capital at Williamsburg was in a stir over the arrival of the delegates who were to take their seats in the Assembly for the fifth and final Virginia Revolutionary Convention. In the confusion, people moved hurriedly down Duke of Gloucester street through its crowded east end to the convention hall. At the hitching posts outside the taverns, tired horses stamped the cobblestones, restlessly awaiting their turn at the watertroughs.

Of the 130[15] members listed in the records of the Convention, only 112 appear to have been present at this assembly.[16] Among these were representatives from the 35 counties on the Tidewater, known as "Old Field Nags,"[17] being mostly "King's people,"[18] members of the "so-called Conservative" faction. In this group were many wealthy planters dressed in ruffled shirts, waistcoats, knee breeches and long coats. Some of these gentry were accompanied by their wives and daughters, who alighted from handsome coaches, dressed in the finest fashions of the day.

But there were other scenes and other circumstances; other men, weatherbeaten, grave looking, pushing their way hurriedly, wearing homespun suits or hunting shirts and buckskin breeches.[19]

---

[12] Boyd, *The Papers of Thomas Jefferson*, I, pp. 462–469. John Page to Thomas Jefferson, July 20, 1776.

[13] *Ibid.*, I, p. 481. Colonel Adam Stephen to Thomas Jefferson.

[14] *Ibid.*, I, p. 470. John Page to Jefferson, July 20, 1776.

[15] J. N. Brenaman, *A History of Virginia Conventions*, May 6, 1776. Note list of delegates.

[16] Henry, *Henry*, I, p. 391.

[17] Morgan, *Henry*, p. 92.

[18] Grigsby, *The Virginia Convention of 1776*, p. 51. Grigsby stated that leading men in the Tidewater counties were in the counsels of the enemy; "As a matter of course, almost all persons who enjoyed office under the Crown became Tories, and these were a large number." J. Franklin Jameson, *The American Revolution as A Social Movement*, p. 13.

[19] Dodd, *Virginia Takes the Road to Revolution*, p. 112. *The Spirit of '76*, Becker, Clark, Dodd.

Comprising this group were members from the 21 upper counties, spoken of as "High blooded Colts."[20] They brought with them their long trusty rifles.

The session, which was to last for two months, was followed with keen interest. The people at large felt that something had to be done to restore law and order in the colony.

The anxiety of the patriot party had become so great as to cause them to single out delegates to the convention who would pledge themselves for independence.[21] In securing new representatives, their efforts were rewarded. Records show that 37 counties out of the 62 had made changes in their delegates since the previous (1775) convention, in which one, or both representatives, were replaced, and in some instances, a third was added.[22] Counties without representation at the previous convention now sent delegates. Before the election it was noted that "the freeholders were all mad and determined to have a new house altogether."[23] Landon Carter, later fuming because his son was not returned to the Assembly, wrote in his diary, "The old delegates were left out . . . and these new ones chosen for this very purpose of an independency in which no gentleman should have the least share. . . ."[24]

In Edmund Pendleton's County of Caroline, it was even doubted that he would be re-elected,[25] but assured of his seat by his "uneasy conservatives," he went in. Carter Braxton, who had taken as his second wife the daughter of Richard Corbin, the King's Receiver General, was suspected of Toryism and lost out in his county of King William for a seat in the convention by a two-to-one landslide.[26] The Corbins were known to be loyal to the King, and Braxton's first marriage into the powerful Robinson family had not helped his reputation, as he was known to have solicited in behalf of the Crown. Nor did his loyalty seem to wane when he became the son-in-law of the receiver general. Braxton, who had a fortune in ships, had lost out in April in his own county for a seat in the Assembly, but he was later sent to Con-

---

[20] Morgan, *Henry*, p. 92.

[21] *Ibid.*, I, p. 373.

[22] Checked from a list of the delegates to the Convention of Dec. 1, 1775, and of May 6, 1776. J. N. Brenaman, *A History of Virginia Conventions.*

[23] Josiah Parker to Landon Carter, April 14, 1776, Landon Carter Papers, University of Virginia.

[24] Brant, *Madison, The Virginia Revolutionist,* op. cit., p. 197. "Diary of Landon Carter," William and Mary Quarterly, XVII, pp. 10–11.

[25] Josiah Parker to Landon Carter, Landon Carter Papers, University of Virginia.

[26] Brant, *Madison, The Virginia Revolutionist,* p. 197.

gress in February to replace Peyton Randolph, having been appointed in the House in December by the "Conservative" faction, while Henry was away in the army, for the express purpose, it was stated, of delaying the independence movement at the same time his fellow Virginians in Congress were turning from reconciliation toward independence.[27]

Elected December 15, Braxton never arrived at Congress until February 23. As late as April 14, Braxton wrote Landon Carter, "Independence and total separation from Great Britain are the interesting Subjects of all ranks of men and often agitate our Body. It is in truth a delusive Bait which men inconsiderately catch at, without knowing the hook to which it is affixed."[28] Braxton was one of those who felt that Congress should await the terms offered by the commissioners.

Pendleton's diplomacy regarding the outcome allowed little consideration for the wishes of the electorate. When Braxton and Harrison were later defeated for re-election to Congress, Pendleton wrote Jefferson: "These things . . . may perhaps have their use, as we shall have those Gentlemen here (in the Assembly) to assist in watching and breaking the Spirit of Party . . ."[29] Patrick Henry was alarmed at such actions. He feared "too great a bias to aristocracy prevailed among the opulent."[30]

But before the Convention opened its meeting, an officer was seen walking through the hall of the House, looking for someone. Gen. Charles Lee was searching out the man who could do him the most good. It was Patrick Henry, of course—former colonel and now a returned delegate "rated in advance as the central figure of the Convention."

Once face-to-face, the British-born Lee and Mr. Henry talked together at length on matters that engaged their deep concern and earnest conviction. General Lee was to leave shortly for the Southern Department of the Army, and his chief worry was the lack of arms, munitions, and the means with which to

---

[27] Burnett, *The Continental Congress*, p. 151; Note also the previous chapter in this book; Braxton's speech on government while in Congress made him no friends and he was not returned at the next session. Note William Fleming to Jefferson, Boyd, *The Papers of Thomas Jefferson*, I, p. 475.

[28] Ibid., p. 151. The proprietary interest in Congress: Pennsylvania, Maryland and Delaware remained so until the Revolution.

[29] Boyd, *The Papers of Thomas Jefferson*, I, Pendleton to Jefferson, July 22, 1776; p. 472. p. 475, William Fleming wrote Jefferson: "Mr. Braxton's address on government made him no friends in Convention, ..."

[30] Henry, *Henry*, I, p. 143; Patrick Henry to John Adams, May 20, 1776.

carry on successful warfare. It was generally known before the meeting that the one powder mill erected at the public expense had made only about 700 lbs. of powder.[31] The general was worried about struggling through a campaign without supplies, fearing defeat and disgrace. Both men recognized the grave danger facing the colony from these shortages. As one military man to another, their conversation must have naturally turned to the ones responsible for the shortages: the Committee of Safety. Doubtless General Lee was made familiar with the difficulties Colonel Henry had had in dealing with the head of the Committee of Safety. As Colonel of the first Virginia Regiment, Henry's experiences in obtaining supplies were the same as General Lee's, and while the two men were talking that May 6, all such necessaries of warfare allocated by Congress, as "cannon, muskets, powder, clothing, etc.," were to be found only on paper.[32]

As the two men parted company, the delegate from Hanover crossed the court green and entered the hall of the House, taking his usual seat on the oval bench. Patrick Henry noted that some of the members from the mountains and back country sections had not arrived, due to the "badness of roads."[33] The men from the western counties, especially Augusta, had had to travel through mountainous country and impassable roads, besides having to cross several rivers and creeks. The North Fork, the South Fork, and the South Branch of the Potomac often were swollen from spring rains and had to be forded.

After most of the delegates present had been seated, the House bell rang. The clerk took the gavel and proceeded with the general routine of calling the roll and electing the President. Edmund Pendleton had presided at the December convention in place of Peyton Randolph, who had died in September.

Immediately one of the old members, Richard Bland, a Conservative, arose and renominated his friend Edmund Pendleton for President. Archibald Cary, another Conservative, seconded Bland's motion.[34] The delegate from Louisa, Thomas Johnson, a

---

[31] Boyd, *The Papers of Thomas Jefferson*, I, p. 288. John Page, Williamsburg, April 26, 1776 had written Jefferson ten days before the meeting.

[32] *Ibid.*

[33] Burnett, *The Continental Congress*, p. 162. A full house was not reported until May 15th. On this date, one hundred and twelve delegates were present. Henry, *Henry*, I, p. 301. George Mason did not take his seat until the 18th of May.

[34] Meade, *Henry*, op. cit., I, p. 272; Pendleton placed his Conservative members in key positions on the committee.

friend of Patrick Henry, who objected to the way things were being run by the head of the Committee of Safety, rose to his feet and nominated Thomas Ludwell Lee, brother of Richard H. Lee, "as a proper person to fill that office." Bartholomew Dandridge, Washington's brother-in-law, who was a successful lawyer and later justice, seconded Johnson's motion, "and on the question being put by the clerk," (according to the Journal), Edmund Pendleton was elected President.

In opening the convention, Pendleton "displayed his usual skill as a politician." He thanked the members for the honor done him in electing him to the high post. He assured them of his unremitting attention to duties which he said he would endeavour to execute with "the utmost impartiality," relying with confidence on their candor to make the "most favorable interpretation" of all his actions.

Pendleton acknowledged the "time truly critical, when subjects of the most important and interesting nature require our serious attention." However, in discussing several resolutions of Congress and several petitions which were not in the power of Congress to determine, Pendleton recommended "calmness, unanimity, and diligence" as the most likely means of bringing them to a happy and prosperous issue. To make sure there would be no agitation, he selected his same old-guard conservatives to strengthen his position. Dudley Digges he appointed chairman of the Committee of Privileges and Elections, to which 30 names were added. Two days later he appointed Robert Carter Nicholas to head the Committee on Propositions and Grievances, although Nicholas was known to oppose independence.[35] He would give the Patriot party a showing on the committees, but he would always have the strong arm of his own party to hold the line. George Mason, writing from Williamsburg May 18, 1776, to Richard Lee in Congress, noted that the committee was "according to custom, overcharged with useless members. You know our Convention," he wrote, "I need not say that it is not mended by the late elections. We shall, in all probability, have a thousand ridiculous and impracticable proposals, and of course a plan formed of heterogeneous, jarring, and unintelligible ingredients." But, Mason noted, "This can be prevented only by a few men of

---

[35] John Page to R. H. Lee, April 12, 1776, "I think almost every man except the Treasurer, (Nicholas) is willing to declare for Independence." Southern Literary Messenger, XXVII, p. 255; Nicholas had been instructed by a majority of his constituents to vote for independence. *American Archives* (4th Series), V., 1046.

integrity and abilities, whose country's interest lies next to their hearts, undertaking this business and defending it ably through every stage of opposition."[36] George Mason knew the man. He knew the "principal member who conducted and prepared whatever resolves and measures" were intended for the preservation of their rights and liberties. In his letter to Martin Cockburn, he had already called Patrick Henry "the first man upon this continent."[37]

Patrick Henry had his stratagem, too. It fell to him to strike the final blow for American independence. Henry's pre-eminence demanded an important place on the committees, and this Pendleton could not ignore. He became a member of the powerful Committees of Privileges and Elections, and of Propositions and Grievances. Although his name appeared next to the chairman of the latter committee, his duties were such in making the numerous reports, etc., as would seem to make him the active chairman.[38] On another committee, he helped prepare an ordinance to encourage the production of the much-needed commodities, salt, saltpetre and gunpowder; during the May sitting alone, Mr. Henry was placed upon six committees. In this, his abilities were clearly indicated, as it was unusual for a member to serve on more than two of the standing committees.[39] In general, his duties were tedious, requiring frequent reports to the floor, and in most instances, several detailed accounts were required on each topic. His influence, "as has been too generally believed," was not confined to public debate.

"At no period of his life did Mr. Henry display his consummate powers as a leader to more advantage than now. He thoroughly informed himself of the temper of the people as displayed in their delegates, and set himself at work to harmonize the various interests in the body, so as to attain, as far as possible, unanimity in their action on the overshadowing question of independence."[40]

And even though President Pendleton at the outset used the most scrupulous care to keep out of sight the subject of independence, which he well knew the party of Henry intended to bring forward[41] by the 14th, Henry had drawn up his resolutions.

---

[36] *Life and Correspondence of George Mason*, p. 226. Virginia Historical Society.
[37] Henry, *Henry*, I, p. 183.
[38] *Ibid.*, I, p. 389.
[39] Mays, *Edmund Pendleton*, I, p. 64.
[40] Henry, *Henry*, I, pp. 389–390.
[41] Grigsby, *The Virginia Convention of 1776*, p. 15.

This resolve, known as Number 1, was proposed by Mr. Henry on the first day. The three were endorsed by the clerk, "Rough Resolutions. Independence."

No. 1. (In handwriting of Patrick Henry):

> As the humble petitions of the Continental Congress have been rejected and treated with contempt; as the parliament of G. B. so far from showing any disposition to redress our grievances, have lately passed an act approving of the ravages that have been committed upon our coasts, and obliging the unhappy men who shall be made captives to bear arms against their families, kindred, friends, and country; and after being plundered themselves, to become accomplices in plundering their brethren, a compulsion not practiced among prisoners of war except among pirates, the outlaws and enemies of human society. As they are not only making every preparation to crush us, which the internal strength of the nation and its alliances with foreign powers afford them, but are using every art to draw the savage Indians upon our frontiers, and are even encouraging insurrection among our slaves, many of whom are now actually in arms against us. And as the King of G. B. by a long series of oppressive acts has proved himself the tyrant instead of the protector of his people. We, the representatives of the Colony of Virginia do declare, that we hold ourselves absolved of our allegiance to the Crown of G.B. and obliged by the eternal laws of self-preservation to pursue such measures as may conduce to the good and happiness of the united colonies; and as a full declaration of Independency appears to us to be the only honourable means under Heaven of obtaining that happiness, and of restoring us again to a tranquil and prosperous situation;
>
> Resolved, That our delegates in Congress, be enjoined in the strongest and most positive manner to exert their ability in procuring an immediate, clear and full Declaration of Independency.[42]

No. 2. (In the handwriting of Meriwether Smith):

> Whereas Lord Dunmore hath assumed a power of suspending by proclamation the laws of this colony, which is supported by a late act of the British Parliament, declaring the colonies in North America to be in actual rebellion and out of the King's protection, confiscating our property wherever found on the water, and legalizing every seizure, robbery and rapine, that their people have heretofore committed on us.

[42] Henry, *Henry,* I, pp. 394–395.

> Resolved, That the government of this Colony as hitherto exercised under the crown of Great Britain be dissolved, and that a Committee be appointed to prepare a Declaration of Rights, and such a Plan of Government, as shall be judged most proper to maintain Peace and Order in this Colony, and secure substantial and equal liberty to the people.[43]

No. 3. (Believed to be in the handwriting of Edmund Pendleton):

> Whereas the Parliament of Great Britain have usurped unlimited authority to bind the inhabitants of the American Colonies in all cases whatsoever, and the British Ministry have attempted to execute their many tyrannical acts in the most inhuman and cruel manner, and King George the third having withdrawn his protection from the said colonies, and jointly with the Ministry and Parliament, has begun and is now pursuing with the utmost violence a barbarous war against the said colonies, in violation of every civil and religious right of the said colonies.
>
> Resolved, That the union that has hitherto subsisted between Great Britain and the American Colonies is thereby totally dissolved, and that the inhabitants of this Colony are discharged from any allegiance to the Crown of Great Britain.[44]

The resolutions, numbered 1, 2, and 3, were among the Convention Papers in the State Library in the year 1890. However, Pendleton's biographer, Dr. David J. Mays, declared, "The only draft of this resolution (No. 3) now to be found in the Convention Papers at the Virginia State Library is not in Pendleton's handwriting, although at a casual glance it is somewhat like it."[45] Patrick Henry's grandson was dubious as to the handwriting and used the word "believed" rather than making a direct statement as he did in the case of the Henry and Smith resolutions. Certainly there was no question in his mind as to who wrote the other two. Pendleton's attitude on the subject of independence was shown in Gen. Charles Lee's letter to Richard Henry Lee in Congress on the day the convention opened. He wrote:

"Pendleton is certainly naturally a man of sense, but I can assure you that the other night, in a conversation I had with him on the subject of independence, he talked or rather stammered

---

[43] *Ibid.*, I, pp. 395–396.

[44] *Ibid.*, I, p. 396.

[45] Mays, *Pendleton,* II, p. 368 n. 12.

nonsense that would have disgraced the lips of an old midwife drunk from bohea tea and gin. . . ."[46]

That there were members among the delegates in the convention opposing independence is seen in George Mason's letter to Richard Henry Lee, May 18, 1776, in which he stated there was a considerable minority.[47] Yet, Pendleton's biographer has seized upon the opportunity to discredit the depth of Henry's convictions on the subject of independence. Mays infers that Henry had become lukewarm:

"But there was one member who was fearful of such an abrupt break with Britain unless all the other Colonies were in the same boat and had the assurances of foreign help besides. That was Patrick Henry. In Convention fourteen months before, when calling upon Virginia to arm, he had shown no such restraint; but now a soberer Henry wanted first to be sure of allies. He had been prompted or strengthened in that view by a letter of April 20th from Richard Henry Lee, written from Philadelphia, in which he argued for independence, but urged that foreign alliances be made at once to avoid a partition of America between Britain and some other power that would demand a slice of America as compensation for helping to conquer her."[48]

To rebut Dr. Mays, one may argue that it was one thing for Patrick Henry to arm Virginia so as to be prepared for any eventuality; but quite another to plunge America into war unless all the colonies were for independence and certain safeguards had been taken. Henry wanted assurances from the Secret Committee. Mays and some other biographers, dubious of Henry's purpose, point to Gen. Charles Lee's letter the day after they had

---

[46] Morgan, *Henry*, p. 252.

[47] Grigsby, *The Virginia Convention of 1776*, pp. 44 n–142 n. George Mason's letter to R. H. Lee, in Congress, May 18, 1776, declared there was a considerable minority, but the opponents being so few that they did not think fit to divide, or contradict the general voice; Brant,*The Virginia Revolutionist*, p. 214, pointed out that Jefferson reversed himself on the matter of independence. On May 16, he wrote Thomas Nelson that nine out of ten were for independence. But in his Notes on Virginia, he declared, Independence, and the establishment of a new form of government, were not even yet the objects of the people at large. Jefferson, who had been out of things for six weeks from illness, did not arrive at Congress until May 16. In 1781, he declared, the idea of independence had not been opened to the minds of the people. Boyd, *The Papers of Thomas Jefferson*, I, p. 292; *Jefferson's Writings*, III, p. 225; Thomas L. Lee to Richard Lee, *Southern Literary Messenger*, XXVII, p. 325.

[48] Mays, *Pendleton,* II, p. 107.

conferred in Williamsburg. General Lee wrote to Patrick Henry the day before he left for the Southern Department:

"The objection you made yesterday, if I understood you rightly, to an immediate declaration, was by many degrees, the most specious; indeed it is the only tolerable one that I have yet heard. You say, and with great justice, that we ought previously to have felt the pulse of France and Spain. I more than believe, I am almost confident, that it has been done; at least I can assert upon recollection, that some of the Committee of Secrecy have assured me that the sentiments of both these Courts, or their agents, had been sounded and were found to be as favorable as could be wished. But admitting that we are utter strangers to their sentiments on the subject, and that we run some risk of this Declaration being coldly received by these powers, such is our situation that the risk must be ventured."

After General Lee cited the advantages of a treaty with France, and the penalties of delay, he emphasized the importance of action: "In the meantime we are to struggle through a campaign, without arms, ammunitions, or any one necessary of war. Disgrace and defeat will infallibly ensue, the soldiers and officers will become so disappointed that they will abandon their colors, and probably never be persuaded to make another effort." The general ended his letter with these words: ". . . I most devoutly pray, that you may not merely recommend, but positively lay injunctions, on your servants in Congress to embrace a measure so necessary to our salvation."[49]

If there seems to have been some hesitancy on the part of Henry in talking with General Lee, Henry's concern may be explained in his letters to Richard Lee and to John Adams. He urged to the latter that confederation and foreign alliances must precede an "open"[50] declaration of independence. It is possible that Mr. Henry, in talking with General Lee, objected to an immediate "open" declaration and Lee misconstrued his meaning.

---

[49] Henry, *Henry,* op. cit., I, pp. 383–384–385; *Charles Lee Papers,* May 7, 1776, General Lee's needs were great: See *Charles Lee Papers,* II, p. 120.

[50] *Ibid.,* I, p. 412; Note also p. 382, and p. 415. Patrick Henry wrote Adams on May 20th that before this reaches you, the resolution for finally separating from Britain will be handed to Congress by Colonel Nelson. But he added: The Confederacy; that must precede an open declaration of independency and foreign alliances. But Adams answered on June 3rd, "I fear we cannot proceed systematically, and that we shall be obliged to declare ourselves independent States before we confederate, and indeed before all the colonies have established their governments."

It is also probable that Mr. Henry did not wish to commit himself fully to the general. Subsequent events showed Lee's double-dealings with General Washington and his treachery in his schemes to aid General Howe.[51] Whether Henry accepted Lee's statements regarding the Secret Committee is not known. The intelligence in the *Gazette* (Purdie's) of June 7, that France would come to the aid of the colonies, may have allayed his fears temporarily when he drew up his resolution.

But between the time he had written his resolution—the 14th—and his letters of May 20, information had reached him of the quibbling in Congress and the ascendancy of Tory elements. Henry was alarmed over the danger of disunion.

Senator Richard Henry Lee had written a letter to Patrick Henry April 20, before Henry left Scotchtown for the convention, pointing to the "indispensable necessity of taking up government immediately," saying, "I leave it with you to judge, whether, whilst we are hesitating about forming alliance, Great Britain may not, and probably will not, seal our ruin by signing a treaty of partition with two or three ambitious powers that may aid in conquering us—upon principles of interest and revenge they surely will. . . . All this danger however may be prevented by a timely alliance with proper and willing powers in Europe. . . . But no State in Europe will either Treat or Trade with us, so long as we consider ourselves subjects of G. B. Honor, dignity and the customs of states forbid them until we take rank as an independent people. . . ."[52]

In his letter, Lee had enclosed a pamphlet on government, written by John Adams, and asked Henry fully to exert his powers in securing the peace and happiness of the country by adopting a wise and free government. He also asked Mr. Henry to inform him of his thoughts on these great subjects as early as possible, as he was impatient to know.[53] Patrick Henry answered him on May 20:

"Your sentiments as to the necessary progress of this great affair correspond with mine. For may not France, ignorant of the great advantages to her commerce we intend to offer, and of the permanency of that separation which is to take place, be allured by the partition you mention? To anticipate therefore the efforts of the enemy by sending instantly American Ambassadors to

---

[51] Morgan, *Henry*, pp. 289–290.

[52] Henry, *Henry*, I, p. 380.

[53] Ballagh, *Lee*, I, p. 180.

France, seems to me absolutely necessary. Delay may bring on us total ruin. But is not a confederacy of our states previously necessary?"[54]

Henry's concern is also expressed in his letter to John Adams of May 20, in which he pointed to what he considered of immense importance: ". . . 'tis to anticipate the enemy at the French Court. The half of our Continent offered to France, may induce her to aid our destruction, which she certainly has the power to accomplish. But pressed, allured, as she will be—but, above all, ignorant of the great things we mean to offer, may we not lose her? The consequence is dreadful," he declared. "The confederacy; that must precede an open declaration of independency and foreign alliances."[55]

Henry's emphasis on the importance of confederation first is seen in the actions of Congress. Jefferson wrote Richard Lee: "The plan of ——— is yet untouched. After being read it was privately printed for the consideration of the members and will come on when we shall have got through the Confederation."[56]

Patrick Henry prudently stressed the importance of an early foreign alliance. From the start, "It had been a race between the British conciliation acts and the French treaty, which should capture the eye and ear of Congress first; and the French treaty had won the race. If the peace commissioners had arrived a few weeks earlier than they did, there is little doubt that the subsequent story of the American Revolution would have been very different from what it became."[57]

In his concern over the perplexing policies in Congress, Patrick Henry was instructing Adams, May 20, a week before the resolutions for independence reached Philadelphia, as to the best course:

"Would it not be sufficient to confine it, for the present, to the objects of offensive and defensive nature, and a guarantee of the respective colonial rights," saying, "If minute arrangements of things is attempted, such as equal representation, etc., you may split and divide . . . and delay French alliance, which with me is everything."[58] Jefferson must have paid strict attention to

[54] Henry, *Henry,* I, p. 410. Patrick Henry to Richard Henry Lee.

[55] *Ibid.*, I, p. 412. Patrick Henry to John Adams.

[56] Boyd, *Jefferson,* I, p. 477. Jefferson to Richard Lee, July 29, 1776.

[57] Ballagh, *Letters of Richard Henry Lee,* I, p. 193; British troops were expected to land on May 21, according to Richard H. Lee.

[58] A secret Committee to probe the minds of the French Ministry had sent its agent April 3.

Henry's suggestions. He wrote Lee: "The minutiae of the Confederation have hitherto engaged us: the great points of representation, boundaries, taxation &c. being left open."[59]

On the same date, May 20, Patrick Henry wrote Richard Henry Lee in Congress, in these words: "I wish to divide you, and have you here, to animate . . . the sometimes drooping spirits of our country, and in Congress . . . to be the vigilant determined foe of tyranny. To give you colleagues of kindred sentiments is my wish. I doubt you have them not at present. . . . Moderation, falsely so called, hath nearly brought on us final ruin. And to see those who have so fatally advised us, still guiding, or at least sharing our public councils alarms me."[60]

When the resolution reached Congress on May 27, six colonies were still holding out for connection.[61] The debate for independence was therefore held up until July 1.

One critic has stated that Henry's resolves for "an immediate, clear, and full declaration of independence" by the Continental Congress "was hardly to be a secret one."[62]

But this writer contends that Henry's resolution *was* intended to be conducted in secret, and not openly. Henry knew the wrangling going on in Congress; that the old delegates had not been instructed to declare independence, and if the new ones had not arrived, the declaration should be effected quietly to prevent a deadlock. He, therefore, had instructed them to "exert their ability in procuring" independence, which could have been conducted in secret, as were most matters in Congress, and apparently this was exactly what was done.[63] Congress would know

---

[59] Boyd, *Jefferson,* I, p. 477. Jefferson to Lee, July 29, 1776.

[60] Henry, *Henry,* I, pp. 410–411.

[61] Burnett, *The Continental Congress,* p. 167; Henry, *Henry,* I, p. 402. These Colonies were: New York, New Jersey, Pennsylvania, Delaware, Maryland and South Carolina. It was not until August that Maryland "excluded from their new Convention all those that have been famous for moderation as it is strangely called . . ." and sent new Delegates to Congress, Alexander and Rogers, Lee wrote Patrick Henry at Scotchtown on August 20, 1776. Ballagh, *Letters of Richard Henry Lee,* I, p. 214. It was not until June 21, that Livingston and the New Jersey delegates were replaced. Brant, *The Virginia Revolutionist,* pp. 217–228. The lack of alertness in Congress was noted in Lee's letter to Henry, April 20, if not sooner. Pennsylvania held out until July.

[62] Brant, *Madison, The Virginia Revolutionist,* p. 222.

[63] Henry, *Henry,* I, pp. 403–404; Note also pp. 400–401. Jefferson held up debate until July 2. After the delegates had arrived with instructions from the new Conventions, and Congress was finally united on independence, they, acting as a body of confederates, cast their votes for independence, except New York,

the time when conditions were right. Yet, because of Henry's prudence in the matter of confederation and alliances, Dr. Mays declared:

"When the Convention met, sentiment for independence was widespread. But Henry was not so sure."[64]

Was this sentiment actually "widespread" among the members of Congress where unanimity was so important? We think not, seeing the delay caused in that body. The final resolution on independence was not cast until July 2, when new members with fresh instructions arrived.[65]

Certainly, Patrick Henry wanted independence. It was his ultimate goal. But he wanted no half-hearted declaration, with some of the members in Congress holding out for commissioners and connection. Mr. Henry's prescience is seen in the fact that France did come to the aid of the colonies. "The morning dawned with the arrival of those aids from France, which Mr. Henry had so long ago predicted; and the sun of American independence arose to set no more."

But before closing the subject regarding the Lee and Adams letters, of which much criticism has been made, one question remains that historians have never asked. Why were the leading men in Congress, and General Lee, writing to Patrick Henry in the first place? Why were they not writing to some of the other so-called "epochal revolutionists" in the convention, if there were such men? Why were they writing to Patrick Henry at all? Apparently, there was no one else who could put independence across to the people, or who, in the face of Dunmore's move nearer inland, had the courage to take over the reins of government.

The answer as to why these men were writing to Patrick Henry is revealed in a statement by Edmund Randolph; it preceded the statement cited by Mays, but was omitted by him.[66] Randolph declared:

---

which did not approve the measure until July 9. Grigsby noted, "The Congress itself was far from being prepared to 'suppress the royal authority' as early as the 10th of May. The debate on the resolution of independence shows that there was much reluctance among the members to declare for independence." Grigsby, *The Virginia Convention of 1776*, p. 144 n.

[64] Mays, *Pendleton*, II, p. 107.

[65] Henry, *Henry*, I, p. 400; Grigsby, *The Virginia Convention of 1776*, p. 144 n.

[66] Mays, *Pendleton*, II, p. 108; Randolph's *Manuscript History*, II, p. 62; Henry, *Henry*, I, pp. 392–393–394; The full text of Randolph.

> It was expected that a declaration of independence would certainly be passed, and for obvious reasons Mr. Henry seemed allotted to crown his political conduct with this supreme stroke.[67]

John Adams also gave the reason why Patrick Henry was so much in demand:

> I know of none so competent to the task as the author of the first Virginia resolutions against the stamp act, who will have the glory with posterity, of beginning and concluding this great revolution. Happy Virginia, whose Constitution is to be framed by so masterly a builder.[68]

Returning to the Virginia Convention and the debates; on May 14, the question of independence was discussed in Committee of the Whole. Archibald Cary was appointed to preside. Patrick Henry selected Thomas Nelson to move independence. Nelson introduced the resolution marked No. 1, which was in the handwriting of Patrick Henry. "The three papers differ not only in the grounds assigned for the step about to be taken, but also in the manner of proceeding. All three declare the union between Virginia and Great Britain dissolved, but Mr. Henry's paper alone, proposed that Congress be asked to make for all the Colonies a "clear and full declaration of independency."[69]

In the debate that followed, the delegate from Hanover found himself in the usual position, faced by the arbitrary rulings of Pendleton's partisans. Robert Carter Nicholas, the Treasurer, arose now to speak. As usual, Henry and Nicholas tangled, this time over the issue of independence. Carter Nicholas spent two days arguing against independence and "demonstrated his title to popularity by despising it. . . ." He doubted "the competency of America in so arduous a contest."[70] Here we see Nicholas opposing the resolutions, even when he had been instructed by a majority of his constituents to vote for independence.[71]

Edmund Randolph, the son of Tory John, who remained behind to look after his father's interest when he was banished from the colony, gave this insight into Henry's argument:

> And yet for a considerable time he talked of the subject, as being critical, but without committing himself by a pointed

[67] Henry, *Henry*, I, p. 393.

[68] *Ibid.*, I, p. 414; John Adams to Patrick Henry, Philadelphia, June 3, 1776.

[69] *Ibid.*, I, p. 397.

[70] Edmund Randolph's *Manuscript History of Virginia*, II, p. 62.

[71] *American Archives*, (4th Series), V., 1046.

> avowal in its favor, or a pointed repudiation of it. He thought that a cause, which put at stake the lives and fortunes of the people, should appear to be their own act, and, that he ought not to place upon the responsibility of his eloquence, a revolution, of which the people might be wearied after the present stimulus should cease to operate.[72]

As the leader, Henry's argument seems sensible in view of conditions. However, Pendleton's biographer offers the opinion that "Henry was in danger of being left out of any part of leadership in the independence movement." But even Edmund Randolph did not withhold his admiration of Henry:

> But after sometime he appeared in an element for which he was born. To cut the knot which calm prudence was puzzled to untie was worthy of the magnificence of his genius. He entered into no subtlety of reasoning, but was aroused by the now apparent spirit of the people. As a pillar of fire, which notwithstanding the darkness of the prospect would conduct to the promised land, he inflamed, and was followed by the convention. His eloquence unlocked the secret springs of the human heart, robbed danger of all its terror, and broke the keystone in the arch of royal power.[73]

Randolph concluded:

> For grand impressions in the defense of liberty, the western world has not yet been able to exhibit a rival.[74]

Let us, therefore, reinstate Patrick Henry at the helm of the independence movement, without which Dr. Mays would not have been able to write revolutionary history at all.

At the close of his speech, even the least perspicacious, the half-hearted, and semi-tories—those who had opposed Patrick Henry from time to time—must have considered his speech the climax to the drama, and the event an historic occasion. Henry had long waited for the hour at hand.

After the committee compared numbers 1, 2 and 3 the best points were taken from the whole. The final draft was made by the President, Edmund Pendleton: "Resolutions of the Virginia Convention Calling for Independence in Convention May the 15th 1776. Present one hundred and twelve members.[75]

---

[72] Randolph's *Manuscript History of Virginia,* II, p. 62.

[73] *Ibid.*

[74] Henry, *Henry,* I, p. 212.

[75] Boyd, *The Papers of Thomas Jefferson,* p. 290; Henry, *Henry,* I, p. 391–392.

Omitting the long preamble in which are found some of Henry's complaints against the British ministry at the first Congress, as well as those in his own preamble (No. 1) written on the first day, the following was preferred:

> Resolved, unanimously, That the delegates appointed to represent this colony in General Congress, be instructed to propose to that respectable body to declare the United Colonies free and independent states, absolved from all allegiance to, or dependence upon, the Crown, or parliament of Great Britain; and that they give the assent of this colony to such declaration, and to whatever measures may be thought proper and necessary by the Congress for forming foreign alliances, and a confederation of the Colonies, at such time, and in the manner, as to them shall seem best: Provided, that the power of forming government for, and the regulations of, the internal concerns of each colony, be left to the respective colonial legislatures. (This added provision took care of Henry's worries over disunion.)
>
> Resolved unanimously, That a Committee be appointed to prepare a Declaration of Rights, and such a plan of government as will be most likely to maintain peace and order in this colony, and secure substantial and equal liberty to the people.[76]

The final resolves were not worded altogether according to Patrick Henry's wishes: "I put up with it in the present form for the sake of unanimity. 'Tis not quite so pointed as I could wish," he wrote John Adams.[77] There were others among the delegates who felt the same as Patrick Henry. George Mason wrote Richard H. Lee, May 18, 1776: "The preamble is tedious, rather timid, and in many instances exceptionable, but I hope it may answer the purpose."[78] Thomas L. Lee wrote his brother Richard Henry Lee: "The preamble is not to be admired in point of composition, nor has the resolve of Independency that pre-emptory, decided air which I could wish."[79] John Augustine Washington wrote: "It is not so full as some would have wished it."[80]

In speaking of Pendleton's preamble, Mays stated: "He took so little pride in the matter of authorship that some, if not most, of the members of the Convention did not know who wrote the

---

[76] Henry, *Henry*, I, p. 392.

[77] *Ibid.*, I, p. 412. Patrick Henry to John Adams, May 20, 1776.

[78] *Life and Correspondence of George Mason*, p. 226, The Virginia Historical Society.

[79] Henry, *Henry*, I, pp. 397–398.

[80] Rowland's, *Mason*, I, p. 225.

final draft, and among the ignorant was no less a person than James Madison."[81]

As President, it was incumbent upon him to write the final resolution decided upon, but the result was not of his own making. His biographer quoted an observer as saying that "while Pendleton went along with the mass of people in separation from Britain, he was on the alert to prevent revolutionary changes within the Colony." The same writer concludes, "Although Pendleton effected the revolution in government, he was strongly opposed, and to his efforts Virginia is strongly indebted, for the prevention of much revolution in Society."[82]

Richard H. Lee had written Patrick Henry on April 20, 1776: "The act of Parliament has . . . dissolved our government, uncommissioned every magistrate, and placed us in the high road to Anarchy. In Virginia we have certainly no Magistrate lawfully qualified to hang a murderer, or any other villain offending ever so atrociously against the state. We cannot be Rebels excluded from the King's protection and Magistrates acting under his authority at the same time. This proves the indispensable necessity of our taking up government immediately, for the preservation of Society. . . ."[83]

Lee, knowing Henry's primacy, was collaborating with him to *preserve society*, perhaps of little consequence to Pendleton, although he had had every opportunity to save it as the head of the Committee of Safety, and as the President of the Conventions. In the latter, he made the committee appointments, controlled the channeling of bills to committees and directed the work of the conventions; yet, many delicate measures for the good of society he had held back, preventing them from reaching the floor. When he saw the "Party of Henry" gathering sufficient strength to put over an energetic measure for the good of the people, Pendleton resorted to his legislative stratagems.

Pendleton wanted no change in government and stated, "I prefer the true English Constitution. . . ."[84] That his heart was not in the cause of independence is shown in Grigsby's statement, that after the convention was over and the motion was carried to

---

[81] Mays, *Pendleton,* op. cit., II, p. 111; Rives' *Madison,* I, p. 128.

[82] Mays, *Pendleton,* II, p. 132.

[83] Henry, *Henry,* I, p. 379.

[84] Mays, *Pendleton,* I, p. 357; II, p. 131. Pendleton declared in his Autobiography, that "when the disputes with Britain began, a redress of grievances, and not a revolution of Government was my wish."

adjourn, Pendleton arose to announce the results, "and the unwonted feelings which agitated his bosom were reflected in his face."[85] In his chagrin he wrote his friend, General Woodford, October 11, 1776: "I wish you were here awhile to see the change of things, a party who were supposed to guide everything last Convention, seem lost."[86]

George Mason, who did not arrive at the Convention until May 17,[87] the day after the instructions for independence were adopted, wrote Patrick Henry:

> I congratulate you, most sincerely, on the accomplishment of what I know was the warmest wish of your heart, the establishment of American independence and the liberty of our country.[88]

Thus was American Union "formed from independent, separate states, each still sovereign within its constitutional sphere." But in its essence, the Declaration suggests a great deal more: "Tyranny does not change; it merely puts on new clothes. Our fathers knew this. And they knew, too, that independence, to be preserved, must be earned anew by each generation. To gain their own independence they made war upon tyranny; in the process of losing ours, we have forgotten what tyranny means."[89] In pointing to the objects to which the Revolution and the Spirit of '76 naturally guide us, John Randolph of Roanoke declared: "It is not a spirit of opposition to foreign nations, but a spirit of resistance to corruption and tyranny here at home."[90]

Colonel Nelson, whom Henry had selected to move independence in convention, gathered up the resolutions and galloped off to Philadelphia, delivering them to Congress May 27, 1776.[91] Eleven days later, June 7, 1776, Richard Henry Lee moved in Congress, as instructed in the resolutions:

"That these united Colonies are and of right ought to be, free and independent States, that they are absolved from all alle-

---

[85] Grigsby, *The Virginia Convention of 1776*, p. 191.

[86] Edmund Pendleton Papers in the Southern Historical Collection, U. N. C. Library, Chapel Hill.

[87] Henry, *Henry*, I, p. 409 n. cites a letter from Thomas L. Lee to Richard H. Lee, Southern Library Messenger, Sept. 1858; Brant, *Madison, The Virginia Revolutionist*, p. 253.

[88] Morgan, *Henry*, p. 311.

[89] From the Editorial Page of the Richmond *News Leader*, July 4, 1956. *Thoughts on the Declaration.* James J. Kilpatrick, Editor.

[90] From Randolph's *Spirit of '76*, as quoted on the Editorial Page, July 4, 1956. John Randolph of Roanoke in the House, April, 1810.

[91] Henry, *Henry*, I, p. 400.

giance to the British Crown, and that all political connection between them and the State of Great Britain is, and ought to be totally dissolved.

"That it is expedient forthwith to take the most effectual measures for forming foreign alliances.

"That a plan of confederation be prepared and transmitted to the respective colonies for their consideration."

Here it is seen that the instructions to secure foreign alliances and confederation, which were urged by Mr. Henry in his letters of May 20 to Lee and Adams, were formally proposed.

The resolutions were seconded by John Adams and were debated on June 8 and 10, but the decision was postponed until July 2. However, a committee was formed on June 11, which was composed of Thomas Jefferson, John Adams, Benjamin Franklin, Roger Sherman and R. R. Livingston,[92] to plan a Declaration of Independence.

The chairman of this committee should have been Lee, since according to rules, the delegate of the colony moving the resolutions usually headed the committees. Instead, Thomas Jefferson was made chairman. This was caused by Richard Lee's decision to attend the Virginia Convention, after stopping off at his home to see Mrs. Lee, who had been ill.[93] Jefferson drew up the formal Declaration of Independence which was finally adopted July 4, 1776.

Among the names of the signers of the Declaration, Patrick Henry is conspicuously absent. It was Henry who threw the torch to his colleagues in Congress. To those who know the preliminaries of the Revolution in the Old Dominion, the omission of Henry's name on this document must have occasioned many questions. Mr. Henry, of course, was busy helping to set up the new government for the sovereign state of Virginia.

In examining the Declaration as written by Mr. Jefferson, no rhetorical innovation is noted. Patrick Henry's arraignment of the King, 13 years before in the "Parson's Cause," already held the very embodiment of the Declaration of Independence. Nevertheless, Dr. Mays has headed a chapter in his book, "The Jefferson Revolution Begins." This does violence to truth.

Prior to the Virginia Convention of 1776, Jefferson had been absent four and a half months, being confined to his home by illness from December 28, 1775, to May 14, 1776. Jefferson had

---

[92] *Ibid.*, I, p. 402.
[93] *Ibid.*

little or no hand in the affairs that called loudly for independence and the prelude to government in the Virginia Convention. In his own words, "I have been so long out of the political world, that I am almost a new man in it."[94]

"Thomas Jefferson, at the age of 26, was elected to the House of Burgesses in 1769 and was one of his Country's representatives thereafter until the end of British rule. His sympathies almost from the outset were with the popular leader of the House of Burgesses, Patrick Henry, who spoke for those who had lost patience with slow-moving compromise. Jefferson worked usefully with Henry and, because of his skill in composition, had a hand in drafting some important papers. He shared in the plan for the establishment of Committees of Correspondence, though the idea itself simply was an adaptation to the inter-Colonial relations of the exchanges legislative bodies in American long had maintained with their agents in England. Jefferson was named to that first general Committee of Correspondence, but he was not a member of what now would be called the Executive Committee of that body of 11. In 1774, when America had been stunned by the parliamentary act closing the port of Boston, Jefferson was one of those whom Henry called into conference to draft a resolution for a day of fasting and prayer. After the adoption of these 'resolves' led Governor Dunmore to dissolve the House of Burgesses, Jefferson was named Delegate from Albemarle to the Convention of 1774, and in anticipation of that meeting he was prompted to write his *Summary View of the Rights of British America*. On his way to the Colonial capital, he fell sick and had to forward the paper (to Mr. Henry) which historically was of the largest importance, though it does not appear to have influenced materially the action of the brief Convention. The next year, 1775, Jefferson came to Richmond in March to attend the second Convention and he doubtless sat in St. John's Church when Patrick Henry delivered the thunderous address with the startling peroration on 'liberty or death.' Jefferson is not mentioned in the all-too-meager accounts of that day's proceedings, nor, strange as it seems, did he ever write at any length about Henry's cry that was 'heard around the world.' "[95]

"During the decade that began with Virginia resistance to the Stamp Act and culminated in Henry's march from Newcastle

[94] Boyd, *The Papers of Thomas Jefferson,* I, p. 293.

[95] Dr. Douglas Southall Freeman, Editor, The Richmond *News Leader,* Editorial Page, *Revision of 'The Common Glory'*, Dec. 13, 1948.

down the Peninsula, proceedings in Jefferson's native Colony were influenced tremendously by eloquence. Here, as in the Continental Congress, there was, in fact, too much oratory, but at the time it was influential and it was an art in which Jefferson was not successful. He used his pen, not his tongue, and when eloquence was the scourge of Kings, he could not contend for first place with Henry or for second place with Richard Henry Lee. Stated still differently, control of Virginia was being transferred in 1765–75 from the older groups dominated by Peyton Randolph and Richard Bland, to the revolutionary group of which Patrick Henry was so indisputably the leader that neither Jefferson nor any one else was mentioned in the same breath with him."[96]

---

[96] *Ibid.*

XV

CONSTITUTIONAL GOVERNMENT

Go, call thy sons, instruct them what a debt
They owe their ancestors; and make them swear
To pay it, by transmitting down entire
Those sacred rights to which themselves were born.
—Source Unknown

THE CONVENTION OF May 6, 1776, held in Williamsburg, was now to replace the old House of Burgesses and witness the last meeting ever attempted by that body—a meeting which neither proceeded to business nor adjourned—as a House of Burgesses.

After the Convention had given its assent to propose to the delegates in Congress to declare the United Colonies free and independent states, the members took upon themselves the institution of government for the sovereign state of Virginia. Without such an administration, the independence resolutions would have little meaning to the people and "to be backward in this act . . . might imply a distrust, whether the rule had been wrested from the King."[1]

However, before further progress could be made, many questions had to be answered, and among them was the delegated power of the Convention to set up constitutional government. Thomas Jefferson, now in Congress to replace Peyton Randolph, who had died in September, had written a friend in the Convention (thought to have been his kinsman, Edmund Randolph) "to oppose a permanent constitution, until the people should elect

[1] Edmund Randolph's "*Manuscript History of Virginia,*" II, p. 63.

deputies for the special purpose. He denied the power of the body elected (as he conceived them to be agents for the management of the war), to exceed some temporary regimen."[2]

"These views were based upon the mistaken idea of the powers of the Convention. The sovereignty of the people was represented by the body, else it had no power to declare independence, the highest act of sovereignty; and representing that sovereignty it was within its powers, and became its duty, to establish a permanent form of government. This view taken by Mr. Henry and others at the time, was afterward unanimously adopted by the Supreme Court of the State in the case of Kamper vs. Hawkins."[3]

Madison's biographer remarks that Jefferson himself did not have such views in the beginning of the Convention. On May 16, 1776, he wrote confidently to Thomas Nelson from Congress:

"Should our Convention propose to establish now a form of government perhaps it might be agreeable to recall for a short time their delegates. It is a work of the most interesting nature and such as every individual would wish to have his voice in. In truth it is the whole object of the present controversy; for should a bad government be instituted for us in future it had been as well to have accepted at first the bad one offered to us from beyond the water without the risk and expense of contest."

Madison's biographer noted further:

"Jefferson's real reason for suggesting that the entire congressional delegation be called to Williamsburg was that he was the last member who could leave Philadelphia under the system of absence in rotation. He had returned to Congress only two days earlier, after a four months' stay in Virginia lengthened by illness. There is not a hint in Jefferson's letter of May 16 that the government which he wished to help establish would lack permanence. Setting it up, he said, was the whole object of the controversy with Great Britain; its nature would determine the future."[4]

In setting up the Constitution, many questions were brought forward. Should it be written or unwritten; and should the State of Virginia form a constitution apart from the other states, leaving each to draft its own, or should Congress be called upon to establish a "uniform plan of government for all the States?"

---

[2] Ibid., II, p. 63, As pointed out by Brant, *Madison, The Virginia Revolutionist*, p. 252.

[3] Henry, *Henry*, I, p. 406.

[4] Brant, *Madison, The Virginia Revolutionist*, pp. 252–253.

The government of Great Britain had always been conducted under an unwritten constitution, but for the new nation it was determined to establish a written constitution, to settle the powers of the different departments of government, to serve as a restraint upon the people themselves in the exercise of their sovereignty, and thus to give permanency to their political institutions.[5]

A written Constitution was to mark a new era in the annals of history; for although attempts to adopt constitutions had been made, "they had been hitherto very crude, and the papers were only intended for temporary use. Indeed, being liable to change by the Legislature, they lacked the feature of permanency." Some ancient states operated under written codes of laws, it is true, but they were codes emanating from the rulers, and their provisions heterogeneously mixed permanent and temporary provisions.[6]

The difficult task of drawing up a declaration of rights and a plan of government for the state of Virginia was begun on May 15, with President Pendleton appointing a committee headed by Archibald Cary. Twenty-eight members were assigned to this work. The next day the president added three more names to the list—thirty-one in all, "loading down the committee with useless members" as was customary with him. George Mason, overcoming the gout, was finally able to make his appearance on May 17, and he was placed on the committee the next day, a Saturday.

Patrick Henry probably noted that the majority were Pendleton's partisans, and under apprehension, he wrote Adams on May 20: "Our session will be very long, during which I cannot count upon one coadjutor of talents equal to the task."[7] Because of Mason's presence on the committee, biographers have chosen to criticize Mr. Henry for his statement. But, as has been pointed out, George Mason was not added to the committee until Saturday, and Mr. Henry's letter was "probably written early on Monday."[8] He must have been sincere in summing up the situation as he saw it at the time. The convention had begun the work of forming the Constitution when Henry wrote Adams, and had there been men of talents equal to the task, they were unwilling, or holding out

[5] Henry, *Henry*, I, pp. 407–408.

[6] *Ibid.*, I, p. 407.

[7] Patrick Henry to John Adams, May 20, 1776. Thomas L. Lee wrote his brother, the Committees were loaded down with useless members; Thomas L. Lee to Richard H. Lee, May 18, 1776, *Southern Literary Messenger*, September, 1858.

[8] Henry, *Henry*, I, p. 409–416 n. It has been said that Mason made his appearance on the 18th, but the letter of T. H. Lee to R. H. Lee states that he appeared in his seat for the first time on May 17.

for connection, no doubt guided by fears for the safety of their property.[9]

Henry wished for the counsel of Richard Lee, but Lee could not leave Congress earlier and most of his assistance was by letter. His name was not placed on the committee until June 29, the day the Constitution was adopted.[10]

George Mason, the "reluctant statesman" up until the previous July, was not convinced of the purpose of the British ministry, and of the only means left to the colonies to regain their basic rights. Patrick Henry had the highest opinion of George Mason's "talents, patriotism, and republican principles."[11] They had collaborated in the conventions and Henry had urged him as a delegate to Congress in August, 1775. Patrick Henry must have showed Mason his prospective plan of government which he called his "most esteemed republican form," and he had written Adams it had "many and powerful enemies."[12]

Even so, it appears that Mason approved Henry's "favorite democratic scheme" and some of the "ablest men . . . united with Mr. Henry in urging it." Whether Patrick Henry brought it forward is not known. It was stated that there was "no great difference of opinion" among the "best speakers," Henry, Mason, Mercer, Dandridge and Smith.[13] Patrick Henry probably yielded his plan in favor of Mason's, which doubtless would have met less opposition in committee. For Henry knew well that his Tidewater antagonists would oppose any plan that he might bring forward.

In this work pertaining to the "rights and liberties of the people," Patrick Henry was no novice. He had made constitution and history his "capital study."[14] Seen in this role, he "acted" as

---

[9] Brant, *Madison, The Virginia Revolutionist*, p. 187. Madison's biographer, Irving Brant, declared: "Madison sided so fully with Patrick Henry and the radical revolutionaries in 1775 that he could by implication charge his father's friend Edmund Pendleton with being ruled by pusillanimous fears for the safety of his property."

[10] Henry, *Henry*, I, p. 442.

[11] Grigsby, *The Virginia Convention of 1776*, p. 148, called Mason the reluctant statesman. As to Henry's admiration for Mason, note Judge Spencer Roane's Memorandum, Morgan, *Henry*, Appendix B. p. 450; Henry, *Henry*, I, p. 417.

[12] Patrick Henry to John Adams, May 20, 1776; Henry, *Henry*, I, p. 413.

[13] *Southern Literary Messenger*, November 1858, p. 330. Henry's *Henry*, I, pp. 421–22.

[14] Henry, *Henry*, I, p. 183; George Mason to Martin Cockburn, May 26, 1774; Grigsby, *The Virginia Convention of 1776*, p. 150; Silas Deane at the first Congress wrote his wife regarding the speakers, Henry and Lee: that they have "made the Constitution and history of Great Britain and America their capital

chairman and was making the numerous reports in the powerful Committee of Propositions and Grievances.[15] He was "exceedingly obliged" to Adams for the pamphlet containing his views on government and promised to make it his "incessant study so that a kindred with New England may be discerned in it," and if all its excellences could not be preserved, he hoped "to retain so much of the likeness, that posterity shall pronounce us descended from the same stock." Henry would "think perfection was obtained" if they had Adams' approbation.[16]

To Adams, Patrick Henry wrote, "Your sentiments are precisely the same I have long since taken up, and they come recommended by you." Adams answered, "I esteem it an honor and a happiness, that my opinion so often coincides with yours." Adams sent his plan to Mr. Henry on June 3. The plan he considered best was that which "communicates . . . happiness, to the greatest number of persons, and in the highest degree; that the happiness and dignity of mankind consist in virtue; that while fear is the foundation of monarchy, and honor of aristocracy, virtue is the foundation of republican government; and as the definition of a republic is 'an empire of laws, and not of men,' that form is best which secures an impartial and exact execution of the laws."[17] Adams' plan, then, was based on a democratic republic with public virtue as its essential mark. His outline was published in the *Gazette*, and parts were used from it in the final draft of the Articles of Rights. The pamphlet on government as visioned by Adams was first given to Lee in Congress and Lee sent it to Mr. Henry on April 20. At the same time Lee enclosed his own "small scheme" on Government that he said he had drawn before he saw Adams' plan.[18] The similarity is striking. Lee "thought the council of the governor should be distinct from the upper House, that the term of the upper House should be longer than one year, and that sheriffs should be appointed as formerly in Virginia; that is, by the Governor, or be elected by the freeholders of the Counties."[19] In other respects, there was no difference from the Adams plan, according to Mr. Henry's

---

study ever since the late troubles between them have arisen." *Collection of Connecticut Historical Society*, II, p. 181; Henry, *Henry*, I, p. 247.

[15] *Ibid.*, I, p. 389.

[16] Patrick Henry to John Adams, May 20, 1776. Henry, *Henry*, I, p. 413.

[17] Adams' Thoughts on Government, Henry's *Henry*, I, p. 417.

[18] Henry, *Henry*, I, p. 381.

[19] *Ibid.*, I, pp. 418–419.

grandson. He also notes that in the *Virginia Gazette* of May 10, 1776, "there appeared a publication which was either the scheme of R. H. Lee, or was drawn by someone who had read it and Mr. Adams' paper. As Mr. Henry had previously received the letter of R. H. Lee, it is highly probable that he inserted the publication in the *Gazette*."[20] The historian Henry declared: "It is so nearly the plan of Mr. Adams, as modified by the suggestions of Colonel Lee, that if it was not Colonel Lee's paper it was doubtless drawn by Mr. Henry from the two papers."[21]

Thomas Jefferson sent a draft of a constitution "which was received on the day on which the Committee of the Whole reported to the Convention," June 24, and "owing to the indisposition of the Convention to open questions which had already caused troublesome debates, they could not be induced to consider his suggestions, except that his preamble was prefixed to the paper adopted."[22] On Jefferson's proposal, George Wythe commented:

"When I came here the plan of government had been committed to the whole house. To those who had the chief hand in forming it the one you put into my hands was shown. Two or three parts of this were, with little alteration, inserted in that: but such was the impatience of sitting long enough to discuss several important points in which they differ, and so many other matters were necessarily to be dispatched before the adjournment that I was persuaded the revision of a subject the members seemed tired of would at that time have been unsuccessfully proposed."[23]

Thomas Ludwell Lee wrote his brother Richard Henry Lee in Congress on June 1, 1776, declaring that the copy of the declaration of rights nearly as it came through committee had been reported to the convention, but they had ever since been stumbling at the threshold, and they were finding such difficulty in laying the foundation stone that he was in "very much fear for that Temple to Liberty which was proposed to be erected thereupon." "I will tell you plainly," he said, "that a certain set of Aristocrats—for we have such monsters here—finding that their execrable system cannot be reared on such foundations, have to this time kept us at bay on the first line, which declares all men to be born

---

[20] *Ibid.*, I, p. 419.

[21] A Government Scheme, Henry, *Henry*, I, pp. 419–420–421.

[22] Mr. Jefferson to Judge A. B. Woodward, April 3, 1825, Henry, *Henry*, op. cit., I, p. 441.

[23] George Wythe to Jefferson, Williamsburg, 27 July, 1776, Boyd, *The Papers of Thomas Jefferson*, I, pp. 476–477.

free and independent. A number of absurd or unmeaning alterations have been proposed. The words as they stand are approved by a very great majority, yet by a thousand masterly fetches and stratagems the business has been so delayed, that the first clause stands yet unassented to by the Convention."[24]

"The struggle in the select committee seems to have resulted, . . . in a victory for a democratic over an aristocratic plan, and the work of framing a Bill of Rights, suited to a democratic Republic, was entered upon at once."[25] Randolph stated, "Many projects of a Bill of Rights and Constitution discovered the ardor for political notice, rather than a ripeness in political wisdom." George Mason's paper "swallowed up all the rest, by fixing the grounds and plan which after great discussion and correction were finally ratified."[26]

Mason acknowledged that his draught of the Declaration of Rights "received few alterations, some of them I think not for the better."[27]

Patrick Henry's grandson, the historian, made this comment:

The Virginia Bill of Rights contained all that was of value in the Bill of Rights of 1689 written by Lord Somers, called the "most complete statement of the principles of government ever attempted," which is said to have embodied the Petition of Rights of 1628, written by Sir Edward Coke.[28]

Every student of American history should have a thorough knowledge of the Virginia Declaration of Rights, often called the Bill of Rights, which is fully explained in W. W. Henry's *Patrick Henry*. The declaration is written in sixteen sections.

The following excerpts are taken from the historian's interpretation:

The first section declares that "men have an inalienable right to enjoy life, liberty, property, and happiness."

The second section declares "all power to be vested in, and derived from, the people."

The third section declares that "government should be for

[24] Thomas L. Lee to Richard H. Lee, June 1, 1776. Henry's *Henry*, I, pp. 424–425.

[25] Henry, *Henry*, I, p. 422.

[26] Randolph's *Manuscript History of Virginia*. Henry, *Henry*, op. cit., I, p. 422.

[27] Col. George Mason to Col. George Mercer of Stafford County, then in England, Oct. 2nd, 1778. *The Virginia Historical Register*, p. 29; The Virginia Historical Society.

[28] Henry, *Henry*, I, p. 424.

the common weal," against maladministration, with the right of the majority to control.

The fourth section "explodes the idea of an inheritance in office, and places the right to fill it on its true basis, merit."

The fifth section "separates the legislative and executive from the judicial department," which was "a radical change of the system which had prevailed in the Colony, where the Governor and his Council were a most important part of the judiciary, and held office for life."

The sixth section "guarantees freedom of elections, and in this copies the Bill of Rights."

The seventh section "declares that the power of suspending laws should only be exercised by that body to which is entrusted the power of making laws, a principle found in the Bill of Rights, and is essential to the proper administration of representative government."

The eighth section "secures to every man the right to a speedy and impartial trial before a jury in all criminal prosecutions," as is also found in the British constitution.

The ninth section, which "prohibits excessive bail and fines, and cruel and unusual punishments, was also borrowed from the Bill of Rights."

The tenth section "prohibits general warrants." The historian pointed to "the experience of the Colonies and the eloquent protest of James Otis in November, 1761."

The eleventh section "recommends the trial by jury as the best mode of settling civil suits, and shows the attachment of Virginians to the methods of English jurisprudence."

The twelfth section secures the freedom of the press.

The thirteenth declares "a trained militia to be the proper defense of a free state, that standing armies in the time of peace are dangerous to liberty," as Patrick Henry pointed out in St. John's Church.

The fourteenth prohibits "the erection of a separate or independent government within the bounds of Virginia."

Edmund Randolph said of the remaining sections:

"The fifteenth, recommending an adherence and frequent recurrence to fundamental principles, and the sixteenth, unfettering the exercise of religion, were proposed by Mr. Henry. The latter, coming from a gentleman who was supposed to be a dissenter, caused an appeal to him, whether it was designed as a prelude to an attack on the established church, and he disclaimed such an object."[29]

The frequent recurrence to fundamental principles in the fifteenth section "bases free government upon the foundation noted in John Adams' pamphlet" and embraces the word "virtue," as "the noblest principles . . . and necessary to lay the foundation for a republican government. . . ."

The sixteenth, "as found in the draft proposed by George Mason, and adopted by the Committee of the Whole, is in these words, doubtless as drawn by Mr. Henry:

"That religion, or the duty we owe to our Creator, and the manner of discharging it, can be directed only by reason and conviction, and not by force or violence; and therefore, that all men should enjoy the fullest toleration in the exercise of religion, according to the dictates of Conscience, unpunished and unrestrained by the Magistrate, unless under the color of religion any Man disturb the peace, the happiness, or the safety of society; and that it is the mutual duty of all to practice Christian forbearance, love, and charity towards each other."[30]

According to Mr. Henry's grandson: "After the section had received the approval of the body in Committee of the Whole, Mr. Madison moved in the House to substitute the following in its stead:

"That religion, or the duty we owe to our Creator, and the manner of discharging it, being under the direction of reason and conviction only, not of violence or compulsion, all men are equally entitled to the full and free exercise of it according to the dictates of conscience, and therefore that no man or class of man ought, on account of religion, to be invested with peculiar emoluments or privileges, nor subjected to any penalties or disabilities, unless, under color of religion, the preservation of equal liberty and the existence of the State be manifestly endangered."[31]

In rewriting the draft, Madison explained that his purpose was "to substitute for the idea expressed by the term 'toleration,' an absolute and equal right in all to the exercise of religion according to the dictates of conscience."[32] Though revised slightly by Madison, the wording of the latter part took care of Mr. Henry's pledges to those who had been denied religious liberty.

---

[29] *Ibid.*, I, p. 430.
[30] *Ibid.*, p. 431.
[31] *Ibid.*
[32] *Works of Madison*, I, p. 24 n.

This section "as adopted, was a more exact expression of what was intended by the body in the draft first adopted." The "paper as amended was adopted by a unanimous vote. The full force of the principles was not at once apprehended by the Convention, as appears from their subsequent history, but it was finally developed into an absolute divorce of Church and State, which was expressly based upon the principle inserted by Mr. Henry," and "has been subsequently engrafted upon every State constitution, and upon the Federal constitution as well."[33]

"Mr. George Mason was the author of the first fourteen articles and Mr. Henry the author of the last two—the last of which was most notable because it was the first formal and official assertion and sanction of the doctrine of religious liberty that had ever been given in Virginia."[34]

In this, the sixteenth, it fell to Patrick Henry to abolish spiritual tyranny, especially the practice of those magistrates acceding to the wishes of the Bishop of London who enforced the vicious acts of 1661[35] in harassing and punishing men of other faiths than the Church of England. Such acts no doubt had helped to cause the defection from the established church.

Such were the conditions when, on June 20, 1776, a petition was brought forward in the convention (and no doubt handed to Patrick Henry) "from sundry Baptists in Prince William County, praying that they be allowed to worship God in their own way without interruption; that they be permitted to maintain their own ministers, and none others; that they may be married, buried, and the like, without paying the clergy of other denominations."[36]

Mr. Henry, who thought nothing of riding fifty miles[37] to

---

[33] Henry, *Henry,* I, p. 432.

[34] Chandler & Thames, *Colonial Virginia,* p. 352.

[35] *Ibid.,* p. 202–203–204–362. Jefferson wrote that his opponents on the religious issue were Pendleton and Nicholas. Ford's *Jefferson* (1904 edition) pp. 1–53–55; Braxton was also among the opponents; Brant, *Madison,* I, pp. 245–247.

[36] Henry, *Henry,* I, pp. 449–450; Later, petitions came from Prince Edward, Buckingham, Culpeper, Amherst, Albemarle, Hanover and Richmond. In his autobiography Jefferson stated that the "petitions to abolish spiritual tyranny" in the assembly of 1776, "brought on the severest contest in which I have ever been engaged." And, as has been pointed out, the principal opponents were "properly placed" in Edmund Pendleton, speaker for the Conservatives, and Robert Carter Nicholas, the Treasurer, who were "never beaten until the doors were locked and the windows barred." Brant, *Madison, The Virginia Revolutionist,* pp. 296–299.

[37] Foote, in his *Virginia Sketches.*

render his services in behalf of the Dissenters, would, in the sixteenth section, grant them all these privileges.

When the General Assembly met in the autumn, they petitioned that body en masse to remove every vestige of tyranny, and implement their rights. Petitions were presented from the Presbytery of Hanover, Augusta, Amherst, Albemarle, Buckingham and Culpeper. Thomas Jefferson would then take up Henry's stand in their behalf and "Pendleton would fight him every inch of the way."

But after "desperate contests," the Dissenters would, in the end, win their fight. A quarter of a century later they would be able, with the help of Judge Spencer Roane, Patrick Henry's son-in-law, to sell the glebes, and Pendleton would go to his death still fighting for the Church of England.[38]

"When we remember that a large number, probably a majority, of the Convention were members of the established church, we may well be surprised that they consented to this section. But it should be remembered, that the discussion of human rights which the period had produced had caused a great enlargement of views, in all classes, on the subject of religious as well as civil rights, and the growth of dissent in the Colony had become so great, that religious liberty could not be withheld when demanded by such a leader as Patrick Henry. . . . If it had been the only act of his public life, it was sufficient to have enrolled his name among the greatest benefactors of the race."[39]

"An article prohibiting bills of attainder was defeated by Mr. Henry." It read:

"That laws having retrospect to crimes and punishing offences committed before the existence of such laws, are generally oppressive, and ought to be avoided."[40]

The article was proposed by Thomas L. Lee. This concluded the Virginia Bill of Rights.

The Select Committee of which George Mason and Patrick Henry were members turned to the task of framing a constitution. Mr. Mason proceeded to make a first draft of an ordinance of government, based somewhat on the plan of John Adams, which had appeared in the *Gazette* with some differences and alterations.[41] James Madison's works preserved copies of the original as written by Mason.

---

[38] Mays, *Pendleton*, II, p. 137.

[39] Henry, *Henry*, pp. 434–435.

[40] Edmund Randolph, *Manuscript History of Virginia*.

[41] Henry, *Henry*, I, p. 436; *Works of Madison*, I, p. 24.

The right of suffrage in choosing the Lower House as proposed by Mason was defeated, the right remaining as was then exercised, to freeholders of 50 acres of unimproved land, or 25 acres which was seated, and to holders of town lots. "This great experiment of republican government determined to trust their destinies with the men who had an interest in the soil."[42]

George Mason's plan for appointing members to the Upper House or Senate called for 24 members to be elected by an "intermediate body to be chosen by the people, and to be divided into four Classes, one of which was to go out of office at the end of each year." This was different from the published plan in the *Gazette*, which called for 24 members to be selected by the Lower House. "The Constitution retained the number 24 and the rotation by classes, but required their election to be directly by the people. . . . "[43]

In commenting on the above, the historian, Henry, had the following to say:

"The mode of selecting the Senate was a question of great difficulty. That body was no longer to represent distinct classes in the community, as did the House of Lords; nor a distinct authority, as did the Colonial Council; but it was to be a representative of the people, and a conservative force in legislation, and a check upon improper action in the Lower House. The Convention determined to have the Senate directly elected by the people, and to trust to the longer term and the rotation to insure a majority of experienced members for the conservatism desired."[44] Mason's proposal for all bills to originate in the Lower House, and money bills not to be liable to amendment in the Senate, was adopted. This was not in the published plan. Mason's plan, like the published plan, called for the election of the Governor to be annually by joint ballot of the Upper and Lower House, which was adopted. But neither George Mason's plan nor the constitution gave the executive a voice in the enactment of laws, as did the published plan. Mr. Henry did not approve of this. He felt that the power of veto should not be withheld from the executive and he urged the convention to grant the right of executive veto. Edmund Randolph noted:

"After creating the office of governor, the Convention gave way to their horror of a powerful chief magistrate, without waiting to reflect how much stronger a governor might be made for

[42] Henry, *Henry*, I, p. 437.
[43] *Ibid.*
[44] *Ibid.*

the benefit of the people, and yet be held with a republican bridle. These were not times of terror, indeed, but every hint of power which might be considered as being of royal origin, obscured for a time a part of that patriotic splendor with which the movers had before shone. No member but Henry could, with impunity to his popularity, have contended as strenously as he did for an executive veto on the acts of the two houses of legislation." He averred that "a governor would be a mere phantom, unable to defend his office from the usurpation of the legislature, unless he could interpose on a vehement impulse or ferment in that body, and that he would otherwise be ultimately a dependent, instead of a coordinate branch of power."[45]

Mr. Randolph seems to have had a keen recollection of what took place in the convention, having served on the select committee with Patrick Henry. Mr. Henry's critics gladly accept the above statement when they wish to make it appear that the convention wished to bridle Mr. Henry's power. But when it comes to Randolph's statement, written at the same time, that Mr. Henry wrote the fifteenth and sixteenth sections in the Virginia Bill of Rights, they declare Randolph's memory did not serve him well.

Was Patrick Henry wise in asking for the power of veto to be vested in the executive? Time proves that he was:

"The profound knowledge of the true principles of government displayed by Mr. Henry in each constitutional Convention in which he sat, shows not only much more extensive reading than he has been credited with, but that accurate thought and thoroughly poised judgment which constituted him a statesman of the highest order. The revulsion which had seized the people and the Convention against Kingly prerogatives, did not affect his clear judgment as to the proper powers to be entrusted to the Executive, and the experience of America has since demonstrated his wisdom. Not only is the veto power vested in the President by the Federal Constitution, but very few of the States of the Union now withhold this power from the Executive."[46]

The Constitution's plan, like Mason's, called for eight members to serve for three years, elected by joint ballot of both Houses of the Assembly, to make up the Governor's Council. The Adams plan fixed the number at twelve, to be chosen annually by joint ballot of the Upper and Lower House. The constitution used

---

[45] Edmund Randolph's *MS History of Virginia;* Henry, *Henry*, pp. 438–439.
[46] Henry, *Henry*, I, p. 439–440.

Mason's plan, adding to it a secretary, to serve during good behavior.

The fixing of the boundaries of Virginia was also a provision inserted in the Constitution. "By the treaty of 1763 between England and France, the Mississippi River became the Western limit." In Mr. Henry's letter to Richard H. Lee on May 20, and to John Adams of the same date, he mentioned the importance of the Mississippi and referred to the great force in San Domingo and Martinique, saying, "The Mississippi should be tho't of." To Adams he wrote that he felt our ambassadors would go thither more safely if routed by way of the Mississippi.[47] He was an "uncompromising advocate of the sovereign right of the State to her western territory, and of the free navigation of the Mississippi."[48]

What changes were made in Colonel Mason's plan by the committee, we have no means of knowing. The historian, Mr. Henry, declared: "The Journal shows that the Committee reported a plan of government to the Convention on June 24, which was considered in Committee of the Whole on the 26th, 27th, and 28th, was reported with amendments on the 28th to the Convention and was adopted on the 29." Mason's plan as originally drawn, and as revised, may be seen in Boyd's *Jefferson*.[49]

It appears that Jefferson had little to do in the adoption of the Constitution and the Bill of Rights of Virginia, which no doubt accounted for his criticism of the constitution in his *Notes on Virginia*. Nevertheless, it has been pointed out that "though not faultless, it remained the fundamental law of the State for fifty-four years, a length of days not accorded to any of its successors, and under its wise provisions the State enjoyed an amount of well-regulated liberty which was without precedent. Being the first written constitution of an independent State in America, it was taken as a pattern by all the other States, and its influence is also distinctly traced in the Federal Constitution."[50]

"There can be no doubt that Mr. Henry took an active part in the preparation and discussion of both the Bill of Rights and

---

[47] *Ibid.*, I, p. 413.
[48] *Ibid.*, I, pp. 146–147–441.
[49] Mason's plan, 8–10 June as originally drawn, Boyd, *Jefferson*, I, p. 366; The Mason plan as revised by the select committee, June 22, Boyd, *Jefferson*, II, p. 369; The Draft reported by the Committee, June 24, considered in Committee of the Whole, Amendments Thereto Offered in Committee, Boyd, *Jefferson*, I, p. 373; Also, Henry, *Henry*, I, pp. 423–441.
[50] *Ibid.*, I, p. 443.

the Constitution, and that it was due to him, in a great measure, that the latter so closely resembled the plan of John Adams, which he declared was an expression of his own sentiments. That these papers were approved by him as a whole, though not containing all he may have suggested, appears by his subsequent correspondence, and by the resistance he made to a revision of the Constitution while he continued in public life."[51]

When George Mason wrote that Patrick Henry's talents would have put him at the head of the Commonwealth of Rome, he was speaking of his "abilities as well as public virtues," and the time that he associated Henry with that glorious Commonwealth, was "during the first Punic war, when the Roman people had arrived at their meridian glory."[52]

"No voice was more eloquent for the independence of our country than that of Henry. No one fought harder to be certain that the fundamental Bill of Rights should become the bedrock of the Constitution, and that the rights of the states should be safeguarded against the potential tyranny of a centralized government."[53]

Under Henry's direction, the framers "went on to provide that the regulation of the internal concerns of each colony be left to respective colonial legislatures. This was a plain declaration of the unassailable fact that the states are the sheet anchors of our institutions. If the federal government should go out of existence, the Common run of people would not detect the difference in the affairs of their daily life for a considerable length of time. But, if the authority of the states were struck down, disorder approaching chaos would be upon us within 24 hours. No method of procedure has ever been devised by which liberty could be divorced from local self-government. No plan of centralization has ever been adopted which did not result in bureaucracy, tyranny, inflexibility, reaction and decline."[54]

These dangers Patrick Henry foresaw, and were his reasons in establishing a republican form of government.

"Henry's hand was quite probably the one which later

---

[51] *Ibid.*, pp. 442–443.

[52] Henry, *Henry,* I, p. 183. George Mason to Martin Cockburn, Williamsburg, May 26, 1774.

[53] State Board of Education, Commonwealth of Virginia, "Superintendent's Memo. No. 3832." May 13, 1960.

[54] The President of the United States, Calvin Coolidge, Speaking at the Sesqui-Centennial at Williamsburg, May 15, 1926, on the signing of the Virginia Resolutions.

qualified the assent of the colony to the formation of the confederation with the clause that no constitution adopted should interfere with the internal concerns of any state—a states' rights reservation, foreshadowing the opposition of Henry to be displayed years later in Richmond, when Washington and Marshall urged Virginia to ratify the Constitution of the United States."[55]

On June 24, the Select Committee reported a plan of government to the convention for the State of Virginia. After it had passed its third reading, it was adopted on June 29. Thus, under the well-established laws of a written constitution, "a rule of laws, not men," Virginia became a Republic.[56]

Implementing the last clause in the constitution which provided that a Governor be elected by the convention to hold office until the next General Assembly, Patrick Henry was nominated. Thomas Nelson, a member of the council, was nominated to oppose Mr. Henry. His name was probably suggested by one of Pendleton's partisans.

Edmund Randolph, in writing of the contest between the two men, noted:

"Nelson had long been secretary of the Colony, and ranked high in the aristocracy, who propagated with zeal the expediency of accommodating ancient prejudices, by electing a man whose pretensions to the chief magistracy were obvious from his being nominally the governor under the old order of things, and out of one hundred and eleven members, forty-five were caught by the desire of bringing all parties together, although Mr. Nelson had not been at all prominent in the revolution. From every period of Henry's life something of a democratic and patriotic cast was collected, so as to accumulate a rate of merit too strong for this last expiring act of aristocracy."[57]

Secretary Nelson, Henry's competitor for the office, was said to have been "beaten easily by Patrick Henry," when considering that Colonel Nelson was "supported by all the aristocracy and by Pendleton and a few others of plebeian standing." Judge Roane pointed out that "Pendleton, the eclipsed rival of Henry, presided in the committee and had his party with him."[58]

In the balloting for Governor, Patrick Henry received 60

---

[55] Governor Harry F. Byrd's review of history, speaking at the Sesqui-Centennial at Williamsburg, May 15, 1926, on the signing of the Virginia Resolutions.

[56] Henry, *Henry*, I, pp. 441–442.

[57] Randolph's *Manuscript History of Virginia;* Henry, *Henry*, I, p. 445.

[58] Morgan, *Henry*, p. 450, Spencer Roane's Memorandum.

votes, Thomas Nelson 45, and John Page one vote. If 112 delegates were present, as stated, six votes are unaccounted for. "Mr. Henry made no effort to secure his election, indeed was so deeply impressed with the responsibilities of the office that he was unwilling even to appear to desire it. He occupied the truly patriotic ground, that the office was neither to be sought nor refused."[59]

However, he was accorded the honor of becoming the Revolutionary War Governor of Virginia. His salary was fixed by the convention at one thousand pounds per annum, which was the sum received by the colonial governors. It was directed that one thousand pounds be used in furnishing the palace.[60]

A committee to devise a proper seal for the commonwealth was appointed on July 5 and George Mason, accordingly, reported the preparation of the device thereof; which was thrice read and agreed to.[61]

George Mason, who it is believed nominated Mr. Henry for Governor, headed the group appointed with Henry Lee, Dudley Digges, John Blair and Bartholomew Dandridge to notify the new governor of his election. The same day the convention elected the members to make up the Governor's Council. They were John Page, Dudley Digges, John Tayloe, John Blair, Benjamin Harrison of Berkeley, Bartholomew Dandridge, Thomas Nelson, and Charles Carter of Shirley. Thomas Nelson declined and Benjamin Harrison of Brandon was later elected in his place.

Although Mr. Henry preferred plain dress and simplicity in living, as Governor he would no longer appear "without a scarlet cloak, black clothes, and a dressed wig, etc., the people being unwilling that the office of Governor in a republican state should be less honored than in a royal colony."[62]

With the announcement of the name of the new Governor and the Henry party now in power under moral order of constitutional government, Pendleton knew that the old order was finished. As head of the Committee of Safety and President of the Conventions he had been an inveterate ruler, but he would now have to step down. On July 6, 1776, Patrick Henry and his Privy Council qualified and took government upon them, thus abolishing the Committee of Safety.[63] Richard Lee wrote Gen.

---

[59] Henry, *Henry*, p. 446.
[60] *Ibid.*, p. 457.
[61] Brenaman, *A History of Virginia Conventions*, p. 37.
[62] Henry, *Henry*, I, p. 457.
[63] Ballagh, *The Letters of Richard Henry Lee*, I, p. 207.

Charles Lee from Williamsburg, July 6, 1776, "The enclosed form of Government will shew you that this Country (Virginia) has in view a permanent system of Liberty. We have in all respects a full and free Government which this day begins the exercise of its powers. Mr. Henry is chosen Governor, and a Privy Council is appointed to assist him."[64] The same letter stated Lord Dunmore still remained at Gwin's Island, but this brought no fear to Henry. Dunmore would be driven out.

The Declaration of Independence was now to be proclaimed from the Governor's Palace at Williamsburg. The central figure was Patrick Henry, first Governor under a written constitution of a sovereign state in the world![65] Standing on the steps of the palace, he began to read slowly from the preamble to the Virginia Bill of Rights, which contained a similar embodiment used by him in his scourge of the King, at Hanover Courthouse: That men by birth were entitled to certain rights in the pursuit of life, liberty and property, and of obtaining happiness and safety, and that whereas George the Third, King of Great Britain, had endeavored to prevent these rights and to pervert the government of Virginia through tyranny, by imposing taxes without the consent of the people, by cutting off their trade, plundering their seas, ravaging their coasts, burning their towns and villages, and destroying lives; and by inciting the Indians to attack, and the Negroes to rise up in arms against the Colony; and since the petitions for the redress of grievances had been answered with further examples of tyranny—that for these and further acts of wanton cruelty—the Government of Virginia was totally dissolved from the Crown of Great Britain.

Patrick Henry raised his hand and took the oath of office as Governor, to administer under a written constitution for the protection of the people and for the maintenance of their rights.

Soldiers from the regiments that he had commanded threw their caps high at the word, "independence." Hurrahs and shouts of gladness were heard from them and from the crowds that had gathered. Bells were ringing and bonfires blazed and sputtered as the British flag went down, never again to be unfurled over the capitol.

Governor Henry was handed the big key and he opened the

---

[64] Ballagh, I, pp. 205–206.

[65] The first Governor under a written constitution of a free State in the annals of the world. Brenaman, *A History of Virginia Conventions*, p. 33 n. See discourse as quoted: Grigsby, *The Virginia Convention of 1776*, pp. 25–26.

Palace door and walked in, taking his seat at Dunmore's desk. When the great door swung to behind him, it was to shut out forever all vestiges of royal authority.

Henry was fearful of anything less than a republic founded on virtue. He had surveyed Rome: "The nation of soldiers, magistrates, and legislators, who composed the thirty-five tribes of the Roman people . . . dissolved into the common mass of mankind, and confounded with millions of servile provincials, who had received the name without adopting the spirit of Romans."[66]

Henry wanted nothing that could circumvent his plan and form for a republic. His definition was explicit. And yet the republic is now called a democracy. This country is not and never has been a democracy. It was established as a republic composed of a union of sovereign states.

The bill of rights, founded on "the rule of laws, not men", makes this nation in its essence, a republic, and distinguishes it from a democracy. "The American colonies sought self-government because they *could* govern themselves, and fulfill the common human destiny through such government." That was the meaning and the lesson of the American Revolution.

---

[66] Gibbon's *Decline and Fall of the Roman Empire.*

XVI

EXECUTIVE YEARS–FIVE TIMES GOVERNOR

AT THE CAPITAL in Williamsburg, Virginia had not awaited the decision of the Continental Congress to establish her sovereign rights, but proceeded on her way by declaring independence, writing her Constitution and electing her Governor. "Congress, instead of giving the impulse to independence, (had) received it from the Colonies."[1]

Before the convention adjourned, vigorous steps had been taken to prosecute the war. Ordinances were drawn for the purpose of building a navy and for increasing troops. The ninth regiment was enlarged and equipped to defend the frontiers. Six troops were added to the cavalry and a general alert was ordered for the entire state militia. Urgently needed salt was to be provided through new salt works to be set up, and Congress was asked to allow exports from abroad to procure further provisions. Whole cargoes of salt, medicines, clothing for the Army, and 900 barrels of flour and some tobacco were stored at Hood's Fort along the James in September.[2] The ordinance called for issuing treasury notes in the amount of one hundred thousand pounds, and a small tax of one shilling three pence was imposed.

In electing the new delegates to Congress, Carter Braxton and Benjamin Harrison were left out, the impression of the convention being that they were "not in full sympathy in their political views,"[3] and the number of delegates was now reduced to five. Later Harrison was exonerated and returned to Congress.

---

[1] Grigsby, *Virginia Convention of 1776*, p. 144 n.

[2] *Virginia, A Guide to the Old Dominion*, p. 580. These provisions were stored, September 13, 1776; note also the situation of naval stores and dockyards, Henry, *Henry*, I, pp. 477–478.

[3] Henry, *Henry*, I, p. 449 n; Randall's *Life of Jefferson*, I, p. 147.

In order to stabilize peace along the boundary with Pennsylvania, a proposed line was drawn until the matter could be properly determined. Commissioners were appointed to investigate conditions in Kentucky concerning Richard Henderson's claims to land purchased from the Cherokees which would dispossess the settlers.[4]

It was directed that any and all reference to the King in the service of the Episcopal Church be omitted and prayers for the colonies' magistrates be substituted.

On July 5, the last day of the Convention, after Mr. Henry had been sworn in as Governor, he left Williamsburg for Scotchtown to attend to his private affairs. After reaching his home he fell sick with fever and for several weeks was confined to his bed.[5] In August the public was informed that "our worthy Governor, who is now at his seat in Hanover is so much recovered from his late severe indisposition that he walks out daily, and it is hoped will soon be able to return to the seat of government to attend to the duties of his high and important office."[6]

Mr. Henry returned to the capital before he had fully recovered. Later, he had to return to his home at the suggestion of his physician. There he gathered sufficient strength to return to the capital to meet with his Council in September.

Within the Governor's palace he would learn to feel at home, for here he lived longer than any other Governor under the constitution of Virginia. In his office he would write his acceptance to the House, and pen letters to the former officers and men under his command in "a graceful specimen of his style."

Proclamations like those that once went out to apprehend "a certain Patrick Henry" by Governor Dunmore, were now given to Gen. Andrew Lewis to capture the said Dunmore himself, or drive him from the country. On July 8, Lewis made the attack, drove Dunmore from Gwin's Island and took possession.[7]

Patrick Henry's election "to the first magistracy of a free people" was "hailed with delight by the patriots not only in his own State, but throughout America, as appeared by letters and addresses sent him."[8] From everywhere came congratulations and good wishes. "It is said that, greatly to the disappointment

---

[4] *Ibid.*, pp. 449–473.
[5] *Ibid.*, I, p. 491.
[6] *Ibid.*, op. cit., I, p. 452, Virginia Gazette, Aug. 2, 1776.
[7] Henry, *Henry*, I, p. 459.
[8] *Ibid.*, I, p. 452.

of his enemies among the aristocrats, he conducted himself as Governor with great dignity, meeting all the requirements and proprieties of the great office with consummate ease and in most excellent taste."[9]

The First and Second Virginia Regiments, trained under his command, sent a cordial letter which speaks for itself:

> May it please Your Excellency:
> Permit us with sincerest sentiments of respect and joy, to congratulate Your Excellency upon your unsolicited promotion to the highest honors a grateful people can bestow.
> Uninfluenced by private ambition, regardless of sordid interest, you have uniformly pursued the general good of your country; and have taught the world, that an ingenious love of the rights of mankind, an inflexible resolution, and a steady perseverance in the practice of every private and public virtue, lead directly to preferment and give the best title to the honours of our uncorrupted and vigorous state.
> Once happy under your military command, we hope for more extensive blessings from your civil administration.
> Intrusted as Your Excellency is, in some measure, with the support of a young empire, our hearts are willing, and arms ready to maintain your authority as chief magistrate; happy that we lived to see the day, when freedom and equal rights, established by the voice of the people, shall prevail through the land. We are, may it please Your Excellency, Your Excellency's most devoted and obedient servants.[10]

It is to be noted that Colonel Woodford, who had disregarded Colonel Henry's position as the head of the army, was now sulking at Pendleton's defeat, and had the following printed in the *Gazette* at Williamsburg:

"Mr. Purdie. Let the public know that Colonel Woodford's name was not among the subscribers of the address to the Governor; that it was not presented as containing the sentiments of the colonel, but of the officers and their men, and that the colonel was not consulted on the occasion. This piece of justice is demanded by the colonel, and cheerfully granted by the officers."[11]

That Woodford had no hand in the matter must have made the letter from the soldiers more noteworthy in the eyes of Patrick Henry. He wrote this answer to the men:

---

[9] Chandler & Thames, *Colonial Virginia*, p. 353.
[10] Henry, *Henry*, I, pp. 452–453.
[11] *Ibid.*, I, p. 454.

Gentlemen of the First and Second Virginia Regiments: Your address does me the highest honour. Be pleased to accept my most cordial thanks for your favourable and kind sentiments of my principles and conduct. The high appointment to which my fellow-citizens have called me, was indeed, unmerited, unsolicited. I am therefore under increased obligations to promote the safety, dignity, and happiness of the commonwealth.

While the civil powers are employed in establishing a system of government, liberal, equitable, in every part of which the genius of equal liberty breathes her blessed influence, to you is assigned the glorious task of saving, by your valor, all that is dear to mankind. Go on, gentlemen, to finish the great work you have so nobly and successfully begun. Convince the tyrants again, that they shall bleed to her last drop, ere their wicked schemes find success.

The remembrance of my former connexion with you shall ever be dear to me. I honour your profession, I revere that patriot virtue, which, in your conduct, hath produced cheerful obedience, exemplary courage, and contempt of hardships and danger. Be assured, gentlemen, I shall feel the highest pleasure in embracing every opportunity to contribute to your happiness and welfare; and I trust the day will come when I shall make one of those that will hail you among the triumphant deliverers of America.

I have the honour to be gentlemen,

Your most obedient and very humble servant.

P. Henry, Jr.[12]

Governor Henry's important letters[13] to Washington during the critical period of the war show his unflagging determination and alertness in helping to win the victory. Although his letter book for the years '76, '77, and '78 are missing,[14] as is also the Executive Journal for 1779, the other volumes of his Journal while Governor "furnish the fullest evidence of his industry, his great executive capacity, and his ardent zeal in the cause of the Revolution."[15] Heading a population of about 400,000, he took office at the most critical period in the history of the country, with an untried government exposed to numberless hazards, not least among them the Indian threat to invade the western frontier.

That his responsibilities were manifold can be seen from his

[12] *Ibid.*, I, pp. 453–454.

[13] These letters were referred to by Tyler, *Patrick Henry:* Oct. 11, 1776, Nov. 19, 1776, Dec. 6, 1776, Jan. 8, 1777, March 20, 1777, March 28, 1777, June 20, 1777; besides he pointed to the letters cited in the text.

[14] Henry, *Henry*, I, p. 458 n.

[15] *Ibid.*, I, p. 458.

letters. He had to protect the frontiers from attack and also to guard the capital; to fortify all strategic points along the bay against marauding Tories, and assure the free passage of Virginia's trading vessels to and from the West Indies. Among his letters during the first year as Governor is one to the Virginia Delegates in Congress, suggesting the use of two officers in the cavalry whose credentials showed their services under the King of Prussia. We see him appoint a commission to alleviate the situation with the Cherokees. He ordered new levies to be placed for the protection of the capital, and row galleys for defense against the enemy's ships and tenders that might go up the rivers, noting that Williamsburg was easily accessible to attack from the James and the York.[16] He fortified Yorktown. He exerted himself to ensure the manufacture of gunpowder, and the mining of lead.

On December 21, 1776, a number of resolutions were passed in the House to meet the perils facing the country. Hearing of General Washington's critical condition, on the south side of the Delaware with only six thousand men to contend against twelve to fifteen thousand approaching British forces, the Legislature "resolved that the governor be fully authorized and empowered, with the advice and consent of the privy council, to carry into execution such requisitions as may be made to the Commonwealth by Congress for encountering or repelling the enemy; to order three battalions, if necessary, to join the Continental Army, or to assist the sister States; to call forth any and such greater military forces as they shall judge requisite, either by embodying and arraying companies or regiments of volunteers, or by raising additional battalions, appointing and commissioning the proper officers, and to direct their operations with this Commonwealth, under the command of the Continental generals or other officers according to their ranks, or order them to march to and act in concert with the Continental Army. . ."[17]

Professor Tyler pointed to the dismal period for the American cause, in the summer and autumn of that year, and gave this "grim procession of dates: August 27, the battle of Long Island; August 29, Washington's retreat across East River; September 15, the panic among the American troops at Kip's Bay, and the American retreat from New York; September 16, the battle of Harlem Plains; September 20, the burning of New York; October

---

[16] *Ibid.*, I, p. 477.

[17] Tyler, *Henry*, p. 231.

28, the battle of White Plains; November 16, the surrender of Fort Washington; November 20, the abandonment of Fort Lee, followed by Washington's retreat across the Jerseys. In the midst of these disasters, Washington found time to write, from the Heights of Harlem, on the 5th of October, to his old friend, Patrick Henry, congratulating him on his election as governor of Virginia and on his recovery from sickness; explaining the military situation at headquarters; advising him about military appointments in Virginia; and especially giving to him important suggestions concerning the immediate military defense of Virginia 'against the enemy's ships and tenders, which,' as Washington told the governor, 'may go up your rivers in quest of provisions, or for the purpose of destroying your towns.' "[18]

Empowered with the necessary authority, the Governor in December proclaimed the critical situation of American affairs and made an earnest appeal for "the utmost exertion of every sister State to put a speedy end to the cruel ravages of a haughty and inveterate enemy, and secure our invaluable rights." He called upon all Virginians, "earnestly exhorting and requiring" their assistance in helping to raise the necessary troops through volunteer companies in order that the quota of troops be met.[19] Heretofore the hope of reconciliation entertained by men in responsible positions had palpably diluted the war effort. Governor Henry vigorously stepped up the number of levies and enlistments.[20]

These, among some of his remaining letters are: To the Lieutenant of Montgomery County, ordering a part of the militia of Montgomery and Botetourt to defend the settlers in Kentucky, 'til further orders. . . . To the Governor of Maryland regarding cooperation of the forces of each state, and notifying him of the use of row galleys along the shoal lines of the Eastern shore. . . . To the Governor of North Carolina, requesting to know the condition of the galleys used for trade, and inquiring where to obtain custody of the unclaimed goods sent to Col. Muhlenberg's Regiment since his march to the North. . . . To George Morgan, Superintendent of Indian Affairs, regarding the delicacy of the business in negotiating with the Chiefs of the Shawnee & Delawares in a measure so necessary for the well-being of the country. . . . To Gen. Adam Stephen to know the num-

---

[18] *Ibid.*, pp. 220–221.

[19] *Ibid.*, p. 235.

[20] Henry, *Henry*, I, pp. 459–488. See also, letters, volume III.

ber of troops necessary to garrison Fort Pitt; pointing to the importance of Pittsburgh: "If lost, we shall retain no post from the Gulf of St. Lawrence to the mouth of the Mississippi. . . ." To the officers who were to command the forces marching to the aid of Kentucky. . . . To the Virginia delegates in Congress. . . . Report to George Washington on the rendezvous of a third part of the militia from eight countries. . . . To Benjamin Franklin, commissioner in France, to assist with his influence the application of Virginia's agents to obtain the arms and stores necessary for defense, in exchange for tobacco or any other production, which will serve to open that commerce with the French nation "with whom it is our wish to form the most interesting Connection. . . ." To General Washington to know the state of the enlistments of the troops, that means may be made for supplying the deficiency. . . . To the Governor of Cuba regarding a quantity of goods sent from Spain for the use of Virginia, and also showing the advantage in the exchange of goods with that island, which could be brought down the Mississippi to New Orleans "from our back country, in exchange for your woolens, linens, wines, military stores, &c.," pointing to the advantage to both from a commercial view. . . . To the Governor of New Orleans regarding trade. . . . To General Washington to know the most effectual means of prosecuting the war vigorously, Oct. 1777. There were several letters from Washington at this time to Governor Henry. Nine wagons went out from the Governor to the Virginia regiments in Continental service in December, 1777. Following were articles from the public store of fifteen thousand pounds worth of woolens, &c., and orders went out at this time over the state for many necessaries: to both Carolinas for blankets and soldiers' clothing. Nothing was left undone in getting whatever the troops needed.[21]

Patrick Henry entered his second term as Governor on May 29, 1777. On October 9, 1777, while still holding his residence at Scotchtown awaiting the renovation of the Capital, he married Dorothea Dandridge,[22] the daughter of Nathaniel West Dandridge of Hanover, and the granddaughter of Governor Alexander Spotswood (1710–22), called "the best of the Colonial Gover-

---

[21] *Ibid.*, III Note Henry, *Henry*, III, Correspondence and Speeches.

[22] Henry, *Henry*, I, p. 618. We are told "that at the time of his second marriage Governor Henry owned, besides his farm in Hanover, (Scotchtown) two small tracts in Botetourt, and ten thousand acres in Kentucky. He was the master of thirty slaves, and received twelve in addition as his wife's marriage portion."

nors."[23] Like her grandmother and mother before her, Dorothea went to live in the palace and was a charming and delightful hostess. This union brought Patrick Henry into a closer relationship with Washington. The latter's wife was the niece of Dorothea's father. The times were pressing and Governor Henry needed the encouragement and love of this daughter of his early neighbor.

He took the oath of office July 2, 1777, at a time of great strain. "So completely had he filled public expectations that all opposition to him vanished. No one was put in nomination against him, and he was appointed Governor for the year commencing with the end of the session, by joint resolution without ballot."[24] Not only did he guard the state, he had also to guard its finances. By way of example, one agent, St. George Tucker, without consulting the Governor, paid on his own £500 for indigo in Charleston in exchange for arms, and came before Governor Henry to ask repayment. The episode is recalled by Mr. Henry's biographer, George Morgan. He quoted Tucker as to what happened:

"I believe I attended twice before I had the honor of admittance to the Council board, when Governor Henry received me like a great man. I was not asked to sit down, I was not thanked for my zeal and expedition, or for advancing my money. Mr. Henry made some remarks upon the high price I had given for the indigo—said it was more than the State had bought it for before (which was very true for depreciation had then begun), and that I appeared to have been too much in a hurry to make the purchase. I felt indignation flash from my eyes, and I feel it in my heart at this moment. I am therefore an unfit person to draw an exact portrait of Mr. Henry, or give a fair estimate of his character."[25]

"It is clear that when Henry was bent upon the execution of public duties, he hardened much in manner. We recall that he mistrusted Carter Braxton and did not cloak his mistrust. We see that he was displeased with young Tucker and did not conceal his displeasure. But it was Henry the official who so appeared. Socially he was a different man. Having met him in company a long while afterwards, Tucker said of him: 'His manners were the perfection of urbanity; his conversation various, entertaining, instructive, and fascinating. I parted from him with

[23] *A Hornbook of Virginia History*, pp. 19–99–100.
[24] Henry, *Henry*, I, p. 521; *Executive Journal*, p. 49.
[25] Morgan, *Henry*, p. 282.

infinite regret, and forgot for the whole time I was with him that I had so many years borne in mind an expression which might not have been intended to wound me as it did.' "[26]

As Governor, Patrick Henry "controlled a navy board which built and equipped seventeen ships, fifteen brigs, nineteen schooners, fifteen galleys, two pilot-boats, and two barges. He established dockyards and naval depots, imported gunpowder, manufactured gunpowder and mined lead. He kept up Virginia's Continental quota of some six thousand men, and was frequently occupied in looking after the four or five thousand militia. He supplied the Virginia soldiers in Washington's army with clothing and foot-leather, and was tireless in his efforts to keep that army from starving. His zeal and vigor in this business entitle him to the highest honor as a guardian of America in her time of trial. It is a great glory of Henry's that he sent all the cattle he could gather to feed the poor fellows at Valley Forge. No one took the troubles of the 'ragged Continentals' more to heart than did the Governor of Virginia."[27]

The biographer, Morgan, cited the "Calendar of State" papers to show that Governor Henry practically exhausted the resources of Virginia in his belief that "the real fighting was likely to continue in the North." Henry learned the "sundry particulars concerning General Mifflin" and the Conway cabal from Mr. Custis, which "much surprised" him. He wrote Washington: "While you face the armed enemies of our liberty in the field, and by that favour of God, have been kept unhurt, I trust your Country will never harbour in her bosom the miscreant who would ruin her best supporter . . ."[28] With Henry's aid, Washington put down the Conway cabal and changed a complacent Congress to the order of business.[29] Washington quelled the disobedient Gen. Charles Lee with "fiery eye" and "biting words."[30] Patrick Henry early recognized that Washington had a positive mind and that his penetration was strong and acute.[31] To Henry, Washington was "the chief figure in his own administrations" and he believed in him and sent him every aid possible.

---

[26] *Ibid.*, pp. 283–284; Henry, *Henry*, II, p. 244.

[27] *Ibid.*, pp. 284–285–286.

[28] Henry, *Henry*, I, p. 548.

[29] Henry, *Henry*, I, pp. 546–547–548–550–551.

[30] *Everybody's Cyclopedia*, V, Edited by Charles Leonard-Stuart, B.A. and George J. Hagar, M.A.; Henry, *Henry*, II, pp. 5–6.

[31] At the First Congress the General had placed in Patrick Henry's hands some queries to be answered.

As an executive, "Henry was not only painstaking in the performance of his particular duties, he was watchful of the larger matters. He secured foreign loans; he looked sagaciously beyond the Alleghenies and he wrote with vigor and effectiveness. Of his twenty-one existing letters to Washington and of Washington's thirty-four letters to him, the greater number deal with the affairs of this period. So with the letters to and from Richard Henry Lee. We note eighteen letters from Henry to Lee, and thirty-six from Lee to Henry. Eight of the latter were found by accident among some of Mayo Cabell's papers at Union Hill, where Henry, who took slight trouble to preserve his Revolutionary correspondence, is supposed to have left them."[32] It should be borne in mind that these letters were in all probability given to Governor Henry's son, Patrick, who married the daughter of Col. William Cabell of Union Hill.

Mr. Henry's correspondence to camp, Congress, and to General Washington was so extensive, that in order to have intelligence of the enemy and make effectual defenses to protect the State as well as meet Washington's requisitions, an agent of correspondence, John Walker, was appointed to go to Washington's headquarters to be placed in a position where he could obtain the best information and dispatch it to the Governor. He was made an extra aide-de-camp at General Washington's headquarters, but as pointed out by Washington, his commission was not to be known, as it would be followed by requests of similar nature from other states.[33] In Washington's letter concerning John Walker, written from Morristown February 24, 1777, the general closed with these words to Governor Henry:

> Let me earnestly entreat, that the troops raised in Virginia for this army be forwarded on by companies, or otherwise, without delay, and as well equipped as possible for the field, or we shall be in no condition to open the campaign. With every sentiment of respect and regard
>
> I am, dear Sir, &c.
>
> Geo. Washington.[34]

Henry showed sound judgment in strengthening the outposts, and in his aid to Col. George Rogers Clark to save Kentucky. In July, while the Governor was recuperating from his

[32] Morgan, *Henry*, pp. 285–286.
[33] Henry, *Henry*, I, pp. 483–484.
[34] *Ibid.*, I, p. 484.

illness at Scotchtown, the young Colonel came to see him there. Clark had been tutored by Patrick Henry's great uncle, Donald Robertson, at his classical school in King & Queen County, and he had also taken up surveying. Later he had gone to Ohio where he fought with Dunmore in the Indian Wars. He turned down a commission in the British service, and noting the importance of the western frontier to Virginia, he left for Kentucky where he was given a commission placing him in charge of the militia. Seeing their meager defense against the Indians, and hoping to share the advantages, Clark became a delegate to Virginia to petition the convention for aid, and for setting off the new County of Kentucky from the County of Fincastle.

Travelling the 500 miles by horseback through the wilds of Kentucky, he reached Williamsburg to find the convention adjourned and Patrick Henry sick in Hanover.[35] Determined to see the Governor, Colonel Clark journeyed on to Scotchtown. Once face-to-face with the Governor, Clark discussed the serious conditions within the outpost of Kentucky, noting that the British emissaries were inciting the Cherokees to attack and the people were in need of gunpowder to defend themselves. Patrick Henry, long in sympathy with the settlers along the frontiers, wrote a letter to the Council "urging that the proper order be made." Clark appeared before the Council in Williamsburg and presented an order for 500 pounds of powder. He was turned down by reason of Henderson's claim to certain lands in Kentucky, since the Council did not know what action the General Assembly might decide to take. Only on the condition that Clark would be responsible in case the legislature rejected the order would they hazard such a risk. Clark declined such an offer, knowing that he could not at his own expense dispatch the powder through enemy territory. He penned a letter to the Council, saying that Kentucky would have to "seek protection elsewhere, which he did not doubt of their getting," stating that "if a country was not worth protecting, it was not worth claiming." At this, the Council recognized that they had made a grave mistake and the order was filled and wagons of powder were dispatched ahead "which secured Kentucky to Virginia."[36] Had Clark's request been denied, there is reason to believe he would have sought the help of the Spaniards, who held the lands west of the Mississippi.[37] Governor Henry's

---

[35] *Ibid.*, I, p. 471.
[36] *Ibid.*, I, p. 472.
[37] *Ibid.*, I, p. 473.

sympathy and vision later brought Colonel Clark back to Virginia on the way to his conquest of the great Northwest.

In reading of the many difficulties facing Patrick Henry during his first year as Governor, it is surprising that he was able to hold out for the first three terms. He served 1776–79, and then served again 1784–86. His Executive Journal covered 424 large folio pages for the first year alone, which did not include the letters written.[38]

On January 9, 1777, Governor Henry wrote Richard Lee in Congress, pointing to the conditions in Virginia during this critical period:

> I congratulate you my dear Sir on our well timed success at Trenton. I trust the honor of our arms will be retrieved.
>
> Our levies go on pretty well in many places; in some the great want of necessary clothing & blankets retards them. Orders issued this day for the officers to hold themselves & soldiers ready to march by companies & parts of companies, & in a little time they'll go off, but in want of everything. . . . I hope all enlistments may be filled, but doubt if it can soon be done. I am endeavoring at vigorous measures. Langour seems to have been diffused thro' the Naval department. However I hope it will mend. The Cherokees are humbled, but I fear hostility about Pittsburgh in the spring, & have provided ammunition and provisions in that quarter, & shall be able to muster a formidable militia thereabouts. The powder is not yet sent, but I wait only for the result of a council of war where to deposit it. Our sea coasts are defenseless almost. Arms & woolens are wanted here most extremely. We are making efforts to secure them. I do indeed pity your situation. I guess at the many perplexities & difficulties that attend you. I know how much the vigorous counsels of America are indebted to you for their support. I know how much you detest the spirit of indecision and lukewarmness that has exposed our country to so much peril. Let me tell you that altho' your fatigue is almost too much to bear, yet you must hold out a little longer. Many people pretend they perceive error in Congress, & some wicked ones are greatly pleased at the hopes of seeing the respect due to that assembly succeeded by contempt.
>
> Make my most affe. compliments to Col. Frank (Francis Lightfoot Lee). Has he forgot me? Indeed he may ask me the same. Tell him that from morning till night I have not a minute from business. I wish it may all do, for there are a thousand things to mend, to begin.

[38] *Ibid.*, I, p. 474.

> Adieu my dear Sir, & believe me your affectionate, humble servant,
>
> P. Henry.[39]

The continued series of stresses were weighing heavily on Patrick Henry and on Lee. Patrick Henry was now feeling the full force of that "bloody touch" that he had predicted would take place, once independence was declared.[40] But it can be said of him, as it was said of Washington, that he did not lose faith: "Nothing shook the firmness of his mind, and with perfect self-possession, he went forward in the performance of his duty, trusting the issue to the Divine Providence in whose keeping were the destinies of mankind."[41]

Conditions became steadily worse, and two months later, March 28, 1777, Governor Henry wrote Senator Lee of further troubles:

> The practice of engrossing all foreign goods & Country produce has gotten to an enormity here, particularly in the latter articles. Corn flour and meat are bought up (as I was informed by Col. Aylett) in so much that it is almost impossible to furnish the public demands, in such time as the necessitys of the army require. A gentleman here in partnership with Mr. Morris, has speculated very largely in such articles as the army wants. The public agent complains he is anticipated. I hope the practice will be effectually stopped, or fatal consequences must ensue. . . .[42]

In meeting the demands, every resource had to be tapped to fill the ranks in Continental service, required by Congress, which called for six new regiments to complete the quota; the ranks of the nine regiments had also to be filled,[43] but this could not be done immediately. Smallpox had taken its toll and re-enlistments were needed. Henry pointed out the overall perplexities to Lee, March 20, 1777:

"Every possible method has been taken to hasten the march of the new Levys . . . I've sent express twice to each colonel, and besides have had public advertisements repeatedly in the papers . . . Two thirds of the Continental Recruits are enlisted, but in broken Quotas. Our three Battalions are more than half

[39] *Ibid.*, I, pp. 511–512–513.
[40] *Ibid.*, I, pp. 207–208.
[41] *Ibid.*, I, p. 489.
[42] *Ibid.*, I, p. 515. See Governor Henry's proclamation, Henry, *Henry*, I, p. 538.
[43] *Ibid.*, I, pp. 510–511.

full." He told Lee he opposed the enlistments for Georgia permitted by the Assembly, and it had "greatly hurt" Virginia's quota.

Added to Washington's need for recruits were the troops necessary for strengthening the forts. A message from one of the outposts told that "a fellow called the 'Dragging Canoe' has seceded from the nation of Cherokees and with 400 warriors has followed his fortune, lying in the woods and making war on us notwithstanding the peace made with Colonel Christian." Governor Henry ordered "three hundred militia" on that service from the neighborhood of Fort Pitt for destroying Pluggy's Town.[44] He wrote further: "Five swift sailing Boats are gone for arms to the West Indies," and "a French ship and two Briggs" had lately arrived with "warlike stores." He "sent to purchase them," he notified Lee, saying, "Perhaps we may arm our own Troops & some others, especially if the importation (that he had solicited) succeeds."

Governor Henry was not satisfied with the way things were being run in Congress. His fear of attack on the Eastern Shore of Virginia was no doubt occasioned by the bands of "plundering Tories along the Bay" and because of the reports of the movements of the British Navy.

In the meantime the success of General Stark and the New England soldiers in routing Burgoyne in August brought Governor Henry reason to rejoice. Later, on October 7, 1777, near Saratoga, a victorious battle ensued, and on the 17th, under Col. Dan Morgan, a Virginian, there followed the surrender of Burgoyne's army.[45] General Howe, who had moved his troops from New Jersey to New York in an endeavor to engage Washington, left New York in August and with his 18,000 troops embarked for Chesapeake Bay. Moving up the bay, he landed and advanced in the direction of Philadelphia. Washington, with only 11,000 troops, encountered Howe at Brandywine in September, and although it was a severe battle, it left the British occupying Philadelphia. An attack was made on Howe at Germantown on October 4, ending in a fierce, unsuccessful struggle due to the fog, which prevented further fall and winter attacks. In December Washington went into winter quarters at Valley Forge,[46] during which

[44] *Ibid.*, I, p. 514.
[45] *Ibid.*, I, p. 531.
[46] *Ibid.*, I, p. 532.

time his army suffered greatly from cold and hunger and from lack of supplies.

In January, Governor Henry had learned to his dismay of the failure of the Quartermaster and Commissary departments to provide the necessaries for the army. "Congress itself never appeared more impotent, nor its members more neglectful of their duties, and at its sittings at York, in Pennsylvania, it was often difficult to secure a quorum."[47] Added to this danger was the serious depreciation of the currency, both State and Continental, which without taxation had put a strain on the progress of the war. At the last meeting of the Assembly, seeing the need to "sustain the credit of the State," Governor Henry had favored taxation,[48] but he hated to place a further burden on the people. He therefore had continued the use of paper money as specie, and relied on export as a basis of credit. But the blockade by the British was having its effect. Conditions had taken a turn for the worse, and in Pennsylvania, where Howe's troops and Washington's were stationed, farm commodities were purchased with British gold instead of paper money.[49]

These alarming conditions were acutely felt by General Washington during the winter of 1777–1778, at Valley Forge. By actual count "there were three thousand men in camp unfit for duty, because they were barefoot and otherwise naked."[50] Washington wrote Governor Henry from Valley Forge, February 19, 1778, of "the melancholy prospect before us, with respect to supplies of provisions" which induced him to trouble him:

> . . . The situation of the Commissary's Department, and of the Army in consequence, is more deplorable than you can easily imagine. We have frequently suffered temporary want & great inconveniences, and for several days past, we have experienced little less than a famine in Camp; and have had much cause to dread a general meeting and dispersion. Our future prospects are if possible still worse. The Magazines laid up, as far as my information reaches, are insignificant, totally incompetent to our necessities, and from every appearance, there has been heretofore so astonishing a deficiency in providing, that unless the most vigorous and effectual measures are at once, everywhere adopted, the language is not too strong to declare, that we shall not be able to make another Campaign.

[47] *Ibid.*, I, p. 553.
[48] *Ibid.*, I, p. 537, See his letter to Senator Lee.
[49] Henry, *Henry,* op. cit., I, p. 554; Irving's *Life of Washington,* III, p. 348.
[50] Shelby Little, *George Washington,* op. cit., p. 218.

> To what causes this is to be attributed; whether to an ill-timed and too general revolution in the Department, in the midst of a Campaign, to its being placed in improper hands, or to a diminution of resources, and increased difficulties in the means of procuring, or to a combination of all these circumstances, I shall not undertake to decide. . . . I address myself to you; convinced that our alarming distresses will engage your most serious consideration, and that the full force of that zeal and vigor you have manifested upon every other occasion, will now operate for our relief, in a matter that so nearly affects the very existence of our contest. . . .[51]

In the plight of Washington as he faced Howe, and the melancholy prospects of conducting a war without supplies and provisions because of the negligence and incompetence of Congress in leaving vacant for three months the post of the Quartermaster General, Governor Henry and General Washington must have found themselves sorely tried.

Disturbed over Washington's description of the distress of the troops, and having had an appraisal from Francis L. Lee from the Committee of Congress regarding the state of affairs, Mr. Henry wrote Lee, January 20, 1778, scoring the inefficiency of the quartermaster and commissary departments:

> Gentlemen: Francis Lightfoot Lee Esqr's. Letter for the Committee on the Subject of provisions filled me with Concern & Astonishment. I applied to the Deputy Commissary General to furnish some active persons for throwing an instant Supply of Provisions to the Army to answer the present Exigency. I was told by him that he could get none such immediately, but he would write to his Deputy to do the Business.
>
> I thought this plan by no means satisfactory, For in the Northwestern parts of the State in that Deputy's Quarter, I found, upon Enquiry, that Eight or ten thousand Hogs & several thousand fine Beeves might have been had very lately in a few Counties convenient to the Camp. In order therefore to avoid blending my Transactions with the Commissary's & to give Dispatch & Efficiency to the measure, I employed Abraham Hite, Thomas Hite & James Barbour Esq[rs], Gentlemen of Character, to purchase instantly Beef, or Pork, if Beef could not be had, to the amount of ten thousand pounds, & drive it to Camp in the most expeditious manner, and advanced them the Cash. I have also directed Colonel Simpson to seize two thousand Bushels of Salt on the Eastern Shore, & send to the Head of Elk for the

---

[51] Henry, *Henry*, III, pp. 148–149.

Grand army, & to reserve a thousand more to answer further orders that may become necessary.

A Galley is also ordered to carry 600 Bushels along the Western Shore to Elk for the same purpose. In the article of flour I have not meddled, thinking from Mr. Lee's Letter that it was not wanting. By these Several Steps, the best which in the sudden Exigency could be taken, I hope a temporary Supply may be obtained.

But Gentlemen I cannot forbear some Reflections on this Occasion, which I beg you will be pleased to lay before Congress as the Sentiments of the Executive Body of this State. It is with the deepest Concern that the Business of Supplying Provisions for the grand army, is seen to fall into a State of uncertainty & Confusion. And while that Executive hath been more than once called upon to make up for Deficiencys in that Department, no Reform in seen to take place. Altho' a great Abundance of Provisions might have been procured from Virginia; yet no Animadversions that I know of, have been made upon the Conduct of those whose Business it was to forward it to the Army. In this Situation of things Intelligence is given to me that from this State it is expected most of the Supplies must be drawn. What may be inferred from this, I do not know. If any kind of Superintendance or Controul over the Commissariate is meant, Congress will please to recollect that the Gentlemen in that Office are not amenable to me. If it is expected that friendly Assistance should be given, I am happy in saying this has been anticipated. Large loans of Flour, Meat and Salt have been made from time to time to great amount, nor will they be withheld but from the most absolute necessity. But I earnestly desire that it may be understood and remembered, once for all, that the Executive power here has nothing to do with the Commissary's Business. That it holds itself guiltless of all the mischief which in future may arise from Delinquency in that office.

It will indeed be unworthy the character of a Zelous American to entrench himself within the strict line of Official duty, and there quietly behold the starving and dispersion of the American Army. The Genius of this Country is not of that Cast.

I do not wish to avoid any Labour which may serve the general Interest and which cannot be executed better by others. But I have the Mortification to know that the present business I have directed will be executed with great Loss to the Public. The pressing occasion puts the price of meat &c. in the power of wicked, avaricious and disaffected men. The value of money will be more and more lessened, the means of supporting public Credit counteracted and defeated. I will not enumerate further the Evils which must follow from suffering Business of this vast import to remain in the Channel where it is now going. Let it suffice to say that this Country abounds with the provisions for which the army is said to be almost starving, particularly that part of it nearest the Camp.

The Executive has no authority over or Connection with the Commissariate. The temporary supply ordered to Camp concludes the Interference which is made in that Business, & is kept as a distinct and Separate Transaction. But if in the Course of future events it should become at any time necessary that the Commissariate should receive any aid within the line of the Executive power of this State, it will be afforded with the greatest pleasure—yet in such a case it is much to be wished that as early notice as possible may be given of such necessity.

The pain which Government feels on this occasion, & which is generally diffused throughout this State, for the melancholy, the perilous situation of the American Army will be relieved when a Reform takes place in that Department, from mismanagement in which have flowed Evils threatening the existence of American Liberty.

I beg leave Gentlemen to apologize for the Freedom of this Letter. Congress will please to be assured of the most perfect Regard of every member of the Executive of Virginia. But that Body would be wanting in the Duty they owe to the great Council of America & to their Country, if they concealed any of their Sentiments on a Subject so alarming as the present. The Honor and Credit of that great Council are conceived to be deeply concerned in rectifying what is wrong in these matters, and nothing but the highest Regard & most anxious Care to preserve that Honor from aspersion, should extort these painful observations from me.

I pray for the prosperity & Happiness of Congress as the Guardians of America, & with the greatest Esteem

I am Gentlemen,
Your very Humble & most obedt. Servant,
P. Henry.[52]

Stronger powers, in the meantime, had been given the Governor by the Assembly in the fall of 1777; his suggestion for a tax was allowed to redeem the paper money[53] that had been issued, thereby stabilizing the currency.[54] Stronger powers were also given the Governor to impress whatever articles or provisions

---

[52] Henry, *Henry*, I, pp. 554–555–556–557.
[53] Henry, *Henry*, op. cit., I, p. 538–539; Hening: *Statutes at Large*, IX, p. 349.
[54] *Ibid.*, I, p. 539.

were needed for the troops.[55] He immediately issued a proclamation pointing to the needs of the army and called upon the people to pen up and feed as many cattle as could be spared to be ready for the army drive in May, June and July.[56] Measures for instant relief were also adopted. Moreover, Governor Henry, being dissatisfied with the inefficiency of the purchasing agent, John Moore, appointed by Congress for Virginia, discharge Moore and selected John Hawkins of Hanover, a man he knew "in every way fitted for the business."[57] Reporting his actions to Congress for their approval, Henry supplied Hawkins with the money and ordered him "to engage and forward with the utmost dispatch to the army, as much beef and bacon as their wants may require." Concerning Moore, Henry wrote Richard Lee, April 7, 1778:

> I am really shocked at the management of Congress in this Department. John Moore's appointment gave me the most painful feelings. Good God! Our fate committed to a man utterly unable to perform the task assigned him! Raw, inexperienced, without weight, consequence, or acquaintance with men or business; called into action at a time when distinguished talent only can save an army from perishing. I tell you, & I grieve at it, Congress will lose the respect due–but I forbear. Tis my business to exert all my powers for the Common Good. I must not be depended on for anything in that line if Hawkins is rejected by Congress. If he is continued, pray supply him with plenty of money. He is really superior to any one in that way, & of established credit to any amount. . . . [58]

John Hawkins did not live long, but his genius and qualifications were noted in a letter to Governor Henry, written by Jefferson with reference to the British prisoners held in Virginia: "I am mistaken, if, for the animal subsistence of the troops hitherto, we are not principally indebted to the genius and exertions of Hawkins, during the very short time he lived after his appointment to the department by your board. His eye immediately pervaded the State, it was reduced at once to a regular machine, to a system, and the whole put into movement and animation by the fiat of a comprehensive mind.[59]

Thus, in this single appointment, can be seen "the zeal and

---

[55] *Ibid.*, I, pp. 539–552.
[56] *Ibid.*, I, pp. 538–558; See *Executive Journal for 1777–1778*, p. 223.
[57] *Ibid.*, I, p. 559.
[58] *Ibid.*, I, pp. 559–560.
[59] *Ibid.*, op. cit., I, p. 561, *The Writings of Jefferson*, I, p. 215.

vigor" of Governor Henry that "contributed largely to the continued existence of the American army during their bitter experience at Valley Forge, if indeed he did not prevent its disbanding."[60]

The disorder in the department of the Quartermaster-General was corrected by Washington himself, in his appointment of General Nathaniel Greene.[61] Expediency and coordination soon followed, with similar changes made in the Commissariat. The spring of 1778 brought better prospects for Washington's campaign. Baron Von Steuben was appointed Inspector General and drillmaster of the troops and fought side by side with Washington.

Intelligence had reached France, through our commissioners, of the results of the battles of Saratoga and Germantown, and the French Court was now ready to acknowledge the independence of the United States by signing a treaty. The treaties of alliance, amity and commerce with France were concluded on February 6, 1778.[62] Governor Henry received this message from the delegates in Congress: "In general we find that his most Christian Majesty has been governed by principles of magnanimity and true generosity, taken no advantages of our circumstances, but acting as if we were in the plentitude of power and in the greatest security . . . with a strong Army, we shall, under God, be perfectly secure, and it will probably compel Great Britain to a speedy recognition of our Independence."[63]

The British Ministry, hearing of the treaty with France, determined on sterner measures against those resisting the British upon land or sea. An act was passed calling for the arrest of all persons suspected of crimes, piracy or treason. The news of the treaty, ratified by Congress on May 4, 1778, lessened the tension and brought encouragement to the American cause. However, Washington's engagements of the previous year had greatly weakened his army and reduced his supplies. The needs of General Gates had caused him to dispatch his fine rifle corps of Virginians from the valley, formerly under Colonel Morgan, for reinforcement. A part of the artillery was also furnished Gates.[64] Beginning with the January 1777 campaign, Washington's progress was slow; he gave battle only twice—at Brandywine and German-

---

[60] *Ibid.*, I, p. 562.
[61] *Ibid.*, I, p. 561.
[62] Burnett, *The Continental Congress*, p. 332.
[63] *Ibid.*, p. 333; Henry, *Henry*, I, p. 533.
[64] Henry, *Henry*, I, p. 530.

town. But he was patient and his spirit did not give way—not even at the sight of his suffering troops at Valley Forge: "That Good God, for man's welfare, and His own purposes, seems at times to have worked slowly, in order perhaps that the material with which He worked might attain to the fibre and fineness and temper requisite to His purpose."[65] In Washington's hours of trial, many of the letters that brought him fresh resolve were those signed by the Governor of Virginia, P. Henry.

Space will not permit coverage of Patrick Henry's full participation as Governor in helping to win the Revolution. The student of history should read his many letters during this period to appreciate his awesome burdens. He had not only to supply Washington's army, but also to strengthen the forts, protect the settlers and equip the forces marching to Kentucky with quantities of provisions, lead and powder, and a great number of pack horses for the officers who were to command these outposts. Responsible for the over-all movements, including the vast western boundaries which were at arms with the Indians, he was placed in a singular position of responsibility and anxiety. Under such a strain, he was "so harassed by the great load of continental Business" thrown on him that he was ready to sink under his "burden" for his "strength" would "not suffice."[66] It is not surprising to find him with recurrent periods of fever in which his physician required him to rest.

But even then, his letters continued to go out, written in his singular style and direction. This is at variance with the statements made by Madison's biographers,[67] "upon the testimony of Mr. Jefferson, that his (James Madison's) skill in foreign languages and readiness with his pen caused him to be so useful as an interpreter, and in preparing papers for the Governor, 'that he bore with many the title of *secretary* as well as *councillor* of state.' "[68]

[65] Embrey, *History of Fredericksburg, Virginia*, p. 114.

[66] Henry, *Henry*, I, p. 560.

[67] Henry, *Henry*, op. cit., I, pp. 616–617; Rives *Madison*, I, pp. 189–190.

[68] Brant, *Madison, The Virginia Revolutionist, 1751–1780*, p. 29. Madison was born March 16, 1752. He became a member of the Council, January 14, 1778; Henry, *Henry*, op. cit., I, p. 616. He married Dolley (Payne) Todd, Henry's cousin. Patrick Henry's sister, Susanna Henry, married Madison's kinsman, Thomas Madison. (The Marshall Family, p. 146, paragraph E.) Agatha Strother m. John Madison, cousin of President Madison.
Issue:
1. Bishop James Madison b. 1749 m. Miss James
2. Richard Madison m. Preston
3. Thomas Madison m. Susanna Henry, Sister of Patrick Henry.

This is another misstatement of facts from the pen of Mr. Jefferson. The Journal of March 26, 1778, records that "The Board having experienced very great inconvenience . . . from the want of a faithful and capable person to act as secretary and interpreter of the French and other foreign languages . . . they advise the Governor to appoint Mr. Charles Bellini to the office of interpreter and secretary for foreign communications, and to apply to the next Assembly to make the office permanent: which was done."[69] It is hardly likely that the great patriot would have trusted his thinking and his policies at this critical period to young Madison, who, when he became a member of the Council, was only 26. "As to the preparation by Mr. Madison of the papers issued by Governor Henry, a comparison of the papers during his service as councillor with these of the other years of Mr. Henry's service, will demonstrate that there is nothing to show that they were by different hands."[70] His letters follow the same style and pattern, and in this short period accounted for—even with the missing letter books—it can be seen how he used every effort at his command in an over-all strategy, covering every department, to meet the exigencies of war. In this, the husbands of his sisters took no small part. No one will question the arduous services rendered by Governor Henry's five brothers-in-law,[71] nor their

---

4. Gabriel Madison b. 1804 m. Meriam Lewis b. 1759 d. 1845 in Jessamine County Kentucky.
5. Roland Madison m. a daughter of Gen. Andrew Lewis. (Information, Miss Mary Winn Shelton, Rural Plains, Hanover County)

[69] Henry, *Henry*, I, p. 617.

[70] *Ibid.*

[71] Patrick Henry's brothers-in-law who had special assignments in the Revolution were the following: Colonel (later General) William Campbell, first husband of his favorite sister, Elizabeth, married April 2, 1776, at the home of Col. Samuel Meredith, "Rocky Mills," Hanover County, (Correction by Miss Nelly Preston, made three years after writing her book, from records of her niece.) Their only surviving child, Sarah, when 15 years old, married Francis Preston, son of Colonel William Preston of "Greenfield" in Botetourt County and of "Smithfield" in Montgomery County. Thus, banding together the Preston patriots in the same cause with Patrick Henry. Sarah Buchanan Campbell married General Francis Preston—born about 1762—second son of Colonel William Preston and his wife, Susanna Smith Preston of Hanover County. General Francis Preston was a Lawyer, a member of the Senate of Virginia, Congressman from Virginia, and Brigadier General in the War of 1812. He married Sarah Buchanan Campbell, daughter of General William Campbell who commanded at King's Mountain. She was a niece of Patrick Henry, her mother was Elizabeth Henry, daughter of John and Sarah Henry, of Hanover County. Elizabeth Henry married, first, General William Campbell, of Fincastle, Virginia, and afterwards General William Russell. She was called in her later years "Madame Russell." General Francis Preston and

unswerving loyalty in the cause. They were given, and accepted, grave responsibility. Gen. William Campbell, the husband of his

---

his wife, Sarah Buchanan Campbell Preston, had ten children, six daughters and four sons:

1. William Campbell Preston, greatly distinguished as an orator and advocate, lived in Columbia, South Carolina. He was twice married—first to Miss Mary E. Coalter, and then to Miss L. P. Davis.
2. Eliza Henry Preston, married General Edward C. Carrington, an officer of distinction in the War of 1812.
3. Susanna Smith Preston, married her cousin, Governor James McDowell, of "Cherry Grove," Rockbridge county.
4. Sarah Buchanan Preston, married her cousin, Governor John B. Floyd.
5. Sophonisba Preston, married her cousin, Dr. Robert Jefferson Breckinridge, who was born at "Cabell's Dale," Kentucky. His mother was Miss Cabell. He was a lawyer, a Presbyterian minister and a writer of note. His second wife was also a cousin, Mrs. Virginia Hart Shelby, widow of Alfred Shelby, son of Governor Isaac Shelby of Kentucky, and daughter of Nathaniel Hart, whose wife was Susanna Preston, sister of General Francis Preston. This Nathaniel Hart was the son of Nathaniel Hart, the Kentucky pioneer, who was born in Hanover county, Virginia, in 1734.
6. Maria T. C. Preston, married her relative, John M. Preston of "Seven Mile Ford," Smyth county, Virginia, from whom Miss Nelly C. Preston is descended.
7. Thomas L. Preston married first his cousin, Miss Elizabeth Watts, and second Miss Ann Saunders.
8. Margaret Brown Preston married Wade Hampton, Governor of South Carolina, a Lieutenant-General in the Confederate Army and a wealthy planter.
9. Charles H. C. Preston married Mary Beale.
10. John S. Preston, of Charleston, South Carolina, a Brigadier General in the Confederate Army, married Caroline Hampton, daughter of Wade Hampton, Senior.

At General Campbell's death, Elizabeth married her husband's good friend, General William Russell in 1783. Other brothers-in-law of Patrick Henry, were Colonels William Christian, Samuel Meredith, Valentine Wood, Thomas Madison, Luke Bowyer, besides the kinsmen among the Winstons and the Flemings. There were also other patriotic connections. Patrick Henry's niece, Agatha Madison, married the hero at Buford's Defeat–Colonel Henry Bowyer. Their son, John, married Lucy Lewis, daughter of General Andrew Lewis. Another niece, Martha Wood, daughter of Lucy and Colonel Valentine Wood, married Major Stephen Southall, a distinguished soldier in the Revolution, and so on to distinguished men in the Civil War, where we see General Joseph H. Johnston and General Wade Hampton. William Henry, was a major of militia. Patrick Henry's daughter, Martha, married Colonel John Fontaine. Elizabeth's husband, Colonel Philip Aylett, was appointed assistant commissary of Virginia. Anne Henry married Judge Spencer Roane of the Court of Appeals of Virginia. Their son, Patrick Henry Roane, was the eminent young United States Senator who lost his life in the Richmond Theater fire. Through the illustrious lineage of Patrick Henry can be traced many distinguished men and soldiers in the Revolution. See Robert D. Stoner, *A Seed Bed of the Republic.*

sister, Elizabeth, in August 1776, took command of the First Virginia Regiment[72] in Williamsburg, protecting the capital. On September 30, 1780, with 400 men from Washington County, Virginia, and other mounted men and riflemen making in all 960, Colonel Campbell, as commander, left the Watauga and with provisions of mostly corn and maple sugar, each man with a tin cup and a blanket, they marched "fifty miles in eighteen hours through mud, rain, and darkness."[73] At King's Mountain, October 7, he attacked the British left wing under Col. Patrick Ferguson and "after a stubborn fight in which Ferguson fell, he killed or captured the entire British army consisting of 1,105 men."[74]

His wife, whom he had met in Williamsburg while visiting her sister, Anne (Mrs. William Christian) and her brother (Patrick Henry), was said to be a toast among the young officers. "She was twenty-six years old, above medium height, with a most attractive face and imposing presence. Both in person and intellect she resembled her brother. She had the same fertile and vivid imagination, the same ready command of language and aptness of illustration, the same flexibility of voice and grace of elocution, and the same play of features expressive of every phase of feeling."[75] Colonel Campbell (later general), was said to be of "a superb physique, six feet two inches high, straight and soldierly in his bearing, quiet and polished in his manners, and always deferential and chivalric toward women. He had the fair complexion and blue eyes which betokened his Scotch descent."[76] Their grandson, William Campbell Preston, when eighteen, visited the White House in 1812. Of this visit to his cousin Dolley, and her husband, President James Madison, the following is recorded:

"She advanced straight to me, and, extending her left hand, said: 'Are you William Campbell Preston, the son of my old friend and most beloved kinswoman, Sally Campbell?' I assented. She said: 'Sit down my son; for you are my son, and I am the first person who ever saw you in this world.' After presenting him to the President, she introduced him to three young ladies and commended him to their special attention, 'Miss Maria Mayo, Miss Worthington, and your kinswoman, Miss Sally Coles. Now,

---

[72] Henry, *Henry*, I, pp. 330–350; Preston, *Paths of Glory*, pp. 111–112–113.

[73] Henry, *Henry*, op. cit., II, p. 66; Draper, *King's Mountain and its Heroes*.

[74] *Ibid.*, II, p. 66. According to the resolutions offered in the House, thanking General Campbell and his men.

[75] *Ibid.*, I, p. 330.

[76] *Ibid.*

young ladies, this young gentleman, if not my son, is my protégé, and I commend him to your special consideration. With you he shall be my guest at the White House as long as he remains in the city. I am his mother's kinswoman, and stand towards him in the relation of a parent.' "[77] He became a member of the United States Senate. "He was maternally related to Patrick Henry and equal to him in oratory. He was the friend of Washington Irving; they made a tramp together in Scotland. He relinquished Senatorial honor rather than abide dictation. He accepted the presidency of the University of South Carolina. He was a Classical scholar and had classic features."[78] It appears that he evinced the same gifts as were observed in his great uncle: "His manners—his wit—his oratory, must all be traditional. One of his distinguished contemporaries mentioned to us, his personification when in circuit, in playfulness, of Mercutio, at a little country inn. Although he had often seen the character portrayed on the stage, he never comprehended it before. A new and sudden blaze, was thrown over the conception of Shakespeare."[79]

The Governor had many kinsmen as well as brothers-in-law holding responsible duties, with whom he kept in close touch. The records show that they were able defenders in the cause. Those dispatched to the frontiers were long-experienced "Over Mountain" men and were no easy prey for Indians or redcoats. William Christian, like William Campbell, had also accompanied Dunmore on his early expeditions. He was lieutenant colonel of the First Virginia Regiment.[80] Later, Governor Henry made him commander-in-chief of all the forces raised for the Indian expedition, with Evan Shelby as his major.[81] Already Charles Lewis and his minutemen had been dispatched after hearing of the Cherokee outbreaks in Clinch Valley. They had been incited by the British emissaries, Stuart, Cameron and Gist. Colonel Christian, after destroying the Indian village, arranged a conference to be held with the warriors. He and William Preston and Major Shelby were appointed commissioners to arrange the terms of the treaty to protect the settlers in Kentucky as well as those living between the Holston River and the Cumberland Mountains.[82] The Gov-

---

77 Clark, *Life and Letters of Dolly Madison*, p. 140.
78 *Ibid.*, p. 295.
79 *Ibid.*, pp. 295–296, citing the Charleston Mercury, May 26, 1860.
80 Henry, *Henry*, I, pp. 320–350.
81 *Ibid.*, I, p. 462.
82 *Ibid.*, I, p. 464.

ernor and his Council completed the treaty, and the commissioners met at Heaton's Station May 26, 1777, where Colonel Christian put into winter quarters.[83] Several chiefs came, but "Dragging Canoe" failed to attend the conference, neither would he make peace. However, hostilities were delayed for a time when a former missionary, James Robertson, was appointed commissioner to dwell among the Cherokees as directed in the treaty. But, as Patrick Henry predicted in his letter, trouble with the Shawanese broke out near Pittsburgh in the spring.

Governor Henry expressed his concern in his letter to Col. William Preston, Lieutenant of Montgomery County, written February 19, 1778. The Indians were being continually incited to attack[84] the Kentucky settlers as well as those settlements east of the Ohio. They were encouraged in their hostilities by British agents[85] who were attempting to divide the country at a time when Governor Henry was making every effort to keep Virginia's quota of troops in the field. The gravity of the situation culminated in the murder of Cornstalk,[86] the mighty chief of the Shawanese and "King of the Northern Confederacy," called one of the greatest of Indian chieftains.

The following letter shows Patrick Henry's vigilance and judgment in his instructions to protect the frontiers:

> Williamsburg February 19, 1778
>
> Colonel William Preston, County
> Lieutenant of Montgomery County.
>
> Sir: The murder of the Shawaneese Indians will no doubt bring on Hostilitys with that people. In order to ward off the Stroke which may be expected, it is necessary to have every Gun in your County put into good order and got ready for action. Lead may be had from the Mines. An order for 1 lb for each man of your Militia accompanys this, Powder it is said is plenty among you. If it can't be had otherwise send to Richmond for it. Let trusty scouts be kept in constant action towards the Enemy's Country to discover their movements, and give information of approaching danger. Proper stockades or Defenses to receive the more helpless part of the people, should be provided in time, and fixed in places judiciously chosen, that the able men may be at liberty to assail the Enemy and range the Frontier

---

[83] *Ibid.*

[84] Henry, *Henry*, op. cit., I, p. 569; Regarding the attacks, see Withers' *Border Warfare* for an account of the Indian depredations upon the Virginians.

[85] *Ibid.*, I, p. 571.

[86] *Ibid.*, I, pp. 573–574.

as occasions may require. These Stockades should be provided at the expense of your people, and are not to be garrisoned, only as particular exigencies may make necessary. I think no neighborhood ought to be without one where the Enemy can possibly penetrate. In case of Attack you are to draw out such Force from the Militia as you judge sufficient to chastise the Invaders. Let the pursuit of scalping parties be close, hot and determined; for if vengeance is taken on the foremost Partys others will be intimidated. I wish to reinforce Captain Arbuckle's Garrison with a Company of 50 men, officered in the usual manner, from your County, and that they should march thither without delay.

Volunteers enlisted for this business to serve 6 months in it, I would prefer. But if they are not to be got without loss of Time, let the Militia be drafted. For I expect the Indians very shortly on the Frontiers. I beg the favor of you to consult with Colonel Fleming, on the propriety of establishing a post to preserve the Communication with Fort Randolph. Perhaps some place near the mouth of Elk river might answer this purpose, and also check the Inroads of the Savages, if the Garrison was alert & diligent to intercept their partys.

I am at a loss for Officers in Green Brier, and wish for a recommendation from your County Court of such as are proper. That place will be attacked it's likely, and if no other expedient can be found I must fill up the Commissions in Council, where the Individuals cannot be known. Rockbridge is in the same situation. Will you please to assist with such information as you can give in finding fit persons for Officers. I wish the Lead to be carefully preserved for the purpose of defence, and not given to the men, but as occassion calls for it, except in exposed places, where people must be trusted with it. I think the Garrison proposed near Elk need not consist of more than 60 men; but I submit it to you and Colonel Fleming to do for the best, being on the spot.

You will perceive that my views go no further than defensive operations. I know how impossible it is to render them completely effectual against the Enemy you have to oppose. But offensive measures set on foot against these Indians at this time, after their late treatment, would be too full of Injustice to escape general execration. Policy and even self preservation may 'ere long call for such measures; But even then it may be doubted whether provisions purchased in your parts would answer the Design.

Having now done everything which I can forsee to be necessary for protecting the Frontiers, I must tell you, Sir, that I really Blush for the occasion of this War with the Shawaneese. I doubt not but you detest the vile assassins who have brought it on us at this Critical Time, when our whole Force was wanted in another Quarter. But why are they not brot to Justice? Tis a few wicked men who committed the Murder. Why do not those among you of a contrary character drag them to Justice? Shall this precedent establish the right of involving Virginia in War, whenever any one in the Back Country shall please? I need not argue to shew you Sir, the fatal tendency of such conduct. You see it and and I fear your Country will feel indiscriminately that misery which ought to Visit only the guilty Authors of the mischief. Some say the people of your Country will not suffer the apprehension of the murderers. I desire it may be remembered that if the Frontier people will not submit to the Laws, but thus set them at defiance, they will not be considered as entitled to the protection of Government; and were it not for the miserable condition of many with you, I should demand the delivery of the offenders previous to any other step. For where is this wretched Business to end? The Cherokees, the Delawares, and every other tribe may be set on in this manner, this Spring for what I know. Is not this the work of Torys? No man but an Enemy to American Independence will do it, and thus oblige our people to be hunting after Indians in the woods, instead of facing General Howe in the field. Search into the matter, & depend upon it the Murderers are Torys. The Honor of your Country is at stake, and it is Time to decide whether these Villains are to meet with punishment, or whether the greater number will espouse their Interests. I desire you to the utmost, at all hazards, & to the last extremity, to support and assist the Civil Magistrate, in apprehending and bringing these Offenders to Justice, If the Shawaneese deserved Death because their countrymen have committed Hostilities, a Jury from the Vicinage will say so, and acquit the accused, who must be judged by their neighbours feeling the same resentments and passions with themselves. But they are Traitors I suspect, & agents for the Enemy, who have taken this method to find employment for the brave back woodsmen at home, and prevent their joining General Washington to strike a decisive stroke for Independency at this Critical Time.

Urge these things, Sir, with the warmth the subject demands; prepare your people for their own Defense against the Indians; to vindicate their honor from the rude attack now made on it; and let them be shown to the world as possessing the other Virtues which usually accompany Courage.

In the confidence that what I now press, I mean bringing the Murderers of the Indians to Justice, will be done, Government will lose no Time in lending its best aids to protect your Country. I fear something essential for the Frontier defense may have escaped me, But your part must be in concert with your

Neighbors to point out what yet remains to be done for your safety. If a reinforcement of 50 men and more is necessary at Fort Randolph, they will be sent when you and Colonel Fleming write to me. I have it much at Heart to bring the Indians to treat on the subject of our difference with them. Perhaps the Grenadier Squaw may be useful in this business. Please to confer on this matter with Colonel Fleming and let every possible effort be made to bring on a Treaty. The expences for the attempt, I will pay on demand. I forbear to mention particulars for beginning this work, as they must be better judged of on this Spot. But at all events try it vigorously.

Wishing safety to you & your people, I remain,

Sir,

Yr mo. hble servant,

P. Henry.

P.S. As there is no officer for Green Brier & 'tis an exposed place, I beg you to receive & distribute the Lead for that county. I will be glad to hear from you.

P. Henry

Colo Preston

2nd P. S. If you judge it best, suspend the sending the fifty men from your County to reinforce Capt. Arbuckle's Garrison 'til you write me. Fifty from Botetourt I've ordered at all Events, & wish the fifty to go from your County if you think it best.

P. Henry[87]

Similar letters were also sent to Col. John Fleming and to Washington County Lieutenant Charles Campbell. The request for 50 men from Botetourt, and 50 from Greenbrier County, to make up a communication post at Kelly's, and 50 from Rockbridge, were dispatched to Fort Randolph.[88] The "assaults of the savages" affected Governor Henry "most sensibly." He offered a reward for the murderer of the chief and made efforts to conciliate the Indians by appointing Andrew Lewis and John Walker to meet with the Shawanese, the Delawares and other tribes at Pittsburgh on July 23, and prevent further trouble. But the Shawanese, determined in their desire for revenge, declined the offer of peace, and in May attacked Fort Randolph, laying siege. But the fort was well guarded and they were driven off. They next raided Greenbrier County and the neighborhood of Lewisburg, but were repulsed. They moved on into the Wyoming Valley of Pennsylvania where they massacred the inhabitants.[89] Fort Randolph, as

[87] Henry, *Henry*, III, pp. 144–145–146–147–148.
[88] *Ibid.*, I, p. 577.
[89] *Ibid.*, I, p. 578.

well as the other two, might well have been captured, had Governor Henry not given orders the previous spring[90] to the lieutenants of the eight counties bordering Fort Pitt to embody as many of the militia as were needed by General Hand, and raised some four or five volunteer companies from Botetourt, Augusta and Greenbrier counties and marched them to Fort Randolph at Point Pleasant to be used by General Hand and Captain Arbuckle.[91]

On November 4, 1785, after the Revolution had ended, Colonel Christian wrote his sister:

> We should be happy enough only the Indians are very troublesome, having been continually in our country this Fall and killed several people. We can't go out in the least safety and expect times will be much worse next Spring and Summer as the Indians have refused the Treaty. As we are very near the frontier we can't think of staying here much longer. We intend to move off to Danville and continue there until some better prospects here. If we had peace here and a trade I should like Beargrass as it is the flower of all Kentucky.[92]

Colonel Christian again wrote:

> Indian affairs begin to be serious and my wife says she will go off from here. My situation is singular, having two frontier places to support. However, another stroke or two will at least move my wife and children and helpless negroes.[93]

The following spring Colonel Christian lost his life in a fight with the Indians. He was 43 years of age.

Regarding her husband's death, Mrs. Anne Christian wrote her brother, Patrick Henry, in September, 1786:

> When the fatal wound was given him he behaved with the greatest fortitude. He never murmured or complained the least, but said, 'My wound is mortal, tho' I hope to get home to my family before I die,' and when the men who carryd him had traveld till late in the night, he then made them stop & got off

[90] *Ibid.*, I, p. 570.

[91] Henry, *Henry*, op. cit., I, pp. 570–571; Executive Journal, p. 33.

[92] *My Life at Oxmoor*, Bullitt, Thomas W. My life at Oxmoor; life on a farm in Kentucky before the War. Privately printed. Louisville, Ky., John P. Morton & Co., cl. 911. p. 9–11. Roosevelt's *The Winning of the West*, Vol. III, pp. 76–77; Draper MSS., 37 J 178, W. C. Bullitt's "To the Voters of Beargrass," June 10, 1869; Draper MSS., 5ZZ 81, Through the courtesy of The Filson Club, Inc., Miss Dorothy Thomas Cullen, Librarian, Louisville, Ky.

[93] *Ibid.*, Draper MSS., 5ZZ 82. Courtesy, The Filson Club, Louisville, Ky.

the litter & rode on horseback 2 miles, but by the great loss of blood was unable to proceed, & had a second litter made in which he was carryd till he desired them to stop for him to rest awhile. He told a friend he was not at all afraid to meet death and died resigned to the will of God, that it would be very melancholy news for his family to hear, and then expired without a groan. They brought the dear remains home on the very day he told me at parting he expected to return.[94]

Patrick Henry's touching letter to his sister on hearing of Colonel Christian's death is worth preserving:

I am at a loss how to address you my dearest sister. Would to God I could say something to give relief to the dearest of women and sisters. My heart has felt in a manner new and strange to me, insomuch that while I am endeavoring to comfort you I want a comforter myself. I forbear to tell you how great was my love for my friend and brother. I turn my eyes to heaven, where he is gone, I trust, and adore with humility the unsearchable ways of that Providence which calls us off this stage of action at such time and in such manner as its wisdom and goodness directs. We can not see the reason of these dispensations now, but we may be assured they are directed by wisdom and mercy. This is one of the occasions that calls your and my attention back to the many precious lessons of piety given us by our honored parents, whose lives were indeed a constant lesson and worthy of imitation. This is one of the trying scenes in which the Christian is eminently superior to all others, and finds a refuge that no misfortune can take away. To this refuge let my dearest sister fly with humble resignation. I think I can see some traces of a kind Providence to you and the children in giving you a good son-in-law, so necessary at this time to take charge of your affairs. It gives me comfort to reflect on this. Pray tell Mr. Bullitt I wish to hear from him and to cultivate an intimacy with him, and that he may command any services from me. I could wish anything remained in my power to do for you or yours. And if at any time you think there is, pray let me know, and depend upon me to do it to the utmost. I need not tell you how much I shall value your letters, particularly now, for I am anxious to hear from you, and how every thing goes on in your affairs. As so few of our family are left, I hope we shall not fail to correspond frequently. It is natural for me to increase in affection to the survivors as the number decreases. I am pained on reflecting that my letters always are penned as dictated by the

[94] Henry, *Henry*, II, p. 478. Colonel Christian's wife died while returning from Antigua, and was buried at sea in the winter of 1790–91; Draper MSS.

> strongest love and affection to you, but that my actions have not kept pace. Opportunity's being wanting must be the excuse. For indeed, my dearest sister, you never knew how much I loved you and your husband. My heart is full. Perhaps I may never see you in this world. O may we meet in heaven, to which the merits of Jesus will carry those who love and serve him. Heaven will, I trust, give you its choicest comfort and preserve your family. Such is the prayer of him who thinks it his honor and pride to be
>
> Yr. Affct. Brother,
> P. Henry[95]

During Patrick Henry's administration as Governor in 1778, he faced more threats than those of General Howe, and the Indian uprisings on the frontiers. The arrival of the peace commissioners from Britain greatly disturbed him. They landed in New York June 6th and "found Sir Henry Clinton, who had superceded Lord Howe, in the act of evacuating the city. They at once set to work to win Congress from France, and did not hesitate to try bribery for the accomplishment of their purpose"[96] Governor Henry "realized that the patriot cause was on the brink of an awful precipice, from which the French alliance only could save it."[97] He wrote Richard H. Lee, June 13, "You will have a different game to play now with the commissioners. How comes Governor Johnstone there? I do not see how it comports with his past life. Surely Congress will never recede from our French friends. Salvation to America depends upon our holding fast our attachment to them. I shall date our ruin from the moment that it is exchanged for anything Great Britain can say or do. She can never be cordial with us. Baffled, defeated, disgraced by her colonies, she will ever meditate revenge. We can find no safety but in her ruin, or at least . . . purged by a revolution, which shall wipe from existence the present king with his connexions, and the present system, with those who aid and abet it."[98]

Congress, however, declined the proposals of the commissioners the day before Patrick Henry wrote his letter. After a second effort failed, they tried to treat separately with the colonies, and "issued a manifesto addressed to Congress, to the *Provincial Assemblies*, and to all the inhabitants of the *Colonies*, offering to treat with assemblies separately, or with the colonies jointly

[95] *Ibid., My Life at Oxmoor*, Courtesy, The Filson Club, Louisville, Ky.
[96] Henry, *Henry*, I, p. 563.
[97] *Ibid.*
[98] *Ibid.*, I, p. 565.

. . ."[99] But the state assemblies were no more impressed than was Congress with their "olive-branch" proposals. The British Government, anticipating the failure of the commissioners beforehand, entered upon a more "cruel prosecution" of the war, "in which the Indians along the western and southern frontier were to play an important part."[100] At Detroit, the seat of the British Governor, Henry Hamilton's efforts to confederate the western tribes and incite them to massacre the Americans were stepped up. Congress, aware of Hamilton's actions, sent the Indian fighter, General McIntosh, to Indian country, at which time Patrick Henry ordered the militia of those counties joining Pittsburgh placed at his command. But the expedition proceeded no further than the Tuscarawas River where Fort Laurens, garrisoned by 150 men, was set up under Col. John Gibson. The rest of the troops returned to Pittsburgh. The expedition was unsuccessful, however, and the fort was abandoned the next year.[101]

"The British occupation of the country between the Ohio and Mississippi was secured by a chain of forts, reaching from Detroit, at the mouth of Lake Huron, to Kaskaskia, very near where the river of that name empties into the Mississippi, above the mouth of the Ohio. These forts were not only military stations, whose garrisons kept the country in subjection, but they were store-houses at which supplies were gathered, which were used in securing the friendship of the native tribes, and in furnishing them with those murderous raids upon the frontiers which have made infamous the British conduct of the American war."[102]

Governor Henry kept a keen eye on the dangers from these outposts. The most far-reaching event during his administration, and his most important decision, was to send George Rogers Clark with a contingent of troops to conquer the Illinois territory. Clark himself, as commander of the Kentucky militia, had seen the evil influence of the British over the Indians in the Kentucky country, and it was for the relief of this settlement that he had come to see Governor Henry in the first place.

Clark saw that "the Americans were as sorely pressed by the English from the seaside, as they were by the Indians from the western wilderness."[103] He discussed the importance of capturing

---

[99] *Ibid.*, p. 566.
[100] *Ibid.*, I, pp. 567–568.
[101] *Ibid.*, I, p. 579.
[102] *Ibid.*, I, pp. 581–582.
[103] *Ibid.*, I, p. 583.

these posts held by the British in the Illinois country, and laid his plan before Governor Henry. The Governor reportedly hesitated at first, no doubt because of the expedition already engaged by General McIntosh. He was probably also sizing up Clark's competence. He decided Clark was the man to send for the job, and when Congress, in the meantime, had planned its own expedition and had requested Governor Henry to raise 2,000 militia, 5,000 horses, ammunition, provisions, military stores, clothing &c. &c. before the winter, the Governor discouraged the idea in his letter written July 8, 1778, as utterly impracticable at that season of the year; "the route they took"[104] and under the existing circumstances.[105] He probably did not like the idea of trusting to the judgment of Congress the selection of the next commander to conduct this most important campaign. He wrote the Virginia delegates in Congress that, feeling a "strong apprehension of incursions on the Frontier Settlements from the savages," the executive power of the state had commanded "Colonel George Rogers Clark on that service sometime last spring."[106] The expedition from Detroit was thought to have been canceled after Clark's operations.[107]

Realizing the importance of such a scheme, the Governor first held a conference with George Wythe, Mason and Jefferson. He later recommended that they take action in behalf of Clark's expedition, pointing to the weak garrison of Kaskaskia. "The Council, after some debate voted £1,200 to be given to George Rogers Clark to organize his expedition. The action was taken under warrant of the law passed by the General Assembly authorizing the Governor and Council to take all necessary means for the protection of the colonists.[108]

"Clark was summoned to attend the Council and was urged to accept the command. He tells us: 'It was far from my inclination at that time . . . . However I accepted it after being told the command of this little army was designed for me.' "[109] He was ordered to raise seven companies of soldiers, consisting of fifty men each. He set out from Williamsburg January 18, 1778, and with a force of 150 men reached Corn Island, at the falls of

---

[104] *Ibid.*, III, p. 230.

[105] *Ibid.*, III, pp. 180–181; See his letter to the President of Congress. Also *Ibid.*, III, p. 205.

[106] *Ibid.*, III, p. 200.

[107] *Ibid.*, II, p. 9.

[108] Chandler & Thames, *Colonial Virginia*, p. 326.

[109] Henry, *Henry*, op. cit., I, p. 584; Clark's *Campaign in the Illinois*, p. 23.

the Ohio. He captured Kaskaskia, and later took possession of Vincennes, which he lost but later recaptured from Hamilton, taking him prisoner.[110]

The bold adventures and the sufferings of Clark and his men in capturing the forts are a volume in themselves. But the particulars and the legality of Virginia's claim to this territory are discussed fully by William Wirt Henry. Hoping that "they may be brought to expel their British Masters, and become fellow citizens of a free State," Governor Henry sent Colonel Clark "some copies of the act of Government and Bill of Rights, together with the French Alliance. These will serve to show our new friends the ground upon which they are to stand, and the support to be expected from their countrymen in France. Equal liberty and happiness are the objects to a participation of which we invite them."[111] Such cordial assurance from Governor Henry must have encouraged the settlers. But Henry cautioned Clark: "I must observe to you that your situation is critical. Far detached from the body of your country, placed among French, Spaniards, and Indian Nations, strangers to our people, anxiously watching your actions and behavior, and ready to receive impressions favourable, or not so, of our Commonwealth and its Government, which impressions will be hard to remove, and will produce lasting good or ill effects to your country. These considerations will make you cautious and circumspect. I feel the delicacy and difficulty of your situation, but I doubt not your virtue will accomplish the arduous work with honor to yourself, and advantage to the Commonwealth. The advice and assistance of discreet good men will be highly necessary. For at the distance of your country, I cannot be consulted. General discretionary powers therefore are given you, to act for the best in all cases where these instructions are silent and the law has made no provision."[112]

The bulk of Governor Henry's instructions to Colonel Clark show his familiarity with all the troublesome aspects of Clark's journey—the tribes; the rivers; the forts and their defenses. His instructions covered every aspect of a successful campaign. He knew of the western country and the proper employment of the men in their approach to the French and Spanish, and to the

---

[110] Chandler & Thames, *Colonial Virginia,* pp. 327–328–329–330.

[111] Henry, *Henry,* III, p. 210. Read his full letter to Clark, beginning p. 209 and page 218. Also his letter to Col. John Todd, p. 212 and to Lieut-Col. John Montgomery, p. 216. Note also Clark's letter to Governor Henry, pp. 220 and 233.

[112] *Ibid.,* III, p. 211.

Indians. His humane admonishment was to win them over to the American side. It was no doubt Governor Henry's precisely prepared instructions, and Clark's execution of them, that accounted for the success of the expedition. Clark wrote Governor Henry, "Your instructions I shall pay implicit regard to, and hope to conduct myself in such a manner as to do honor to my country."[113] Thus do we see the "greatest military achievement in the history of America," through Clark's conquest of the Great Northwest Territory. An act passed by Parliament in 1774, known as the "Quebec Act," had annexed to the Province of Quebec all the territory between the Ohio and the Mississippi Rivers south of the Great Lakes.[114] This province, by remaining loyal to England throughout the Revolution, would have extended the boundaries of Quebec to include all this territory west of the Ohio as a British possession, and established it as the western boundary of the United Colonies. Today this territory would conceivably be a part of Canada.

But through the vision of Governor Patrick Henry, and the courage of George Rogers Clark, the states of Ohio, Indiana, Illinois, Michigan, Wisconsin and half of Minnesota became part of the United States of America.

So impressed was the Governor with the importance of Clark's expedition, that he wrote the Virginia delegates in Congress assuring them that he would give the necessary orders for Colonel Clark's cooperation in any expedition that Congress might be pursuing in the western country, pointing out: "Were it possible to secure the St. Lawrence, and prevent the English attempts up that river by seizing some post on it, peace with the Indians would seem to me to be secured.[115] Through an act passed by the Assembly, he lost no time in establishing claim to the County of Illinois, embracing all the territory between the Ohio and the Mississippi as a county within the Commonwealth of Virginia. He dispatched Col. John Todd of Kentucky as Commandant, with 500 men to take charge and establish a trade with New Orleans.[116] His instructions as to the general course of his conduct were similar to those given Clark. "You are on all occasions to inculcate on the people the value of liberty, and the difference between the state of free citizens of this Common-

---

[113] *Ibid.*, III, p. 238.

[114] Henry, *Henry*, op. cit., II, p. 105, American Archives, 4th Series, I, p. 215.

[115] *Ibid.*, III, pp. 201–202.

[116] *Ibid.*, I, p. 594.

wealth, and that Slavery to which Illinois was destined. . . . You will embrace every opportunity to manifest the high regard and friendly sentiments of this Commonwealth towards all the subjects of his Catholic Majesty, for whose safety, prosperity and advancement, you will give every possible advantage. You will make a tender of the Friendship and services of your people to the Spanish Commandant near the Kaskaskias, and cultivate the strictest connection with him and his people. I deliver you a letter which you will hand him in person. . . .[117] Governor Henry wanted to make sure that all were extended a warm welcome into the Commonwealth, and he, himself, "prepared the instructions to Colonels Clark, Todd, and Montgomery."[118]

The story is told of a prominent Virginian who visited the State of Illinois, and while there, called on Governor Adlai Stevenson. He took the visitor and showed him a portrait of the first Governor of Illinois. It was Patrick Henry! Illinois remained a county included in the Commonwealth up to 1782. In 1783 it was turned over to the Federal Government.

About the same time as the Clark expedition, the Governor dispatched Col. David Rogers to establish and command a military post on the lower Mississippi for the purpose of navigation. His instructions to Colonel Rogers called for "a proper place to fix a post for facilitating and securing the trade to New Orleans, and Consult the Spanish Governor on it." He was also to "Describe to that Gentleman the real strength and situation of Virginia; the progress of the war, and whatever else he may wish to know of the American Confederacy." Governor Henry also requested to know the strength of the English possessions on the Mississippi; whether they supplied the West Indies, and with what materials, etc.[119] But the expedition was unsuccessful, as Colonel Rogers and his men fell upon Indians and were slain.

Patrick Henry was informed of his nomination to a third term as Governor on May 29, 1778.[120] He was unopposed and was appointed without ballot. Thomas Jefferson was chairman of the committee to notify the Governor of his appointment, which suggests that he nominated Patrick Henry for the third term. If so, this hardly comports with the idea that Patrick Henry

---

[117] *Ibid.*, III, pp. 214–215.

[118] Henry, *Henry*, op. cit., I, p. 594. "These papers were spread upon the Journal, and are thus preserved for us." See post, III, pp. 208–218.

[119] *Ibid.*, I, pp. 607–608.

[120] Henry, *Henry*, op. cit., I, p. 621; *House Journal*, p. 26.

was trying to establish himself as a dictator, as Jefferson would have us to believe in his *Notes on Virginia*,[121] and in his letter to Wirt.[122]

During his third term as Governor, Patrick Henry devoted his services to raising the necessary troops ordered by Congress and requested by the General Assembly. He dispatched 150 men for the protection of the people of Kentucky. He commissioned Brig. Gen. Thomas Nelson to raise a regiment of cavalry. He appointed several officers to recruit volunteer battalions for Washington's army, and commissioned others to raise the necessary divisions to garrison the state. The following report made by the Secretary of War, H. Knox, May 11, 1790, shows Governor Henry's efforts in raising Virginia's quota—remarkable "considering the difficulties which surrounded him":

> Virginia furnished 6,181 men to the Continental army in 1776; that her quota fixed by Congress for 1777 was 10,200 men, of which she had on the Continental rolls, 5,744, and furnished besides 5,269 militia; that in 1778 her quota was fixed at 7,830 men, of which she furnished the Continental rolls 5,230, besides 600 as a guard for the Saratoga prisoners, and 2,000 militia; and that in 1779 her quota was 5,742, and she is credited by 3,973 regulars, 600 as a guard for the prisoners and 4,000 militia.[123]

This did not include the "number of State troops, and of men sent to the Northwest, to the defence of Kentucky, and to the Indian wars . . ." which if "added to the Virginians in the Continental army, it will appear that the State during Governor Henry's terms had many more men in continuous service than her Continental quota, and this without estimating her militia, so often called out for service in the State, nor the Virginians serving in the regiments of other States."[124]

The depreciation of the currency, "which increased from a ratio of five to one to that of twenty to one for gold," greatly increased the difficulty of raising troops and keeping them in the field during Governor Henry's third term.[125]

The Governor was requested by Congress to furnish armed

---

[121] *Ibid.*, I, p. 622; *Ibid.*, II, p. 145; Morgan, *Henry*, p. 309.
[122] *The Confidential Letters from Thomas Jefferson to William Wirt*, p. 17. In the collection of Mr. John Gribbel.
[123] Henry, *Henry*, II, p. 9.
[124] *Ibid.*, II, p. 10. See also, pp. 154–155.
[125] *Ibid.*

galleys for an attack upon East Florida, with orders to rendezvous at Charles Town, and requisitions further called for 1,000 troops for the defense of South Carolina and Georgia for immediate march, November 16, 1778. The Governor disliked the proposal to withdraw his armed vessels from Virginia, and wrote to Congress pointing to the necessity of protecting Chesapeake Bay, not only for the State, but because of its importance in safeguarding Pennsylvania, Maryland and North Carolina. The folly of such actions was seen and the plan to attack Florida was called off.[126] In the meantime, "owing to the inefficiency of Congress," Savannah was attacked on December 29, 1779, and being defended by only 1,500 men, it was captured, giving the British a direct and open communication with the Cherokees.[127]

Supplied now with munitions of war by the British, the Cherokees were ready and waiting to aid Hamilton in his planned march southward from Detroit to attack Kentucky and the western borders of Virginia. Governor Henry dispatched General Shelby with 1,000 men in all—from Virginia, North Carolina, and the Watauga settlement—against the Cherokees who had penetrated the Chickamauga towns, preventing navigation on the Tennessee River.[128]

These were perhaps Governor Henry's most important decisions in sending first Clark, then later Evan Shelby and Montgomery to reinforce Clark, against the outrages upon the frontiers. On April 10, 1779, the small army of 750 men under Montgomery set out in their canoes during a freshet, and floated down the waters of Big Creek in Tennessee, and three days later reached the camping ground of Dragging Canoe at the mouth of the Chickamauga Creek. The Indians were surprised and fled, leaving behind forty dead. Colonel Shelby "burnt their towns and destroyed their provisions. He captured stores and goods valued at £20,000, which had been collected by the British agents for distribution at the grand council, to be had with Hamilton and the Northern Indians at the mouth of the Tennessee."[129]

This expedition "left the Chickamaugas impotent for war, and checked the disposition of the Cherokees to unite in the attack upon the frontier, while the union of the Northern and

---

[126] *Ibid.*, II, pp. 20–21–22.

[127] *Ibid.*

[128] *Ibid.*, p. 22–23. See his letter to General Washington, March 13, 1779, III, pp. 229–230.

[129] Henry, *Henry*, op. cit., II, pp. 24–25; Ramsey's *History of Tennessee*, p. 187.

Southern Indians had been effectually prevented by the capture of Hamilton the preceding month.

"Thus it was the good fortune of Governor Henry, by the two expeditions he sent out, the one under Clark and the other under Shelby, to defeat the murderous design of the Royal Government to combine the Indian tribes in savage war upon the West, while the British regulars were engaging the American forces in the East. The wisdom displayed in selecting the commanders of these expeditions insured their success, and was in strong contrast with the want of judgment shown by Congress in the selection of commanders for the western frontier and the South."[130]

The previous month, he had urged the conquest of the lower Mississippi, seeing the danger to our trade. He wrote Washington on March 13, 1779, that he had requested Congress to authorize the conquest of Forts Natchez and Morishac, which had fallen into enemy hands, "and from thence they infest and ruin our trade on the Mississippi, on which river the Spaniards wish to open a very interesting commerce with us."[131] He pointed out that "the possession of them would give a colorable pretence to retain all West Florida when a treaty may be opened, and in the meantime, ruin our trade in that quarter, which would otherwise be so beneficial." But, he told the General, "I can get no answer to this application, although it is interesting to our back settlements, and not more than four hundred men required for the service."[132]

The "poison of wicked faction" in Congress[133] was no doubt having its effect. "Had the application of Governor Henry been followed, the United States would have been in possession of the posts commanding the lower Mississippi above New Orleans when Spain declared war with Britain. After that declaration Spain seized upon these herself, and in consequence retained possession of the Floridas at the peace."[134]

These complicated negotiations were begun in the year 1782, and by the Treaty of Paris the Mississippi was left open to American shipping.[135] Washington knew the reason why Patrick Henry had no response from his suggestion to Congress. Four-

---

[130] *Ibid.*, II, p. 25.

[131] *Ibid.*

[132] *Ibid.* See also his letter to General Washington, III, pp. 230–231.

[133] *Ibid.*, III, p. 227.

[134] *Ibid.*, II, p. 26.

[135] *Ibid.*, II, See pages 177 through 182.

teen days after Henry's letter, Washington wrote George Mason ". . . it is a fact too notorious to be concealed, that Congress is rent by party, that much business of a trifling nature and personal concernment withdraws their attention from matters of great moment at this critical period—when it is also known that idleness and dissipation take the place of close attention and application. . . ." Washington also referred to the speculators—various tribes of money-makers and stock-jobbers of all denominations who wished to continue the war for their own private gain without considering that their avarice must plunge everything (including themselves) in a common ruin. He noted that ". . . from the present state of our currency, dissensions, and other circumstances," matters were pushed to "the utmost extremity."[136]

On December 4, 1778, Governor Henry sent an urgent appeal to Congress for naval assistance in protecting Chesapeake Bay,[137] having "no armed vessels of our own of sufficient strength to oppose even privateers," except two that were found to be too slow. He feared depredations from the enemy, especially since the departure in July from the Capes of Delaware of the French fleet, which had been damaged after a severe storm and had sailed to the West Indies.

As he feared, on May 8, 1779, a small fleet under Sir George Collier, and a landing force of about 2,000 men under General Matthews, entered Chesapeake Bay and did considerable damage. Governor Henry lost no time in defending against the attack and "between two and three thousand militia" were soon under arms.[138] He again applied to Congress on May 12 for naval assistance.

Spain declared war on England in June, as was predicted by Patrick Henry, but the alliance with the American Confederacy had yet to be made. The Governor made foreign loans from France through the aid of Captain Lemaire and Philip Mazzei "which greatly aided Virginia in maintaining her military establishments during the remaining years of the Revolution."[139]

Patrick Henry's third term as Governor expired June 1, 1779, and under the constitution he was ineligible for another term.

---

[136] *Ibid.*, II, pp. 45–46–47. Washington to George Mason, March 27, 1779. The General was writing about the "present state of our currency, dissensions, and other circumstances."

[137] *Ibid.*, III, pp. 207–208.

[138] *Ibid.*, II, p. 29. See also, pp. 149–150.

[139] *Ibid.*, II, pp. 14–16.

Thomas Jefferson was his successor by a close vote. The first ballot showed 55 for Jefferson, 38 for John Page and 32 for Gen. Thomas Nelson. The second ballot showed 67 for Jefferson and 61 for Page.[140]

That Patrick Henry had faithfully discharged the important trust is seen in his election by the Assembly on June 17 to a seat in Congress. This he declined, because of the condition of his health, which he said he was "satisfied, will never again permit a close application to sedentary business, and I even doubt whether I can remain below long enough to serve in the Assembly. I will however make the trial and be down on the next Assembly, if I am chosen."[141]

At the close of his term as Governor he moved with his family to "Leatherwood," on the famous Leatherwood Creek, in Henry County, "seven miles from the Court House, on the road leading to Danville." Among friends in the county named for him, he was elected delegate to the next meeting of the Assembly in May, which he accepted, though he was not well. Patrick Henry was not only sick, he was despondent, as were many others in the winter of 1779–80, watching the conditions which he could not control: the depreciation of the currency, the inefficiency of Congress and the gradual dissipation in the people's morals. General Lincoln had been forced to capitulate at Charleston on May 12, 1780, surrendering about 2,000 men composed mostly of Virginians, besides "500 militia, 1,000 seamen, 400 pieces of ordnance, and a large supply of military and naval stores. The Americans lost in addition, all the shipping in the harbor."[142] That same month Washington had had to quell a mutiny by two Connecticut regiments at Morristown.[143]

Governor Thomas Jefferson was now occupying the uncomfortable seat formerly held by Patrick Henry, and in the winter of 1779–80, he communicated with Patrick Henry, to which Mr. Henry replied:

> Leatherwood, Feb. 15, 1780
>
> Dear Sir: I return many thanks for your favour by Mr. Sanders. . . . I have had many anxieties for our commonwealth, principally occasioned by the depreciation of our money. To judge

---

[140] Henry, *Henry*, op. cit., II, p. 39; *House Journal*, p. 29.
[141] *Ibid.*, II, p. 49; Wirt, *Henry*, p. 242, (1836) on Constitutionality . . .
[142] *Ibid.*, II, p. 45.
[143] *Ibid.*, II, p. 47. See also, p. 160.

by this which somebody has called the pulse of the State, I have feared that our body politic was dangerously sick. God forbid it may not be unto death. But I cannot forbear thinking, the present increase of prices is in great part owing to a kind of habit which is now of four or five years growth, which is fostered by a mistaken avarice, and like other habits hard to part with—for there is really very little money hereabouts. What you say of the practices of our disguised tories perfectly agrees with my own observation, and the attempts to raise prejudices against the French, I know, were begun when I lived below. What gave me the utmost pain was to see some men, indeed very many, who were thought good whigs, keep company with the miscreants, wretches, who, I am satisfied, were labouring for our destruction. This countenance shewn them is of fatal tendency. They should be shunned and execrated, and this is the only way to supply the place of legal conviction and punishment. But this is an effort of virtue, small as it seems, of which our countrymen are not capable. Indeed, I will own to you, my dear sir, that observing this impunity, and even respect, which some wicked individuals have met with while their guilt was clear as the sun, has sickened me, and made me sometimes wish to be in retirement for the rest of my life. . . But tell me, do you remember any instance where tyranny was destroyed and freedom established on its ruins, among a people possessing so small a share of virtue and public spirit? I recollect none, and this more than the British arms makes me fearful of final success, without a reform. But when or how this is to be effected, I have not the means of judging. I most sincerely wish you health and prosperity. If you can spare time to drop me a line now and then, it will be highly obliging to, Dear Sir, your affectionate friend & obt Servt,

P. Henry.[144]

Besides the mischief of the Tories, Patrick Henry decried such actions as consorting with the enemy, particularly in view of the brutal treatment of the American prisoners by the British and in their other actions, "unknown to civilized nations."[145] The same brutal pattern was followed throughout the other southern colonies, as in the instance of the writer's forebear, Col. Roger Gordon. He was a very active patriot, fighting under command of Gen. Francis Marion. In 1781 near the close of the war,

---

[144] *Ibid.*, II, pp. 48–49.

[145] *Ibid.*, II, pp. 28–30–32; Boyd, *The Papers of Thomas Jefferson*, XIII, pp. 363–364.

Colonel Gordon and his men were on a scouting mission and were sent to patrol Lynch's Creek in what is now Williamsburg County, S. C.[146] The enemy was already entrenched, but Colonel Gordon and his men were surprised by a larger force of Tories under Captain Britton. Finding that they were entirely surrounded, Colonel Gordon and his men surrendered, giving up their arms. The British officer immediately turned them over to the Tories, who with the aid of the Indians, promptly murdered Colonel Gordon and his entire command.

Tarleton, with a superior force, attempted to capture General Marion. Following him for many miles, he looked over the way Marion had gone and exclaimed: "This miry waste, Come my boys! Let us go back! We will soon find the Game Cock (meaning Sumter) but as for this 'Swamp Fox,' the Devil himself could not catch him." From this expression, General Marion received the nickname "Swamp Fox."[147]

After the war, Cornwallis at one point was being taunted because of his inability to destroy Marion in Williamsburg. "I could not capture webfooted men who could subsist on roots and berries," he replied. He was thinking, of course, "of the ability of Marion's men to cross the swamps of Williamsburg and of their potato diet."[148]

Patrick Henry's return to the Assembly in 1780 raised the hopes and spirits of the populace. His record in this body was well known and his abilities as Governor had produced the highest admiration. The depreciation of the currency was the first matter of importance to be discussed. "Already Congress had issued over two hundred and sixty millions of dollars of paper money, and the several States had issued as much more, while no adequate provision had been made for the redemption of either issue." Having depreciated in value to one-fortieth of specie, "it could not be relied on to purchase food for the army."[149] Mr. Henry resented the scheme of Congress to replace the old paper money with new bills to be redeemable in six years in specie. He did not wish to put off with new promises what had been "solemnly declared would be paid in full" at one-twentieth of its face value, which had been such a disappointment to the men in uniform and was

---

[146] Boddie, *History of Williamsburg, S.C.*, p. 122.
[147] *Ibid.*, pp. 107–108.
[148] *Ibid.*, p. 112.
[149] Henry, *Henry*, II, p. 52.

discouraging the recruiting system. His counter-proposals for strengthening by taxation the public credit and for keeping faith with the people declared:

> 1st. That ample and certain funds ought to be established for sinking the quota of the Continental debt due from this state in fifteen years.
>
> 2nd. That certain funds ought to be established, for furnishing to the Continent the quota of this State, for the support of the war for the current year.
>
> 3rd. That a specific tax ought to be laid for the use of the Continent, in full proportion to the abilities of the people.[150]

Patrick Henry had seen how these conditions handicapped him in conducting the essential business, and he did not wish the war effort to be further jeopardized. Lee and Mason supported the scheme of Congress, "as being the only expedient remaining for the restoration of public credit." But Patrick Henry eloquently opposed it, and his proposals carried by a vote of 59 to 25. Later, however, he had to leave the session for reasons of his health and the paper-money project was again brought forward and adopted. But Mr. Henry's predictions came true and "the plan failed to stop the depreciation of the currency," with the same results of "over-issue and depreciation" as were seen in the French Revolution and in the Civil War.[151] But before Patrick Henry left the legislature, new and vigorous measures were taken during the 20 days he sat to defend Virginia and the Southern States, and Congress was "urged to send speedily a strong Continental force" to aid Virginia and North Carolina.[152] Governor Jefferson sent an appeal to George Washington also for arms.

The people generally appeared more hopeful of their cause, and in Philadelphia a bank was established with available funds for the much-needed army supplies. Washington appeared encouraged for the first time and we find him in June, 1780, writing to Governor Trumbull: "As I always speak to your Excellency in the confidence of friendship, I shall not scruple to confess that the prevailing politics for a considerable time past have filled me with inexpressible anxiety and apprehension, and have uniformly appeared to me to threaten the subversion of our independence.

---

[150] *Ibid.*, II, p. 53.
[151] *Ibid.*, II, p. 54.
[152] *Ibid.*, II, p. 51.

I hope a period to them is now arrived, and that a change of measures will save us from ruin."[153]

Hopes began to brighten as affairs in Europe became more favorable. Lafayette had returned from France in April with the promise of "six men-of-war and six thousand regular troops" to aid the spring campaigns. The "Armed Neutrality" generally approved by the States of Europe had resulted in open war between Britain and the Netherlands, due to Holland's extensive trade. Thus was Mr. Henry's prediction at "Plain Dealing" in Hanover County verified, when he said that France, Spain and Holland would come to the aid of the Americans.[154] In June, Congress corrected its error by calling on Washington to replace General Gates for his lack of leadership at Camden. He appointed Gen. Nathaniel Greene to take over the Southern department and oppose Cornwallis.[155] Greene, in the meantime, realizing his inferior force, retreated through North Carolina into Virginia in February, crossing the Dan.[156] Remembering Patrick Henry's success at raising troops, he wrote him "to collect fourteen or fifteen hundred volunteers to aid us"[157] against Cornwallis. Mr. Henry was living near the waters of the Dan and he rallied the militia from all the four counties, as well as the adjoining counties, and sent them promptly to General Greene. Virginia gave Greene every support. The looked-for aid from the French Fleet finally arrived at Rhode Island on July 10, 1780, but Britain's superior fleet appeared on the 13th and confined it at Newport.

During these serious times when New York was bottled up by the British fleet and Arnold had attempted treason, the Virginia Assembly met in Richmond, October 16, 1780. Patrick Henry was made chairman of the Committee of Privileges and Elections, and of the committee to bring in a bill for the better defense of the Southern frontier, and was placed upon the Committee of Propositions and Grievances, and of Courts of Justice. We also find him during the session on Committees to form a plan for the defenses of the eastern frontier of the State, to prepare bills for raising the State's quota of men and money, to settle the accounts of the delegates to Congress, and the accounts of the State with the United States, to draw bills for the organization and main-

---

[153] *Ibid.*, II, pp. 55–56.
[154] *Ibid.*, II, p. 59. See also Henry, *Henry*, I, pp. 207–208.
[155] *Ibid.*, II, pp. 62–67.
[156] Henry, *Henry*, op. cit., II, p. 67.
[157] *Ibid.*, II, pp. 67–68.

tenance of the navy, the better regulation and discipline of the militia, and supplying the army with clothes and provisions. Of some of these committees he was chairman.[158]

The British fleet entered the Virginia Capes on December 30, 1780, and in the spring a serious attempt was made by the British to subdue Virginia. Cornwallis abandoned North Carolina for Virginia and General Greene advanced again into the southern states and retook the larger part of Georgia and both Carolinas.[159] Leaving Wilmington, Cornwallis arrived in Petersburg May 20, and joined forces with the invading army. This gave him 5,000 men, and he was later reinforced by a body of 1,700 from New York. In comparison, Lafayette had "only about one thousand regulars, two thousand militia and fifty dragoons.[160] But he soon "effected a junction with Wayne" bringing 900 regulars from Pennsylvania.[161]

Tarleton, with his mounted men, moved in the direction of Louisa County with orders to seize the legislature, which had reassembled at Charlottesville, and to capture Governor Jefferson, who had left the capital. Like Congress, which had had to change its location twice, the legislature found itself in a position where it either had to move or risk capture. Seeing Tarleton's men passing Cuckoo Tavern, John Jouette mounted his horse and taking the short cut, he sped to Charlottesville and gave the alarm in time for the assemblymen's escape. On the way, Tarleton stopped at the homes of Dr. Thomas and John Walker for the purpose of seizing some prominent citizens. He surprised two men in their beds—Judge Peter Lyon, and Patrick Henry's half brother, Col. John Syme, a member of the Senate of Virginia. "It is related as an instance of Tarleton's humor, that when Colonel Syme, who was remarkably homely, was brought from his bedroom undressed, and with dishevelled hair, the celebrated cavalry man threw himself into the attitude of Hamlet upon discovering his father's ghost, and exclaimed:

'Angels and ministers of grace, defend us!
Be thou a spirit of health, or goblin damned?' "[162]

Too late, the British arrived at Charlottesville to find that the legislature had left for Staunton. Neither did they capture

---

[158] Henry, *Henry*, op. cit., p. 71; *Journal*, pp. 7–8–10–14–24–45–50–51.
[159] *Ibid.*, II, p. 124.
[160] Henry, *Henry*, op. cit., II, p. 126.
[161] *Ibid.*, II, p. 127.
[162] *Ibid.*, II, pp. 128–129; Morgan, *Henry*, p. 304.

Jefferson, who had taken refuge at his farm in Bedford. Regarding the flight of the legislators to Staunton, this story is taken from Able's *Life of John Tyler*:[163]

> It is said that as Patrick Henry, Benjamin Harrison, Judge Tyler, and Colonel Christian were hurrying along, they saw a little hut in the forest. An old woman was chopping wood by the door. The men were hungry, and stopped to ask her for food.
>
> 'Who are you?' she asked.
>
> 'We are members of the legislature,' said Patrick Henry; 'we have just been compelled to leave Charlottesville on account of the British.'
>
> 'Ride on, then, ye cowardly knaves!' she said in wrath. 'Here are my husband and sons just gone to Charlottesville to fight for ye, and you running away with all your might. Clear out! Ye shall have nothing here.'
>
> 'But,' replied Mr. Henry, 'we were obliged to flee. It would not do for the legislature to be broken up by the enemy. Here is Mr. Benjamin Harrison; you don't think he would have fled had it not been necessary?'
>
> 'I always thought a great deal of Mr. Harrison till now,' answered the old woman, 'but he'd no business to run from the enemy.' And she started to shut the door in their faces.
>
> 'Wait a moment, my good woman,' cried Mr. Henry; 'would you believe that Judge Tyler or Colonel Christian would take to flight if there were not good cause for so doing?'
>
> 'No, indeed, that I wouldn't.'
>
> 'But,' he said, 'Judge Tyler and Colonel Christian are here.'
>
> 'They are? Well, I would never have thought it. I didn't suppose they would ever run from the British; but since they have, they shall have nothing to eat in my house. You may ride along.'
>
> Things were getting desperate. Then Judge Tyler stepped forward: 'What would you say, my good woman, if I were to tell you that Patrick Henry fled with the rest of us?'
>
> 'Patrick Henry!' she answered angrily, 'I should tell you there wasn't a word of truth in it! Patrick Henry would never do such a cowardly thing.'
>
> 'But this is Patrick Henry,' said Judge Tyler.
>
> The old woman was astonished; but she stammered and pulled at her apron string, and said: 'Well, if that's Patrick Henry, it must be all right. Come in, and ye shall have the best I have in the house.'[164]

---

[163] Morgan, *Henry*, p. 305; Henry, *Henry*, II, pp. 139–140.

[164] Burton, *The Story of Patrick Henry*, pp. 56–57–58–59; Henry, *Henry*, II pp. 139–140.

This story is said to be "inconsistent with tradition," since it is pointed out that the alarm reached Staunton on Sunday morning, and in case the rumor had been true, the legislature was to have met at Warm Springs. But the rumor "having been discovered to be false during Sunday," and by Mr. Henry's "being in his place early Monday morning, it is most probable that he never left town at all, certainly not within a few hours of the meeting of the House."[165]

According to Richard Henry Lee: "The Assembly adjourned to Charlottesville, where they were never able to collect members sufficient to form the Legislature before they were dispersed by 500 of the enemies light horse with as many light infantry mounted behind as we learn from some of the flying delegates."[166] Hence the reason for their withdrawal to Staunton. But Mr. Jefferson's departure from the seat of government was not dismissed quite so lightly. The House met June 11, 1781, and during the session he received censure which "was supported at the time by some of the most intelligent men in Virginia."[167] When he left the office as Governor and retired to Bedford, his term of office had expired only two days before, and when on June 12 the Legislature proceeded to elect the new Governor, the state had been without an executive for ten days. Gen. Thomas Nelson was elected the next Governor, and afterward, a resolution was placed in the Journal, calling for an inquiry at the next session of the Assembly into the conduct of the executive of the state for the preceding 12 months.[168] ". . . Two persons were named with acrimony as delinquent: Baron Von Steuben, for not having succeeded in protecting the stores in the vicinity of the Point of Fork, and Thomas Jefferson, the governor at the time of Arnold's invasion, as not having made some exertions which he might have made for the defense of the country. . . . Colonel George Nicholas and Mr. Patrick Henry were those who charged Mr. Jefferson. They aimed to express themselves with delicacy toward him, without weakening the ground on which they supposed that their suspicions would be found ultimately to stand. But, probably without design, they wounded by their

---

[165] Henry, *Henry*, II, pp. 141–142; Note the record of the Journal.

[166] Ballagh, *The Letters of Richard Henry Lee*, II, p. 234.

[167] Henry, *Henry*, op. cit., II, p. 150. See letter of John Page to Colonel Bland, *Virginia Historical Register*, IV, p. 195, and Henry Lee's *Memoirs of War in* the South.

[168] *Ibid.*, II, p. 143. See charges by Georgia Nicholas, and Jefferson's answers. Boyd, *The Papers of Thomas Jefferson* v.6. pp. 104–105–106–107–108–109.

measured endeavor to avoid the infliction of a wound. . . ."[169] The motion was made at the next session by Colonel Nicholas and carried by his "friends and foes." Mr. Jefferson furnished Col. Nicholas with the answers to his objections regarding his official conduct at the succeeding session. 'But the question still remains whether Mr. Jefferson did his duty in protecting the State against Arnold's invasion, and in defending him in this matter, his apologists have not failed to institute comparisons with the conduct of his predecessor under similar circumstances. The facts give them no comfort, however, from this source," as can be seen:

"In the case of Collier's invasion, Governor Henry had no warning until the enemy entered the Capes, while Governor Jefferson was warned when the Arnold expedition was being prepared in New York. When the enemy entered the Capes Governor Henry received exact information within less than two days, through vessels he had posted to watch the entrance of the Bay, some of which engaged the ships which were detached from the British fleet;[170] while Governor Jefferson, who had discontinued the spy vessels, got his information through a private letter written to another person, and was not assured of the destination of the fleet, nor indeed whether it was French or English, for two days afterward; at the Collier invasion Governor Henry had a regiment of regular troops posted so as to resist their landing at different points along the Bay, and to be easily concentrated for the protection of the capital; while Governor Jefferson had no such force. Governor Henry promptly assembled a sufficient force to prevent the advance of the enemy, 2,000 strong, farther than Suffolk, near the Bay. Governor Jefferson, on the contrary, did not assemble a sufficient force to meet half of that number of invaders, until they had taken Richmond, much further in the interior, and were retiring after their work of destruction."[171]

"Mr. Jefferson, in his defense furnished to Mr. Nicholas,[172] admits the information received in December, and excuses himself for neglecting the warning on the ground that the embarkation of the British was said to be for the southward, but not certainly for

[169] Henry, *Henry*, op. cit., II, p. 144. Edmund Randolph.

[170] Henry, *Henry*, op. cit., II, p. 149 n. Account of the Expedition by one with it, *Virginia Historical Register*, IV, p. 186. *The Journal of the House* of May 10, 1779, shows information of the hostile fleet which entered the Bay the evening of the 8th.

[171] *Ibid.*

[172] *Ibid.*, op. cit., p. 149. Randall's *Life of Jefferson*, I, p. 354.

Virginia, and it was too expensive and harassing to call out the militia upon such an uncertainty. Even if this could excuse him for not calling out the militia at once, it would not excuse him for failing to send a swift vessel to the capes, to watch and report the first appearance of the enemy coming in; and for not having everything ready to bring out the militia on the first warning. He in fact paid little or no attention to the warning sent him. . . . Mr. Jefferson himself, in his autobiography, admitted his inability to properly fill the office of Governor during the invasion, and on that based his 'resignation,' as he termed it, in favor of General Nelson."[173]

The war was practically over at the next session, and the people were in such a state of jubilation that "no one appeared to prosecute the charges against Mr. Jefferson." Instead, resolutions were passed by the Assembly extending its sincere thanks to the former Governor, "for his impartial, upright and attentive administration whilst in office." But Jefferson's letters showed "deep resentment" and he never forgave Patrick Henry,[174] which no doubt accounted for the malignity manifested throughout Wirt's biography of Henry, as revised by Jefferson.

"Henry, for his part, never abused Jefferson. He would not have prompted the Jefferson inquiry if he had not felt it to be his sworn duty to do so. No man was kinder hearted—no man less envious of other men in the public service. But he was not afraid. As it proved the resolution of inquiry was superfluous. Nicholas regretted that he had made it, apologized to Jefferson, and became his ardent follower. The inquiry was held, but by that time something had happened—something that caused the sun to burst forth and shine from one end of America to the other, something truly glorious and unforgettable. Tarleton was trapped—Cornwallis—all of them. It was Yorktown that lifted the clouds. The war was as good as over."[175]

At this session of the legislature, larger powers were invested in the Governor and Council which were a little less than dictatorial, and placed all the forces and resources of the state at their command. Mr. Henry spoke in behalf of stronger powers in the hands of the executive,[176] of which in after years Mr.

[173] Henry, *Henry*, op. cit., II, pp. 149–150 n. See letter of John Page to Colonel Bland, *Virginia Historical Register*, IV, p. 195, and Henry Lee's *Memoirs of the War in the South*, Morgan, *Henry*, 304–305.

[174] *Ibid.*, II, p. 145.

[175] Morgan, *Henry*, p. 309.

[176] Henry, *Henry*, II, p. 145.

Jefferson wrote Wirt, referring to the proposition in the legislature, which he called a scheme for a dictator.[177]

Patrick Henry was placed on several committees at this session. One called for effectively regulating and disciplining the militia. He headed several committees that reported "bills for raising Virginia's quota of Continental troops; for relief of residents on the western waters; for establishing courts of claims; for making the money emitted at this session legal tender; for stopping the expedition lately ordered to Detroit; and for suppressing certain insurgents in the western and northwestern frontiers," and no doubt introduced the measures.[178] Among the resolutions he introduced was one requesting the Executive to present to Captain John Jouette, on behalf of the Assembly, "an elegant sword and pair of pistols."[179]

But Jack Jouette did not need to use the sword and pistols at his side. The war was actually over.

The inspiration of Patrick Henry's words had done its work. "The glorious task" he had assigned to his soldiers of saving by their valor "all that is dear to Mankind," had been accomplished.[180]

He served as Governor from 1776 to 1779. He returned to the House in 1780, serving until 1784. He was again elected Governor 1784 to 1786, and was once more returned to the House, where he served 1787 to 1790.

After the war was over George Mason wrote to Patrick Henry:

> I congratulate you most sincerely, on the accomplishment of what I know was the warmest wish of your heart, the establishment of American independence and the liberty of our country. We are now to rank among the nations of the world; but whether our independence will prove a blessing or a curse, must depend upon our own wisdom or folly, virtue or wickedness. Judging of the future from the past, the prospect is not promising. Justice and virtue are the vital principles of republican government; but among us a depravity of manners and morals prevails, to the destruction of all confidence between man and man. It greatly behooves the Assembly to revise several of our laws, and to

---

[177] *Ibid.*, II, p. 145; Wirt, *Henry*, p. 248, (1836 ed.) See Morgan, *Henry*, pp. 308–309.

[178] *Ibid.*, II, p. 152.

[179] Henry, *Henry*, op. cit., II, p. 152: *Journal* for June 15, 1781, p. 19, Also June 19, 22, 25, 26, 27.

[180] *Ibid.*, I, pp. 453–454, Colonel Henry's letter to his officers and men of the First and Second Virginia Regiment.

> abolish all such as are contrary to the fundamental principles of justice. . . . It is in your power, my dear sir, to do more good and prevent more mischief than any man in this State; and I doubt not that you will exert the great talents with which God has blessed you, in promoting the public happiness and prosperity.[181]

[181] Morgan, *Henry*, p. 311.

XVII

THE ARTICLES OF CONFEDERATION

THE WAR OF THE Revolution was now over. Tarleton's last engagement ended October 3, 1781, at Gloucester Point. On the 19th, with the aid of the French fleet under Count de Grasse guarding the mouth of Chesapeake Bay, and with Washington's and Lafayette's forces, "estimated at 16,000, of whom 7,000 were French, 5,500 Continentals, and 3,500 Virginia Militia," Cornwallis found that he was "not only cut off from retreat by sea, but hemmed in also by an allied army of sixteen thousand men, more than twice the number of British in Yorktown."[1] Thus, "the ball of the revolution rested in the same state in which it had received the first impulse."

The close of the war brought great rejoicing among the colonies, but there remained problems of gravest importance, as well as painful readjustments facing the infant nation. New laws were needed for immediate action. Old laws had to be revised. If Congress disbanded, there was no president to head the government. The states, through their constitutions, had assumed sovereign rights, but the demands of war called for "unity of action, and the problem of union, always evaded in colonial times, had now to be faced."[2] The Articles of Confederation, recommended to the states November 15, 1777, which had kept the colonies together, assigned no more power to Congress than "had been exercised to a large extent by the imperial government . . . and the states in reality denied themselves few privileges that they had ever held as colonies."[3] Congress had been given "only such powers as were definitely assigned to it; the states had all the

[1] Henry, *Henry*, II, p. 164; Hicks, *The Federal Union*, p. 146.

[2] Hicks, *The Federal Union*, p. 156.

[3] *Ibid.*, p. 157.

rest." The right was given the states to conduct the finances, levy taxes and regulate commerce, while "even the most general sort of regulations" were denied Congress. It had freedom in the matter "to work out as best it could a plan for the discharge of its executive duties."[4] The function of the judiciary was handicapped by a lack of authority. There was no national court system adequate to the needs. In cases of disputes, Congress was the court of appeal for the states. It established the appellate courts in certain states and selected state courts to try acts of piracy and felony, but there was "no well-rounded national system of courts." The states were denied the powers to "make treaties alone with foreign countries; receive ambassadors, or engage in war." The regulation of delegates called for "not less than two, nor more than seven" representatives from each of the states, and "regardless of the number of delegates" sent to Congress, each state had but one vote, and "a delegate might serve only three years out of each six."[5]

The provisions left Congress "no room for doubt as to where sovereignty lay under the Articles of Confederation, for they pointedly declared that each state retain its 'sovereignty, freedom, and independence.' Congress in a sense was merely an assembly of diplomats to whom had been entrusted the control of certain common problems. It derived its authority wholly from the states, as whose agent it acted. It was in no sense responsible to the people of the United States, nor could any of its actions bear directly upon them."[6]

In the light of these facts, it seems that there would have been little delay in adopting the Articles. But the serious question over the settlement of the western lands caused concern, and "one by one the various states gave their consent until only Maryland remained." Maryland held out for a portion, collectively, of the western back lands and petitioned Congress that it be considered "common stock" to be "parceled out" to the independent governments. This Congress refused to do, and Maryland refused to accept the Articles. However, Thomas Paine's essay called "The Public Good" caused Congress to reconsider. Virginia adopted resolutions to cede the northwestern territory, on reasonable terms, to the United States,[7] and "there was no

---

[4] *Ibid.*, p. 159.
[5] *Ibid.*, pp. 157–159.
[6] *Ibid.*
[7] Henry, *Henry*, II, p. 86.

better claim than that of Virginia, which was now based not only on the original grant,[8] but also upon the military exploits of George Rogers Clark, so when Virginia agreed to relinquish her claim to Congress, Maryland was content."[9]

The matter respecting Virginia's western territory was taken up in the House while Mr. Henry was a member of the legislature in December, 1779. The terms were fully debated, and upon the condition that Maryland sign the Confederation, the Virginia Assembly ceded the territory for the happiness, strength, and safety of the United States.[10] Virginia's "readiness to make these great sacrifices for the common welfare, was in keeping with her noble conduct during the entire Revolutionary struggle. . . . It not only effected the completion of the Confederation, but by endowing it with so large a property, it gave it credit, and the characteristic of a nation." Spain, however, "was not willing to treat on any terms, and as soon as the emergency passed, Virginia recalled her resolution, and Congress returned to her first instruction on the subject,"[11] The Articles, nevertheless, were adopted and carried into effect on March 1, 1781, and remained as the supreme law "until the first Wednesday of March, 1789."

But Congress was to find itself seriously handicapped by the Articles of Confederation. To meet the critical problems, "the new nation had only a makeshift government, lacking even in the all-important power of taxation. The financial embarrassment of the Confederation government was always acute . . . and this impotence with which it was cursed soon made the Congress of the Confederation a joke."[12] In February, a month before all the states had ratified, Congress became aware "that a change must be made in its finances to avoid utter ruin. Robert Morris, a man competent to the task of restoring its credit, was made Superintendent of Finance, February 20, 1781. Under his direction a return to specie payments was determined on. The debt due in paper money was ordered to be reduced to a specie value and funded as an interest-bearing loan. The quotas of money asked for from the States were fixed in specie, and it was recommended that all tender laws be repealed. A bank was also chartered to aid the government, upon a plan prepared by Gouverneur Morris, the

---

[8] See Henry, *Henry*, II, pp. 97–101–103–105–107.

[9] Hicks, *The Federal Union*, p. 159.

[10] Henry, *Henry*, II, p. 85–86.

[11] *Ibid.*, II, p. 87–88.

[12] Hicks, *The Federal Union*, pp. 165–166.

Assistant Superintendent of Finance. These measures, with the loan of six millions of livres from France, effected by Colonel Laurens, had the desired effect. Paper money soon went out of use, and prices were adjusted upon a specie basis."[13]

But Congress had no independent source of revenue. It required an income of about a half million dollars a year to meet its ordinary expenditures, and the United States war debt alone was well over forty million dollars. To meet its obligation, Congress had to rely upon the "requisitions levied upon the states," which had proved to be inadequate. In 1781, Congress had tried to make alterations in the Articles by asking for "a five per cent ad-valorem duty on imports, from the proceeds of which the interest on the national debt might be paid and a beginning made toward the payment of the principal."[14] This was defeated, because some of the states were as much opposed to tax collectors from Congress within the states as they were to British tax agents. Two years later, 1783, Congress requested "the power to levy duties on imports for twenty-five years only, the states themselves to appoint the revenue officers." But this also was a failure, and Congress had to tolerate the Articles as best it could, content with the insufficient requisitions from the states. Added to this was a small sum from the sales of public lands, and the "ten or fifteen thousand dollars a year" brought in by the post office department.[15]

The finances of the southern states had "long gone to ruin." Within the year past, "twenty millions of dollars" had been "emitted in state money from the Virginia Treasury" and there still remained a sum of "enormous amount" for recent expenses of the war beyond the abilities to discharge.[16] Whether the constitution that had served them well in war would answer their needs now at the close of the contest, remained to be seen.

At this critical time in Virginia's history we find Patrick Henry in the legislature, "to nurse the new-born nation into health and strength; to develop its resources, moral and physical; and thus to give security and permanence to its liberties." He "continued to represent the county of his residence (Henry) and controlled the proceedings of that body, with a weight of personal

[13] *Ibid.*, Henry, *Henry*, II, p. 161.

[14] Hicks, *The Federal Union*, p. 166

[15] *Ibid.*

[16] Henry, *Henry*, II, p. 153. An address to Congress from the Virginia Legislature, June 22, 1781, "which had been prepared and presented by Mr. Henry under a previous order." See *Journal*, 1781, p. 23.

authority, and a power of eloquence, which it was extremely difficult, and indeed almost impossible to resist."[17]

Serving on a number of committees affecting the serious condition of affairs, November 1781, he introduced several bills at this time that deserve special mention:

"A tax bill, carefully prepared, and admirably adjusted to the conditions of the State, which was in great need of a sound circulating medium. Paper money had ceased to circulate, and the little specie derived from the Spanish trade, and the French troops, was utterly inadequate to the wants of the people. The bill introduced by Mr. Henry imposed a tax of one pound on every one hundred pounds value of land, two shillings on every horse and mule, three pence a head on cattle, five shillings per wheel on pleasure carriages, fifty pounds on every billiard-table, five pounds on every ordinary license, and ten shillings capitation on white males above twenty-one, and on all slaves. This might be paid one half in specie, tobacco, hemp, or flour, except the tax on land, and one-tenth of that might be paid in the Continental bills emitted under the act of March 18, 1780, which, when received, were to be destroyed by the State Treasurer.[18]

"A bill for calling in and funding the paper money of the State. By this act the paper money issued by the State was to be no longer a legal tender, except for the taxes of 1781. All holders of it were required to bring it to the treasury on or before October 1, 1782, when it might be exchanged for specie certificates, carrying six per cent interest, at the rate of one thousand for one,[19] the last value affixed to the paper currency.

"A bill to adjust the pay of the Virginia Officers and soldiers in Continental or State service, and of the sailors and marines in the State service. By this act all accounts were to be audited, and what was due in paper money scaled to specie as of due day, according to a scale fixed by the act for every month from January 1, 1777, to January 1, 1782; the tract of land between the Mississippi, Ohio, and Tennessee Rivers was substituted for the land lost to the State by the running of the Tennessee line, in the location of military warrants; and the proceeds of confiscated estates were devoted to the payment of the arrears of military pay.[20]

[17] Wirt, *Henry*, (1836,) p. 249.

[18] Henry, *Henry*, op. cit., II, p. 170. *Journal*, p. 44; Hening, *Statutes at Large*, X., p. 501.

[19] *Ibid.*, op. cit., *Journal*, p. 43. Hening, *Statutes at Large*, X., p. 456.

[20] *Ibid.*, op. cit., *Journal*, p. 29. Hening, *Statutes at Large*, X., p. 462.

"A bill for adjusting all debts and contracts entered into between January 1, 1777, and January 1, 1782, payable in paper money.[21] This authorized the debtor to settle his obligation by paying the scaled value in specie of the paper money as of the date of the contract, by the scale given in the act; required partial payments already made to be first credited at their nominal amount; and gave a stay of execution on judgments until December 1, 1783, except on debts to the commonwealth, or for rents or hires. No wiser measures could have been devised for bringing order out of the prevailing confusion."[22]

However, Thomas Jefferson, in a letter to William Wirt, declared that, "At the close of the war many of us wished to re-open all accounts which had been paid in depreciated money, and have them settled by the scale of depreciation. But on this he (Mr. Henry) frowned most indignantly, and knowing the general indisposition of the Legislature, it was considered hopeless to attempt it with such an opponent at their head as Henry."[23]

In commenting upon the above, Mr. Henry's grandson made the following observations:

"It seems very apparent that of the two, Mr. Henry's sense of justice was the more correct. The Legislature could not properly release men from their contracts. All it should have attempted was to establish a just specie scale for the settlement of outstanding obligations payable in an exploded paper currency. To have set aside, or scaled, payments accepted in paper money, would have been to avoid the agreements of the creditors to receive the payments at their nominal value, and make other and different contracts for the parties. This can never be right. That Mr. Henry's bill was just and proper was not only the testimony of the Legislature of 1781, but of the Legislature of 1865, which enacted a similar law upon the close of the war between the States and the collapse of the Confederate paper currency. The principle has been also approved by similar legislation in other States at each period."[24]

Patrick Henry was again in his seat in the legislature, May 6, 1782, when there was universal rejoicing over the news that the House of Commons on Feb. 28, 1782, had determined to put an end to the war. The business of the session at this time cannot be traced, due to the loss of the Journal from the State archives.

[21] *Ibid.*

[22] *Ibid.*, p. 171.

[23] *Ibid.*, op. cit., See *Historical Magazine* for 1867, p. 91.

[24] Henry, *Henry*, II, p. 172.

However, an act was passed calling for the manumission of slaves.[25] Mr. Henry may have introduced the bill; if not, he certainly supported it. At this time it was realized that "the scarcity of specie made it a serious matter to raise even the proportion which was required by the tax bill of the preceding session. Under the lead of Mr. Henry,[26] the tax was divided and one-half made payable by July 1, and the other half by November 1."[27]

At this time, the legislature "withdrew their consent to the abandonment of the claim to the first navigation of the Mississippi, and also instructed their delegates in Congress upon the question of the fisheries, and the admission of Vermont."

The American commissioners were sent to Paris in 1782 to conduct the very complicated negotiations for peace. Benjamin Franklin, John Jay and John Adams, with Henry Laurens added, represented the United States, acting under instructions from Congress. The Comte de Vergennes acted on behalf of France, and the Count D'Aranda represented Spain. By a secret treaty, France was bound to Spain, with the promise that Gibraltar, or its equivalent, would be acquired. Already Spain, in her grasp for power, had taken Baton Rouge, Natchez and Mobile, which Mr. Henry had predicted, as basis for her claim to the lower Mississippi, and she had sent an expedition in 1781 from St. Louis and seized St. Joseph, now within the present state of Missouri, to strengthen her covetous hand on the upper Mississippi. But the United States had already established "a more extensive claim to it."[28]

France and Spain failing in their final attempt to take Gibraltar in September, and England being now ready to treat for peace, France found herself embarrassed over her obligations to Spain and yielded to her demands for "an equivalent in America, and by restricting the western border of the United States, and depriving them of their fisheries, they both hoped to dwarf a republican power which they feared would become dangerous to monarchy, and which they proposed, with the aid of England, to confine to the east of the Alleghenies."[29] The British, "hoping to gain at least enough territory to make compensation for the losses of the Tory refugees," laid claim to the lands between the

[25] *Ibid.*, op. cit., II, p. 174. Hening, *Statutes at Large,* II, p. 39.

[26] *Ibid.*, op. cit., II, p. 175, *Bland Papers,* II, p. 83.

[27] *Ibid.*, op. cit., Hening, *Statutes at Large,* II, p. 66.

[28] See Henry, *Henry,* II, pp. 105–106–107–178.

[29] *Ibid.*, pp. 180–181. See their scheme during Jay's interview with the commissioners.

Mississippi and the Alleghenies, as Patrick Henry had feared. But the commissioners were able "to refute the Spanish and British claims to this coveted territory in the conclusive arguments . . . of the rights of the United States in the letter of Congress of October 17, 1780; namely, their charter limits, the actual occupation of the territory by many American settlers, and of that north of the Ohio by Virginia, with a military and civil government since the conquest of Clark. The principle of *uti possidetis* prevailed."[30]

Thus were the provisional articles of peace signed "which became definitive in 1783, and which secured to the United States their independence, with a boundary along the St. Croix on the east, the lakes on the North, the Mississippi on the west, and the Floridas on the south, with the right of fisheries in the waters of Newfoundland."[31]

The treaty of 1783 has been called one of the most brilliant triumphs in the whole history of modern diplomacy. "Had the affair been managed by men of ordinary ability, the greatest results of the Revolutionary War would probably have been lost; the new republic would have been cooped up between the Atlantic and the Alleghenies; our westward expansions would have been impossible without further warfare; and the formation of our Federal Union would doubtless have been effectively hindered or prevented."[32] It is fair to say that, had it not been for the vision of Governor Henry and the bravery and patriotism of Clark, these results would not have been achieved.

"The boundaries agreed on suggested extensions, and by the acquisition of Louisiana in 1803, of Florida in 1819, of Texas in 1845, of Oregon in 1846, of California in 1848, and of Alaska in 1867, millions of acres have been added to the original area fixed by the treaty."[33]

The May session of 1783 found Mr. Henry again seated in the House, where he was "made chairman of the committee on Propositions and Grievances, and a member of the committees on Privileges and Elections, Religion, and Courts of Justice." Because of an indisposition, he remained at home after June 13, although there are several recorded votes afterward. He did not make his appearance at the October session until seven days after

---

[30] *Ibid.*

[31] *Ibid.*, p. 182.

[32] *Ibid.*, p. 182–183.

[33] *Ibid.*

the House convened, when he was placed on the Committees of Privileges and Elections, Propositions and Grievances, Claims and Commerce. He remained until December 13, and no doubt being still indisposed, he did not return for the remaining nine days of the session. In May, 1784, he was absent until the 15th, being eleven days late, but he stayed on throughout the rest of the session. At this time he served on Committees of Religion, Privileges and Elections, Propositions and Grievances, and Courts of Justice. The first day of the October session, 1784, found him in his seat, and he was made chairman of the Committees on Religion, Propositions and Grievances, and Commerce. On November 17, he was elected Governor for a fourth term, which commenced on November 30.[34]

The importance of Mr. Henry's influence and leadership at the time the Legislature convened in May, 1783, is revealed in a letter to him from George Mason. It discusses among other things the news that "the Assembly intend to dissolve itself, to make way for a General Convention, to new model the constitution of government." He discussed British debts, taxes, and other weighty matters, and apologized for the long letter, which he ascribed to "its true cause, the unfeign'd esteem and regard with which I am dear sir, Your affectionate & obd^t^ sert., G. Mason."[35]

During the first day of the May session, Mr. Henry offered a bill to relieve restraints on British Commerce, "before any treaty was entered into," when he was opposed by his friend Judge Tyler. Mr. Henry took the ground that "that measure would expel from this country the trade of every other nation, on account of our habits, language, and the manner of conducting business on credit between us and them; also on this ground, in addition to the one above, that if we changed the then current of commerce, we should drive away all competition, and never perhaps regain it (which has literally happened)."[36]

In referring to Mr. Henry's observations in the matter, Judge Tyler said, "he was beyond all expression eloquent and sublime. After painting the distress of the people, struggling through a perilous war, cut off from commerce so long that they were naked and unclothed, he concluded with a figure, or rather a series of figures, which I shall never forget, because beautiful as they were in themselves, their effect was heightened beyond all

[34] Henry, *Henry*, II, p. 190.
[35] *Ibid.*, II, Beginning at page 184 through 189.
[36] *Ibid.*, II, p. 191.

description, by the manner in which he acted what he spoke:—'Why,' said he, 'should we fetter commerce? If a man is in chains, he droops and bows to the earth, for his spirits are broken (looking sorrowfully at his feet); but let him twist the fetters from his legs, and he will stand erect'; straightening himself, and assuming a look of proud defiance. —'Fetter not commerce, sir—let her be as free as the air—she will range the whole creation, and return on the wings of the four winds of heaven, to bless the land with plenty.' "[37]

His measure carried, "against a strong opposition, embracing his friend [Judge Tyler] whom he had just made speaker."[38]

At the fall session, a similar bill which he had introduced in May was taken up in Committee of the Whole. It called for repealing the act that had excluded the Tories from the rights of citizenship, and granting them permission to return to the state.[39]

During the war, great prejudice had arisen over the actions of the Tories, as well as against the Tories themselves. It was too early after the war for a change of heart, and many of the members felt a violent opposition and antipathy toward the Tories. The proposal of such a measure by Mr. Henry, of all people, took them by surprise. During the argument, his good friend, Judge Tyler, opposing it "with great warmth," inquired of Mr. Henry, "how he, above all other men, could think of inviting into his family an enemy from whose insults and injuries he had suffered so severely?" To this Mr. Henry answered:

"The personal feelings of a politician ought not to be permitted to enter those walls. The question (he said) was a national one, and in deciding it, if they acted wisely, nothing would be regarded but the interest of the nation. On the altar of his country's good he was willing to sacrifice all personal resentments, all private wrongs—and he flattered himself that he was not the only man in the House who was capable of making such a sacrifice. 'We have, sir' (said he), 'an extensive country, without population—what can be more obvious policy than that this country ought to be populated? People sir, form the strength and constitute the wealth of a nation. I want to see our vast forests filled up by some process a little more speedy than the ordinary course of nature. I wish to see these states rapidly ascending to the rank which their natural advantages authorize them to hold among

[37] *Ibid.*, II, pp. 191–192; Wirt, *Henry*, pp. 254–255, (1836 edition).

[38] *Ibid.*, op. cit., *Journal*, p. 586; Hening, *Statutes at Large*, II, p. 195.

[39] *Ibid.*, op. cit., *Journal*, pp. 22–76; Hening, *Statutes at Large*, II, p. 324.

the nations of the earth. . . . If you prefer the latter course, as I trust you do, encourage emigration—encourage the husbandmen, the mechanics, the merchants of the old world, to come out and settle in this land of promise—make it the home of the skilful, the industrious, the fortunate, as well as the asylum of the distressed—fill up the measure of your population as speedily as you can, by the means which heaven has placed in your hands—and I venture to prophesy there are those now living who will see this favored land among the most powerful on earth—able, sir, to take care of herself, without resorting to that policy which is always so dangerous, though sometimes unavoidable, of calling in foreign aid.' Here Patrick Henry referred to 'the golden harvests waving over fields of immeasurable extent; her commerce penetrating the most distant seas, and her cannon silencing the vain boasts of those who now proudly affect to rule the waves; your timber must be worked up into ships to transport the productions of the soil from which it has been cleared—then you must have commercial men and commercial capital to take off your productions, and find the best markets for them abroad—your great want, sir, is the want of men; and these you must have, and will have speedly, if you are wise.

" 'Do you ask how you are to get them? Open your doors, sir, and they will come in—. . . They see here a land blessed with natural and political advantages which are not equalled by those of any other country upon earth—a land on which Providence hath emptied the horn of abundance—a land over which peace hath now stretched forth her white wings, and where content and plenty lie down at every door! Sir, they see something more attractive than all this—they see a land in which liberty hath taken up her abode— . . . they see here a real divinity—her altars rising on every hand throughout these happy states—her glories chanted by three millions of tongues—and the whole region smiling under her blessed influence. Sir, let but this . . . Liberty, stretch forth her fair hand toward the people of the old world—tell them to come, and bid them welcome—and you will see them pouring in from the north, from the south, from the east, and from the west—your wilderness will be cleared and settled—your deserts will smile—your ranks will be filled, and you will soon be in a condition to defy the powers of any adversary. . . . Let us have the magnanimity, sir, to lay aside our antipathies and prejudices, and consider the subject in a political light. Those are an enterprising, moneyed people, they will be serviceable in taking off surplus produce of our lands, and supplying us with necessaries, during the infant state of our manufactures. Even if they be inimical to us in point of feeling and principle, I can see no objection in a political view, in making them tributary to our advantage. And as I have no prejudices to prevent my making this use of them, so, sir, I have no fear of any mischief that they can do us. Afraid of *them!* What, sir,' said he, rising to one of his loftiest attitudes, and assuming a look of the most indignant and sovereign contempt. 'Shall we who have laid the proud British *lion* at our feet, now be afraid of his whelps?' "[40]

Needless to say, Mr. Henry's proposal, calling for the repeal of the act excluding the Tories, carried.

At this same session, Patrick Henry "introduced and carried through a bill 'for clearing the Roanoke River'; was on a committee 'for cutting a navigable canal from the waters of the Elizabeth River to the waters of Albemarle Sound.' This became the Dismal Swamp Canal."[41] He was also a member of a committee "that reported charters for an Academy in Northampton County, and for Hampden-Sydney College, in Prince Edward County."[42] His name as a trustee appears "next to the President of the College, the distinguished Presbyterian divine, the Reverend John Blair Smith." It was these college students who had marched with the Rev. Mr. Smith at their head "when Governor Henry had called for men to defend the capital," and some of these same men had volunteered with Mr. Smith "when General Green crossed the Dan, and needed recruits." These colleges grew as the result of the effort to "pass an act to support religious teachers by taxation." The tax for supporting the ministers of the Episcopal Church had been suspended in 1776, at which time "the Legislature invited an expression of the public opinion on the question of a general assessment for the support of religion." The next spring, the Hanover Presbytery opposed it in a memorial laid before the legislature. The Baptist General Association also sent their memorial opposing it the following October, 1778. Mr. Jefferson's bill for establishing religious freedom, with a provision calling "for a

---

[40] Henry, *Henry,* op. cit., II, pp. 193–196. Wirt, *Henry,* pp. 250–254. Mr. Wirt states that Chancellor Wythe used to quote this figure to his law class at William and Mary.

[41] *Ibid.,* op. cit., II, pp. 197–198, *Journal,* p. 29; Hening, *Statutes at Large,* II, p. 332.

[42] *Ibid.,* op. cit., *Journal* for 1783, pp. 8-43; *Journal,* pp. 8–12; Hening, *Statutes at Large,* II, pp. 250–272.

general assessment, putting all denominations on the same footing," had been proposed in the House at the May session of 1779. It had gone through two readings in the House, where it was held up, waiting until further public opinion could be learned. At the following session, "the act for the support of the Episcopal clergy, which had been suspended from year to year since 1776, was repealed."

The Baptist Association met in October 1779 and presented a memorial to the legislature, calling for the passage of Mr. Jefferson's bill. Similar memorials were presented at the same session in November "from Amherst County, signed by Episcopalians, Presbyterians, Baptists, and Methodists." Other memorials were also presented: The Hanover Presbytery urged the Assembly that "they abstain from interfering in the government of the church, and also that the exclusive privileges enjoyed by the Episcopal Church be done away with." The Episcopalians urged "an assessment for the support of religion, and the passage of an act incorporating the Episcopal Church. Some of them also distinctly opposed the passage of Mr. Jefferson's bill."[43]

However, "the decay of religion and morality was so apparent, that thinking men, who had planned republican government on the basis of the virtue of the people, became greatly alarmed." And although "Virginia had ninety-one clergymen, officiating in one hundred and sixty-four churches and chapels" at the beginning of the Revolution, "at its close, only twenty-eight ministers were found laboring in the less desolate parishes of the State." The effects of the war were demoralizing, with the result that the church and religion were left in a deplorable condition. "The Sabbath had been almost forgotten, and public morals sadly deteriorated."[44] The volunteer contributions for the support of religious teachers "seemed destined to be a failure," as the people "were impoverished and demoralized by the late war," and the "pious patriotism of Mr. Henry shuddered for the event." The subject was brought up in the House at the May session of 1784, when further petitions and complaints were received. Memorials were received from the Hanover Presbytery and the Baptist Association, "praying that the Episcopal Church, still clinging to some remnants of the establishment, be put upon the same footing as

---

[43] *Ibid.*, op. cit., p. 202; Foote's *Sketches of Virginia*, p. 330; Hening, *Statutes at Large*, X, p. 197; Meade's *Old Churches*, II, p. 444; Foote's *Sketches*, p. 332.

[44] *Ibid.*, op. cit., p. 203; Meade's *Old Churches*, I. p. 17; Foote's *Sketches*, p. 412; Semple's *History of Baptists*, p. 36.

the other denominations." They complained of "the retention of the glebe land, unnecessary restrictions on other ministers performing marriages, and requiring members of vestries to be Episcopalians." The Episcopal Church, on the other hand, "petitioned for further security for their glebe lands and other property, and for an act of incorporation. . . ." One petition from some of the citizens of Powhatan County stated that "they are of the opinion a reasonable and moderate contribution of the people for the support of ministers of the Gospel and the Christian religion in the public worship of God is essential to the good and prosperity of the Commonwealth."[45]

Several papers were reported on by the Committee for Religion. One calling for the incorporation of the Episcopal Church was discussed, but was postponed until the November session, when "the question of the incorporation of the churches, and of a general assessment for the support of religion, again came up for discussion, but under very different circumstances. The subject of assessment was introduced by a petition from the Isle of Wight County, urging the necessity of such a measure; and by a memorial of Hanover Presbytery, adopted at its October session, 1784, consenting to what they deemed inevitable."[46]

Madison, having conferred with Jefferson about the assessment, wrote that "many petitions from below the Blue Ridge had prayed for such a law; and though several from the Presbyterian laity beyond it were in a contrary style, the clergy of that sect favored it. The other sects seemed passive."[47]

Patrick Henry was chairman of the committee given the task of drafting the bill, which was reported on November 11, 1784. The Committee of the Whole "reported in favor of 'a moderate assessment for the support of the Christian religion'; and the report was agreed to by a recorded vote of 47 to 32." The Presbyterian and Baptist proposals on the subjects of marriages and vestries, and also "that acts ought to pass for the incorporation of all societies of the Christian religion which may apply for same" were taken up on November 17 and the Committee of the Whole reported in favor of the memorials. "The last was agreed to by a recorded vote of 62 to 23, and Mr. Henry was one of the committee ordered to bring in a bill to 'incorporate the clergy of the

---

[45] *Ibid.*, op. cit., p. 204, *Journal,* p. 36. See their change of position, p. 205.

[46] *Ibid.*, p. 205.

[47] *Ibid.*, op. cit., Mr. Madison to Mr. Jefferson concerning the assessment. Letter of January, 1785, Madison's *Works,* I, p. 130.

Protestant Episcopal Church.' " However, Mr. Henry was due at the capital on November 1 to take on his duties as Governor, and had to leave the body "before either of these bills were reported, but it is quite certain that he approved of them." Unlike some of the features of the bill as first proposed, "it was not for the incorporation of the clergy of the Episcopal Church, as distinct from the laity, but of 'the Protestant Episcopal Church,' embracing both clergy and laity. Although Mr. Madison voted against the resolution of the Committee of the Whole on the subject, he voted for the bill reported."[48]

The assessment bill allowed the taxpayer to apply his taxes to the "support of the religious teachers of his own denomination"; it had been "stripped of nearly every objectionable feature," and was said to be "as perfect as a measure could well be," proposing "only a small tax on all taxable property." However, James Madison "led the opposition to it, and counted largely on Mr. Henry's absence for its defeat. He wrote, November 27, 'Mr. Henry, the father of the scheme is gone up to his seat for his family, and will no more sit in the House of Delegates—a circumstance very inauspicious to his offspring.' "[49] In "the absence of 'the father of the scheme' its opponents found themselves in the minority." The bill had gone through its third reading on December 23 when "Madison proposed and carried a resolution to postpone its further consideration till the next session, with a request that the people then signify their opinion on the subject." Intense interest was aroused over the question. Madison drafted for its opponents "a masterly discussion of the subject, and presented with great force the argument for entire separation of Church and State, based upon the principle introduced into the Bill of Rights by Mr. Henry himself. At first Mr. Madison was greatly incensed with the Presbyterian clergy for the memorial of Hanover Presbytery of October 1784, in which he declared that they had misrepresented the laity of that church.[50] But the Presbyterian clergy soon regained their old attitude on the subject." In May 1785, at the next meeting of the Presbytery, "the body unanimously disapproved of 'any kind of assessment for the support of religion,' " and at their convention in August, "adopted a strong memorial to the Legislature opposing the proposed bill, and asking that Mr. Jefferson's bill, reported in 1779, be adopted."

[48] *Ibid.*, p. 206.

[49] *Ibid.*, op. cit., p. 207; Rives' *Madison,* I, p. 606.

[50] *Ibid.*, op. cit., II, p. 208, Letter to Monroe, *Madison's Works,* I, p. 144.

It was supported by the bulk of the Scotch-Irish Presbyterians, as well as the Baptist General Association, and some Episcopalians. Thus, "the Legislature of 1785 did not stop with the defeat of the assessment bill. It took up and passed Mr. Jefferson's bill 'for the establishment of religious freedom,' which had been reported by the revisers in 1779. Even this bill has been attacked from time to time, as seen in one memorial of October 22, 1779, from Essex County, denouncing it as a 'diabolical scheme.' . . . But it is nothing more than an exposition of the principle inserted by Mr. Henry into the Bill of Rights, that religion is a matter to be determined by every man's conscience in accordance with his convictions."[51]

The fact that Patrick Henry was a patron of the bill calling for the incorporation of the Episcopal church has been used as proof that he favored the established church. "To test the justness of this charge, the journals of the house of delegates have been examined, and this is the result of the evidence which they furnish: on the 17th of November, 1784, Mr. Matthews reported from the Committee of the Whole house, on the state of the Commonwealth, the following resolution:—

"Resolved, That it is the opinion of this committee, that acts ought to pass for the incorporation of all societies of the Christian religion, which may apply for the same."

". . . How a measure which holds out to all religious societies, *equally*, the same benefit, can be charged with partiality, because accepted by one only, it is not very easy to discern."[52] Special criticism has been made of Mr. Henry because of the assessment, which accounts for the space given to these bills. "Mr. Henry's advocacy of the assessment bill, and the incorporation act, has been considered a blunder" by some clergymen and critics. But Patrick Henry always did what he thought was best for the people. His views regarding these bills "were approved by Washington, Richard Henry Lee, John Marshall and Henry Tazewell, and whatever may have been his error, it was on the side of virtue. His design was to support Christianity against French infidelity. Doubtless much of the opposition to the assessment bill came from the poverty of the people, and the difficulty they experienced in paying the taxes necessary for the support of

---

[51] *Ibid.*, pp. 209–210. See the sixteenth section of the Bill of Rights as written by Patrick Henry, Henry, *Henry,* I, pp. 430–431; Also what the Rev. Caleb Wallace, and Edmund Randolph have to say on the subject, I, pp. 495–496–497–498.
[52] Wirt, *Henry,* (1836) pp. 260–261.

government, and the payment of the public debt incurred during the war. In this distress Mr. Henry keenly sympathized, and under his leadership several bills were passed, during 1783 and 1784, for temporarily postponing the collection of taxes."[53]

A description surrounding one such bill in which Patrick Henry opposed an increase in taxation is given in writing by Judge Archibald Stuart for the purpose of showing Mr. Henry's eloquence in the Virginia Legislature, about the year 1784, when Judge Stuart sat in that body. He says:

"The finances of the country had been much deranged during the war, and public credit was at a low ebb; a party in the legislature thought it then high time to place the character and credit of the state on a more respectable footing, by laying taxes commensurate with all the public demands. With this view, a bill had been brought into the house, and referred to a committee of the whole; in support of which the then speaker (Mr. Tyler), Henry Tazewell, Mann Page, William Ronald, and many other members of great respectability (including, to the best of my recollection, Richard H. Lee, and perhaps, Mr. Madison) took an active part. Mr. Henry, on the other hand, was of the opinion that this was a premature attempt; that policy required that the people should have some repose after the fatigues and privations to which they had been subjected, during a long and arduous struggle for independence.

"The advocates of the bill, in committee of the whole house, used their utmost efforts, and were successful in conforming it to their views, by such a majority (say thirty) as seemed to ensure its passage. When the committee rose, the bill was instantly reported to the house; when Mr. Henry, who had been excited and roused by his recent defeat, came forward again in all the majesty of his power. For some time after he commenced speaking, the countenances of his opponents indicated no apprehension of danger to their cause.

"The feelings of Mr. Tyler, which were sometime warm, could not on that occasion be concealed, even in the chair. His countenance was forbidding, even repulsive, and his face turned from the speaker. Mr. Tazewell was reading a pamphlet, and Mr. Page was more than usually grave. After some time, however, it was discovered that Mr. Tyler's countenance gradually began

[53] Henry, *Henry*, pp. 211–212. See what Bishop Meade has to say about French infidelity permeating the State: Meade, *History of Old Churches and Families of Virginia*, I, p. 175.

to relax; he would occasionally look at Mr. Henry; sometimes smile, his attention by degrees became more fixed; at length it became completely so:—he next appeared to be in good humor; he leaned toward Mr. Henry—appeared charmed and delighted, and finally lost in wonder and amazement. The progress of these feelings was legible in his countenance.

"Mr. Henry drew a most affecting picture of the state of poverty and suffering in which the people of the upper counties had been left by the war. His delineation of their wants and wretchedness was so minute, so full of feeling, and withal so true, that he could scarcely fail to enlist on his side every sympathetic mind. He contrasted the severe toil by which *they* had to gain their daily subsistence, with the facilities enjoyed by the people of the lower counties. The latter, he said, residing on the salt rivers and creeks, could draw their supplies at pleasure, from the waters that flowed by their doors; and then he presented such a ludicrous image of the members who had advocated the bill (the most of whom were from the lower counties) peeping and peering along the shores of the creeks, to pick up their mess of crabs, or addling off to the oyster-rocks, to rake for *their daily bread*, as filled the house with a roar of merriment. Mr. Tazewell laid down his pamphlet, and shook his sides with laughter; even the gravity of Mr. Page was affected; a corresponding change of countenance prevailed through the ranks of the advocates of the bill, and you might discover that they had surrendered their cause. In this they were not disappointed; for on a division, Mr. Henry had a majority of upward of thirty against the bill."[54]

Another incidence of Patrick Henry's wit and "good-natured pleasantry" was related by Judge Tyler: "During one of the sessions of the Legislature, he and R. H. Lee were of a party who spent a night at the home of Mr. Edmund Randolph, near Richmond. Colonel Lee, who was a brilliant conversationalist, entertained the company to a very late hour, descanting on the genius of Cervantes, especially as it was displayed in 'Don Quixote.' Finally the company began to yawn, but Colonel Lee did not observe it and continued his remarks. Mr. Henry took in the situation, and rising slowly from his chair, walked across the room, remarking that 'Don Quixote' was certainly a most excellent work, and most skilfully adapted to the purpose of the author; 'but,' said he, 'Mr. Lee,' stopping before him with a most significant archness of look, 'you have overlooked, in your eulogy, one

[54] Wirt, *Henry,* pp. 271–272–273; Henry, *Henry,* op. cit., pp. 212–213–214.

of the finest things in the book.' 'What is that?' asked Lee. 'It is,' said Mr. Henry, 'that divine exclamation of Sancho, "Blessed be the man that first invented sleep; it covers one all over, like a cloak."' Mr. Lee took the hint, and the company broke up in good humor."[55]

These reminiscences of Mr. Henry cover the sessions when he sat as a member of the legislature, 1783–1784. Further bills offered at this time included one "demanding that Congress take steps to obtain the free navigation of the Mississippi"; and resolutions instructing the delegates in Congress of the importance of forming treaties with the Indians in the southern department. Mr. Henry moved the resolutions requesting the adoption of such measures necessary "to avert the danger of hostilities with the Indians, and to incline them to treat with the commissioners of Congress. . . ." But Patrick Henry realized that treaties were only temporary measures. He looked for a permanent remedy that would relieve "the feverish hostility" that existed "between the whites and the red men. . . . This he could only hope for by replacing the hatred between the races by kindly affection. To his generous mind the best way to accomplish this was to unite the two by ties of blood." On November 16 he introduced a resolution for the "encouragement of marriages with the Indians," which he advocated "with irresistible earnestness and eloquence," and it carried. The bill read in part:

"Whereas, intermarriages between the citizens of this commonwealth and the Indians living in its neighbourhood, may have great effect in conciliating the friendship and confidence of the latter, whereby not only their civilization may in some degree be finally brought about, but in the meantime, their hostile inroads be prevented. . . ."[56] Special inducements were offered as encouragement, which included pecuniary bounties on certificates of marriage and at the birth of each child, exemption from taxes, and a provision for free schools for the children. Introduced in accordance with the resolution, the bill would have passed unimpeded had Mr. Henry continued a member of the House. It passed its first and second readings and was prepared for its final passage when "his election as governor took effect, and displaced him from the floor: on the third day after which event the bill was read a third time and rejected."[57]

---

[55] *Ibid.*, p. 425; Henry, *Henry*, op. cit., II, pp. 214–215.
[56] *Ibid.*, pp. 258–259 n. See also *Henry*, II, pp. 218–219.
[57] *Ibid.*, pp. 259–260.

In this bill, Mr. Henry's great humanity of character is seen and his policy should not be thought unwise. Many families today proudly claim descent from Pocahontas. It must be admitted that his purpose "does honor to his heart, and is another evidence of the boldness and independence of his statesmanship." It was also John Marshall's opinion that the bill for encouraging intermarriages with the Indians "would have been advantageous to this country."[58]

At the meeting of the legislature in May 1783, the matter of the cession of Virginia's Northwestern territory to the United States had been put off because of the deepest irritation brought on by the action of Congress. However, at the fall assembly, the proposal of Congress "to accept the cession of Virginia with some slight and not material alterations in her conditions, brought a change in Virginia's attitude." Patrick Henry was the advocate of the measure as proposed by Congress and was a member of the committee "ordered to bring in a bill pursuant to this resolution."

The Committee of the Whole on December 9 "Resolved that the delegates of this state to the Congress of the United States, be instructed to convey . . . all right, title and claim, which the said Commonwealth hath to the lands northward of the river, Ohio, upon the terms contained in the act of Congress of September 13 last. . . ." This bill passed the House on December 19 with epochal consequences for the future of America.[59]

Also considered were the neglected Congressional requisitions and the need for greater powers for the collection of revenue from the states to meet the public obligations. This aroused considerable interest as well as many proposals for amending the Articles of Confederation. In February, 1781, Congress had requested the power to levy duty of five percent on imports, which was approved by Mr. Henry and was acceded to by the Assembly at its June session.[60] But since several of the states had failed to take similar action, the act was suspended at its next session until the other states should give their consent. However, at the fall session, October, 1782, when Patrick Henry was at home sick, Richard Lee led a successful move to have the act repealed. On Mr. Henry's return in the spring, 1783, he advocated a modified measure to aid Congress with its finances and he was a member of a committee charged with drawing a proper bill. This doubt-

---

[58] Henry, *Henry*, II, p. 219.

[59] *Ibid.*, op. cit., II, p. 220, *The Journal*, pp. 53, 62 and 71.

[60] *Ibid.*, II, p. 221.

less would have passed except for the alarm aroused over a paper drawn by Alexander Hamilton suggesting that Congress, "by having the power to contract debts binding upon the States, had the constructive power to provide the means for their payment regardless of the agency of the States." This article was looked upon "as destructive of the reserved rights of the States and members were unwilling to vest additional powers in a body disposed to extend its powers so dangerously by construction."[61] Patrick Henry was influenced by Hamilton's paper; it brought a change in his sentiments, and in most of those who would otherwise have supported the bill. Regarding this, Jefferson wrote Madison, June 17, 1783, "Mr. Henry had declared in favor of the impost, but when the question came on he was utterly silent." But its opposition was evident: "The vote against it was so large that no division was called for." It was resolved, however, that a committee be appointed (of which Mr. Henry was a member) to bring in an alternate bill favored by the legislature to "levy the duty asked for by Congress with its own officers, and to apply the proceeds to the State's quota of the continental debt, any deficiency to be made up from the tax on land and slaves." Mr. Henry "carried the measure against Richard H. Lee."

In the meantime, General Washington, disbanding his army, had written to the several states, pointing to "the weakness of the Confederation, and the consequent danger to the liberties which had been so dearly bought, and urged that Congress be vested with power to collect its revenue without reliance on the States, thus endorsing specifically the plan proposed" by Congress. This was not received until after the vote had been taken in the legislature on June 11. However, at the November session, two days after Mr. Henry took his seat, "a resolution was adopted to that effect, and Mr. Henry was one of the Committee to frame the bill."[62] But even now, the other states would not assent to this grant of power.

Disturbed over the need to "strengthen the Federal arm," Patrick Henry decided again to offer himself for the legislature, and May 1784 found him in Richmond for this purpose. His sentiments on the subject were expressed in the coffeehouse to James Madison and Joseph Jones, according to William Short, who reported the conversation in a letter to Thomas Jefferson. "The event of it was that Mr. Jones and Mr. Madison should

---

[61] *Ibid.*, op. cit., II, p. 224, Rives' *Madison,* I, p. 435.

[62] See references, *Ibid.*, II, pp. 224–225.

sketch out some plan for giving greater power to the federal government, and that Mr. Henry should support it on the floor. It was thought a bold example set by Virginia would have influence on the other States. Mr. Henry declared that it was the only inducement he had for coming to the present assembly. He saw ruin inevitable unless something was done to give Congress a compulsory process on delinquent States, etc."[63]

In consequence, a series of resolutions were introduced four days after Mr. Henry took his seat and were adopted in the Committee of the Whole. The appropriate remedy for giving greater strength to the Confederation is suggested in the following:

> In agreeing to the alteration of the eighth article of the Confederation proposed by Congress, so as to make the basis of requisitions all free white inhabitants and three-fifths of all others, instead of the value of lands;
>
> In urging a prompt compliance by the States with all requisitions, on whatever basis made;
>
> In urging Congress to make speedy settlement of its accounts with the several States, by estimation, if necessary, and declaring that the balance due 'ought to be enforced, if necessary, by such distress on the property of the defaulting States or of their citizens, as the United States, in Congress assembled, may deem adequate and most eligible'; and
>
> In declaring that Congress ought to be invested, for fifteen years, with power to prohibit imports and exports by citizens of other nations not having commercial treaties with the United States. This was to meet the illiberal policy of Great Britain.[64]

Regarding this, Madison wrote Jefferson, May 15, "Mr. Henry arrived yesterday, and from a short conversation I find him strenuous for invigorating the federal government, though without any precise plan." However, Patrick Henry lost no time in determining on a plan, which was offered on the 18th and apparently had the approval of the whole committee. These resolutions were later used against Mr. Henry in the Virginia Convention of 1788, when George Nicholas referred to them as coercive of the states, saying to Mr. Henry: "I am sure that the gentleman recognizes his child," and since it was not disowned, the plan must have been Patrick Henry's own.

But if, as claimed, it was a power of coercion, it was "different

---

[63] Morgan, *Henry*, p. 332; Henry, *Henry*, op. cit., II, pp. 225–226, Bancroft's *History of the Constitution*, I, p. 361.

[64] Henry, *Henry*, op. cit., II, pp. 226–227, *Journal*, pp. 11–12.

from the right claimed by Hamilton in the reply of Congress to the Legislature of Rhode Island, touching the impost duty. That was a claim to a power to levy a duty on the commerce of the States, nowhere granted in the articles of confederation. This was a claim to force the States to comply with the lawful requisitions of Congress, and it was based on the acknowledged common law of confederacies, both ancient and modern. Such was the construction of the power of Congress, not only by Mr. Henry and Mr. Madison, but by Mr. Jefferson as well."[65]

Patrick Henry's grandson, W. W. Henry, made no apologies for his States-Righter-grandfather and his efforts to strengthen the power of Congress over commerce and in the matter of requisitions. If the Articles of Confederation were inefficient, and only "provided for just such a Congress as already existed," and no more powers were granted than those while conducting the war, it is not surprising to find Mr. Henry and General Washington urging stronger measures to the central government, seeing that under such conditions the war effort had been greatly impeded.[66]

Nevertheless, Patrick Henry's actions in lending aid to Congress in its distress would cause Madison and others to refer to him as the "champion of the federal cause," until he suddenly took an about-face two years later. The question is asked, what brought about this sudden change in Mr. Henry's policies? One of Mr. Henry's most able biographers explained it as "the discovery of some new influence which came into his life between 1784, and 1786, and which was powerful enough to reverse entirely the habitual direction of his political thought and conduct. Just what that influence was can now be easily shown.

"On the 3rd of August, 1786, John Jay, as secretary for foreign affairs, presented to Congress some results of his negotiations with the Spanish envoy, Gardoqui, respecting a treaty with Spain; and he then urged that Congress, in view of certain vast advantages to our foreign commerce, should consent to surrender the navigation of the Mississippi for twenty-five or thirty years,—[67] a proposal which, very naturally, seemed to the six Southern States

---

[65] *Ibid.*, op. cit., II, p. 227, Letter to Edward Coles, August 4, 1787, *Jefferson's Writings*, II, p. 203. Rives' *Madison*, I, p. 303.

[66] See Governor Henry's and General Washington's exchange of letters in the previous chapter; Washington, writing to Governor Trumbull, June 1780, hoped "that a change of measures will save us from ruin." Chapter 18, footnote, 161.

[67] Tyler, *Henry, American Statesman*, op. cit., p. 307, *Secret Journal of Congress*, IV, pp. 44–63.

as nothing less than a cool invitation to them to sacrifice their own most important interests for the next quarter of a century, in order to build up during that period the interests of the seven States of the North. The revelation of this project, and of the ability of the Northern States to force it through, sent a shock of alarm and of distrust into every Southern community. Moreover, full details of these transactions in Congress were promptly conveyed to Governor Henry by James Monroe, who added this pungent item,—that a secret project was then under the serious consideration of 'committees' of Northern men, for a dismemberment of the Union, and for setting the Southern States adrift, after having thus bartered away from them the use of the Mississippi."[68]

Monroe's letter was full of portents for the future. The occlusion of the Mississippi was not the only danger revealed. Another object was "to break up the settlement on the western waters. . . . To throw the weight of population eastward and keep it there, to appreciate the vacant lands of New York and Massachusetts. In short, it is a system of policy which has for its object the keeping the weight of government and population of this quarter, and is proposed by a set of men so flagitious, unprincipled, and determained in their pursuits, as to satisfy me beyond a doubt they have extended their views to the dismemberment of the gov't . . . and resolved either that sooner than fail it shall be the case, or being only desirous of that event have adopted this as the necessary means of effecting it. . . ."[69]

Governor Henry's reaction to the reported scheme of Congress to yield the navigation of the Mississippi, and to dissolve the Union, was so bitter as to cause him to decline the appointment to the proposed Federal Convention to meet in the spring of 1787 at Philadelphia. His refusal showed, to put it colloquially, that he "smelt a rat." But it must be agreed that this attempt by Congress in secret session, August 25, 1786, by a vote of seven states to five,[70] in the face of the constitutional provision which

---

[68] *Ibid.*, op. cit., Rives' *Life of Madison,* II, p. 122; See full letter from James Monroe to Governor Henry; Henry, *Henry,* II, pp. 291–292–293–294–295–296–297–298.

[69] Monroe to Henry, See also Madison's letter to Jefferson, Tyler, *Henry,* p. 308.

[70] If Patrick Henry now turned his back on the central government after his willingness to strengthen Congress, his actions were perfectly obvious and justified: It was the intrigue of Congress in secret session, August 25, 1786, in its attempt to grant the occlusion of the Mississippi by a vote of seven States

required nine states to enter into a treaty, must have been most offensive to the patriot, who had early recognized the Mississippi's commercial advantages to the Southern states, and its contribution to the defense and security of the western frontiers. Such a threat by Congress had brought about a disposition among the Eastern states to "secede from the Union." Mr. Henry himself was heard to say "that he would rather part with the Confederation than relinquish the navigation of the Mississippi."[71]

Two months later, November 9, a bill was passed in the Virginia House of Delegates, calling for the appointment of seven commissioners to be sent to the proposed convention to aid "in devising and discussing all such alterations and further provisions as may be necessary to render the federal constitution adequate to the exigencies of the Union," the results of which would be subject to the approval of Congress and the states.

On the 29th of the same month, the following resolutions were passed in the House and were unanimously adopted:

> That the common right of navigating the river Mississippi, and of communicating with other nations through that channel, ought to be considered as the bountiful gift of nature to the United States, as proprietors of the territories watered by the said river and its eastern branches, and as moreover secured to them by the late revolution.
>
> That the Confederacy, having been formed on the broad basis of equal rights, in every part thereof, to the protection and guardianship of the whole, a sacrifice of the rights of any one part, to the supposed or real interest of another part, would be a flagrant violation of justice, a direct contravention of the end for which the federal government was instituted, and an alarming innovation in the system of the Union. . .[72]

"Henry and Mason had put so much of themselves into the existing State government that they were naturally partial to it." As to the west and southwest, "there had always been a magnet in that part of the country, drawing him thither in his dreams.

(Northern) as opposed by the five Southern States, including Maryland, directly in violation of the Constitutional provision, requiring nine states to enter into a treaty, as well as the plot to dissolve the Union. Henry, *Henry*, II, pp. 290–291–295. Read Monroe's complete letter to Governor Henry.

[71] Henry, *Henry*, II, p. 301, John Marshall to Arthur Lee, March 5, 1787, *Life of Arthur Lee*, II, p. 321.

[72] Tyler, *Henry*, op. cit., pp. 308–309, *Journal*, Virginia House Delegates, pp. 66–67; Henry, *Henry*, II, pp. 299–300.

He loved it." Yet, for the sake of the Confederation, he had induced Virginia to cede her western territory, and when the Articles had proved weak, he had been "the champion of amendments" to make them strong. "That the Northern States, for which Virginia had done so much, should, from a purely selfish policy attempt to barter away the navigation of the Mississippi, so valuable to her, at the risk of losing the all-important Western country and dividing the Union, was a shock to him indeed."[73]

In the light of such conditions in Congress, it is not surprising to find the revulsion engendered in the bosom of Patrick Henry that kept him from accepting the appointment as commissioner to the convention. He was in "no state of mind to surrender sovereign attributes of any sort for the sake of strengthening a general government which had just demonstrated that it might become a curse instead of a blessing. . . . Washington at first declined to go to the Convention, but his reason for declining was altogether different from Henry's. With Henry, liberty was an emotion, a passion; he was republican to the core, and when stirred was intensely imaginative. He and Mason still distrusted the old aristocrats."[74]

Madison, who was among the seven delegates chosen to go to the convention in Philadelphia, wrote Washington on December 7: "I am entirely convinced from what I observe here, that unless the project of Congress can be reversed, the hopes of carrying this State into a proper federal system will be demolished. Many of our most federal leading men are extremely soured with what has already passed. Mr. Henry, who has been hitherto the champion of the federal cause, has become a cold advocate, and, in the event of an actual sacrifice of the Mississippi by Congress, will unquestionably go over to the opposite side."[75]

During the same month Madison again wrote Washington: "I hear from Richmond, with much concern, that Mr. Henry has positively declined his mission to Philadelphia. Besides the loss of his services on that theatre, there is danger, I fear, that this step has proceeded from a wish to leave his conduct unfettered on another theatre, where the result of the convention will receive its destiny from his omnipotence."[76]

At this same time, December 6, Edmund Randolph wrote to

---

[73] Henry, *Henry*, II, p. 300.
[74] Morgan, *Henry*, pp. 337–338.
[75] Tyler, *Henry*, op. cit., p. 310, Madison, *Letters*, etc., I, p. 264.
[76] *Ibid.*, p. 311; Henry, *Henry*, II, p. 312.

Mr. Henry with the sincere wish for his presence at the federal convention: "From the experience of your late administration, you must be persuaded that every day dawns with peril to the United States. To whom, then can they resort for assistance with firmer expectation, than to those who first kindled the Revolution?" Mr. Henry replied to Randolph: "It is with much concern that I feel myself constrained to decline acting under this appointment, so honorable to me from the objects of it as well as the characters with whom I am joined."[77]

The offer was made to General Nelson to substitute for Mr. Henry, and upon his declining, it was next made to Richard Lee, who also declined. Dr. James McClurg, a friend of Henry's and "a patriot, a 'character,' and a true man," thus substituted. The Virginia Federalists were "Madison, Randolph, and Marshall," while the State Sovereignty men were "Colonel William Grayson, Monroe, and Mason."[78]

Edmund Randolph, who had now succeeded Mr. Henry in the chair as governor, wrote Madison on March 1 that "Congress must have done with all talk of shutting up the Mississippi," adding: "It will not be sufficient to negative it merely; but a negative with some emphasis can alone secure Mr. Henry to the objects of the Convention at Philadelphia."[79] On March 19, Madison wrote Jefferson in Paris regarding conditions and added: "But although it appears that the intended sacrifice of the Mississippi will not be made, the consequences of the intention and the attempt are likely to be serious. Mr. Henry's disgust exceeds all measure, and I am not singular in ascribing his refusal to attend the convention to the policy of keeping himself free to combat or espouse the result of it, according to the result of the Mississippi business, among other circumstances."[80]

The friends of the new system, who were watching Mr. Henry with "great solicitude," were beginning to realize that he meant what he said and he would not go to the convention in Philadelphia. Washington was, with difficulty, prevailed on to attend.[81]

Mr. Henry closed his fifth term as Governor, which had begun November 30, 1784, and ended November 30, 1786. He declined reelection. During this term he had lived at "Salisbury"

[77] Henry, *Henry*, II, p. 311.
[78] Morgan, *Henry*, pp. 338–339.
[79] *Ibid.*, pp. 336–337.
[80] Henry, *Henry*, II, p. 313; *Madison Papers*, II, p. 623.
[81] *Ibid.*, II, p. 314. He was persuaded by Governor Randolph and others.

in Chesterfield County, 13 miles from Richmond. His son-in-law, Judge Spencer Roane, who married his daughter, Ann Henry, says: "With respect to his family, they were furnished with an excellent coach (at a time when these vehicles were not so common as at present [1814]); they lived as genteelly and associated with as polished society as those of any Governor before or since have done. He entertained as much company as others, and in as genteel a style, and when at the end of two years he resigned the office, he had greatly exceeded the salary, and was in debt, which was one cause that induced him to resume the practice of law."[82] But Mr. Henry had put his "spare money into land." He owned two tracts in Botetourt and 10,000 acres in Kentucky in 1778, and the same year he bought three-fifths part of 16,650 acres on Leatherwood Creek. He now had seven children by his second marriage to Dorothea Dandridge. They were: Dorothea, Sarah, Martha Catharine, Patrick, Fayette, Alexander Spotswood and Nathaniel. Richard died as a baby, and Jane Robertson when four days old. Later, at Red Hill, he would have two other sons, Edward Winston and John.[83] By his first wife there were six children, making seventeen in all.

From Leatherwood, Patrick Henry's thoughts turned homeward again, to Hanover. He was tired of the "bustle" he lived in at Leatherwood and besides, his "fine and promising children" would soon need to enter college. Some land in Hanover he had set his eyes upon and hoped to get from General Nelson. Whether the property was too costly, or had already been sold, is not known, but instead he moved in a different direction—80 miles southwest of Richmond to Prince Edward County, where he could enter his sons in Hampden-Sydney College.[84] Here he once again took up the practice of law which he had discontinued since 1774. And although he had declined to serve further as chief magistrate, this did not mean that he would discontinue his interest in the state government. There was no time for retirement now. The next year, 1787, he would return to the Virginia legislature and serve as a member of the House until December 1790.

He had "closed his administration with honour, as the first republican governor of Virginia, and was the most considerable man in the commonwealth."[85]

---

[82] Morgan, *Henry*, p. 323; See also Henry, *Henry*, II, p. 521.

[83] *Ibid.*, p. 325. See chapter XIV, (this book). Also, Henry, *Henry*, II, p. 631.

[84] *Ibid.*, p. 323.

[85] Wirt, *Henry*, (1836) p. 245 n.

XVIII

FOE OF THE FEDERAL CONSTITUTION: INCREASE TO GREATNESS

THE FEDERAL CONVENTION met in Philadelphia on May 25, 1787, behind closed doors, with George Washington as the presiding officer. Acting on the recommendations of the Annapolis Convention of five states, and later, by the respective legislatures themselves, the twelve states "who were no longer opposed to a reform in the federal constitution" dispatched their deputies. Only Rhode Island refused to take any part and did not attend.

The threatened dangers to the plan of Congress to conclude the Spanish treaty with a provision for the occlusion of the Mississippi had become so alarming as to cause the abandonment of the effort. Had Congress not done so, the people of Kentucky and Tennessee would have declared their independence from the United States and they, undoubtedly, would have been followed by the states to the southward.[1] The dissolution of the Union was the hope of Spain and England, and was even expected, and had this occurred, they were making plans to divide the territory between themselves. These dangers as well as others were no doubt responsible for the willingness of the states to overcome their difficulties and make their attendance upon Congress. Mr. Henry's vigorous proposition, offered as an amendment to the bill, in its form providing for "the repeal of all acts repugnant to the treaty of peace," had carried in the House of Delegates by a vote of 80

[1] Henry, *Henry*, op. cit., II, pp. 316–317. See the opinion of Jefferson, Curtis, *History of Constitution*, I, p. 321.

to 31, which was called "one of the most remarkable exhibitions of his power in debate" and "was believed to be without parallel in the history of legislative bodies."[2]

When the convention opened in Philadelphia, the Virginia delegates—Edmund Randolph, John Blair, James Madison, George Mason and George Wythe—were in their seats, but not Patrick Henry. And had he been present and answered to the roll in the order in which the relative vote was received by him, his name would have been next to Washington. His absence must have been conspicuous. It seems to have caused considerable worry among some of his colleagues, and no doubt his recent decision, like his earlier ones, discomfited them also. Jefferson, who had missed out in framing the government of his own state, was destined to have no hand now in the proposed plan agreed on by the Virginia delegates. The 15 resolutions setting forth the "Virginia plan" were introduced by Edmund Randolph. This proposed that the Articles of Confederation be set aside, and in their place, "a National government, consisting of a supreme legislative, executive, and judiciary"[3] be established. (The word National was later stricken out). These branches of government formed the basis for the construction of the Constitution, and on June 13, 19 resolutions based on the Virginia plan were reported by the Committee of the Whole.[4] But the difficult problem "of framing a supreme federal government, acting directly upon the people, without duly restricting the sovereignty of the several States," remained to be solved. And when the work was completed, and time came for signing the Constitution on the last day—September 17—even then 16 deputies would refuse to sign it, among whom were "Mason, Randolph and Gerry. Mason said that he would 'sooner chop off his right hand than put it to the Constitution as it then stood.' Franklin said: 'Several parts of this Constitution I do not at present approve, but I am not sure I shall never approve them. It astonishes me to find this system approaching so near to perfection. I assent to this Constitution because I am not sure it is not the best. The opinions I have had of its errors I sacrifice to the public good.' "[5]

[2] *Ibid.*, II, p. 326. See also pp. 325–327. Congress recommended the repeal of the acts to the several states. Mr. Henry's amendment to the bill came up in the fall session of the Virginia Legislature on December 3, 1787, upsetting the previous vote.

[3] Henry, *Henry*, op. cit., II, p. 318; Journal of Convention for May 30, 1787.

[4] Morgan, *Henry*, p. 339; Henry, *Henry*, II, pp. 318–323.

[5] *Ibid.*, pp. 339–340.

But how did others feel regarding the Federal Constitution? Were they hopeful of bringing it to a conclusion? Jefferson, who was now living in Paris as commissioner and minister to France, wrote Lewis Littlepage, Aug. 12, 1787:

> A federal convention is now sitting at Philadelphia, of which Genl. Washington is President. Its object is to amend the confederation by strengthening more the hands of Congress. Much good is hoped from it. It is composed of the greatest characters in America, every state having appointed to it except Rhode Island. They will go on without her.[6]

Three months of convention wrangling made little headway in coming to a solution, and James Madison, among others, appears to have lost much of his enthusiasm. He wrote Jefferson from Philadelphia, September 6, 1787, and in mentioning the powers of Congress, he enclosed some outlines, saying: "I hazard an opinion nevertheless that the *plan should it be adopted* will neither effectually *answer* its *national object* nor prevent the local *mischiefs* which every where *excite disgust* against the *state* governments. The grounds of this opinion will be the subject of a future letter."[7]

Madison's "future letter" to Jefferson was written after the Philadelphia Convention had closed September 17. It was dated October 24, 1787. He mentioned the issues that were involved and declared:

> It will not escape you that three names only from Virginia are subscribed to the Act. Mr. Wythe did not return after the death of his lady. Docr. McClurg left the Convention sometime before the adjournment. The Governor and Col. Mason refused to be parties to it. Mr. Gerry was the only other member who refused. . . . Col. Mason left Philadelphia in an exceeding ill humor indeed. . . . My information from Virginia is as yet imperfect. I have a letter from General Washington which speaks favorably of the impression within a circle of some extent, and another from Chancellor Pendleton which expresses his full acceptance of the plan, and the popularity of it in his district. I am told also that Innis and Marshall are patrons of it. In the opposite scale are Mr. James Mercer, Mr. R. H. Lee, Docr. Lee and their connections of course, Mr. M. Page according to Report, and most of the Judges and Bar of the general Court. The part which Mr. Henry will take is unknown here. Much will depend

[6] Boyd, *The Papers of Thomas Jefferson*, XII, p. 27.
[7] *Ibid.*, p. 103.

on it. I had taken it for granted from a variety of circumstances that he would be in the opposition, and still think that will be the case. There are reports however which favor a contrary supposition. . . . A very decided majority of the Assembly is said to be zealous in favor of the New Constitution. The same is said of the Country at large. It appears however that individuals of great weight both within and without the Legislature are opposed to it. A letter I just have from Mr. A. Stuart names Mr. Henry, Genel. Nelson, W. Nelson, the family of Cabels, St. George Tucker, John Taylor and the Judges of the General Court except P. Carrington. The other opponents he described as of too little note to be mentioned, which gives a negative information of the Characters on the other side. All are agreed that the plan must be submitted to a Convention.[8]

The new system seemed to be causing considerable conjecture and it appears that Patrick Henry was not alone in his decision. Edward Carrington wrote Thomas Jefferson from New York, November 10, 1787: "We have learned from Virginia that several men of considerable influence are in the opposition, amongst whom Mr. Henry is numbered. It appears however, by the papers, that the new project is getting much into fashion in that state."[9]

Washington had just returned to Mount Vernon from Philadelphia and wrote at once to Patrick Henry on September 24, in the hope of obtaining his support:

In the first moment after my return, I take the liberty of sending to you a copy of the constitution, which the federal convention has submitted to the people of the States. I accompany it with no observations. Your own judgment will at once discover the good and the exceptionable parts of it; and your experience of the difficulties, which have ever arisen when attempts have been made to reconcile such a variety of interests and local prejudices, as pervade the several States, will render explanation unnecessary. I wish the constitution, which is offered, had been more perfect; but I sincerely believe it is the best that could be obtained at this time. And, as a constitutional door is opened for amendments hereafter, the adoption of it, under the present circumstances of the Union, is in my opinion desirable.

From a variety of concurring accounts, it appears to me that the political concerns of this country are in a manner suspended by a thread, and that the convention has been looked

---

[8] Boyd, *The Papers of Thomas Jefferson*, XII, pp. 279–280–281–287.

[9] *Ibid.*, XII, p. 335.

up to, by the reflecting part of the community, with a solicitude that is hardly to be conceived; and, if nothing has been agreed on by that body, anarchy would soon have ensued, the seeds being deeply sown in every soil.[10]

Patrick Henry's response to Washington's letter must have been painful indeed, recalling their close association. It was under "the strongest sense of duty, and with the greatest pain," that he penned the following:

> . . . I have to lament that I cannot bring my mind to accord with the proposed Constitution. The Concern I feel on this account is really greater than I am able to express. Perhaps mature Reflections may furnish me Reasons to change my present Sentiments into a Conformity with the opinions of those personages for whom I have the highest Reverence. Be that as it may, I beg you will be persuaded of the unalterable Regard & attachment with which I ever shall be,
>
> Dear Sir, your obliged and very humble servant,
>
> P. Henry.

The following January 8, Washington wrote Edmund Randolph, "There are some things in the new form, I will readily acknowledge, which never did, and I am persuaded never will, obtain my cordial approbation."[11] This opinion was also held by "Franklin, Hamilton, and Gouverneur Morris," who have left on record "the fact that the Constitution was not approved in all of its parts by them."

The Virginia Assembly convened its fall session in Richmond, October, 1787. Among the important matters that came up in the legislature was the question of renewing the issues of irredeemable paper money. A unanimous vote as shown in the Journal in behalf of the resolution "that an emission of paper currency would be ruinous to trade and commerce, and highly injurious to the good people of this Commonwealth," showed the wisdom of this body. Mr. Thurston was chairman of the Committee of the Whole and Mr. Henry's name was second to the chairman.[12]

At this time the country was called upon to act on the new system. Patrick Henry was a delegate to the House from Prince Edward County. George Mason had also taken his seat, and in

---

[10] Henry, *Henry, II*, pp. 319–320.

[11] *Ibid.*, op. cit., II, p. 319 n, *Writings of Washington*, IX, p. 297. For the others who disapproved, See *Ibid.*, II, p. 318.

[12] *Ibid.*, II, p. 328. For George Mason's statement, see p. 323.

reporting on the Federal Constitution declared: "I thought it wrong, Mr. Chairman—I thought it repugnant to our highest interests—and if with these sentiments I had subscribed to it, I might have been justly regarded as a traitor to my country. I would have lost this hand before it should have marked my name to the new government."

Mr. Corbin on October 25 offered resolutions in the legislature calling for a convention to "ratify or reject the proposed Constitution" as recommended by Congress. Mr. Henry, fearing Virginia would not be allowed to propose amendments—only to adopt or reject them—asked that the power of proposing amendments be added to the resolution. Mr. George Nicholas arose to Corbin's defense, saying the amendments might have the appearance that the Virginia legislature "thought amendments might be made to the new government, whereas he believed there was a decided majority in its favor," and he accordingly seconded Corbin's resolutions. It was then that George Mason arose to tell his embarrassing situation: he had had an honored seat in the Federal Convention and "all knew that he had refused to subscribe to its proceedings." John Marshall spoke next and proposed that the Constitution be "submitted to a convention of the people for full and free investigation and discussion." This had no opposition and was adopted. Mr. Henry's bill, calling for "the expenses of any delegate the body might send to sister States with a view to consulting as to proper amendments, and of delegates to another Federal Convention, if one was determined on," carried.[13]

Shortly after the session of the Assembly began, a correspondent wrote Washington: "I have not met with one in all my inquiries (and I have made them with diligence) opposed to it, except Mr. Henry, who I have heard is so, but could only conjecture it from a conversation with him on the subject. . . . The transmissory note of Congress was before us to-day, when Mr. Henry declared that it transcended our powers to decide on the Constitution, and that it must go before a convention. As it was insinuated he would aim at preventing this, much pleasure was discovered at the declaration."[14]

But two months later in December, this same friend of Washington wrote a different story when he stated that " 'it was doubtful whether it had any longer a majority of the body in its favor.'

---

[13] *Ibid.*, II, pp. 323–324.
[14] Tyler, *Henry*, pp. 314–315.

And Mr. Henry carried his proposals looking to previous amendments by fifteen majority."[15]

Patrick Henry being placed in his customary position as leader, upon the powerful standing committees of Privileges and Elections, Propositions and Grievances, Commerce, and Courts of Justice, the latter of which he was chairman, it is not surprising to find Madison and other proponents of the Constitution fearing his power. But Washington was writing frightening letters:

"There is no alternative between the adoption of the Constitution and anarchy. Should one State (meaning Virginia), however important it may conceive itself to be, or a minority of the States, suppose that they can dictate a constitution to the majority, unless they have the power of administering the *ultima ratio*, they will find themselves deceived. Opposition to it is addressed more to the passions than to reason. If another federal convention is attempted, the members will be more discordant than the last. They will agree upon no general plan. The constitution or disunion is before us. If the first is our choice, a constitutional door is open for amendments in a peaceable manner, without tumult or disorder."[16]

Madison, Hamilton and Jay had lost no time in making public a series of articles on the proposed Constitution, which has served as a textbook on the subject under the title of "The Federalist." Madison was solicitous, nay eager, in his efforts at putting the plan over to the people, and there were certain methods in his exertions. However, "every one of consequence understood the issue. It was strict Federalism, with new and nationalistic attributes, against a loose union of local governments. Every one of clear comprehension understood the binding effect of the final yea and nay. Madison was blunt, but not too blunt, when he declared: 'The Constitution requires an adoption *in toto* and forever.' Many of the members likewise appreciated the dramatic aspects of this grand game in fundamental politics. The New York Convention was to meet on the 17th and the New Hampshire Convention on the 18th, and the news of the three was to be borne to and fro by men riding express. It was a device set up by Hamilton and Madison, with the idea that they might thus be able to utilize the inspiring effect of a victory in one State to win votes in another. So do generals in a critical campaign send off

---

[15] Henry, *Henry*, op. cit., II, p. 325; Rives' *Madison*, II, pp. 535–537–538.

[16] *Ibid.*, op. cit., II, p. 334. Washington to Charles Carter, Dec. 14, 1787; Bancroft's *History of the Constitution*, II, p. 297.

their couriers breakneck and sound their fanfares to animate their men. Henry's party had no such arrangement; yet the Anti-Constitutionalists were active indoors and out. Mason was chairman of the Virginia branch of the 'Federal Republicans,' a society organized in New York, under the guidance of General John Lamb, with whom Henry was in correspondence. Its purpose was to bring the amendments to be proposed in the several States into close order and uniformity, so that they might continue a rear line of entrenchments in the event of defeat at the outstart of battle."[17]

Mr. Henry wrote General Lamb on June 9: ". . . It is a matter of great consolation, to find that the sentiments of a vast majority of Virginians are in unison with those of our northern friends. I am satisfied four-fifths of our inhabitants are opposed to the new scheme of government. Indeed, in the part of this country lying south of James River, I am confident nine-tenths are opposed to it. . . . The friends and seekers of power, have, with their usual subtilty wriggled themselves into the choice of the people, by assuming shapes as various as the faces of the men they address on such occasions. If they carry their point, and preclude previous amendments, which we have ready to offer, it will become highly necessary to form the society you mention. Indeed, it appears the only chance to secure a remnant of those invaluable rights which are yielded by the new plan. Colonel George Mason has agreed to act as chairman of our republican society. His character I need not describe. He is in every way fit; and we have concluded to send you . . . a copy of the Bill of Rights, and of the particular amendments we intend to propose in our convention."[18]

Madison was keeping Jefferson informed and from New York, Dec. 9, 1787, he related further news:

"All the Legislatures except that of R. Island, which have been assembled, have agreed in submitting it to State Conventions. Virginia has set the example of opening a door for amendments, if the Convention there should choose to propose them. . . . What change may be produced by the united influence of exertions of Mr. Henry, Mr. Mason, and the Governor with some pretty able auxiliaries, is uncertain. . . . Mr. Harrison the late Governor is with Mr. Henry. So are a number of others. The General and Admiralty Courts with most of the Bar, oppose the

[17] Morgan, *Henry*, pp. 343–344.
[18] Henry, *Henry*, II, pp. 342–343.

constitution, but on what particular grounds I am unable to say. Genl. Nelson, Mr. Jno. Page, Col. Bland, &c. are also opponents, but on what principle and to what extent, I am equally at a loss to say."

With respect to the names, Madison stated that he spoke "from information that may not be accurate. . . . Mr. Henry is the great adversary who will render the event precarious. He is I find with his usual address, working up every possible interest, into a spirit of opposition."[19]

Madison's next letter, written to Jefferson February 9, from New York, noted: "The temper of Virginia, as far as I can learn, has undergone but little change of late. At first there was an enthusiasm for the Constitution. The tide next took a sudden and strong turn in the opposite direction. The influence and exertions of Mr. Henry, and Col. Mason and some others will account for this. . . . The previous adoption of nine States must have a very persuasive effect on the minds of the opposition, though I am told that a very bold language is held by Mr. H——y and some of his partisans."[20]

Patrick Henry's influence is seen throughout the letters, and the course he would take was causing considerable concern. It must have been heartening to him to know that Mason had been on guard at the Convention. George Mason had attended, but he, likewise, had suspicions which were well founded. He wrote Jefferson on May 26, 1788, concerning the government framed at Philadelphia, saying:

"Upon the most mature Consideration I was capable of, and from Motives of sincere Patriotism, I was under the Necessity of refusing my Signature, as one of the Virginia Delegates; and drew up some general Objections; which I intended to offer, by Way of Protest; but was discouraged from doing so. . . ."

Mason enclosed a copy of some of his objections to the Federal Constitution, "conceived in general Terms," and further noted: "Delaware—Pennsylvania—Jersey—Connecticut—Georgia, and Maryland have ratified the new Government (for surely it is not a Confederation) without Amendments. Massachusetts has accompanied the Ratification with proposed Amendments. Rhode Island has rejected it. New Hampshire, after some deliberation, adjourned their Convention to June. The Convention of South

---

[19] Boyd, *The Papers of Thomas Jefferson*, XII, pp. 409–410.
[20] *Ibid.*, XII, p. 609.

Carolina is now sitting. The Convention of New York meets in June, that of North Carolina in July, and the Convention of Virginia meets on the first Monday in June. I shall set out for Richmond this week, in order to attend it.—From the best information I have had, the Members of the Virginia Convention are so equally divided upon the Subject, that no man can, at present, form any certain Judgment of the Issue. There seems to be a great Majority for Amendments; but many are for ratifying first, and amending afterwards. This Idea appears to me so utterly absurd, that I can not think any Man of Sense candid in proposing it. . . ."[21]

Mason's idea of amending first and ratifying afterward was in direct opposition to Jefferson's views. Thomas Jefferson wrote Madison from Paris, December 20, 1787: "If they approve the proposed Convention in all its parts, I shall concur in it cheerfully, in hopes that they will amend it whenever they shall find it work wrong."[22] Later, February 7, 1788, Jefferson wrote from Paris to Alexander Donald: "I wish with all my soul that the nine first Conventions may accept the new Constitution, because this will secure to us the good it contains, which I think great and important. But I equally wish that the four latest Conventions, whichever they be, may refuse to accede to it till a declaration of rights be annexed."[23]

These letters, the dates of which follow in sequence, are cited in order to document the different opinions of Patrick Henry's colleagues, and the politics which ensued.

From his home in Orange County, Virginia, Madison next wrote to Jefferson in Paris. This letter concerned the members elected to the convention to be held at Richmond, June 1788:

> The proposed Constitution still engrosses the public attention. The elections for the Convention here are but just over and promulgated. From the returns (excluding those from Kentucky which are not yet known) it seems probable, though not absolutely certain that a majority of the members elect are friends to the Constitution. The superiority of abilities at least seems to lie on that side. The characters of most note which occur to me, are marshalled thus. For the Constitution, Pendleton, Wythe, Blair, Innis, Marshal, Doctr. W. Jones, G. Nicholas, Wilson Nicholas, Gabl. Jones, Thos. Lewis, F. Corbin, Ralph Wormley, Jr. White of Frederik, Genl. Gates, Genl. A. Stephens,

---

[21] *Ibid.*, XIII, p. 205–206.

[22] *Ibid.*, XII, pp. 439–440–441–442.

[23] *Ibid.*, XII, p. 571. See Jefferson's complete letter to Madison.

> Archd. Stuart Zachy. Johnson, Docr. Stuart, Parson Andrews, H. Lee Jr, Bushrod Washington considered as a young Gentleman of talents: against the Constitution, Mr. Henry, Mason, Harrison, Grayson, Tyler, M. Smith, W. Ronald, Lawson, Bland, Wm. Cabell, Dawson. The Governor is so temperate in his opposition and goes so far with the friends of the Constitution that he cannot properly be classed with its enemies. Monroe is considered by some as an enemy, but I believe him to be a friend though a cool one. There are other individuals of weight whose opinions are unknown to me. R. H. Lee is not elected. His brother F. L. Lee is a warm friend to the Constitution, as I am told, but also is not elected. So are Jno. and Mann Page.[24]

If Madison's estimate was true as to the strength of parties, that "the majority of the members elect are friends to the Constitution," it appears that the 21 hand-picked members would hold the whip over the opposition, with only 11 members, even before the convention in Richmond started. Madison's statement, then, that Mr. Henry had "rendered the event precarious" by "working up every possible interest into a spirit of opposition" must have been exaggerated. The facts surrounding the election show "that the contest for seats in the Virginia Convention had been warm. The advocates of immediate ratification had shown great tact in selecting their candidates. All citizens were eligible under the act calling the body, and they persuaded the judges and the distinguished soldiers, nearly all of whom were advocates of ratification, to offer for seats. In some cases rich men, who had been Tories, but whose money brought them influence, were selected, and by these means counties considered doubtful, and even some distinctly opposed, were carried at the polls for the party for ratification, now known as Federalists. When the result of the elections was made public, the people of the State, a majority of whom were decidedly opposed to immediate ratification, as appeared in the Legislature elected about the same time, were astonished to find that the Federalists claimed a majority. This had been the more easily obtained by the manner of constituting the body, the small counties in the east, which were Federal, having the same weight as the larger ones in the interior, which were anti-Federal."[25] Moreover, the date for holding the Virginia Convention was said to be fixed by "the opposition in the Legislature, in order that the State, which had so long led the Confederacy, might be in a posi-

[24] *Ibid.*, XIII, p. 98.

[25] Henry, *Henry*, II, pp. 339–340.

tion to act as arbitrator between the States accepting and those rejecting the Constitution."[26]

Eight states had now ratified and the interest in the outcome of Virginia's decision was intense, because it was felt that without her, Massachusetts might withdraw her decision and the plan could not be effected. Thus, the fate of the new government was believed to rest with Virginia.

* * *

The Virginia Convention was called for the first Monday in the month, which fell on June 2, 1788. A full house was reported. Each county and city had two delegates, with the exception of Williamsburg and Norfolk, which had only one each, making a total of 170 members. This assemblage comprised some of the most distinguished men in Virginia, except for the absence of four: Washington, who decided he would serve the cause from Mount Vernon; Jefferson, who was in France; Richard H. Lee, who was not elected; and Colonel Nelson, who was too feeble to attend. But for the absence of these gentlemen, such a collection of illustrious men had not been seen before in the annals of their country, and such a large and imposing body were hardly collected before under one roof. They assembled in the old capitol building on the northwest corner of Fourteenth and Cary Streets for the first day of the session, but the large gathering of men from every part of the state made it necessary to adjourn the next day to the largest room in the city that would accommodate such an audience—the new Academy, located on the north side of Broad, between Twelfth and Thirteenth Streets, on Shockoe Hill.[27]

The arrival of Henry and Pendleton at Richmond on the opening day made an interesting picture. "Though not personal enemies, they rarely thought alike on the greatest questions of that age, and they came aptly enough by different roads. One was seen advancing from the south side of the James, driving a plain and topless stick gig. He was tall, and seemed capable of enduring fatigue, but was bending forward as if worn with travel. His dress was the production of his own loom, and was covered with dust. He was to be the master-spirit of the Convention. The other approached from the north side of the river in an elegant vehicle,

---

[26] *Ibid.*, II, pp. 338–339.
[27] *Ibid.*, pp. 340–341.

then known as a phaeton. . . . They met on the steps of the Swan and exchanged salutations. Public expectation was at its height when it was known that Patrick Henry and Edmund Pendleton, who for a quarter of a century had been at the head of the two great parties of that day, were about to engage in another fierce conflict in the councils of their country. We have another picture of Henry and Mason walking arm in arm from the Swan to the Convention hall—Mason 'dressed in a full suit of black,' and remarkable for the 'urbanity and dignity' of his bearing."[28]

Edmund Pendleton, a proponent, was elected to preside over the convention, but when this body "sat in Committee of the Whole, as it usually did, he gave Chancellor Wythe the gavel and took the floor, that he might chasten the logic and confute the arguments of his old time enemy."[29] The secretary was John Beckley, and the chaplain was the Rev. Abner Waugh; while seated in "an ineligible seat"—all he could secure—was the reporter, David Robertson, of Petersburg. Through his published report, the convention became history, but regarding Mr. Henry's performance, he confessed "his inability to follow him in his overpowering bursts of eloquence, and the incompleteness of the report which is given, attests, with the concurrent testimony of the hearers, the fact that it falls far short of doing him justice."[30]

Judge St. George Tucker wrote Patrick Henry's first biographer, William Wirt: "His speeches were then taken in shorthand. I do not think them accurately taken. At that time it appeared to me that Mr. Henry was sometimes as great as on former occasion. I recollect the fine image he gave of Virginia seated on an eminence and holding in her hand the balance in which the fate of America was weighing. . . . The variety of arguments which Mr. Henry generally presented in his speeches, addressed to the capacities, prejudices, and individual interests of his hearers, made his speeches unequal. . . . If he soared at times like the eagle, and seemed, like the bird of Jove, to be armed with his thunder, he did not disdain to stoop like the hawk to seize his prey, but the instant he had done it, rose in pursuit of another quarry."[31]

The effect of Mr. Henry's speeches upon the audience was

---

[28] Morgan, *Henry*, p. 342 n.

[29] *Ibid.*, p. 343.

[30] Henry, *Henry*, op. cit., II, p. 345 n. He refers to the statement by both Judges, Tucker and Roane, in their letters to Mr. Wirt, MS.

[31] *Ibid.*, op. cit., II, pp. 346–347. MS.

described by Judge Edmund Winston: "While he was speaking there was a perfect stillness throughout the House, and in the galleries. There was no inattention or appearance of weariness. When any other member spoke, the members and the audience would in half an hour be going out or moving from their seats."[32]

In the debates recorded by Robertson, which fill a volume of 663 pages, one of Mr. Henry's speeches "fills eight pages, another ten pages, another sixteen, another twenty-one, another forty; while in the aggregate, his speeches constitute nearly one quarter of the entire book. . . . Upon him alone fell the brunt of the battle. Out of the twenty-three days of that splendid tourney, there were but five days in which he did not take the floor. On each of several days he made three speeches; on one day he made five speeches; on another day eight. In one speech alone, he was on his feet for seven hours,"[33] as he lashed out against the dangers of centralized government and pointed to the loopholes in the federal constitution.

One of his biographers noted: "Any one who has fallen under the impression, so industriously propagated by the ingenious enmity of Jefferson's old age, that Patrick Henry was a man of but meagre information and of extremely slender intellectual resources, ignorant especially of law, of political science, and of history, totally lacking in logical power and in precision of statement, with nothing to offset these deficiencies excepting a strange gift of overpowering, dithyrambic eloquence, will find it hard, as he turns over the leaves on which are recorded the debates of the Virginia Convention to understand just how such a person could have made the speeches which are there attributed to Patrick Henry, or how a mere rhapsodist could have thus held his ground, in close hand-to-hand combat, for twenty-three days, against such antagonists, on all the difficult subjects of law, political science, and history involved in the Constitution of the United States,—while showing at the same time every quality of good generalship as a tactician and as a party leader. 'There has been, I am aware,' says an eminent historian of the Constitution, 'a modern skepticism concerning Patrick Henry's abilities; but I cannot share it. . . . The manner in which he carried on the opposition to the Constitution in the Convention of Virginia, for nearly a whole month,

---

[32] *Ibid.*, op. cit., II, p. 347–, His MS. letter to William Wirt.

[33] Tyler, *Henry*, pp. 320–321; Henry, *Henry*, II, pp. 350–351. See Elliot, *Debates*, III.

shows that he possessed other powers besides those of great natural eloquence.' "[34]

Patrick Henry was only fifty-two years of age when he took up his fight in the convention against changing the existing Confederation of sovereign States into a great national government. The pressing years during the many terms as Governor, in his efforts toward winning the Revolution, had borne heavily upon him and left him "ill in health and with the appearance of an old man." And "although his body had been affected by disease, his mental powers were as great as ever, and the deep interest he took in the subject under debate caused him to exert them to the utmost. It was said that whenever he arose, a death-like silence prevailed, and the eager listeners did not fail to catch every syllable he uttered."[35]

In Madison's letter to Jefferson, he showed the majority of the delegates elected to be in favor of the Constitution. It should be noted that "within the Convention itself, at the opening of the session, it was claimed by the friends of the new government that they then outnumbered their opponents by at least fifty votes. Their great champion in debate was James Madison, who was powerfully assisted, first or last, by Edmund Pendleton, John Marshall, George Nicholas, Francis Corbin, George Wythe, James Innes, General Henry Lee, and especially by that same Governor Randolph, who after denouncing the Constitution for 'features so odious' that he could not 'agree to it,' had finally swung completely around to its support. Against all this array of genius, learning, character, logical acumen, and eloquence, Patrick Henry held the field as protagonist for twenty-three days,—his chief lieutenants in the fight being Mason, Grayson, and John Dawson, with occasional help from Harrison, Monroe, and Tyler."[36] However, the brunt of the battle fell upon Henry alone.

Previous to the meeting of the convention, Patrick Henry was accused by Madison and others as aiming at disunion. Edward Carrington had written Jefferson: " 'Mr. H. does not openly declare for a dismemberment of the Union, but his arguments in support of his opposition to the Constitution go directly to that issue. He says that three confederacies would be practicable, and better suited to the good of commerce than one.' On April 28, Washington wrote to Lafayette an account of the struggle then going forward; and after naming some of the leading champions

---

[34] *Ibid.*, op. cit., pp. 321–322; Curtis, *History of Constitution*, II, p. 561, n.
[35] Henry, *Henry*, II, p. 346.
[36] Tyler, *Henry;* op. cit., p. 320, *Historical Magazine* for 1873, p. 274.

of the Constitution, he added sorrowfully: 'Henry and Mason are its great adversaries.' "[37]

Anyone reading Mr. Henry's question following the opening of the debates on the preamble, after two sections of Article I were read and Wilson Nicholas yielded the floor, will know that disunion was not his purpose. In his reply to Randolph he stated, "I am persuaded . . . that separate confederacies will ruin us . . . I am a lover of the American Union; the dissolution of the union is most abhorrent to my mind . . ."

Mr. Henry took the floor on June 4, and disregarding Nicholas's argument on the preposed plan for a House of Representatives, he aimed his question directly at the language of the compact. He had not forgotten the full title of the confederate establishment: "The Articles of Confederation and Perpetual Union *between the States*," and if, as the object was, "to amend the Confederation,"[38] it was still a compact between the States, and not the people. He declared:

"Mr. Chairman: The public mind, as well as my own, is extremely uneasy at the proposed change of government. Give me leave to form one of the number of those who wish to be thoroughly acquainted with the reasons of this perilous and uneasy situation, and why we are brought hither to decide on this great national question. I consider myself as a servant of the people of this commonwealth, as a sentinel over their rights, liberty, and happiness. . . . Before the meeting of the late Federal Convention at Philadelphia, a general peace, and an universal tranquility prevailed in this country, and the minds of our citizens were at perfect repose; but since that period they are exceedingly uneasy and disquieted. . . . I conceive the republic to be in extreme danger. . . . It arises from this fatal system . . . a proposal to change our government—a proposal that goes to the utter annihilation of the most solemn engagements of the States—a proposal of establishing nine States into a confederacy, to the eventual exclusion of four States. It goes to the annihilation of those solemn treaties we have formed with foreign nations. . . . This proposal of altering our federal government is of a most alarming nature . . . you ought to be extremely cautious, watchful, jealous of your liberty; for instead of securing your rights, you may lose

---

[37] *Ibid.*, op. cit., p. 317. Bancroft, *History of the Constitution,* II, p. 465; *Writings of Washington,* IX, p. 356.

[38] Jefferson wrote Littlepage, Aug. 12, 1787, "Its object is to amend the Confederation by strengthening, more the hands of Congress." (See his letter in this chapter.)

them forever. . . . That this is a consolidated government is demonstrably clear; and the danger of such a government is, to my mind, very striking. . . . Give me leave to demand, what right had they to say, 'We the People,' instead of 'We the States?' States are the characteristics, and the soul of a confederation. If the States be not the agents of this compact, it must be one great consolidated national government of the people of all the States. I have the highest respect for those gentlemen who formed the convention. . . . America had on a former occasion put the utmost confidence in them; I would cheerfully confide in them as my representatives. But, sir, on this great occasion, I would demand the cause of their conduct. Even from that illustrious man, who saved us by his valor, I would have a reason for his conduct—that liberty which he has given us by his valor, tells me to ask this reason—and sure I am, were he here, he would give us that reason. . . . Had the delegates, who were sent to Philadelphia a power to propose a consolidated government instead of a confederacy? Were they not deputed by States, and not by the people? The assent of the people, in their collective capacity, is not necessary to the formation of a federal government. The people have no right to enter into leagues, alliances, or confederations: they are not the proper agents for this purpose: States and sovereign powers are the only proper agents for this kind of government. Show me an instance where the people have exercised this business: has it not always gone through the legislatures? I refer you to the treaties with France, Holland, and other nations: how were they made? Were they not made by the States? Are the people, therefore, in their aggregate capacity, the proper persons to form a confederacy? This, therefore, ought to depend on the consent of the legislatures. . . . The people gave them no power to use their name. That they exceeded their power is perfectly clear. . . . Difference in opinion has gone to a degree of inflammatory resentment, in different parts of the country, which has been occasioned by this perilous innovation. The federal convention ought to have amended the old system; for this purpose they were solely delegated: the object of their mission extended to no other consideration. You must therefore forgive the solicitation of one unworthy member, to know what danger could have arisen under the present confederation, and what are the causes of this proposal to change our government."[39]

[39] *The World's Great Classics, Orations of American Orators,* With a Special Introduction by Julian Hawthorne, 1900, I, pp. 61 to 63; Elliot, *Debates.*

Mr. Henry's inquiry was answered by Governor Edmund Randolph, who, though refusing to sign his name to the adoption of the Federal Convention "because of its serious defects," had now changed his mind and declared his purpose to vote for the unamended Constitution. Regarding his actions, James Monroe wrote Jefferson, July 12, 1788: "The Governor exhibited a curious spectacle to view: having refused to sign the paper, every body supposed him against it. But he afterwards had written a letter and having taken a part which might be called rather vehement than active he was constantly labouring to show that his present conduct (was) consistent with that letter and the letter with his refusal to sign."[40]

Randolph answered Mr. Henry with a powerful speech, justifying his change of attitude by the fear of disunion, and declared, the honorable gentleman attacks the constitution, as he thinks it contrary to our bill of rights. The debate next passed into George Mason's hands. He discussed the dangers of a consolidated government and objected to the plan for the House of Representatives, as the number of members would be too small[41] to know the needs of the people. James Madison closed the first day's debate with a short reply.

The following day, June 5, Mr. Henry took up where he had left off, after Edmund Pendleton and Richard H. Lee had addressed the body. This speech, in which he "laid down the theme he was to develop constantly for the next three weeks," was regarded by many as his greatest effort.

"Mr. Chairman: I am much obliged to the very worthy gentleman[42] for his encomium. I wish I were possessed of talents . . . that might enable me to elucidate this great subject. I am not free from suspicion: I am apt to entertain doubts: I rose yesterday to ask a question, which arose in my mind. When I asked that question, I thought the meaning of my interrogation was obvious: the fate of this question and of America may depend on this. Have they said, We, the states? Have they made a proposal of a compact between states? If they had, this would be a confederation: it is otherwise most clearly a consolidated government. The question turns, sir, on the expression, We, the People,

---

[40] Boyd, *The Papers of Thomas Jefferson,* XIII, p. 352; The letter referred to was the one Randolph had addressed to the Speaker of the House of Delegates.

[41] Following Mason's speech, Mr. Henry pointed to, "the strangest language" that there shall not be more representatives than one for every 30,000.

[42] Mr. Lee, of Westmoreland.

instead of, the States of America. I need not take much pains to show that the principles of this system are extremely pernicious, impolitic, and dangerous. Is this a monarchy, like England—a compact between prince and people: with checks on the former to secure the liberty of the latter? Is this a confederacy, like Holland—an association of a number of independent States, each of which retains its individual sovereignty? . . . Had these principles been adhered to, we should not have been brought to this alarming transition, from a confederacy to a consolidated government. We have no detail of those great considerations which, in my opinion, ought to have abounded before we should recur to a government of this kind. Here is a revolution as radical as that which separated us from Great Britain. It is as radical, if, in this transition, our rights and privileges are endangered, and the sovereignty of the States relinquished. And cannot we plainly see, that this is actually the case? The rights of conscience, trial by jury, liberty of the press, all your immunities and franchises, all pretentions to human rights and privileges, are rendered insecure, if not lost, by this change . . .

"Is this tame relinquishment of rights worthy of freemen? Is it worthy of that manly fortitude that ought to characterize republicans? It is said eight States have adopted this plan. I declare that if twelve States and a half had adopted it, I would, with manly firmness, and in spite of an erring world, reject it. You are not to inquire how your trade may be increased, nor how you are to become a great and powerful people, but how your liberties can be secured; for liberty ought to be the direct end of your government.

". . . Will the abandonment of your most sacred rights tend to the security of your liberty? Liberty, the greatest of all earthly blessings—give us that precious jewel, and you may take everything else. But I am fearful I have lived long enough to become an old-fashioned fellow. Perhaps an invincible attachment to the dearest rights of man may, in these refined, enlightened days, be deemed old-fashioned: if so, I am contented to be so. I say the time has been when every pulse of my heart beat for American liberty, and which, I believe, had a counterpart in the breast of every true American. But suspicions have gone forth—suspicions of my integrity. It has been publicly reported that my professions are not real. Twenty-three years ago was I supposed a traitor to my country: I was then said to be a bane of sedition, because I supported the rights of my country: I may be thought suspicious, when I say our privileges and rights are in danger; but, sir, a number of people of this country are weak enough to think these things are too true. I am happy to find that the gentlemen on the other side declare they are groundless: but sir, suspicion is a virtue as long as its object is the preservation of the public good, and as long at it stays within proper bounds: should it fall on me, I am contented: conscious recititude is a powerful consolation: I trust there are many who think my professions for the public good to be real.

". . . Guard with jealous attention the public liberty. Suspect every one who approaches that jewel. Unfortunately, nothing will preserve it but downright force. Whenever you give up that force, you are inevitably ruined.

". . . I shall be told I am continually afraid; but, sir, I have strong cause of apprehension. In some parts of the plan before you, the great rights of freemen are endangered, in other parts absolutely taken away. How does your trial by jury stand? In civil cases gone—not sufficiently secured in criminal—this best privilege is gone. But we are told, that we need not fear, because those in power, being our representatives, will not abuse the power we put in their hands. I am not well versed in history; but I will submit to your recollection, whether liberty has been destroyed most often by the licentiousness of the people, or by the tyranny of the rulers. I imagine, sir, you will find the balance on the side of Tyranny. Happy will you be, if you miss the fate of those nations, who omitting to resist their oppressors, or negligently suffering their liberty to be wrested from them, have groaned under intolerable despotism! . . . Let not gentlemen be told that it is not safe to reject this government. Wherefore is it not safe? . . . To encourage us to adopt it, they tell us, that there is a plain, easy way of getting amendments. When I come to contemplate this part, I suppose that I am mad, or that my countrymen are so. The way to amendments is, in my conception, shut.

"Hence it appears, that three fourths of the states must ultimately agree to any amendments that may be necessary. Let us consider the consequence of this. . . . Let us suppose (for the case is supposable, possible, and probable), that you happen to deal these powers to unworthy hands; will they relinquish powers already in their possession, or agree to amendments? Two thirds of the Congress, or of the state legislatures, are necessary even to propose amendments. If one third of these be unworthy men, they may prevent the application for amendments; but a destructive and mischievous feature is, that three-fourths of the State legislatures, or of the State conventions, must concur in the amendments when proposed. In such numerous bodies, there must necessarily be some designing, bad men. To suppose that so large a number as three-fourths of the States will concur, is to suppose that they will possess genius, intelligence, and integrity, approaching to miraculous. It would, indeed, be miraculous, that they should concur in the same amendments, or, even in such as would bear some likeness to one another. For four of the smallest States, that do not collectively contain one-tenth of the population of the United States, may obstruct the most salutary and necessary. Nay, in these four States, six-tenths of the people may reject these amendments. . . . A bare majority in these four small States, may hinder the adoption of amendments; so that we may fairly and justly conclude, that one-twentieth part of the American people may prevent the removal of the most grievous inconveniences and oppression, by refusing to accede to amendments. Will the great rights of the people be secured? Is this an easy mode of securing the public liberty? It is, sir, a most fearful situation, when the most contemptible minority can prevent the alteration of the most oppressive government; for it may, in many respects, prove to be such. Is this the spirit of republicanism? . . . Our bill of rights declares, 'That a majority of the community hath an indubitable, *unalienable and indefeasible right to reform, alter, or abolish it, in such manner as shall be judged most conducive to the public weal.*' I have just proved, that one-tenth, or less, of the people of America—a most despicable minority, may prevent this reform, or alteration. Suppose the people of Virginia should wish to alter their government, can a majority of them do it? No, because they are connected with other men; or, in other words, consolidated with other States. When the people of Virginia, at a future day, shall wish to alter their government, though they should be unanimous in this desire, yet they may be prevented therefrom by a despicable minority at the extremity of the United States. The founders of your own constitution made your government changeable: but the power of changing it is gone from you! Whither it is gone? It is placed in the same hands that hold the rights of twelve other States; and those, who hold those rights, have right and power to keep them. It is not the particular government of Virginia; one of the leading features of that government is, that a majority can alter it, when necessary for the public good. This government is not a Virginian, but an American government. Is is not therefore a consolidated government? How different from the sentiments of freemen. . . . If then, gentlemen, standing on this ground, are come to that point, that they are willing to bind themselves and their posterity to be oppressed, I am amazed and inexpressibly astonished. We have heard that there is a great deal of bribery practiced in the House of Commons in England. . . . But, sir, the tenth part of that body cannot continue oppressions on the rest of the people. English liberty is, in this case, on a firmer foundation than American liberty. It will be easily contrived to procure the opposition of one tenth of the people to any alteration, however judicious.

"The honorable gentleman who presides, told us, that to prevent abuses in our government, we will assemble in Convention, recall our delegated powers, and punish our servants for abusing the trust reposed in them. Oh, sir, we should have fine times indeed, if to punish tyrants, it were only sufficient to assemble the people. Your arms, wherewith you could defend yourselves, are gone . . .

"Let me here call your attention to that part which gives the Congress power 'To provide for organizing, arming and disciplining the militia, and for governing such parts of them as may be employed in the service of the United States, reserving to the States respectively the appointment of the officers, and the authority of training the militia, according to the discipline prescribed by Congress.' By this, sir, you see that their control over our last and best defense is unlimited. If they neglect or refuse to discipline or arm our militia, they will be useless: the States can do neither, this power being exclusively given to Congress. The power of appointing officers over men not disciplined or armed, is ridiculous: so that this pretended little remnant of power, left to the States, may, at the pleasure of Congress, be rendered nugatory. Our situation will be deplorable indeed: nor can we ever expect to get this government amended; since I have already shown, that a very small minority may prevent it . . . Will the oppressor let go the oppressed? Was there ever an instance? Can the annals of mankind exhibit one single example, where rulers, overcharged with power, willingly let go the oppressed, though solicited and requested most earnestly? The application for amendments will therefore be fruitless. We drew the spirit of liberty from our British ancestors: by that spirit we have triumphed over every difficulty. But now, sir, the American spirit, assisted by the ropes and chains of consolidation, is about to convert this country into a powerful and mighty empire. If you make the citizens of this country agree to become the subjects of one great consolidated empire of America, your government will not have sufficient energy to keep them together: such a government is incompatible with the genius of republicanism.

"Where are the checks in this Constitution? There will be no checks, no real balances, in this government. What can avail your specious, imaginary balances, your rope-dancing, chain-rattling, ridiculous ideal checks and contrivances?

"The clause under consideration gives an unlimited and unbounded power of taxation. Suppose every delegate from Virginia opposes a law laying a tax, what will it avail? They are opposed by a majority; eleven members can destroy their efforts: those feeble ten cannot prevent the passing the most oppressive tax-law. So that in direct opposition to the spirit and express language of your declaration of rights, you are taxed, not by your own consent, but by people who have no connection with you.

"The clause of our Bill of Rights tells you, '*That all power of suspending law, or the execution of laws, by any authority, without the consent of the representatives of the people, is injurious to their rights, and ought not to be exercised.*' This tells us that there can be no suspension of government, or laws, without our own consent; yet this constitution can counteract and suspend any of our laws, that contravene its oppressive operation; for they have the power of direct taxation, which suspends our Bill of Rights; and it is expressly provided that they can make all laws necessary for carrying their powers into execution; and it is declared paramount to the laws and constitutions of the States. Consider how the only remaining defense, we have left, is destroyed in this manner. . . . The voice of tradition, I trust, will inform posterity of our struggles for freedom . . . for I never will give up the power of direct taxation, but for a scourge.

"Sir, the dissolution of the Union is most abhorrent to my mind. The first thing I have at heart is American liberty; the second thing is American union; and I hope the people of Virginia will endeavor to preserve that union.

"Gentlemen have told us, within these walls, that the union is gone—or that the union will be gone. Is not this trifling with the judgment of their fellow-citizens? Till they tell us the ground of their fears, I will consider them as imaginary. I rose to make inquiry where those dangers were: they could make no answer. I believe I never shall have that answer.

"The most valuable end of government is the liberty of the inhabitants. No possible advantages can compensate for the loss of this privilege. Show me the reason why the American Union is to be dissolved. Who are those eight adopting States? Are they averse to give us a little time to consider, before we conclude? Would such a disposition render a junction with them eligible; or, is it the genius of that kind of government, to precipitate a people hastily into measures of the utmost importance, and grant no indulgence? If it be, sir, is it for us to accede to such a government? We have a right to have time to consider—we shall therefore insist upon it. Unless the government be amended, we can never accept it.

"The honorable gentleman has told us that these powers given to Congress, are accompanied by a judiciary which will correct all. On examination, you will find this very judiciary oppressively constructed, your jury-trial destroyed, and the judges dependent on Congress. In this scheme of energetic government, the people will find two sets of tax-gatherers—the State and the federal sheriffs. This, it seems to me, will produce such dreadful oppression, as the people cannot possibly bear. The sheriff comes to-day as a State collector—next day he is federal—how are you to fix him? Will not his ingenuity perplex the simple, honest planter? . . . When you fix him, where are you to punish him? For, I suppose, they will not stay in our courts: they must go to the federal court; for, if I understand that paper right, all controversies arising under that constitution, or under the laws made in pursuance thereof, are to be tried in that court.

". . . I am not well acquainted with federal jurisprudence; but it appears to me that these oppressions must result from this part of the plan. It is at least doubtful, and where there is even a possibility of such evils, they ought to be guarded against.

". . . I see great jeopardy in this new government, I see none, from the present one. This Constitution is said to have beautiful features; but when I come to examine these features, sir, they appear to be horribly frightful. Among other deformities, it has an awful squinting; it squints toward monarchy; and does not this raise indignation in the breasts of every true American?

"Your president may easily become King, your senate is so imperfectly constructed, that your dearest rights may be sacrificed by what may be a small minority; and a very small minority may continue forever unchangeably this government, although horribly defective. Where are your checks in this government? Your strongholds will be in the hands of your enemies. . . . Show me that age and country where the rights and liberties of the people were placed on the sole chance of their rulers being good men, without a consequent loss of liberty. I say that the loss of that dearest privilege has ever followed, with absolute certainty, every such mad attempt. If your American chief be a man of ambition and abilities, how easy will it be for him to render himself absolute! . . . And, sir, will the American spirit solely relieve you when this happens? I would rather infinitely . . . have a king, lords and commons, than a government so replete with such insupportable evils. If we make a king, we may prescribe the rules by which he shall rule his people, and interpose such checks as shall prevent him from infringing them: but the President in the field, at the head of his army, can prescribe the terms on which he shall reign master, so far that it will puzzle any American ever to get his neck from under the galling yoke. I cannot, with patience, think of this idea. . . . Where is the existing force to punish him? What will then become of you and your rights? Will not absolute despotism ensue? . . . If you have a good President, senators and representatives, there is no danger. But can this be expected from human nature? Without real checks, it will not suffice that some of them are good. A good President, or senator, or representative will have a natural weakness. Virtue will slumber: the wicked will be continually watching: consequently you will be undone. . . . If you depend on your President's and senator's patriotism, you are gone. . . . Their checks upon paper are inefficient and nugatory. Can you search your President's closet? Is this a real check? We ought to be exceedingly cautious in giving up this life, this soul—our money—this power of taxation to Congress.

[On war, Mr. Henry noted:]

"A republic can never enter into a war, unless it be a national war, unless it be approved of, or desired by the whole community. Did ever a republic fail to use the utmost resources of the community when a war was necessary? I call for an example. I call also for an example, when a republic has been engaged in a war contrary to the wishes of its people. There are thousands of examples where the ambition of its prince has precipitated a nation into the most destructive war. No nation ever withheld power when its object was just and right. I will hazard an observation: I find fault with the paper before you because the same power that declares war has the ability to carry it on. . . . The Congress can both declare war and carry it on, and levy your money as long as you have a shilling to pay. . . . We are told by that paper, that a regular statement and account of the receipts and expenditures of all public money shall be published from time to time.

Here is a beautiful check! What time? Here is the utmost latitude left. If those who are in Congress please to put that construction upon it, the words of the constitution will be satisfied by publishing those accounts once in one hundred years. They may publish or not, as they please. . . . Grant that any of them are wicked, they may squander the public money so as to ruin you, and yet this expression will give you no redress. I say, they may ruin you; for where, sir, is the responsibility? Have you any sufficient, decided means of preventing them from sucking your blood by peculations, commissions, and fees? Thus thousands of your people will be most shamefully robbed. . . . Is this like the present despised system, whereby the accounts are to be published monthly? . . . When these harpies are aided by excisemen, who may search, at any time, your houses and most secret recesses, will the people bear it? If you think so, you differ from me. In the country from which we are descended, they have real, and not imaginary responsibility; for there, maladministration has cost their heads to some of the most saucy geniuses that ever were. . . . While other nations, precipitated by the rage of ambition or folly, have, in the pursuit of the most magnificent projects, riveted the fetters of bondage on themselves and their descendants, these republicans have secured their political happiness and freedom.

"Congress, by the power of taxation, by that of raising an army, and by their control over the militia, have the sword in one hand and the purse in the other. Shall we be safe without either? Congress have an unlimited power over both: they are entirely given up by us. Let him candidly tell me, where and when did freedom exist, when the sword and purse were given up by the people? Unless a miracle in human affairs interposed, no nation ever retained its liberty after the loss of the sword and purse. . . . If you give them up, you are gone. Give us at least a plausible apology why Congress should keep their proceedings in secret. They have the power of keeping them secret as long as they please; for the provision for a periodical publication is too inexplicit and ambiguous to avail anything. . . . They may carry on the most wicked and pernicious of schemes under the dark veil of secrecy. The liberties of a people never were nor ever will be secure, when the transactions of their rulers may be concealed from them. . . . To cover, with the veil of secrecy, the common routine of business, is an abomination in the eyes of every intelligent man, and every friend to his country.

"The Senate, by making treaties, may destroy your liberty and laws, for want of responsibility. Two-thirds of those that shall happen to be present, can, with the President, make treaties that shall be the supreme law of the land: they may make the most ruinous treaties, and yet there is no punishment for them. . . . The transactions of Congress may be concealed a century from the public consistently with the constitution. This, sir, is a laudable imitation of the *transactions of the Spanish treaty*. We have not forgotten with what a thick veil of secrecy those transactions were covered. . . . Whoever shows me a punishment provided for them, will oblige me.

"What can be more defective than the clause concerning the elections? The control given to Congress, over the time, place and manner of holding elections, will totally destroy the end of suffrage. . . . The power over the manner admits of the most dangerous latitude . . ."

During his argument, Mr. Henry pointed several times to the history of Switzerland and to the freedom of her people. His purpose was obvious: Switzerland and the Confederated States, or United States, were federal republics. He referred to the government of Holland to prove that that confederation was adequate to every purpose of human association. He saw a great difference between a democracy with one strong central government, elected and controlled by votes of the people, and a federal republic of severeign states. He cited ancient Greece and Rome: on how the public liberty of Rome was trifled with by the mode of voting, etc. He declared, "In great danger this power has been given. Rome has furnished us with an illustrous example." He made reference to Cincinnatus; to the patricians and plebeians.

In Mr. Henry's argument of June 5, when he was making his greatest effort in developing his objections to the Constitution, an incident occurred which "shows that his feelings as a husband were never lost in those of a patriot." In the audience "he recognized the face of his son, whom he had left to protect his family in his absence, and he knew that some important domestic event had brought him to Richmond. He hesitated a moment, stooped down, and with a full heart whispered to a friend near him: 'Dawson, I see my son in the hall; take him out.' Mr. Dawson at once withdrew with young Henry, and soon returned with the grateful intelligence that Mrs. Henry had given birth to a son, and that both mother and child were doing well. The new-born babe was named Alexander Spotswood, and lived to be familiar with his father's features and to enjoy his fame, and at the age of sixty-five was laid by his side in the quiet burial-ground at Red Hill."[43]

[Mr. Henry continued his discourse as follows:]

"This government is so new, it wants a name. I wish its other novelties were as harmless as this. . . . My worthy friend said that a republican form of government would not suit a very extensive country; but that if a government were judiciously organized and limits prescribed to it, an attention to these principles might render it possible for it to exist in an extensive territory. Whoever will be bold to say that a continent can be governed by that system contradicts all the experience of the world. . . . I tell him that a government may be trimmed up according to gentlemen's fancy, but it never can operate; it will be but very short-lived."

"This government, collectively taken, is without an example; that it is national in this part, and federal in that part, etc. We may be amused, if we please, by a treatise of political anatomy. In the brain it is national: the *stamina* are federal—some limbs are federal, others national. The senators are voted for by the State Legislatures: so far it is federal. Individuals choose the members of the first branch; here it is national. It is federal in conferring general powers, but national in retaining them. It is not to be supported by the States—the pockets of individuals are to be searched for its maintenance. What signifies it to me, that you have the most curious anatomical description of it in its creation? To all the common purposes of legislation it is a great consolidation of government. . . . This is not imaginary. It is a formidable reality.

"If consolidation proves to be as mischievous to this country as it has been to other countries, what will the poor inhabitants do? This government will operate like an ambuscade. It will destroy the State governments, and swallow the liberties of the people. If gentlemen are willing to run the hazard, let them run it; but I shall exculpate myself by my opposition, and monitory warnings within these walls."

[Mr. Henry wished to know the duties left to the states.]

"You are not to have the right to legislate in any but trivial cases: You are not to touch private contracts: You are not to have the right of having arms in your own defense: You cannot be trusted with dealing out justice between man and man. What shall the States have to do?—Take care of the poor, repair and make highways, erect bridges, and so on . . . Abolish the State

---

[43] Henry, *Henry*, op. cit., II, p. 359; Grigsby's *Convention of 1788*, p. 119.

legislatures at once. What purposes should they be continued for? Our legislature will indeed be a ludicrous spectacle—one hundred and eighty men marching in solemn, farcical procession, exhibiting a mournful proof of the lost liberty of their country, without the power of restoring it. Is the government of Virginia a state government after this government is adopted? I grant that it is a republican government; but for what purposes? For some trivial, domestic considerations, as render it unworthy the name of a legislature. But, sir, we have the consolation that it is a mixed government; that is, it may work sorely on your neck, but you will have some comfort by saying that it was a federal government in its origin."

Following Mr. Henry in debate were Governor Randolph, Mr. Madison, Mr. Nicholas and Mr. Corbin. Randolph and Madison each spoke twice. Mr. Henry resumed his remarks on June 7.

"Mr. Chairman: I have thought, and still think, that a full investigation of the actual situation of America ought to precede any decision on this great and important question. That government is no more than a choice among evils, is acknowledged by the most intelligent among mankind, and has been a standing maxim for ages. . . . Gentlemen strongly urge that its adoption will be a mighty benefit to us: but, sir, I am made of such incredulous materials, that assertions and declarations do not satisfy me.

"There are certain maxims, by which every wise and enlightened people will regulate their conduct. There are certain political maxims, which no free people ought ever to abandon: maxims, of which the observance is essential to the security of happiness. It is impiously irritating the avenging hand of Heaven, when a people, who are in the full enjoyment of freedom, launch out into the wide ocean of human affairs, and desert those maxims which alone can preserve liberty.

"We have one, sir, that all men are by nature free and independent, and have certain inherent rights, of which, when they enter into society, they cannot, by any compact, deprive or divest their posterity. We have a set of maxims of the same spirit, which must be beloved by every friend to liberty, to virtue, to mankind—our Bill of Rights contains those admirable maxims.

"Now, sir, I say, let us consider whether the picture given of American affairs ought to drive us from those beloved maxims.

"The honorable gentleman (Mr. Randolph) has said, that it is too late in the day for us to reject this new plan. That system which was once execrated by the honorable member, must now be adopted, let its defects be ever so glaring. That honorable member will not accuse me of want of candor, when I cast in my mind what he has given the public, and compare it to what has happened since. It seems to me very strange and unaccountable, that what was the object of his execration should now receive his encomiums. Something extraordinary must have operated so great a change in his opinion. It is too late in the day! Gentlemen must excuse me, if they should declare again and again, that it is too late, and I should think differently. I never can believe, sir, that it is too late to save all that is precious. I have, I fear, fatigued the committee, yet I have not said the one hundred thousandth part of what I have on my mind, and wish to impart.

"The honorable member has given you an elaborate account of what he judges tyrannical legislation, and an *ex post facto* law in the case of Josiah Phillips. He has misrepresented the facts. That man was not executed by a tyrannical stroke of power; nor was he a Socrates. He was a fugitive murderer and an outlaw; a man who commanded an infamous banditti, at a time when the war was at the most perilous stage. He committed the most cruel and shocking barbarities. He was an enemy to the human name. Those who declare war against the human race may be struck out of existence as soon as they are apprehended. He was not executed according to those beautiful legal ceremonies which are pointed out by the laws, in criminal cases. The enormity of his crimes did not entitle him to it. I am truly a friend to legal forms and methods; but, sir, the occasion warranted the measure. A pirate, an outlaw, or a common enemy to all mankind, may be put to death at any time. It is justified by the laws of *nature and nations*.

"The honorable member tells us then that there are burnings and discontents in the hearts of our citizens in general, and that they are dissatisfied with their government. I have no doubt the honorable member believes this to be the case, because he says so. But I have the comfortable assurance, that it is a certain fact, that it is not so. Sir, I fear this change will ultimately lead to our ruin. My fears are not the force of imagination; they are but too well founded. I tremble for my country: but, sir, I trust, I rely, and I am confident, that this political speculation has not taken so strong a hold of men's minds as some would make us believe.

"Another gentleman tells us, that no inconvenience will result from the exercise of the power of taxation by the general government; that two shillings out of ten may be saved by the impost; and that four shillings may be paid to the federal collector, and four to the State collector. A change of government will not pay money. If from the probable amount of the impost, you take the enormous and extravagant expenses, which will certainly attend the support of this great consolidated government, I believe you will find no reduction of the public burdens by this new system. The splendid maintenance of the President and of the members of both Houses; and the salaries and fees of the swarm of officers and dependents on the government will cost this continent immense sums . . .

"The style of the government (we the people) was introduced, perhaps, to recommend it to the people at large; to those citizens who are to be levelled and degraded to the lowest degree, who are likened to a herd, and who, by the operation of this blessed system, are to be transformed from respectable, independent citizens, to abject, dependent subjects or slaves. The honorable gentleman has anticipated what we are to be reduced to, by degradingly assimilating our citizens to a herd."

Governor Randolph answered Mr. Henry, declaring that he "did not use that word to excite any odium, but merely to convey the idea of a multitude. Mr. Henry replied, that it made a deep impression on his mind, and that he verily believed that system would operate as he had said."

Randolph's third speech, in which he painted a terrible picture of the dangers to which Virginia would be subjected should she refuse to ratify, was too much for Patrick Henry. He did not lack candor in his interrogation as to why Randolph changed his mind. In biting words Mr. Henry asked to know how his present doctrine was consistent with what had happened. "This seems to me strange and unaccountable. Something extraordinary must have operated to produce so great a change in his opinion? . . . What alteration has a few months brought about? The eternal difference between right and wrong does not fluctuate. It is immutable."

Greatly angered, Randolph replied: "I find myself attacked in the most illiberal manner by the honorable gentleman. I disdain his aspersions and his insinuations. His asperity is warranted by no principle of parliamentary decency, nor compatible with the least shadow of friendship; and if our friendship must fall, *let it fall like Lucifer, never to rise again!*"

No doubt in the recesses of his mind, Mr. Henry was remembering the "various devices" resorted to by the Federalists. One in particular concerned Governor Randolph's withholding the communication to the Governor of New York, inviting that State to unite with Virginia in the effort to secure amendments.[44] The bill, proposed by Mr. Henry in the legislature, was sent to each of the governors of the other states and was dated December 27, 1787, but "the one Governor Randolph addressed to Governor Clinton, did not reach its destination until March 7, 1788," too late for action to be taken by the legislature of that state. Governor Clinton's favorable reply, considered by the Council to be of public nature, was not transmitted to the convention, but was reserved for the special meeting of the legislature. This letter was not sent to the Assembly until after the final vote in the convention had been taken.[45] (George Mason offered a resolution asking for a committee to investigate Governor Randolph's conduct). Had Governor Randolph not destroyed the effect of the letter upon the convention, that body might have determined "to send a delegation to New York and await their report, which would have been very certainly favorable to the opposition; and in the meantime the fact that New Hampshire had made the ninth State to ratify, might have determined Virginia to follow Jefferson's advice, and hold off for satisfactory amendments."

There were other scenes on the floor not confined to Mr. Henry and Governor Randolph. George Mason, in discussing the judiciary, declared:

"There are many gentlemen in the United States who think it right that we should have one great, national, consolidated government, and that it is better to bring it about slowly and imperceptibly rather than all at once. . . . I know from my own knowledge many worthy gentlemen of this opinion."

Mason was interrupted by Mr. Madison who "demanded an unequivocal explanation, and a statement of who the gentlemen were to whom he alluded." Colonel Mason replied:

"I shall never refuse to explain myself. It is notorious that this is a prevailing principle. It was at least the opinion of many gentlemen in convention, and many in the United States. I do not know what explanation the honorable gentleman asks. I can say with great truth, that the honorable gentleman, in private conversation with me, expressed himself against it; neither did I ever hear any of the delegates from this state advocate it."[46]

Here the fact "that Pendleton, Wythe, and others in Virginia, who opposed the earlier measures of the Revolution, and showed

---

[44] *Ibid.*, op. cit. II, pp. 362–363. Hening's *Statutes at Large*, XII, p. 463.

[45] *Ibid.*, See footnote, p. 363.

[46] *Ibid.*, II, p. 357; Elliot, *Debates*, III, p. 522.

an indisposition to give up a kingly government, were now the earnest advocates of the proposed plan, was sarcastically alluded to by Colonel Mason in the following words:

"I have some acquaintances with a great many characters who favor this government, their connections, their conduct, their political principles, and a number of other circumstances. There are a great many wise and good men among them. But when I look round the number of my acquaintances in Virginia, the country wherein I was born and have lived so many years, and observe who are the warmest and the most zealous friends to this new government, it makes me think of the story of the cat transformed into a fine lady; forgetting her transformation, and happening to see a rat, she could not restrain herself, but sprang upon it out of the chair."[47]

Mr. Henry had the same grounds of distrust as Mason, when he interrogated Randolph.

In his reference to other nations which, "precipitated by the rage of ambition or folly," had "*riveted the fetters of bondage* on themselves and their descendants," his eloquence was said to be overpowering. So fervid was Mr. Henry's description of the slavery to which the people would be levelled and degraded under a federal executive, that it "caused a Mr. Best of Nansemond County, to unconsciously feel his wrists to assure himself that the fetters were not already pressing his flesh, and the gallery in which he sat seemed to become dark as a dungeon."[48]

[Concerning requisitions, Mr. Henry noted:]

"On this depends our political prosperity. I never will give up that darling word, requisitions; my country may give it up; a majority may wrest it from me, but I will never give it up till my grave. Requisitions are attended with one singular advantage. They are attended by deliberation. They secure to the States the benefit of correcting oppressive errors.

". . . The power of direct taxation was called by the honorable gentleman the soul of the government: another gentleman called it the lungs of the government. We all agree that it is the most important part of the body politic. If the power of raising money be necessary for the general government, it is no less so for the States. If money be the vitals of Congress, is it not precious for those individuals from whom it is to be taken? Must I give my soul, my lungs, to Congress? Congress must have our souls; the State must have our souls. This is dishonorable and disgraceful.

[47] *Ibid.*, II, p. 358.
[48] *Ibid.*, II, p. 359.

These two co-ordinate, interfering, unlimited powers of harassing the community, are unexampled—unprecedented in history; they are the visionary projects of modern politicians: tell me not of imaginary means, but of reality: this political solecism will never tend to the benefit of the community. It will be as oppressive in practice as it is absurd in theory. If you part from this, which the honorable gentleman tells you is the soul of Congress, you will be inevitably ruined. I tell you, they shall not have the soul of Virginia."

Taking the floor again after an interruption by Randolph, Mr. Henry pointed to the danger of implied power:

"If we are to have one representative for every 30,000 souls, it must be by implication. The constitution does not positively secure it. Even say it is a natural implication, why not give us a right to that proportion in express terms, in language that could not admit of evasions or subterfuges? If they can use implication for us, they can also use implication against us. We are giving power; they are getting power; judge, then, on which side the implication will be used. When we once put it in their option to assume constructive power, danger will follow. Trial by jury, and liberty of the press, are also on this foundation of implication. If they encroach on these rights, and you give your implication for a plea, you are lost; for they will be justified by the last part of it, which gives them full power 'to make all laws which shall be necessary and proper to carry their powers into execution'; Implication is dangerous, because it is unbounded . . ."

The importance of the Mississippi engaged his most serious attention. He referred to it again and again:

". . . By the confederation, the rights of territory are secured. No treaty can be made without the consent of nine States. While the consent of nine States is necessary to the cession of territory, you are safe. If it be put in the power of a less number, you will most infallibly lose the Mississippi. As long as we can preserve our unalienable rights, we are in safety. This new constitution will involve in its operation the loss of the navigation of that valuable river. The honorable gentleman cannot be ignorant of the Spanish transactions. A treaty had been nearly entered into with Spain, to relinquish that navigation, and that relinquishment would absolutely have taken place, had the consent of seven States been sufficient. . . . This dispute has sprung from the federal government. I wish a great deal to be said on this subject. . . .In my opinion, the preservation of that river calls for our most serious consideration. It has been agitated in Congress.

Seven States have voted so that it is known to the Spainards, that under our existing system the Mississippi shall be taken from them. Seven States wished to relinquish this river to them. The six Southern States opposed it. Seven States not being sufficient to convey it away, it remains now ours. . . .This new government, I conceive, will enable those States, who have already discovered their inclination that way, to give away this river. Will the honorable gentleman advise us to relinquish this inestimable navigation, and place formidable enemies to our backs? . . . To preserve the balance of American power it is essentially necessary that the right to the Mississippi should be secured . . . federal measures will lose it to us forever. If a bare majority of Congress can make laws, the situation of our Western citizens is dreadful. . . . The efforts of our ten men will avail very little when opposed by the Northern majority. . . . The Northern States will never assent to regulation promotive of the Southern aggrandizement. . . . There is a striking difference, and great contrariety of interest between the States. . . . This government subjects everything to the Northern majority. Is there not then a settled purpose to check the Southern interest? We thus put unbounded power over our property in hands not having a common interest with us. Sir, this is a picture so horrid, so wretched, so dreadful, that I need no longer dwell upon it.

"We are threatened with danger for the non-payment of the debt due to France. We have information from an illustrious citizen of Virginia (Jefferson), who is now in Paris, which disproves the suggestions of such danger. The honorable gentleman tells us, that hostile fleets are to be sent to make reprisals upon us; our ambassador tells you, that the King of France has taken into consideration to enter into commercial regulations on reciprocal terms with us, which will be of peculiar advantage to us. Does this look like hostility? . . . This illustrious citizen advises you to reject this government, till it be amended. His sentiments coincide entirely with ours. . . . Living amidst splendor and dissipation, he thinks yet of bills of rights—thinks of those little despised things called maxims. Let us follow the sage advice of this common friend of our happiness. It is little usual for nations to send armies to collect debts . . .

"The necessity of amendments is universally admitted. It is a word which is reechoed from every part of the continent. A majority of those who hear me think amendments are necessary. . . . Reason, self-preservation, and every idea of propriety, powerfully urge us to secure the dearest rights of human nature. . . ."

On the next day, Edmund Randolph answered Patrick Henry's allusion to Jefferson, saying: ". . . I trust that his name was not mentioned to influence any member of this house. Notwithstanding the celebrity of his character, his name cannot be used as authority against the Constitution. . . . As far as my information goes, it is only a report circulated through the town, that he wished nine states to adopt, and the others to reject it in order to get amendments. . . ."

But Mr. Henry knew that it was more than just a report, having probably seen the Donald letter,[49] wherein Jefferson wished with all his soul "that the nine first Conventions may accept the new Constitution," and "the four latest Conventions . . . may refuse to accede to it till a declaration of rights be annexed." Thus, he showed that Jefferson was for amendments, and did not imply that he was for adoption. He pointed to the eight states that had already ratified, and if, as asserted, New Hampshire would certainly do so, Henry wanted to know, "Where then, will four states be found to reject, if we adopt it? If we do, the counsel of this enlightened and worthy countryman of ours will be thrown away; and for what? He wishes to secure amendments and a bill of rights, if I am not mistaken. . . . His amendments go to that despised thing, called a *bill of rights*, and all the rights which are dear to human nature—trial by jury, the liberty of religion and the press, &c. Do not gentlemen see that, if we adopt, under the idea of following Mr. Jefferson's opinion, we amuse ourselves with the shadow, while the substance is given away? If Virginia be for adoption, what states will be left, of sufficient respectability and importance to secure amendments by their rejection? . . . Where will you find attachment to the rights of mankind, when Massachusetts, the great northern state, Pennsylvania, the great middle state, and Virginia, the great southern state, shall

---

[49] Boyd, *The Papers of Thomas Jefferson*, XII, p. 571. See Jefferson's letter to Alexander Donald, Feb. 7, 1788. Also, his similar views as expressed to James Monroe, Aug. 9, 1788. *Ibid.*, XIII, pp. 489–490; Henry, *Henry*, op. cit., II, p. 360; Jefferson *Works*, II, p. 355. On May 27, 1788, Jefferson wrote Carrington: "My first wish was that 9 states would adopt it in order to ensure what was good in it, and that the others might, by holding off, produce the necessary amendments. . . . There are two amendments only which I am anxious for: 1. A bill of rights, which is so much the interest of all to have, that I conceive it must be yielded. The 1st amendment proposed by Massachusetts will in some degree answer this end, but not so well. It will do too much in some instances and too little in others. It will cripple the federal government in some cases where it ought to be free, and not restrain it in some others where restraint would be right. . . ." *Ibid.*, XIII, p. 208.

have adopted this government? Where will you find magnanimity enough to reject it?"[50]

Madison arose to answer Mr. Henry and proposed to show that Jefferson had changed his mind since writing the Donald letter. But lacking the evidence to prove that Jefferson now favored the Massachusetts plan for obtaining amendments, he could only lament that "the opinion of a citizen who is an ornament to this state" had been mentioned by Henry. "Is it come to this, then, that we are not to follow our own reason? Is it proper to introduce the opinions of respectable men not within these walls? . . . I believe that, were that gentleman now on this floor, he would be for the adoption of this Constitution. I wish his name had never been mentioned. I . . . know that the delicacy of his feelings will be wounded, when he will see in print what has and may be said concerning him on this occasion. I am, in some measure, acquainted with his sentiments on this subject. . . . But, whatever be the opinion of that illustrious citizen, considerations of personal delicacy should dissuade us from introducing it here."[51]

Jefferson had not only written to Alexander Donald; he had expressed the same views to Monroe and to Carrington. (See footnote 49) When or if he changed his mind is not known. According to Madison's biographer, Jefferson feared that objection to the new form might produce a schism . . . "whereas, all of us going together, we shall be sure to cure the evils of our new Constitution before they do great harm." He thought the plan of Massachusetts best—"that is, to accept and amend afterwards."[52]

Mr. Henry continued:

"If there be a real check intended to be left on Congress, it must be left in the State governments. There will be some check, as long as the judges are incorrupt. As long as they are upright, you may preserve your liberty. But what will the judges determine when the State and federal authority come to be contrasted? Will your liberty then be secure, when the congressional laws are declared paramount to the laws of your State, and the judges are sworn to support them?"

"I am constrained to make a few remarks on the absurdity of

---

[50] Boyd, *The Papers of Thomas Jefferson,* XIII, p. 355. Elliot, *Debates, Philadelphia, 1901,* III, pp. 152–153–199–200, 314–315, 329–330.

[51] *Ibid.,* op. cit., XIII, pp. 354–355 n. Elliot, *Debates, 1901,* III, pp. 152–153–199–200, 314–315, 329–330. See also, Madison to Jefferson, 24 July, 1788.

[52] Rives' *Life and Times of James Madison,* II, pp. 556–557; Randall, *Writings of Jefferson,* II, pp. 303–340; Jefferson's *Writings,* II, p. 270.

adopting this system, and relying on the chance of getting it amended afterwards. When it is confessed to be replete with defects, is it not offering to insult your understandings, to attempt to reason you out of the propriety of rejecting it, till it be amended? Does it not insult your judgments to tell you—adopt first, and then amend? Is your rage for novelty so great, that you are first to sign and seal, and then to retract? Is it possible to conceive a greater solecism? I am at a loss what to say. You agree to bind yourselves hand and foot—for the sake of what? Of being unbound. You go into a dungeon—for what? To get out. Is there no danger when you go in, that the bolts of federal authority shall shut you in? . . . I ask you again, where is the example that a government was amended by those who instituted it? . . . I look on that paper as the most fatal plan that could possibly be conceived to enslave a free people. If such be your rage for novelty, take it and welcome, but you never shall have my consent. . . .

". . . I should be led to take that man for a lunatic, who should tell me to run into the adoption of a government avowedly defective, in hopes of having it amended afterwards. Were I about to give away the meanest particle of my own property, I should act with more prudence and discretion. My anxiety and fears are great, lest America, by the adoption of this system, should be cast into a fathomless abyss."[53]

Mr. Henry found it "exceedingly painful" to be objecting, but he wished for further time to answer Madison, Randolph, Pendleton, John Marshall and Henry Lee:

"An honorable gentleman several days ago observed that the great object of this government was justice. . . . Why is the trial by jury taken away? . . . A state may be sued in the federal court by the paper on your table. . . . The honorable member told us that he had doubts with respect to the judiciary department. Trial by jury is the best appendage of free men. Does it secure this? Does it secure the other great rights of mankind?

"The honorable gentlemen did our judiciary honor in saying that they had firmness to counteract the legislature in some cases. We have this landmark to guide us."

[Mr. Henry inquired of Madison to know:]

"Is that judiciary so well constructed and so independent of the other branches as our State judiciary?"

---

[53] *The World's Great Classics, Orations of American Orators,* With a Special Introduction by Julian Hawthorne, 1900, I, pp. 63 to 124.

"The State governments," said Madison, "will possess greater advantages than the general government, and will consequently prevail."

[Henry disagreed:]

"His opinion and mine are diametrically opposite. Bring forth the Federal allurements, and compare them with the poor, contemptible things that the State Legislatures can bring forth . . . There are rich, fat, Federal emoluments. Your rich, snug, fine, fat Federal officers—the collectors of taxes and excises—will out-number anything from the States. Who can cope with the excise man and the tax man?"

"Then the honorable gentleman, Madison, said that the two judiciaries and legislatures would go in a parallel line and never interfere—that as long as each was confined to its proper objects, that there would be no danger of interference—that like two parallel lines as long as they continued in their parallel direction they never would meet.

"With submission to the honorable gentleman's opinion, there is danger of interference, because no line is drawn between the powers of the two governments in many instances; and where there is a line, there is no check to prevent the one from encroaching upon the power of the other. I therefore contend that they must interfere, and that this interference must subvert the State government, as being less powerful."[54]

Henry hoped "they will not have federal courts in every county. If they will, the State courts will be debased and stripped of their cognizance, and utterly abolished. . . . If you give too little power today, you may give more tomorrow. But the reverse of the proposition will not hold. If you give too much power today, you cannot retake it tomorrow, for tomorrow will never come for that purpose.

". . . It was expressly declared in Confederation that every right was obtained by the states, respectively, which was not given up to the government of the United States. But there is no such thing here, you, therefore, by a natural and unavoidable implication, give up your rights to the general government. . . . If you give up these powers without a bill of rights, you will exhibit the most absurd thing to mankind that ever the world saw—a government that has abandoned all its powers—the power of direct taxation, the sword and the purse. . . .

"Mr. Chairman, I have already expressed painful sensations

[54] Elliot, *Debates*, III, pp. 323–325–327–385–446–539.

at the surrender of our great rights, and I am again driven to the mournful recollection. The purse is gone; the sword is gone; and here is the only thing of any importance that is to remain with us. As I think this is a more fatal defect than any we have yet considered, forgive me if I attempt to refute the observations made by the honorable member in the chair, and last up.

"I consider the Virginia judiciary as one of the best barriers against strides of power—against that power which, we are told by the honorable gentleman, has threatened the destruction of liberty . . .

". . . I see arising out of that paper, a tribunal, that is to be recurred to in all cases, when the destruction of the State judiciaries shall happen; and from the extensive jurisdiction of these paramount courts, the State courts must soon be annihilated."

The debates on the expediency of adopting the Federal Constitution had now reached June 23. Its defects were recognized and were admitted, and the question of adoption or rejection remained to be decided. Anxiety filled every heart and mind over its outcome. Patrick Henry "partook most deeply of this feeling, and while engaged as it were in his last effort, availed himself of the strong sensations which he knew to pervade the house, and made an appeal to it which, in point of sublimity, has never been surpassed in any age or country of the world."[55]

On completing the examination of the Constitution by sections, it appeared that a majority was for amendments. But the Federalists "resorted to the tactics of their party in Massachusetts": Upon the resolution of Mr. Wythe, their speaker, it was proposed, "That the committee should ratify the Constitution, and that whatsoever amendments might be deemed necessary should be recommended to the consideration of the Congress which should first assemble under the Constitution, to be acted upon according to the mode prescribed therein." The resolution of ratification[56] was read, and later reported by a committee of five, Randolph, Nicholas, Madison, Marshall and Corbin.

---

[55] Henry, *Henry*, op. cit., II, pp. 370–371 n.; William Wirt, quoting Judge Archibald Stuart.

[56] *Ibid.*, II, pp. 365–366.

"We, the delegates to the People of Virginia duly elected in pursuance of a recommendation from the General Assembly and now met in Convention, having fully and freely investigated and discussed the proceedings of the Federal Convention and being prepared as well as the most mature deliberation hath enabled us to decide thereon, do in the name and in behalf of the People of Virginia declare and make known that the powers granted under

Mr. Henry arose at once in opposition to the resolutions with the following speech, June 24, 1788:

"Mr. Chairman: The proposal of ratification is premature. The importance of the subject requires the most mature deliberation. The honorable member must forgive me for declaring my dissent from it, because, if I understand it rightly, it admits that the new system is defective, and most capitally; for, immediately after the proposed ratification, there comes a declaration, that the paper before you is not intended to violate any of these three great rights—the liberty of religion, liberty of the press, and the trial by jury. What is the inference, when you enumerate the rights which you are to enjoy? That those not enumerated are relinquished. There are only three things to be retained—religion, freedom of the press, and jury trial. Will not the ratification carry every thing, without excepting these three things? Will not all the world pronounce, that we intended to give up all the rest? Every thing it speaks of, by way of rights, is comprised in these three things. Your subsequent amendments only go to these three amendments. I feel my self distressed, because the necessity of securing our personal rights seems not to have pervaded the minds of men; for any other valuable things are omitted. . . .

"Another most fatal omission is, with respect to standing armies. In your bill of rights of Virginia, they are said to be dan-

---

the Constitution being derived from the People of the United States may be resumed by them whensoever the same shall be perverted to their injury or oppression *and that every power not granted thereby remains with them and at their will:* that therefore no right of any denomination can be cancelled abridged restrained or modified by the Congress by the Senate or House of Representatives acting in any Capacity by the President or any Department or Officer of the United States except in those instances in which power is given by the Constitution for those purposes: & that among other essential rights the liberty of Conscience and of the Press cannot be cancelled, abridged, restrained, or modified by any authority of the United States.

With these impressions, with a solemn appeal to the Searcher of hearts for the purity of our intentions, and under the conviction that whatsoever imperfections may exist in the Constitution ought rather to be examined in the mode prescribed therein than to bring the Union into danger by a delay with a hope of obtaining Amendments previous to the Ratification, We the said Delegates in the name and in behalf of the People of Virginia do by these presents assent to and ratify the Constitution recommended on the seventeenth day of September one thousand seven hundred and eighty seven by the Federal Convention for the Government of the United States hereby announcing to all those whom it may concern that the said Constitution is binding upon the said People according to an authentic Copy hereto annexed."

gerous to liberty; and it tells you, that the proper defense of a free state consists in militia; and so I might go on to ten or eleven things of immense consequence secured in your bill of rights. . . .

"I exhort gentlemen to think seriously before they ratify this constitution, and persuade themselves that they will succeed in making a feeble effort to get amendments after adoption. With respect to that part of the proposal which says that every power not granted remains with the people, it must be previous to adoption, or it will involve this country in inevitable destruction. To talk of it as a thing subsequent, not as one of your inalienable rights, is leaving it to the casual opinion of the congress who shall take up the consideration of that matter. They will not reason with you about the effect of this constitution. They will not take the opinion of this committee concerning its operation. They will construe it as they please.

". . . With respect to subsequent amendments, proposed by the worthy member, I am distressed when I hear the expression. It is a new one altogether, and such a one as stands against every idea of fortitude and manliness. . . . Evils admitted, in order to be removed subsequently, and tyranny submitted to, in order to be excluded by a subsequent alteration, are things totally new to me. But I am sure he meant nothing but to amuse the committee. I know his candor. His proposal is an idea dreadful to me. I ask, Does experience warrant such a thing from the beginning of the world to this day? Do you enter into a compact of government first, and afterwards settle the terms of the government? It is admitted by every one, that this is a compact. . . . I confess I never heard of such an idea before. It is most abhorrent to my mind.

"Anxious as I am to be as little troublesome as possible, I cannot leave this part of the subject without adverting to one remark of the honorable gentleman. He says, that, rather than bring the union into danger, he will adopt it with its imperfections. . . . A previous ratification will raise insurmountable obstacles to union. New York is an insurmountable obstacle to it, and North Carolina also.—They will never accede to it till it be amended. A great part of Virginia is opposed, most decidedly, to it, as it stands. . . . There was a majority of only nineteen in Massachusetts. We are told that only ten thousand were represented in Pennsylvania, although seventy thousand had a right to be represented. Is not this a serious thing? Is it not worth while to turn your eyes for a moment, from subsequent amendments, to the situation of your country? Can you have a lasting union in these circumstances? It will be in vain to expect it. But if you agree to previous amendments, you shall have union, firm and solid. I cannot conclude without saying that I shall have nothing to do with it, if subsequent amendments be determined upon. . . . I conceive it my duty, if this government is adopted before it is amended, to go home. . . . Previous amendments, in my opinion, are necessary to procure peace and tranquillity. I fear if they be not agreed to, every movement and operation of government will cease; and how long that baneful thing, civil discord, will stay from this country, God only knows. When men are free from restraint, how long will you suspend their fury? The interval between this and bloodshed is but a moment. The licentious and wicked of the community will seize with avidity every thing you hold. In this unhappy situation, what is to be done? It surpasses my stock of wisdom. If you will, in the language of freemen, stipulate that there are rights which no man under heaven can take from you, you shall have me going along with you, and not otherwise.—"

Here Mr. Henry informed the committee, that he had "a resolution prepared, to refer a declaration of rights, with certain amendments to the most exceptionable parts of the constitution, to the other states in the confederacy, for their consideration, previous to its ratification. The clerk then read the resolution, the declaration of rights, and amendments, which were nearly the same as those ultimately proposed by the convention, for the consideration of congress. He then resumed the subject."

"I have thus candidly submitted to you, Mr. Chairman, and this committee, what occurred to me as proper amendments to the constitution, and a declaration of rights containing those fundamental, inalienable privileges, which I conceive to be essential to liberty and happiness. I believe that, on a review of these amendments, it will still be found that the arm of power will be sufficiently strong for national purposes when these restrictions shall be a part of the government. I believe no gentleman, who opposes me in sentiments, will be able to discover that any one feature of a strong government is altered; and at the same time your inalienable rights are secured by them. . . . If the government be constructed to satisfy the people and remove their apprehensions, the wealth and strength of the continent will go where public utility shall direct. This government, with these restrictions, will be a strong government united with the privileges of the people. . . . The language of this paper is not dictatorial, but merely a proposition for amendments. The proposition of Virginia met with a favorable reception before. We proposed that convention which met at Annapolis. It was not called dictatorial. We proposed that at Philadelphia. Was Virginia thought dictatorial? But Virginia is now to lose her preeminence. Those rights to which the meanest individual in the community is entitled. . . . Have we not a right to say, Hear our propositions? . . . What do we require? Not preeminence, but safety; that our citizens may be able to sit down in peace and security under their own figtrees. . . . I could not withhold from my fellow-citizens any thing so reasonable. I fear you will have no union, unless you remove the cause of opposition. Will you sit down contented with the name of union without any solid foundation?

"The great and direct end of government is liberty. Secure our liberty and privileges, and the end of government is answered."[57]

Mr. Henry's speech of the next day, June 24, was made during a violent thunderstorm that shook the whole building, when the very heavens seemed to be protesting against the calamities that would befall the nation from the actions to be taken. In the severe lightning, thunder, and torrents of rain, the scene was described as something sublime and appalling. But Patrick Henry's eloquence, like the storm, did not cease. Instead, "with a master's art, he seemed to . . . seize upon the artillery of heaven, and direct its fiercest thunders against the heads of his adversaries."[58]

On the next day, June 25, he concluded his last speech with these words:

"I beg pardon of this House for having taken up more time than came to my share, and I thank them for their patience and polite attention with which I have been heard. If I shall be in the minority I shall have those painful sensations which arise from a conviction of being overpowered in a good cause. Yet I will be a peaceable citizen. My head, my hand, and my heart shall be at liberty to retrieve the loss of liberty, and to remove the defects of that system in a constitutional way. I wish not to go to violence, but will wait with hopes that the spirit which predominated in the revolution is not gone, nor the cause of those who are attached to the revolution, lost. I shall, therefore, patiently wait in expectation of seeing that government changed so as to be compatible with the safety, liberty, and happiness of the people."

---

[57] *American Oratory*, or *Selections From the Speeches of Eminent Americans*, Compiled by A Member of The Philadelphia Bar. Philadelphia: Desilver, Thomas, & Co., 253 Market Street, 1836.

[58] Tyler, *Henry*, op. cit., p. 338; Wirt, *Henry*, pp. 296–297. Also, Henry, *Henry*, II, pp. 370–371.

In place of the resolution of ratification Mr. Henry moved the following:

"That previous to the ratification of the new constitution of government recommended by the late convention, a declaration of rights, asserting and securing from encroachment the great principles of civil and religious liberty, and the unalienable rights of the people, together with amendments to the most exceptionable parts of the said constitution of government, ought to be referred by this convention to the other States in the American confederacy for their consideration."[59]

However, his motion "was lost by a vote of 80 ayes to 88 noes, and the vote being then taken on the resolution to ratify, it was carried by a vote of 89 ayes to 79 noes."

Thus the final vote brought the debate over the ratification of the Federal Constitution to an end. The die was cast. However, Mr. Henry prevailed in the matter of his amendments, which were carried by a large majority.[60] But the outcome might have been different except for the extraordinary influence of Washington. He was in "constant communication with Madison and others." Added to this was "the danger of disunion and anarchy in case of delay" used by the Federalists, "a danger altogether chimerical, as was afterward proved on the refusal of North Carolina and Rhode Island to ratify."[61] But even Washington's influence might have failed, "had the Convention known that New Hampshire had made the ninth State to ratify on June 21, or had Governor Clinton's letter to Randolph been laid before the body. As it was, the result was attained by inducing several of the delegates to vote against the wishes of their constituents.[62] Among these may be mentioned Humphrey Marshall of Fayette County, Kentucky; Andrew Moore, and William McKee, of Rockbridge;[63] George Parker, of Accomac; Paul Carrington, of Charlotte; Levin Powell, of Loudon; William Overton Callis, of Louisa; and William McClerry, of Mongolia. Had these voted the sentiments of their constituents as indicated by instructions, or by the votes of their associated delegates, the result would have been against ratification without previous amendments."[64]

---

[59] Henry, *Henry,* II, pp. 372–373.

[60] *Ibid.,* II, p., 375.

[61] *Ibid.,* II, pp. 363–364–377.

[62] *Ibid.,* op. cit., II, p. 377 n. "This is an able review of the Convention by John Scott, Esq., of Virginia, in a volume entitled *The Lost Principle.*"

[63] *Ibid.,* op. cit., "He admits this in his *History of Kentucky.* These were instructed to vote against ratification without previous amendments."

[64] *Ibid.,* II, p. 377.

Upon hearing the results, Patrick Henry and the Anti-Federalists must have felt their defeat keenly. For 18 days he had thrown his whole soul into the debate, as he expounded and admonished upon the dangers in the Federal Constitution. Yet, the historian, after carefully examining his political acuity, must concede the soundness of Henry's interpretations. Future events would bear out his predictions with tragic swiftness.

His discernment in the Virginia Convention 180 years ago is astonishing and merits singular praise in light of the events of today. He prophesied the fate of the agricultural South at the hands of the industrial North. He foretold the baneful effects of a supreme judiciary beholden to no one.[65] Patrick Henry declared that this government would not last a century. He had not been in his grave 65 years before his predictions came to pass, "by the result of the greatest civil war history has recorded, brought about by the endeavor of the Southern States to exercise the asserted right of secession."[66]

The framers of the unamended Constitution would not be around to reap the whirlwind that Henry plainly saw: the inadequacy of checks and balances; the Federal government's power of direct taxation; the unlimited power of judicial intervention, as well as that very real risk of having a President of the United States entrench himself in office. The evils of judicial usurpation disquieted him most of all, and his fears were not premature. The abuses in this department began with the injudicious and hostile Judiciary Act of 1789, written by United States Senator Oliver Ellsworth. This bill was made the basis of the federal court system and established its powers, which permit the Supreme Court to overturn state court decisions and acts of the legislatures, as well as to change federal laws. However, nowhere in the Constitution, itself, is the Supreme Court specifically empowered to make judicial interpretation, or to reverse the decisions of the state courts. Ellsworth became Chief Justice of the United States, retiring in the fall of 1800. This was ironical, because he had to be replaced barely six weeks before President Adams went out of office. "The appointment which would have gone to Spencer Roane, had Jefferson come into office soon enough to make it, instead was accepted in February of 1801 by another Virginian: John Marshall. What happened thereafter needs no review. Mar-

[65] See the cases and opinions that had arisen in the Supreme Court under the Constitution up to the year 1891, as cited by Patrick Henry's grandson, William W. Henry, Henry, *Henry*, II, beginning with page 381.
[66] Henry, *Henry*, II, p. 382.

shall shaped the Constitution to his own centralist philosophy. He impressed upon the country his own ideas of loose construction, national domination, subordination of the States."[67]

Spencer Roane, the son-in-law of Patrick Henry, was, like him, a libertarian, and an avowed States'-Righter. "He perceived that the Supreme Court of the United States, if unchecked by the States themselves, would by degrees elevate itself to a judicial oligarchy, as powerful as any prince or tyrant. Judge Roane's great political aim was to see the Union preserved as just that—a *Union of States*, in which each separate sovereign State exercised full authority over its internal affairs."[68]

Another Virginian, complaining of the Court in 1802, declared: "I fear if things are allowed to stand, our destiny will be like that of Rome. Since the Judges have with strong hand, seized their courts, and bent them to their will." He said further: "There is no independent part of this government; in popular governments, the force of every department, as well as the government itself, must depend upon popular opinion."[69]

In the convention, Patrick Henry fought hard to prevent the ineluctable erosion of the sovereignty of the states. It was not his intention that the states should lie at the mercy of the supreme judiciary. He felt certain of the possibility of judicial vandalism, and this conviction underlies his Requisitions, the source of *interposition.* If a law were passed by Congress, injurious to the rights, then it was indubitable that Congress change the law, or curb any and all acts repugnant to the people, which is the duty of all appointed representatives. And should the judges attempt to force the sovereignty of the states to bow before them, this was cause for impeachment.

If in the convention Mr. Henry had lost the struggle against ratification, he was not finished. He was "unremitting in his efforts to procure the amendments he deemed of such vital importance," and this would be his next object. In the meantime, he would remain a peaceful citizen. He had fought a good fight and kept the faith without malevolence and without rancor.

On the same evening that concluded the bitter fight, some of the delegates from among the Anti-Federalists gathered to regroup

---

[67] From the Editorial Page of the Richmond News Leader, by James J. Kilpatrick, Editor, September 4, 1956: *Here Lived a States' Righter.*

[68] *Ibid.*

[69] *American Oratory*, Mr. Giles from Virginia, speaking in the United States Senate, January 13, 1802.

their forces and formulate a plan of resistance to the government. Mr. Henry was asked to take the chair, which he did. However, upon hearing their purpose, he turned them aside, saying "He had done his duty strenuously in opposing the constitution, in the proper place, and with all the powers he possessed. The question had been fully discussed, and settled, and that, as true and faithful republicans, they had all better go home; they should cherish it and give it fair play and support it, too."[70]

Several days before the convention closed, word was received of the meeting of the New York convention beginning June 17. Among the 65 delegates present, "two-thirds were opposed to unconditional ratification." The opposition was led by Governor Clinton, and the Federalists, by Hamilton. However, a compromise was reached, and ratification was agreed to, with the proposal of numerous amendments, and that "a circular letter be sent to the legislatures of the several States, recommended the call of another General Convention to act upon the amendments proposed by the States."[71] There was a unanimous vote in favor of the letter. Next heard from was New Hampshire, which had ratified on the 24th, making the ninth State, but the decision still rested with Virginia. North Carolina held its convention next on July 21, and noting the results in Virginia and New York, that body deferred ratification with the proposal that amendments be adopted similar to those suggested by Virginia. The motion carried by a vote of 184 to 84, with heartening results for the Anti-Federalists.

However burdened Patrick Henry had been with anxieties over the new government, and dreading its consequences, he spent the summer in restful contemplation after the rigors of the convention, and awaited the coming of the legislature. In the meantime, Madison and Washington were speculating as to what his next move might be. Madison wrote Washington on June 27 that he hoped Mr. Henry's efforts would be directed toward peacemaking; that he had promised to submit as a quiet citizen, although he had declared he would "seize the first moment that offered for shaking off the yoke in a *constitutional way*." Madison suspected the plan of Henry and the Anti-Federalists would be

---

[70] Henry, *Henry,* op. cit., II, p. 412, *Southern Literary Messenger,* I, p. 332. "This account was also substantially given by Mr. Richard Venable, of Prince Edward County, to Hon. James W. Bouldin, who related it in a letter to the author's father."

[71] *Ibid.,* II, pp. 410–411.

"to engage two-thirds of the legislature to the task of undoing the work; or to get a Congress appointed in the first instance that will commit suicide on their own authority."[72] On September 21 Washington wrote Madison urging the election of Federalists to Congress, saying: "To be shipwrecked in sight of the port would be the severest of all possible aggravations to our misery, and I assure you I am under painful apprehensions from the single circumstance of Mr. Henry having the whole game to play in the Assembly of this State; and the effect it may have in others should be counteracted if possible."[73] Little did Washington realize that he would later call on Patrick Henry to help him tow the Federal bark into a port of safety.

Edward Carrington, another apprehensive Federalist returning from Mount Vernon after talking with Washington over "the probable politics in the Assembly," wrote Madison October 19: "He is fully persuaded that anti-federalism will be the actuating principle, and that great circumspection is necessary to prevent very mischievous effects from a cooperation in the insidious proposition of New York. He is particularly alarmed from a prospect of an election for the Senate, entirely anti-Federal. It is said in this part of the State that Mr. Henry and Mr. R. H. Lee are to be pushed. I believe it is founded only in conjecture, but the General is apprehensive it may prove true; that to exclude the former will be impossible; and that the latter being supported by his influence, will also get in, unless a Federalist very well established in the confidence of the people can be opposed. He is decided in his wishes that you may be brought forward upon this occasion."[74]

Here had emerged "two divided parties" with "two conflicting theories as to the nature of the United States Constitution,"[75] each attempting to line up their forces for the final showdown within Congress.

In October Patrick Henry again journeyed to Richmond for the meeting of the Assembly to convene on the 20th. His leadership unabated, he was seen as "the master spirit of the Assembly," holding an "omnipotent" sway over that body. He served on four standing committees and was chairman of the Committee of Courts of Justice. In the second week of the session, Mr. Henry seized the moment he had been looking for, and let it be known "that he

---

[72] *Ibid.*, op. cit., II, pp. 413–414; Madison's *Works*, I, p. 402.
[73] *Ibid.*, pp. 415–416; *Writings of Washington, IX*, p. 433.
[74] *Ibid.*, op. cit., Bancroft's *Constitution*, II, p. 480.
[75] *Ibid.*, II, p. 382.

should oppose every measure tending to the organization of the Government, unless accompanied with measures for the amendment of the Constitution; for which purpose he proposed that another general convention of deputies from the different States shall be held, as soon as practicable." The preamble to his resolutions is particularly noteworthy:

"Whereas, the Convention of delegates of the people of this Commonwealth did ratify a Constitution or form of government for the United States, referred to them for their consideration, and did also declare that sundry amendments to exceptionable parts of the same ought to be adopted. And whereas, the subject-matter of the amendments agreed to by the said convention involves all the great essential and unalienable rights, liberties, and privileges of freemen, many of which, if not cancelled, are rendered insecure under the said Constitution until the same shall be altered and amended."

The first resolution read:

"That for quieting the minds of the good citizens of this commonwealth, and securing their dearest rights and liberties, and preventing those disorders which must arise under a government not founded on the confidence of the people, application be made to the Congress of the United States, as soon as they shall assemble under the said Constitution, to call a convention for proposing amendments to the same according to the mode therein directed."

Further resolutions were offered "for appointing a committee to draft a proper application to Congress, a reply to Governor Clinton's communication as president of the New York Convention, and a circular to the other States. These resolutions were a bitter pill to the Federalists, for they not only asked for the dreaded new Convention, but described the friends of the proposed plan as betrayers of the dearest rights of the people. When they came up for action the Federalists offered as a substitute a resolution calling on Congress to pass an act, 'recommending to the Legislatures of the several States the ratification of a bill of rights, and of certain articles of amendment proposed by the Convention of this State for the adoption of the United States, and that until the said act shall be ratified in pursuance of the fifth article of the said constitution of government for the United States, Congress do conform their ordinances to the true spirit of the said bill of rights.' "[76]

---

[76] *Ibid.*, op. cit., p. 417. *Journal of the House of Delegates*, pp. 16–27.

In trying to prevent the threat of a new convention, "the Federalists were forced to urge the adoption of Mr. Henry's proposed amendments." But even here they failed, as the vote on the substitute bill shows 39 for, 85 against, carrying Patrick Henry's resolutions without division.

Washington, following the progress of the session closely, wrote Madison, November 17: "The accounts from Richmond are indeed very impropitious to Federal measures. In one word it is said that the edicts of Mr. H. are enregistered with less opposition in the Virginia Assembly than those of the grand monarch by his parliaments. He has only to say, let this be law, and it is law."[77]

His "edicts," then: "the Communication to Congress, the reply to Governor Clinton's letter, and the circular letter to the States, all written by Patrick Henry were approved by the House" and accomplished within less than a month. His debate in behalf of these measures should be read fully, but the scope of this chapter will not permit space. However, the Communication to Congress is given in full as it is said to be from the pen of Patrick Henry, exhibiting in his words "the spirit and purpose of a measure then, and since, so greatly misconstrued."

Omitting the last two, it reads as follows:

> To the Congress of the United States
>
> The good people of this Commonwealth in Convention assembled, having ratified the Constitution submitted to their consideration, this Legislature has in conformity to that act, and the resolutions of the United States in Congress assembled to them transmitted, thought proper to make arrangements that were necessary for carrying it into effect. Having thus shown themselves obedient to the voice of their constitutients, all Americans will find, that so far as it depends on them, that plan of government will be carried into immediate operation.
>
> But the sense of the people of Virginia, would be but in part complied with, and but little regarded, if we went no further. In the very moment of adoption, and coeval with the ratification of the new plan of government, the general voice of the convention of this State pointed to objects no less interesting to the people we represent, and equally entitled to your attention. At the same time that, from motives of affection for our sister States, the convention yielded their assent to the ratification,

[77] *Ibid.*, p. 432, Bancroft's *History of the Constitution*, II, p. 483.

they gave the most unequivocal proofs that they dreaded its operation under the present form.

In acceding to a government under this impression, painful must have been the prospect, had they not derived consolation from a full expectation of its imperfections being speedily amended. In this resource, therefore, they placed their confidence,—a confidence that will continue to support them whilst they have reason to believe they have not calculated upon it in vain.

In making known to you the objections of the people of this Commonwealth to the new plan of government, we deem it unnecessary to enter into a particular detail of its defects, which they consider as involving all the great and unalienable rights of freemen: for their sense on this subject, we refer you to the proceedings of their late convention, and the sense of this General Assembly, as expressed in their resolutions of the 30th day of October.

We think proper, however, to declare that in our opinion, as those objections were not founded in speculative theory, but deduced from principles which have been established by the melancholy example of other nations, in different ages, so they will never be removed until the cause itself shall cease to exist. The sooner, therefore, the public apprehensions are quieted, and the government is possessed of the confidence of the people, the more salutary will be its operations, and the longer its duration.

The cause of amendments we consider as a common cause; and since concessions have been made from political motives, which we conceive may endanger the republic, we trust that a commendable zeal will be shown for obtaining those provisions which, experience has taught us, are necessary to secure from danger the unalienable rights of human nature.

The anxiety with which our countrymen press for the accomplishment of this important end, will ill admit of delay. The slow forms of congressional discussion and recommendation, if indeed they should ever agree to any change, would, we fear, be less certain of success. Happily for their wishes, the Constitution hath presented an alternative, by admitting the submission to a convention of the States. To this, therefore, we resort, as the source from whence they are to derive relief from their present apprehensions. We do, therefore, in behalf of our constituents, in the most earnest and solemn manner, make this application to Congress, that a convention be immediately called, of deputies from the several States, with full power to take into their consideration the defects of this Constitution, that have been suggested by the state conventions, and report such amendments thereto, as they shall find best suited to promote our common interests, and secure to ourselves and our latest posterity the great and unalienable rights of mankind.[78]

Thus committed to another convention, the House under the leadership of Mr. Henry took up next the election of the delegates to make their attendance upon Congress. Convinced of the urgency of the amendments, he knew that the outcome would depend upon the ability of the men sent to Congress. His concern in this matter was greater than that of Washington or Madison. Hamilton had written Madison, "Our chances of success depend on you." Henry knew his men. They were R. H. Lee and William Grayson for the Senate. Washington was urging Madison as the man to be put in nomination. The electors for President, as well as the members of Congress, were to be voted on, and Washington was considered the choice for the first seat. Prior to the election on October 31, Mr. Henry, in deference to the wishes of the Federalists, "caused the State to be divided into twelve districts for the selection of presidential electors, and ten districts for the selection of members of Congress, and in either case the person chosen by the district was required to be a resident."[79]

In this bill districting the state for Senate seats, the word "henrymandering" has been leveled at Patrick Henry, suggesting that it helped to defeat Madison. If this were an advantage to the Anti-Federalists, the facts do not show any unfairness in the division, though no doubt Mr. Henry's experience as Governor made him conscious of what was patriot territory. Where he was then living, "in near 20 adjoining counties . . . at least 19/20th were anti-federal."[80] There was no better advantage than that of putting the decision before those who cherished their dearest rights and liberties under a sovereign State. . . . Of the committee of 15 appointed to district the State, "seven were staunch Federalists." Mr. Henry, knowing Madison's views on the amendments, "he, very naturally, was unwilling to trust the fate of the proposed amendments to his care, with his avowed hostility to some of the most important ones." When time came for the election of Senators, October 29, he nominated Richard Henry Lee and William Grayson. Madison was also put in nomination for the Senate, but was defeated. The votes showed 98 for Lee,

[78] Henry, *Henry*, II, pp. 423–424–425; Also Wirt, *Henry*, pp. 324–325–326.
[79] *Ibid.*, p. 425.
[80] *Ibid.*, p. 429, Letter from Patrick Henry to Richard H. Lee, Richmond, Nov. 15, 1788, written while the Legislature was sitting.

86 for Grayson, and 77 for Madison.[81] Some votes went to others not nominated. Patrick Henry, who let it be known that he would not take "any part in deliberations held out of this state" would not allow his name to be placed in nomination. Even so, he received 26 of the votes cast away.

One thing that defeated Madison was the matter of instructions: It was doubted whether he would obey instructions which should direct him to vote "against direct taxation," to which Mr. Henry rejoined: "Thus, gentlemen, the secret is out." Madison wrote Jefferson regarding the election: " 'They made me a candidate for the Senate, for which I had not alloted my pretensions. The attempt was defeated by Mr. Henry, who is omnipotent in the present legislature, and who added to the expedients common on such occasions a philippic against my federal principles.' "[82]

In speaking of Madison's policy, Judge Spencer Roane declared, "Patrick Henry was astonished that Madison could take the Constitution, admitting its defects, and in a season of perfect peace, and believed him too friendly to a strong government and too hostile to the Governments of the States." (MS. to Wirt)

Henry wrote Lee congratulating him on his election to the Senate, and added: "The friends of the system are much displeased that Mr. Madison was left out of the choice. They urged his election most warmly, claiming as a sort of right the admission of one Federal member; but in vain—For to no purpose must the efforts of Virginia have been expected to procure amendments, if one of her senators had been found adverse to the scheme. The universal cry is for amendments, & the Federals are obliged to join in it; but whether to amuse, or conceal other views seems dubious. . . . I firmly believe the American union depends on the success of amendments. God grant I may never see the day when it shall be the duty of whiggish Americans to seek for shelter under any other government than that of the United States."[83]

Lee and Grayson both "had expressed themselves as advocates of the measures necessary to put the government in operation without embarrassments,"[84] and Patrick Henry had faith in their ability.

Although Madison was defeated for the Senate, he secured his election to the House of Representatives by running against

---

[81] *Ibid.*, pp. 427–428, Governor Randolph to Madison.

[82] Tyler, *Henry*, p. 351.

[83] *Ibid.*, II, pp. 428–429–430.

[84] *Ibid.*, op. cit., II, p. 430; *Writings of Washington,* I, p. 448.

James Monroe. It was the impression that Monroe opposed the amendments, "even to that securing the freedom of religion, Mr. Madison openly advocated them, and pledged himself to their support."[85] Regarding the districting bill for the House, Edward Carrington wrote Madison: "The *Antes* have levelled every effort at you. The point of residence in the district is carried by some of the *Feds* having at an early period committed themselves on that side. Your district is composed of the counties of Amherst, Albemarle, Louisa, Orange, Culpeper, Spotsylvania, Goochland, and Fluvanna. We wished to get Fauquier, but the power of the *Antes* was too strong for us."

Patrick Henry was not a member of the committee that prepared this bill. Yet, "Mr. Madison and his friends charged him with arranging the district in which Madison resided, so as to put a majority of republican counties in it, with a design of preventing his election to the lower house." But Carrington in his letter did "not charge Mr. Henry with the arrangement of the district," which certainly he would have done had it been true. But, "The letter shows that the friends of Mr. Madison tried to fix a district which would certainly have elected him by including Fauquier. This was a strong Federal county, and would have taken the place of Amherst and Goochland, which were anti-Federal in the Convention."[86]

No doubt both sides were contending for this district, in which the anti-Federals were the winners. Patrick Henry "was a generous opponent, and was incapable of petty warfare against any adversary." If he controlled anything it was the legislature, as Washington's secretary noted in his letter to the Governor of New Hampshire regarding his course in this body: "In plain English, he ruled a majority of the Assembly. . . ."

In less than a month from the opening of the session, "he had succeeded in pressing through the legislature, in the exact form he wished, all these measures for giving effect to Virginia's demand upon Congress for amendments."[87] On November 19, "after he had settled everything relative to the government wholly, I suppose, to his satisfaction, he mounted his horse and rode home, leaving the little business of the State to be done by anybody who chose to give themselves the trouble of attending to it."[88]

[85] *Ibid.*, Madison's *Works*, I, pp. 446–449.

[86] *Ibid.*, Rives' *Madison*, II, p. 654, n.

[87] Tyler, *Henry*, p. 352.

[88] Henry, *Henry*, II, p. 433; Bancroft's *History of the Constitution*, II, pp. 488–485.

Mr. Henry's departure for home was due to the illness of his daughter, Betsy Aylett, and his sister, Anne Christian. The latter's husband, Colonel Christian, had been killed by the Indians, and she had arrived from Kentucky in ill health, with the intention of making a trip to the West Indies in hopes that climate would be beneficial. She was waiting impatiently to see her brother, for whom she had a tender regard. It was fortunate that he came at this time, as they were not to see each other again. She died on board the vessel on her return from the West Indies and was buried at sea in the winter of 1790–91.[89]

As soon as Mr. Henry reached home he was attacked through a series of articles aimed primarily at him and the leaders of the Republican party. The scurrilous attacks were written under the name "Decius," thought to be John Nicholas. However, from letters received by Mr. Henry, he was gratified in knowing that the assertions were not confined to his political friends. He maintained a dignified silence, conscious that he needed no defense, and as his friend, Senator Grayson, pointed out in the words of Addison: "Envy and detraction is a tax which every man pays for being eminent and conspicuous. You have certainly adopted the dignified line of conduct, and I trust, & hope, you will persevere in it."[90] "Washington was soon to experience a similar bitterness, which he bore with 'less equanimity.' "

In the spring of 1789, the first Congress of the United States was organized. A majority of Federalists were elected from Virginia in the hope of giving the Constitution a fair trial. Patrick Henry was elected as a member of the Electoral College from his district, casting his vote for President for George Washington, who received 69 votes, and John Adams, 34. The inauguration took place on May 1.

On June 8, Madison in Congress now took a complete about-face, "presenting a striking contrast to Mr. Madison on the floor of the Virginia Convention. Knowing the *vis a tergo* which impelled him to accomplish the task," he moved for some of the amendments in Congress with this apology: "I consider myself bound in honor and in duty to do what I have done on the subject." The preliminary discussion was laid aside until August 13, when the amendments became the subject of debate lasting until the 24th. Completing its work, the House sent 17 articles of amendment to the Senate. "Only twelve of these articles succeeded

[89] Henry, *Henry,* II, p. 478, Whitsitt's, *Rev. Cabeb Wallace,* p. 119.
[90] *Ibid.,* II, p. 438.

in passing the Senate; and of these twelve, only ten received from the States that approval which was necessary to their ratification. This was obtained on the 15th of December, 1791." The dread of a new convention "drove Madison and his brethren in Congress into the prompt concession of amendments they themselves did not care for." It was attributed, "in no small degree, to the bitter and implacable urgency of the popular feeling in Virginia, under the stimulus of Patrick Henry's leadership, that Congress was induced by Madison to pay any attention to the subject. In the matter of amendments, therefore, Patrick Henry and his party did not get all that they demanded, nor in the way that they demanded; but even so much as they did get, they would not then have got at all, had they not demanded more, and demanded more. . . ."[91]

In fact, "the articles proposed by Mr. Madison were but little more than a bill of rights, and the addition of the substance of the first, second, seventeenth, and a part of the fourteenth amendments proposed by the Virginia Convention. The modification of the fourteenth Virginia amendment left out all of it except the provision for trying appeals in jury cases according to the provisions of the common law. Mr. Madison proposed none of those amendments of the Virginia Convention which, by restricting the judicial power, and the power of Congress over standing armies, taxation, commerce, treaties, and elections, secured the States from the encroachment of the Federal government. The action of Mr. Madison was as predicted by Mr. Henry, who knew his hostility to the omitted amendments. It seems to have been backed up by a strong party, which doubtless he was active in forming."[92]

The effects of these omitted amendments are seen today, particularly in the commerce clause, as well as the implied power of judicial interpretation. Three days before the amendments passed, Senator Grayson wrote Patrick Henry, June 12, 1789:

"Some gentlemen here, from motive of policy, have it in contemplation to effect amendments which shall affect personal liberty alone, leaving the great points of the judiciary, direct taxation, etc., to stand as they are; their object is in my opinion unquestionably to break the spirit of the party by divisions; after this I presume many of the most sanguine expect to go on coolly in sapping the independence of the State legislatures."[93]

---

[91] Tyler, *Henry*, pp. 355–356; Henry, *Henry*, II, pp. 444–445.
[92] Henry, *Henry*, II, p. 443.
[93] *Ibid.*

This news from his friend, Grayson, greatly troubled Mr. Henry. In the convention he had pointed to the importance of those amendments now proposed, and "he plainly saw that the effects of those proposed amendments (by Madison) would be to silence the demand for others he deemed of vital importance." Fearing the outcome, he kept constantly in touch with Lee and Grayson, and they, in return, consulted him as to the "proper course to be pursued in the important measures which were discussed in the first Federal Congress."

Perhaps, as Madison said, "he accomplished all that it was possible for him to do, even if he had approved of, and urged, all the amendments proposed by the Virginia Convention."[94] However, had he obeyed the orders of this body, and offered all the amendments written by Patrick Henry (a bill of rights and twenty additional articles)[95] there would not have followed the abuses to which the Federal Constitution has led. When the "Virginia Senators moved the addition of the omitted Virginia amendments" without success, Colonel Grayson wrote Patrick Henry, they might as well have tried "to carry Mount Atlas on their shoulders."

Yet, hardly a year had passed when the states saw in the proposal of the Assumption Act, "the most bitter and angry contests ever known in Congress, before or since the union of the States."[96] In the financial policy of Alexander Hamilton as Secretary of the Treasury, the proposal of the assumption of the debts of the several states was countenanced with the conclusion from his arguments that "a national debt is a national blessing." As the "great leader of the Federalists, his idea for a good administration was, 'to acquire for the Federal government more consistency than the Constitution seems to promise for so great a country. It may thus triumph altogether over the State governments, and reduce them to an entire subordination, dividing the larger States into smaller districts.' "[97]

The proposal of the Assumption Act was fought vigorously in the Virginia legislature of October, 1790, and it was condemned throughout the state. The resolution that was adopted, and passed by a vote of 75 to 52, read:

"An act making provisions for the debt of the United States, as assumes the payment of the State debts, is repugnant

---

[94] *Ibid.*, op. cit., II, p. 446; Rives, *Madison*, III, p. 44.

[95] *Ibid.*, II, pp. 369–373–374; See Elliott, *Debates*, post, III, p. 593.

[96] *Ibid.*, II, p. 454, According to Thomas Jefferson.

[97] *Ibid.*, op. cit., II, p. 454, *Hamilton Works*, II, p. 421.

to the Constitution of the United States, as it goes to the exercise of a power not expressly granted to the General government."[98]

Mr. Henry was a member of a committee to prepare a memorial to Congress on the subject of the Assumption Act. This was the first state legislative act against an Act of Congress. This memorial was put off until the next meeting of the legislature, in hopes that Congress in the meantime might be forced to add to the amendments by the new delegates lately elected to the government. This was Patrick Henry's last act in the Virginia legislature. However, at this sitting, an unprecedented compliment was paid him after he had returned home: Henry County was divided in two, and the new county was given the name "Patrick."

The second election saw no changes in the sentiment of Congress, and thus emerged the two-party system, the Federalists under Hamilton, and the Republicans under Jefferson. Writing to James Monroe, who had been elected to replace Colonel Grayson in Congress at Grayson's death, Mr. Henry noted, "The form of Government into which my Countrymen determined to place themselves, had my Enmity, yet as we are one & all imbarked, it is natural to care for the crazy Machine, at least so long as we are out of Sight of a Port to refit. I have therefore my Anxietys to hear and to know what is doing, & to keep up the Metaphor, whether there is no Appearance of Storms in our Horizon? . . . I console myself with hoping that the Advocates of Oppression may find the Time when the Measures of Iniquity shall give place to just and enlightened Policy. . . ."[99]

The storms referred to by Mr. Henry were on the horizon. The usurpation of power by the Federal government was begun in less than a decade, in the summer of 1798, when the fifth Congress enacted three laws that came to be known as the "Alien and Sedition Acts." It was because of these unwise laws that Thomas Jefferson "either revised, or drew up some resolves, later offered in the Kentucky Legislature, known as the First Kentucky Resolution of 1798; a copy of which was sent to Madison as a guide in drafting the Virginia Resolutions of 1798, both professing the rights of the States, but skilfully worded so as not to commit the legislature too distinctly to nullification."[100] Only then, from the trend of events, did Madison and Jefferson begin to see the errors of *subsequent* amendments.

---

[98] *Ibid., Journal,* pp. 35–36.
[99] Henry, *Henry,* II, p. 460.
[100] *Ibid.,* II, p. 584.

Later, in 1828, another oppressive enactment affecting four of the southern states, known as the Tariff of Abominations, resulted in a strongly worded resolution in the Virginia legislature. Furthermore, in the year 1814, delegates gathered at Hartford, Connecticut, from five New England states, for the purpose of settling their problems by drafting resolutions against the infractions of the Constitution.

After the War between the States, in 1870, Patrick Henry's great-grandson, the Rev. Edward Fontaine,[101] had the grim satisfaction of recalling his forebear's predictions:

> Patrick Henry left the Capitol resolved to be a peaceful citizen, but with little hope of the perpetuity, or success of the form of Government. He was again elected Governor of Virginia which office he declined. General Washington, who was elected President, under the new Constitution, offered him a place in his Cabinet, which he also refused to accept. Whether he had conscientious scruples about holding office under a government which he could not support; or whether the necessity of attending to his private affairs caused his refusal of these flattering honors, cannot now be ascertained. Perhaps he was actuated by both of these motives to retire to the shade of private life. While living in retirement with his family, as planter, and practicing lawyer, the pamphlet containing the Constitution and the additional 12 amendments adopted by the majority of States requisite to make them a part of the instrument, was brought to him and examined by him most carefully in the presence of my father and Mr. Dandridge. He seemed to have been suspicious of the character of some of the framers of the Constitution, and of the crafty politicians through whose hands it had passed since its adoption by Virginia, that he feared they had not only altered the amendments adopted by the Virginia convention, but had tampered with the body of the instrument itself. After reading it carefully, satisfying himself that they had not changed the original paper, he read carefully the amendments to the tenth. When he read this he threw down the pamphlet upon the table, and remarked with

[101] The Rev. Edward Fontaine was descended from Col. John Fontaine, who married Patrick Henry's daughter, Martha. Col. Fontaine was born at Beaver Dam, Virginia, June 8, 1750 and died of malarial fever in Henry County, April 17, 1790. His son Col. Patrick Henry Fontaine was born Feb. 22, 1775 and died Sept. 2, 1852 at Pontotoc, Miss. The Rev. Edward Fontaine was born at Martinsville, Virginia, Aug. 5, 1814 and died on Belvedere plantation, Jackson, Miss., Jan. 19, 1884. (Information by the late Rev. Patrick Henry Fontaine, Jackson, Miss., Jan. 7, 1953). Another among this eminent family is Mr. John Winston Fontaine of Paces, Virginia.

great solemnity: "I find that these shrewd Northern Statesmen have outwitted our Southern men again in the wording of these amendments. They determined when this Constitution was framed to make this a great consolidated National Government of all the people of the States. To secure this object they inserted in its preamble the words 'We, *the people of the United States,*' instead of *We, the States.* Their object was to make it a Government of a majority of the whole people; that is a Government of the *Northern people;* for they have this *majority;* and under such a government holding this power they can and will exercise it oppressively to the South for their own advantage. To prevent this, and to hinder this majority from doing whatever they may think proper for 'the general welfare,' which they will construe to mean their own sectional welfare, I wrote the first 20 amendments adopted, and recommended by the Convention of Virginia in these words: '*Each* State *in the Union* shall *respectively retain* every *power, jurisdiction,* and *right* which is not by this Constitution *delegated* to the Congress of the United States, or to the departments of the Federal Government.' This was intended to secure the rights of the States, and to prevent the exercise of doubtful powers by the Federal Government but they have omitted it, and substituted for it this *equivocal* thing to which they have tacked the objectionable and dangerous words of 'the people.' 'The powers not delegated to the United States by the Constitution, nor prohibited by it to the States, are reserved to the *States respectively,* or to the people.' Why did they add, 'or to the people?' They determined to make it a consolidated government. They added these words to neutralize the amendment of Virginia, and they have done it effectually. This government cannot last. It will not last a century. We can only get rid of its oppression by a most violent and bloody struggle."

He at once discerned the craft displayed by this ingenious amendment, worded to deceive the conventions of the different States. They were intended to persuade them that they embraced the strong safe-guard to their rights furnished by the clear and explicit amendment of Patrick Henry. The amendment does this to the word *respectively.* If the amendment had ended there, its meaning could not have been perverted. But the trickery is veiled in the words added "or to the people." They are superfluous verbiage, if they were added to curb federal power, and guard state sovereignty, which the amendment was adopted to effect. But the cunning politicians who inserted them did so with a design of using them to suit their purpose when occasion should arise in the future. We are not "states respectively" with any reserved and sovereign rights. "We are a nation" ruled first by a northern majority, and then by a "con-

> temptible minority" of oligarchs. The violent and bloody struggle has ensued, and it is not yet ended. The Constitution is destroyed. The Government has been over-turned, and the century has not yet rolled away. Our present Government is not that framed in Philadelphia; *that* did not last a century. The new dominion, which has arisen out of it, is changing continually. What it is now is difficult to define. It requires another Henry to predict.[102]

In the unfolding of Patrick Henry's prophecy we recognize his genius and his increase to greatness!

---

[102] *De Bows' Review*, 1870, *The Character and Opinions of Patrick Henry*, pp. 829–830, by the Rev. Edward Fontaine.

XIX

THE BRITISH DEBT CASE and PATRICK HENRY'S RETIREMENT

MR. HENRY'S RETIREMENT from public life at this time was due to the exhausting demands upon his strength as Governor during the war, and to his strenuous fight against the Federal Constitution. Furthermore, he wished now to give some attention to his private fortune, which had been greatly neglected, and devote some time to the practice of law. It was in the practice of criminal law that his manner and oratory made him the master of his audience. Among his many important civil court cases, the greatest was the British Debt (case), in which he "astonished the public not less by the matter than manner of his speech." This case was the result of suits brought by British creditors to recover debts contracted by Virginia debtors before the Revolution, wherein Mr. Henry defended the debtor, Dr. Thomas Walker, in an action by the plaintiff, William Jones.

The suit began in Federal Court in Richmond, November, 1791. The case "involved many subtle and difficult points of law, municipal, national, and international. . . . Some idea of the importance attached to the case may be inferred from the assertion of Wirt that 'the whole power of the bar of Virginia was embarked' in it; and that the 'learning, argument, and eloquence' exhibited in the discussion were such 'as to have placed that bar, in the estimation of the federal judges . . . above all others in the United States.' "[1] The defendants engaged in the case were

[1] Tyler, *Henry*, p. 360.

Patrick Henry, John Marshall, Alexander Campbell and James Innes, whose names appear in the order in which they spoke. For several weeks before the case Mr. Henry made no engagements, and secluded himself from his family for three days, his food being handed by a servant through the office door, at which time he settled down to intense study in the retirement of his country home.[2] Also, weather permitting, he walked and meditated under the shade of the locust trees with his notebook in hand for several days before he started for Richmond. The result was that he "came forth, on this occasion, a perfect master of every law, national and municipal, which touched the subject of investigation in the most distant point."[3]

There were five difficult points to which the defendant pleaded. On November 25, in a crowded courtroom, Mr. Henry arose, when "every eye in front of the bar was riveted upon him, and so still and deep was the silence, that every one might hear the throbbing of his own heart."

On the first point, in which he wished to establish that debts became subject to forfeiture in common wars, he cited and read "copious extracts from Grotius, and Vattel's 'Law of Nations' to support his position and to show that this nation had unlimited powers. In his further efforts to show "that war gives the same right *over the debts* as over the other goods of the enemy," he illustrated Vattel's doctrine by "the instance of Alexander's remitting to the Thessalians a debt due by them to the Theban commonwealth." He declared, "Every consideration must give way to the public safety. That admirable Roman maxim, *salus populi suprema lex*, governed that people in every emergency. It is a maxim that ought to govern every community. It was not peculiar to the Roman people."[4] He declared, "When the war commenced, these things called British debts, lost their quality of external obligation, and became matters of internal obligation, because the creditors had no right of constraint over the debtors." Respecting public justice, he declared, the states of America, being a sovereign and complete nation . . . not like those nations whose crude systems of jurisprudence originated in the ages of barbarity and ignorance of human rights, "stepped forth to resist

[2] Morgan, *Henry*, p. 386; Tyler, *Henry*, p. 361.

[3] Tyler, *Henry*, op. cit., p. 362; Wirt, *Henry*, p. 312. Wirt "devoted fifty of the four hundred and sixty-seven pages of his book to Henry's argument," according to Morgan, *Henry*, p. 386.

[4] Henry, *Henry*, III, pp. 607–608–609.

the unjust hand of oppression, and declared themselves independent. The consent of Great Britain was not necessary to create us a nation. . . . We were a nation long before the monarch of that little island in the Atlantic ocean gave his puny assent to it."

In his exordium, in which he referred to long-established rules and old forgotten laws, Patrick Henry showed from Vattel the certain maxims and customs observed by nations: that a *customary law of nations*, founded on a tacit convention *of the nations that observe it with respect to each other*, was binding only to those nations that have adopted it and are parties to the custom. He declared that there was no customary law to this effect when America announced her will to be free in 1776, or when the law concerning British debts passed in 1777. There was nothing in our constitution or laws which tied our hands, since to make this customary law obligatory, the assent of all the parties to be bound by it is necessary. "There must be an interchange of it." Nor did the creditors trust to this customary law of nations. Instead, "they trusted to what they thought as firm, the statute and common law of England."

Mr. Henry showed from Vattel the situation of America, "that right goes hand in hand with necessity" and that in attack upon an enemy, "the end of a just war is to revenge or prevent injury," or "whatever is necessary in bringing him to reason, and obtaining justice and security from him." He contrasted the late war with wars in general, and recited many instances of misrule by the King of England, showing the consequences to America if we had been conquered by England. He pointed to "the most horrid forfeitures, confiscations, and attainders" in English history from the time of William the First, saying, "Were not his *Normans* gratified with the confiscations of the richest estates in England?" He pointed further to the "inhabitants stripped of the dearest privileges of humanity—degraded with the most ignominious badges of bondage—and totally deprived of the power of resistance to usurpation and tyranny . . . continued to the time of Henry the Eighth," as well as "the sad and lamentable effects of the York and Lancastrian wars"; the rebellions of 1715 and 1745; the fate of the people of Ireland. "What confiscations and punishments were inflicted in Scotland? The plains of *Culloden*, and the neighbouring gibbets, would show you. I thank Heaven that the spirit of liberty, under the protection of the Almighty, saved us from experiencing so hard a destiny,"[5] he declared.

[5] *Ibid.*, p. 629.

Before Mr. Henry completed his arguments, he had established without question "that debts are subject to confiscation in common wars and much more so in the war of the revolution." That the plaintiff had derived his claim "through perfidy, through a polluted channel," and that such a claim "would have come better from our side of the question, than from theirs" he proved fully.

Wirt declared, "He adapted himself, without effort to the character of the cause; seized with the quickness of intuition its defensible point, and never permitted the jury to lose sight of it. . . . In like manner, Mr. Henry by a few master-strokes upon the evidence, could in general stamp upon the cause whatever image or character he pleased; and convert it into tragedy or comedy, at his sovereign will, and with a power which no efforts of his adversary could counteract. He never wearied the jury by a dry and minute analysis of the evidence. . . ." Jefferson, who was stinting in his appraisal of Mr. Henry, said of him as a lawyer, "I believe he never distinguished himself so much as on the question of British debts in the case of Jones against Walker."[6]

John Randolph, observing the courtroom as Mr. Henry ascended the heights in his description of the cruelty of England and of our fate had we lost, declared, "The color began to come and go in the face of the Chief-Justice, John Jay, while the Associate Justice, James Iredell, sat with eyes stretched open in perfect wonder." When Patrick Henry "raised his hands in one of his grand and solemn pauses, Randolph said his hands seemed to cover the whole house. There was a tumultuous burst of applause, and Judge Iredell exclaimed: 'Gracious God! He is an orator indeed!' "[7]

Other important cases during Mr. Henry's last labors at the bar included Carter vs. Carter, Defense of Holland, The Turkey Case, Defense of Richard Randolph, besides the case involving the Commonwealth known as the Manor of Leeds Case, offered him by Governor Robert Brooke, involving 90,000 acres of land. Of this latter, he declined the retainer because of his determination to retire. He had not fully recovered from the spell of sickness of the past fall, and the long journeys to and from the distant courthouses were taxing. His success as a lawyer and his astute handling

[6] Henry, *Henry,* op. cit., II, p. 472. Letter to Mr. Wirt, *Historical Magazine,* August, 1867, p. 93.

[7] *Ibid.,* II, p. 474, "MS. Letter of Hon. James W. Bouldin, a countryman of Randolph, who heard his description of the scene."

of his affairs had made him a wealthy man; thus, he decided in the year 1794, at the age of 58, to give up the practice of law.

In 1792 he sold his farm in Prince Edward County and purchased an estate known as "Long Island" in Campbell County, where he removed in December. In 1794 he acquired another fine estate 18 miles below, in Charlotte County, known as Red Hill. He divided his residence between the two places, sometimes spending eight months at Red Hill; but during the sickly season, returned to Long Island.[8] Red Hill stands on an elevated ridge, within a quarter of a mile of the junction of Falling River with the Staunton. Here, "under the trees in full view of the beautiful valley, Patrick Henry was accustomed in pleasant weather to sit mornings and evenings, with his chair leaning against one of the trunks, and a can of cool spring water by his side, from which he took frequent draughts. Occasionally he walked to and fro in the yard from one clump of trees to the other, buried in revery, at which time he was never interrupted. His great delight was in conversation in the society of his friends and family, and in the resources of his own mind."[9]

His domestic life has been described as most amiable. "In every relation, as a husband, father, master, and neighbor, he was entirely exemplary. As to the disposition of Mr. Henry, it was the best imaginable. He was never seen in a passion, nor apparently out of temper. Circumstances which would have highly irritated other men had no visible effect on him, he was always calm and collected." Judge Roane further wrote Wirt, "with many sublime virtues, he had no vice that I knew or ever heard of, and scarcely a foible." Judge Winston declared, "His children were on the most familiar footing with him, and he treated them as companions and friends." "In his habits of living he was remarkably temperate and frugal. He was very abstemious in his diet and used no wine or alcoholic stimulants. He seldom drank anything but water, and his table, though abundantly spread in the Virginia fashion, was furnished with the simplest viands. His manners were those of the Virginia gentleman: kind, open, candid, and conciliating; warm without insincerity, and polite without pomp. He did not chill by reserve, nor fatigue by loquacity, but adapted himself without an effort to the character of his company.

---

[8] Morgan, *Henry*, op. cit., p. 396, Patrick Henry to his daughter, Betsy Aylett, Oct. 26, 1793; again in the autumn of 1794, he wrote her again: "We go to Red Hill in August for five weeks."

[9] Henry, *Henry*, II, p. 515. As described by Judge Spencer Roane.

He had himself a vein of pleasantry which was extremely amusing without detracting from his dignity. His conversation was pure and chaste . . . He had not even the habit of using tobacco, so common in Virginia. In fact tobacco-smoke became offensive to him as he grew older, and it is said he required his house servants to give up their pipes, and was very sure to detect them if they came where he was with the least smell of tobacco upon them. One of his neighbors going to see him found him reading the Bible. Holding it up in his hand, he said: 'This book is worth all the books that ever were printed, and it has been my misfortune that I have never found time to read it with the proper attention and feeling till lately. I trust in the mercy of Heaven that it is not yet too late.' "[10] According to his daughter, Sarah Butler, "It was his habit to seat himself in his dining-room every morning directly after rising, and read his Bible, and as his children would pass him for the first time he would raise his eyes from his book and greet them with a 'good morrow.' And this he would never neglect." In his retirement he was able to give himself "more than ever to the study of the Bible, and of the great English divines, particularly Tillotson, Butler, and Sherlock. The sermons of the latter, he declared had removed all his doubts of the truth of Christianity, and from a volume which contained them and which was full of his pencilled notes, he was accustomed to read every Sunday evening to his family, after which they all joined in sacred music, while he accompanied them on the violin."[11] Like his father, and his uncle, the Rev. Patrick Henry, he was, and remained, an Episcopalian. His concern over "the spread, and the undermining influence of French infidelity" had caused him to have published at his own expense during his second term as Governor, an edition of Soame Jenyns's "View of the Internal Evidence of Christianity," and an edition of "Butler's Analogy."[12]

But the conditions now in France had increased his apprehensions even more and had brought over him a feeling of despondency. His good friends, Colonels Mason and Grayson, were dead, and Richard H. Lee had passed away in June. The eyes of all America had been turned to our former ally, France, whose revolution had followed ours. In this, the nobility and educated

[10] Henry, *Henry*, op. cit., II, pp. 516–519–520. Wirt, *Henry*, pp. 417–428. Taken from the MS. Letters to Mr. Wirt, from Judge Roane, Judge Winston, Samuel Meredith, Patrick Henry Fontaine and George Dabney.

[11] *Ibid.*, op. cit., II, p. 519, *Life of A. Alexander*, p. 193; Howe's *History of Virginia*, p. 221.

[12] Tyler, *Henry*, p. 394.

classes "had been corrupted by the infidel writings" of the period, in which "the church and the army shared in the general corruption and afforded no check to the rising tide." The conditions from which the French Revolution developed were seen from the letter of our Minister to France, Gouverneur Morris, to General Washington, April 29, 1789:

"The materials for a revolution in this country are very indifferent. Everybody agrees that there is an utter prostration of morals; but this general position can never convey to an American mind the degree of depravity. It is not by any figure of rhetoric, or force of language, that the idea can be communicated. A hundred anecdotes and a hundred thousand examples are required to show the extreme rottenness of every member. There are men and women who are gentle and eminently virtuous. I have the pleasure to number many in my own acquaintance. But they stand forward from a background deeply and darkly shaded. It is however from such crumbling matter that the great edifice of freedom is to be erected here . . . but it seems quite as likely that it will fall and crush the builders. I own to you that I am not without such apprehensions, for there is one fatal principle which pervades all ranks. It is a perfect indifference to the violation of engagements. Inconsistency is so mingled in the blood, marrow, and very essence of this people, that when a man of high rank and importance laughs to-day at what he seriously asserted yesterday, it is considered as in the natural order of things. Consistency is a phenomenon. Judge then what would be the value of an association, should such a thing be proposed, and even adopted. The great mass of common people have no religion but the priests, no law but their superiors, no morals but their interest. These are the creatures who, led by drunken curates, are now on the high road à la liberté."[13]

In January, 1793, the King of France had been put to death; Lafayette, America's friend in the Revolution, had been cast in prison; and in April, France declared war against England. When news of the declaration of war was learned, there arose a great feeling of sympathy for our former ally, and "gratitude for the great services rendered by France on the one hand, and a deep resentment of the conduct of Great Britain during and after the revolutionary struggle on the other, produced a desire to help France which could with difficulty be restrained."[14]

---

[13] Henry, *Henry*, II, pp. 524–525.

[14] Henry, *Henry*, II, p. 527.

Washington no doubt shared the keenest sympathy for the young republic, but he was determined to keep America neutral, in which he was supported by his cabinet, where side by side sat Jefferson, the Secretary of State, and Hamilton, the Treasurer. On April 22, 1793, Washington's proclamation of neutrality was announced. In the meantime the French Minister, Genet, arrived in the United States for the purpose of fitting out privateers to apprehend British merchantmen. Washington, however, was firm in his policy affecting the United States. In June, British instructions "directing the capture of all neutral vessels laden with provisions bound for France, then threatened with famine, and the orders of the French government soon afterward, directing the seizure and carrying into France of all neutral vessels laden with provisions bound for other countries, added to the perplexities of the Administration." In view of the danger that was likely to arise from hostilities, Chief Justice John Jay was sent to England in 1794 to negotiate a treaty of amity and commerce with the British government. His appointment was said to be unfortunate, since "he had already committed himself to the position that the United States were guilty of the first infraction of the treaty of 1783, on which ground the British had withheld the western posts." In Jay's treaty, which was not received in America until March, 1795, he had disobeyed orders and "yielded much to which the United States were entitled," and it was "justly liable to the severest criticism," the Republicans denouncing it "as dictated by the English in their own interest, and to the injury of France. . . . The western posts, which should have been given up in 1783, were to be withheld till June, 1796, and no compensation was allowed for their unlawful detention." This fixed "the northern and eastern boundary of the United States, and the British ports were opened to American commerce, which was secured in them now for the first time by treaty." It passed by a "bare constitutional vote" in the Senate, Washington finally fixing his signature to it after much deliberation, "without running the risk of further delay and open hostilities with Great Britain."[15] When news of the treaty was learned, it brought about the bitterest party feelings, headed by Hamilton and Jefferson. The Federalists sided with Washington, while the Republicans leaned toward Jefferson and the French Minister, aided by certain political organizations known as "Democratic Societies."

In Washington's decision to maintain neutrality, during his

[15] *Ibid.*, II, pp. 530–531.

second term as President, he "had hoped that the United States might avoid the hazards of party politics, but his hopes were not to be realized. For a time he kept men of such divergent views as Hamilton and Jefferson in his cabinet. But the two could not see eye-to-eye, for Hamilton was ever the spokesman of wealth and privilege, whereas Jefferson's interest lay in the welfare of the common man, in whose capacities he earnestly believed. . . . Hamilton favored the greatest possible centralization of power in the hands of the national government, whereas Jefferson championed the rights of the states, and believed firmly in the adage 'the less government the better.' Around the views of these two men parties took form, the Federalists reflecting Hamilton, and the Republicans, Jefferson."[16]

Madison, who had worked closely with Hamilton in the Federal Constitution, was now seen to be pulling away, joining Jefferson. Observing Hamilton's plan for funding the debts owed by the United States, and for the assumption of the state debts, Madison feared the tyranny of taxation seen in his fiscal policy. When the Senate came to the decision of voting the necessary funds for carrying Jay's treaty into effect, Madison denied in the House of Representatives that such authority had been placed in the hands of the Senate by the Constitution, and held to the doctrine that it had only such powers as were specifically stated; taking the position "that it could control the treaty-making power by refusing the necessary appropriation."[17] Washington, however, held to the policy that "the treaty-making power had been exclusively vested by the Constitution in the president and the Senate," and he determined to carry it into effect. Only now were Madison and Jefferson feeling the full effects of their Constitutional errors: to accept first and amend afterwards. Consequently, they would later have to conform with Henry's states' rights policy, recur to fundamental principles affecting the sovereign states and assert in strong language their answer to the offensive Alien and Sedition Acts with their Kentucky-Virginia Resolutions.

Hamilton's broad financial policy was pushed through Congress for the purpose of favoring the wealthy manufacturers, and "the commercial interest of the Northwest, whereas Jefferson favored agriculture, and saw in the small free farmer of the South and West the ideal citizen." The central government thus favored the wealthy classes and had aroused the deep resentment of the

[16] Hicks, *The Federal Union,* Third Edition, p. 198.
[17] Henry, *Henry,* II, p. 531.

people of the agricultural sections, who did not share in the profits. Hamilton's proposal to levy an excise tax on domestic distilled spirits was enacted by Congress in 1791, which dealt a blow to the small farmers who used their surplus grain in making whiskey. The tax was offensive, "not merely for the money it took, but also for its prying nature," and the "burdensome system of enforcement, which required for the accused an expensive trip across the mountains to Philadelphia, where the delays of justice might detain the victim for months." This resulted in many protest meetings, the main body of the trouble arising in the four Pennsylvania counties west of the Alleghenies. "The pioneer farmer set high store by his personal freedom, and he felt outraged at the tax-collectors who pried into his private business and told him what he must and must not do." Open rebellion broke out in which stills that paid the tax were raided, and the tax collectors were handled roughly by the "whiskey boys." Force finally had to be used when the disorders continued after Washington's warning, and 15,000 militia from the four adjoining states were dispatched to the area in 1794 under Gen. Henry Lee, Governor of Virginia. The "Whiskey Rebellion" was put down without further trouble or bloodshed. The strong hand of the federal government was thus fully demonstrated and the residents looked on "aghast at the ruthless power. . . . In consequence, they gave their support the more willingly to Thomas Jefferson and the Republicans."[18]

Washington believed these disorders were fomented by the Democratic Societies. At this time the press, particularly, was engendering "the bitterest party feelings," in which the two party leaders, Hamilton and Jefferson, "were the chief objects of attack in their public and private relations. But the Republicans' attacks upon the Administration did not stop with the characters of the Federal members; they were aimed at the venerated character of Washington himself, and strange to say, some of the most violent appeared in the columns of the *National Gazette*, edited by Philip Freneau, a clerk in Mr. Jefferson's department."[19]

Thomas Jefferson had not become disaffected with France after its ruthless barbarity. Instead, he wrote the Minister to Holland, January 3, 1793, regarding the revolution:

> . . . The liberty of the whole earth was depending on the issue of the contest, and was ever such a prize won with so

[18] Hicks, *The Federal Union,* Third Edition, pp. 206–207

[19] Henry, *Henry,* II, p. 532.

> little innocent blood? My own affections have been deeply wounded by some of the martyrs to this cause, but rather than it should have failed I would have seen half the earth desolated; were there but an Adam and Eve left in every country, and left free, it would be better than it now is.[20]

Nor with such feelings could Mr. Jefferson be expected to condemn the rioters in the Pennsylvania rebellion. We find him, instead, "sneering at Washington's account of their suppression in his speech to Congress in December, 1794." Concerning it, he wrote James Madison:

> I expected to have some justification of arming one part of society against another, of declaring a civil war the moment before the meeting of that body which has the sole right of declaring war; of being so patient of the kicks and scoffs of our enemies, and rising at a feather against our friends.[21]

Jefferson as the leader in opposition to Washington's Administration, aided by the Democratic clubs, "hung upon, and, in every way in their power, clogged the wheels of government, which they charged was conducted in the interest of England in her war with France. They openly espoused the cause of France, and by the revolutionary methods resorted to, seemed to threaten the country with something of the anarchy which was cursing that land. Such at least were the fears of Washington and many others."[22] There were other societies, known as Republican clubs, that were "formed out of sympathy for France" and had "multiplied amazingly, particularly in the South and West. Many of the Republicans were ready to make common cause with France in a war against the British in Canada and the Spanish on the Gulf of Mexico. To Jefferson the French Revolution was still 'the most sacred cause that man was ever engaged in.' "[23]

Washington on his Federal bark was drifting in troubled seas, fearing anarchy. In these developments, "Hamilton did not disguise his disgust for the French Revolution, and to most of the Federalists it now seemed that Great Britain was fighting for the preservation of civilization while France had become a public enemy. . . . On the question of the French treaties Hamilton

---

[20] *Ibid.*, op. cit., II, p. 533, Randall's *Jefferson,* II, p. 108.

[21] *Ibid.*, op. cit., Jefferson's *Works*, IV, p. 112.

[22] *Ibid.*, p. 534.

[23] Hicks, *The Federal Union,* Third Edition, p. 211.

and Jefferson divided sharply. Hamilton took the ground that the treaties were with the King of France, and the King's government being done away with, they were no longer binding. Jefferson took the more correct view that treaties were between nations, and that the existing French government had the same claims upon the United States that the King's government had had. All agreed that for the present, at least, neutrality was the only possible course."[24] However, before long, "French violations of American neutral rights began to be about as offensive as anything the British had ever done."

Patrick Henry, now in retirement, sympathized with Washington, particularly in his dealings with the French ministry. Henry held a feeling of gratitude and affection for Lafayette, for whom he had named one of his sons. But he could not accept the infidelity, debased condition, and "bloody horrors of French democracy."[25] He knew that the United States was in no condition to become engaged in another conflict, and he supported Washington's policy of neutrality. But he looked upon Jay's treaty with the British government, in which it had unlawfully held onto the western posts, as repugnant to the principles of the American Revolution. He recalled his warnings in the convention against the treaty-making power vested exclusively in the President and the Senate.[26] He feared Hamilton's grasp for power and his fiscal recklessness. Yet, "having with his own eyes beheld Virginia take up the pen that wrote away certain of her own powers, and with that pen subscribe to the nationalization of the United States, he knew exactly where his allegiance belonged."[27] He saw the new government well established and he had become reconciled to it through the ten amendments, although they were not all he wished. In the legislature of 1790, it was gratifying to him to learn that many Federalists in that body openly objected to the power granted Congress under Hamilton's direction. He wrote his friend, Robert Walker, in November:

> Truth obliges me to declare that I perceive in the Federal characters I converse with in this country an honest and patriotic care of the general good.[28]

---

[24] *Ibid.*

[25] Morgan, *Henry*, p. 367.

[26] See his letter written to his daughter Mrs. Aylett, Aug. 20, 1796, given later in this chapter.

[27] Morgan, *Henry*, p. 407.

[28] Henry, *Henry*, II, p. 535.

To Mr. Henry, there remained no good reason "why he should any longer hold himself aloof from the cordial support of the new government, especially as directed by Washington, and afterwards by John Adams,—two men with whom, both personally and politically, he had always been in great harmony, excepting only upon this single matter of the Constitution in its original form. Undoubtedly, the contest which he had waged on that question had been so hot and so bitter that, even after it was ended, some time would be required for his recovery from the soreness of spirit, from the tone of suspicion and even of enmity, which it had occasioned. Accordingly, in the correspondence and other records of the time, we catch some glimpses of him which show that even after Congress had passed the great amendments, and after their approval by the States had become a thing assured, he still looked askance at the administration, and particularly at some of the financial measures proposed by Hamilton.[29] Nevertheless, as year by year went on, and as Washington and his associates continued to deal fairly, wisely, and, on the whole, successfully, with the enormous problems which they encountered; moreover, as Jefferson and Madison gradually drew off from Washington, and formed a party in opposition, which seemed to connive at the proceedings of Genet, and to encourage the formation among us of political clubs in apparent sympathy with the wildest and most anarchic doctrines which were then flung into words and into deeds in the streets of Paris, it happened that Patrick Henry found himself, like Richard Henry Lee, and many another of his companions in the old struggle against the Constitution, drawn more and more into support of the new government."[30]

Governor Henry Lee, knowing Patrick Henry's respect for George Washington, as well as the President's "determination to keep aloof from party alliances, conceived the idea of adding if possible, the great influence of Mr. Henry's name to the support of the administration. With this in mind, Lee had the opportunity while on business in Philadelphia to discuss with the President the matter of placing Henry in the office of the Federal Government. The most suitable position determined on, and the one that was felt he would most likely accept, was the Supreme Court. When

---

[29] Tyler, *Henry*, op. cit. p. 397, For example, D. Stuart's letter, in *Writings of Washington*, X, pp. 94–96; also, *Journal*, Virginia House of Delegates, November 3, 1790.

[30] *Ibid.*, pp. 397–398.

the offer was tendered Mr. Henry, he declined, remembering a deeply wounding remark by General Washington in 1791. Reporting to Washington the result of his offer to Mr. Henry, Governor Lee wrote from Richmond, August 17, 1794:

> When I saw you in Philadelphia, I had many conversations with you respecting Mr. Henry, and since my return I have talked very freely and confidentially with that gentleman. I plainly perceive that he has credited some information, which he has received (from whom I know not), which induces him to believe that you consider him a factious, seditious character, and that you expressed yourself to this effect on your return from South Carolina, in your journey through this state, as well as elsewhere. Assured in my own mind that his opinions are groundless, I have uniformly combatted them, and lament that my endeavors have been unavailing.
>
> He seems to be deeply and sorely affected. It is very much to be regretted, for he is a man of positive virtue as well as transcendent talents, and were it not for his feelings above expressed, I verily believe he would be found among the most active supporters of your administration. Excuse me for mentioning this matter to you. I have long wished to do it, in the hope that it will lead to a refutation of the sentiments entertained by Mr. Henry.[31]

The President replied to Governor Lee's letter nine days later, August 26, 1794, refuting the information sent him by Lee. Regarding this, he declared:

> With solemn truth . . . I can declare that I never expressed such sentiment of that gentleman as from your letter he has been led to believe. I had heard, it is true, that he retained his enmity to the constitution; but with very peculiar pleasure I learnt from Colonel Coles, who, I am sure will recollect it, that Mr. Henry was acquiescent in his conduct, and that, though he could not give up his opinion respecting the constitution, yet, unless he should be called upon by official duty, he would express no sentiment unfriendly to the exercise of the powers of a government which had been chosen by a majority of the people, or words to this effect.

After expressing his respect and esteem for Mr. Henry, Washington continued:

> Anything short of one of the great offices it could not be presumed he would accept, nor would there, under any opinion

[31] Henry, *Henry,* II, pp. 539–540; *Writings of Washington,* X, p. 561.

> he might entertain, have been propriety in. What is it then you have in contemplation, that you conceive would be relished? And ought there not be a moral certainty of its acceptance? This being the case, there would not be wanting a disposition on my part, but strong inducements on public and private grounds, to invite Mr. Henry into any employment under the general government to which his inclination might lead, and not opposed by those maxims which have been the invariable rule of my conduct.[32]

Before Governor Lee addressed his letter to President Washington, a vacancy occurred in the United States Senate. The seat was offered to Patrick Henry by the Governor and his Council. Mr. Henry declined the offer.

The President, no doubt remembering Mr. Henry's insistence on the free navigation of the Mississippi,[33] now offered him the mission to Spain in the interest of concluding a treaty. This appointment, which was most gratifying to him, he had to decline because of "the consciousness of failing health," and the necessity of putting his affairs in order. The offer was then extended to Thomas Pinckney, who was successful in concluding a treaty in which the boundaries and free navigation of the Mississippi as claimed by the United States were finally conceded.[34]

In the meantime Governor Lee sent to Mr. Henry Washington's letter, wherein he had refuted the charges made against him. Mr. Henry made the following reply to Lee:

> Red Hill, 27 June, 1795
>
> My Dear Sir,—Your very friendly communication of so much of the President's letter as relates to me, demands my sincere thanks. Retired as I am from the busy world, it is still grateful to me to know that some portion of regard remains for me amongst my countrymen. . . . But the esteem of that personage, who is contemplated in this correspondence, is highly flattering indeed.
>
> The American Revolution was the grand operation, which seemed to be assigned by the Deity to the men of this age in our country. . . . I ever prized the superior privilege of being one in that chosen age. . . . To the man, especially, who led

[32] *Ibid.*, op. cit., pp. 543–545; *Writings of Washington*, X, p. 428.

[33] Henry, *Henry*, III, p. 521, Patrick Henry declared in the Convention June 13, 1788: "If Congress should, for a base purpose, give away this dearest right of the people, your Western brethren will be ruined. We ought to secure to them that navigation which is necessary to their very existence. If we do not, they will look upon us as betrayers of their interest."

[34] *Ibid.*, II, p. 549, See Marshall's *Washington*, V, p. 541.

our armies . . . it is not in nature for one with my feelings to revere the Revolution, without including him who stood foremost in its establishment.

Every insinuation that taught me to believe I had forfeited the good-will of that personage . . . must give me pain; particularly as he had opportunities of knowing my character both in public and in private life. The intimation now given me, that there was no ground to believe I had incurred his censure, gives very great pleasure.

Since the adoption of the present Constitution, I have generally moved in a narrow circle. But in that I have never omitted to inculcate a strict adherence to the principles of it. And I have the satisfaction to think, that in no part of the Union have the laws been more pointedly obeyed, than in that where I have resided and spent my time. . . . Although a democrat myself, I like not the late democratic societies. As little do I like their suppression by law. Silly things may amuse for awhile, but in a little time men will perceive their delusions. The way to preserve in men's minds a value for them is to enact laws against them.

My present views are to spend my days in privacy. If, however, it shall please God, during my life, so to order the course of events as to render my feeble efforts necessary for the safety of the country . . . that little which I can do shall be done. Whenever you may have an opportunity, I shall be much obliged by your presenting my best respects and duty to the President, assuring him of my gratitude for his favorable sentiments towards me.

Be assured, my dear sir, of the esteem and regard with which I am yours, etc.,

Patrick Henry.[35]

General Lee sent Mr. Henry's letter to the President, after which Washington undertook to offer Henry the office of Secretary of State, which Henry also declined. Three months later, through the offices of General Lee, Washington offered Henry the chief justiceship of the United States. This offer Mr. Henry also felt obliged to turn down.

Mr. Jefferson, who was no doubt watching "all these overtures" with envy, and had not forgiven Patrick Henry for urging an inquiry into his actions as Governor in 1781, wrote James Monroe, July 10, 1796, respecting the Federalists and Mr. Henry. He declared:

---

[35] Tyler, *Henry*, pp. 400–401; *Writings of Washington*, X, pp. 562–563.

> Most assiduous court is paid to Patrick Henry. He has been offered every thing which they knew he would not accept. Some impression is thought to be made on him, but we do not believe it is radical. If they thought they could count on him they would run him for their vice-president, their firm object being to produce a schism in this State.[36]

Patrick Henry answered Washington's letter October 16, 1795. In making his decision regarding the offer of Secretary of State it is certain he found nothing in Washington's policy incompatible with his own. What was of "decisive weight" with him was the condition of his health and strength which he believed "unequal to the dutys" offered him; his health having been "injured" by resuming his profession at the Bar "at a time of life too advanced to support the fatigues of it."

In after years, Mr. Jefferson alleged that Mr. Henry changed his political views. Respecting this, Judge Spencer Roane, who like Jefferson was an ardent Republican, wrote the following to William Wirt:

> When I was last with him in October, 1794, there was no difference between his opinions and mine that I could discover. I was extremely well pleased with all his opinions, which he communicated freely. He had, after the adoption of the Constitution, taken the anti-federal side in the Assembly on all occasions—After this, matters seeming to come to extremity in relation to our foreign affairs, I understood, for I never again saw him, that he disapproved the policy of embarking in the cause of France and running the risk of a war with Britain. Possibly his sagacious mind foresaw the issue of the French Revolution, and dreaded the effect of a war with England upon our free government, and upon the finances of the United States. After it began to be rumored that he had changed his opinions, he wrote me several letters alluding to the report, and averring that his opinions were not changed, and that he was too old to change them, but admitting that he differed from the republican leaders as to some of their measures, which he considered unwise and impolitic. . . . The alleged change must, I presume have been subsequent to the fall of 1796, for in that session he was elected governor for the third time, (he means the 3rd series of terms, really his sixth election) with a view to keep out General Wood, who was deemed a federalist. Mr. Henry was voted for zealously by the republicans.[37]

[36] Henry, *Henry,* II, p. 572.

[37] *Ibid., II,* p. 574–575. Judge Roane wrote Wirt, that "the offers were made to

The great advantage that was likely to result at this time by having Mr. Henry occupy the Governor's seat was doubtless recognized, and it was in the fall session of 1796 that the Virginia Assembly elected him Governor for a sixth time. This offer by the Republicans Mr. Henry declined, as he likewise had declined the offers of Governor Lee and Washington. Thus it appears that each of the contending parties was vying for his influence; and, moving in the small circle that Mr. Henry was at this time, away from the public scene, his opinions as to party issues could have easily been misrepresented.

Mr. Henry's whole life bears evidence of the purity of his republicanism. He had his own reservations and convictions regarding certain unwise measures, but the patriot never betrayed his principles. His innate greatness lay in the fact that he was willing to lay aside certain prejudices for the over-all good of the republic.

His letter to his daughter in which he refers to the reports that he had changed his political sentiments is his best vindication:

> Red Hill, August 20th, 1796
>
> My Dear Betsy:
>
> [The first paragraph relates to the family.]
>
> As to the reports you have heard of my changing sides in politics, I can only say they are not true. I am too old to exchange my former opinions, which have grown up into fixed habits of thinking. True it is, I have condemned the conduct of our members in Congress, because in refusing to raise money for the purpose of the British treaty, they, in effect, would have surrendered our country bound, hand and foot, to the power of the British nation. This must have been the consequence, I think; but the reasons for thinking so are too tedious to trouble you with. The treaty is, in my opinion, a very bad one indeed. But what must I think of those men, whom I myself warned of the danger of giving the power of making laws by means of treaty, to the president and senate, when I see these same men denying the existence of that power, which they insisted, in our convention, ought properly to be exercised, by the president and senate, and by none other? The policy of these

---

Patrick Henry after he began to diverge from the Republican party, and measures were afterward taken to widen the breach and to inflame him against the Republican leaders. He further stated that the difference was in some degree as to policy, in some instances; in some of which, perhaps, time has shown that he was not mistaken. As to fundamentals, however, I must always believe he remained a true and genuine Republican." MS to Wirt.

men, both then and now, appears to me quite void of wisdom and foresight. These sentiments I did mention in conversation in Richmond, and perhaps others which I don't remember; but sure I am, my first principle is, that from the British we have everything to dread, when opportunities of oppressing us shall offer. It seems that every word was watched which I casually dropped, and wrested to answer party views. Who can have been so meanly employed, I know not—nor do I care; for I no longer consider myself as an actor on the stage of public life. It is time for me to retire; and I shall never more appear in a public character, unless some unlooked-for circumstance shall demand from me a transient effort, not inconsistent with private life—in which I have determined to continue. I see with concern our old commander-in-chief most abusively treated—nor are his long and great services remembered, as an apology for his mistakes in an office to which he was totally unaccustomed. If he, whose character as our leader during the whole war was above all praise, is so roughly handled in his old age, what may be expected by men of the common standard of character. I ever wished he might keep himself clear of the office he bears, and its attendant difficulties—but I am sorry to see the gross abuse which is published of him. . . .

Perhaps Mr. Roane and Anne may have heard the reports you mention. If it will be any object with them to see what I write, show them this. But my wish is to pass the rest of my days as much as may be, unobserved by the critics of the world, who show but little sympathy for the deficiencies to which old age is so liable. May God bless you my dear Betsy, and your children. Give my love to Mr. Aylett, and believe me ever

Your affectionate father,
P. Henry.[38]

The gentleman responsible for the report regarding Mr. Henry had left the cabinet and retired to his home at Monticello, from whence he now floated the French tricolor. As the former Minister to France, Jefferson had "served during the stormiest period" of the Revolution in which its "liberal and destructive spirit had great influence upon him, and his subsequent views and acts were more or less shaped by it." He well knew Mr. Henry's sentiments as to French infidelity, and he knew also that "his French cookery at Monticello had excited Mr. Henry's keen humor, and that he had been heard to say that he 'did not approve of gentlemen abjuring their native victuals.' "[39]

[38] *Ibid.*, II, pp. 568–569–570–571.

[39] *Ibid.*, op. cit., II, p. 549, Randall's *Jefferson*, III, p. 508.

Although Washington and Henry were both hoping to see the differences of party resolved, the bitterness of faction prevented a compromise. The year 1796 ended Washington's second term as President and he declined to serve longer. The Federalists selected John Adams as their candidate, while the Republicans chose Jefferson. At the same time, there was a plan afoot to run Patrick Henry for the vicepresidency, but he had shown no inclination to take any part in politics in the previous five years.[40] Meantime, some members of the Electoral College, two of whom were Levin Rowell and Charles Simons, "professed a willingness to vote for Henry as President, but not for Jefferson." However, he was "impenetrable" to attempts of this kind and declined the honor by a short notification in the *Gazette*.[41] John Adams won in the Electoral College by a vote of 71 to Jefferson's 68. The outcome of the election was said to be due to the French minister Adet's efforts in aiding Jefferson, and to Hamilton's rift with Adams in which he threw his weight to Thomas Pinckney for the presidency. Hamilton's scheme "was foiled by the action of many New England electors who voted for Adams, but refused to support Pinckney." Thus Hamilton's plan, revealing "a rift in the party," almost "cost the Federalists the election"; Jefferson, who received the next highest number of votes, became Vice President.

Washington did not leave the presidency with reluctance. The conditions under which he had served had borne heavily upon him. In his Farewell Address to the people of the United States, published September 17, 1796, he pled for loyalty to the Union, and pointed to those habits of religion and morality which lead to political prosperity. He declared:

"Of all the dispositions and habits which lead to political prosperity, religion and morality are indispensable supports. In vain would that man claim the tribute of patriotism, who should labor to subvert these great pillars of human happiness, these firmest props of the destinies of men and citizens. The mere politician, equally with the pious man, ought to respect and to cherish them. A volume could not trace all their connection with private and public felicity. Let it simply be asked, where is the security for property, for reputation, for life, if the sense of religious obligation desert the oaths, which are the instruments of investigation in courts of justice. And let us with caution indulge

---

[40] *Ibid.*, op. cit., II, p. 571, Gibb's *Washington and Adams*, I, p. 337.

[41] *Ibid.*, op. cit., Judge Roane in MS. letter to Mr. Wirt

the supposition, that morality can be maintained without religion. Whatever may be conceded to the influence of refined education on minds of peculiar structure, reason and experience both forbid us to expect, that national morality can prevail in exclusion of religious principles."[42]

In these sentiments, he and Henry were one.

John Adams assumed the office of President in 1797. He had supported the policies of Washington and Hamilton, and his opposition to the principles of the French revolution were already defined in an article, "Discourses on Davila," published by him in 1790. His election over Thomas Jefferson increased the already strained relations with France, in which public opinion was badly divided, and everywhere there was "an increasing bitterness and even violence in partisan feelings." France clung to the treaty of 1778, that "free ships should make free goods, while England, which had always claimed the contrary rule, had it now accorded her by Jay's treaty. This put France under a serious disadvantage in her war with England, and Washington had intimated to Adet, that the United States were ready to change the treaty with France in that respect if desired."[43] In her continuous spoliation of American commerce, the long-irritating relations between the two countries were almost at a breaking point. James Monroe, a Republican, whose sympathies lay with France, was now called home, and as his successor Adams appointed Charles Cotesworth Pinckney, a Federalist. This change angered France, and Pinckney was not received. Adams, therefore, hoping to establish good relations, decided to send a mission to France and appointed Elbridge Gerry, a Republican, and two Federalists, John Marshall and the same C. C. Pinckney, to Paris. The ministers, likewise, were shown no formal recognition, but were informed by representatives of Talleyrand that any recognition was contingent upon "a *douceur* of £50,000 to the Directory and Ministers, and an agreement to make a large loan to the French Government."[44] Refusing to meet such demands, Marshall and Pinckney returned to America. Gerry, however, remained on to continue discussions. In these difficult and apparently hopeless relations, Congress decided to repeal the treaty with France and prepare for war. Defense measures were taken to create a new and strong navy and to strengthen the army; large appropriations were made.

---

[42] *The World's Great Classics, Orations of American Orators,* I, p. 40.

[43] Henry, *Henry,* op. cit., II, p. 580, Marshall's *Washington,* V, p. 679.

[44] *Ibid.,* II, p. 582; Hicks, *The Federal Union,* Third Edition, p. 225.

Washington was again called into the service as Lieutenant General and Commander-in-Chief to lead the American forces.

In these measures Congress had proceeded wisely, and had it stopped here, Patrick Henry would not have had to point to his warnings against the cession of powers into the hands of the President and Congress. But "the Federal majority, with a singular lack of wisdom, marred their legislation with two other war measures, which became famous as the 'alien and sedition laws,' and finally proved the ruin of their party. By the alien laws, the President was authorized to order out of the country all such aliens as he should judge to be dangerous to the peace and safety of the United States; and in case of invasion, actual or threatened, all subjects of hostile powers, not naturalized, were liable to arrest and confinement, or deportation. By the sedition act, fine and imprisonment were imposed for unlawful conspiracies to oppose the operations of the Government, and for counselling insurrections, riots, or unlawful combinations against its authority."[45]

These acts caused considerable consternation among the Republicans and "were attacked on the ground that they were oppressive, and contrary to the constitutional provisions securing personal rights." Jefferson, their leader, determined to test the constitutionality of the acts, in which he planned to use his influence with the party through the legislatures of the states. Therefore, "he either drew, or revised,[46] the resolutions which were afterward offered in the Kentucky Legislature, and which were adopted by that body in November, 1798."[47] He sent a copy of these resolutions to Madison, which he used as a guide in drawing the Virginia resolutions, both protesting against the usurpation of Congress. These resolutions "created intense excitement upon their publication. Taken in their obvious meaning, they set forth the doctrine that the States, as sovereignties, had entered into a compact known as the United States Constitution, and each State had the right to judge of the infraction of this compact and to apply such remedy as it deemed proper, even to a nullification of the Federal act. Such was the interpretation put upon them by the seven States responding to the Virginia resolutions, as their

---

[45] *Ibid.*, II, p. 583.

[46] *Ibid.*, op. cit., II, p. 584, Letter of Jefferson, December 11, 1821, *Works*, VII, p. 229. "It is claimed on strong evidence that John Breckenridge wrote the original draft, and submitted it to Mr. Jefferson, notwithstanding Mr. Jefferson's claim to authorship."

[47] *Ibid.* See these eight resolutions with interpretations given in Henry's *Henry*.

answers more or less indicate . . ."[48] These laws, added to the already bitter feelings, raised new party issues in which the government of Virginia was secretly making preparations for armed resistance to the United States government.[49]

General Washington, in the meantime, hearing of the passage of the Virginia resolutions in opposition to the defense measures taken by Congress, looked with alarm upon the actions of the Republicans against the general government. In his concern, he wrote John Marshall, lately returned from his ministry to Paris, and urged him to run for the seat in Congress representing the five counties in the Richmond district, largely Republican. John Clopten, then serving in that district, was an ardent Republican, while Marshall, though far removed from the extreme wing of Hamilton, was, to a moderate degree, a Federalist. The contest, in which Patrick Henry's district was involved, was looked upon with the keenest interest and it was rumored that he favored Clopton in the election. Concerned over the report, the Clerk of the Executive Council, Archibald Blair, decided to write Mr. Henry, and in his letter of December 28, 1798, he enclosed a copy of the resolutions passed by the legislature. He appealed to Mr. Henry "for some written expression of his views upon the troubled situation, with the immediate object of aiding in the election of John Marshall . . ."

Mr. Henry made the following reply:

> Red Hill, Charlotte, 8 January, 1799.
>
> Dear Sir,—Your favor of the 28th of last month I have received. Its contents are a fresh proof that there is cause for much lamentation over the present state of things in Virginia. It is possible that most of the individuals who compose the contending factions are sincere, and act from honest motives. But it is more than probable, that certain leaders meditate a change in government. To effect this, I see no way so practicable as dissolving the confederacy. And I am free to own, that, in my judgment, most of the measures lately pursued by the opposition party, directly and certainly lead to that end. If this is not the system of the party, they have none, and act 'extempore.'
>
> I do acknowledge that I am not capable to form a correct judgment on the present politics of the world. The wide extent to which the present contentions have gone will scarcely permit

[48] *Ibid.*, op. cit., II, p. 589. See answers of Delaware, Rhode Island, Massachusetts, New York, Connecticut, New Hampshire, and Vermont, Elliott's *Debates*, IV, p. 532.

[49] Tyler, *Henry*, op. cit., Henry Adams, *Life of J. Randolph*, pp. 27–28.

any observer to see enough in detail to enable him to form anything like a tolerable judgment on the final result, as it may respect the nations in general. But, as to France, I have no doubt in saying that to her it will be calamitous. Her conduct has made it the interest of the great family of mankind to wish the downfall of her present government; because its existence is incompatible with that of all others within its reach. And, whilst I see the dangers that threaten ours from her intrigues and her arms, I am not so much alarmed as at the apprehension of her destroying the great pillars of all government and of social life,—I mean virtue, morality, and religion. This is the armor, my friend, and this alone, that renders us invincible. These are the tactics we should study. If we lose these, we are conquered, fallen indeed. In vain may France show and vaunt her diplomatic skill, and brave troops: so long as our manners and principles remain sound, there is no danger. But believing, as I do, that these are in danger, that infidelity in its broadest sense, under the name of philosophy, is fast spreading, and that, under the patronage of French manners and principles, everything that ought to be dear to man is covertly but successfully assailed, I feel the value of those men amongst us, who hold out to the world the idea that our continent is to exhibit an originality of character; and that, instead of that imitation and inferiority which the countries of the old world have been in the habit of exacting from the new, we shall maintain that high ground upon which nature has placed us, and that Europe will alike cease to rule us and give us modes of thinking.

But I must stop short, or else this letter will be all preface. These prefatory remarks, however, I thought proper to make, as they point out the kind of character amongst our countrymen most estimable in my eyes. General Marshall and his colleagues exhibited the American character as respectable. France, in the period of her most triumphant fortune, beheld them as unappalled. Her threats left them, as she found them, mild, temperate, firm. Can it be thought that, with these sentiments, I should utter anything tending to prejudice General Marshall's election? Very far from it indeed. Independently of the high gratification I felt from his public ministry, he ever stood high in my esteem as a private citizen. His temper and disposition were always pleasant, his talents and integrity unquestioned. These things are sufficient to place that gentleman far above any competitor in the district for Congress. But, when you add the particular information and insight which he has gained, and is able to communicate to our public councils, it is really astonishing that even blindness itself should hesitate in the choice. . . . Tell Marshall I love him, because he felt and acted as a republican, as an American. . . . I am too old and infirm ever again to undertake public concerns. I live much retired, amidst a multiplicity of blessings from that Gracious Ruler of all things, to whom I owe unceasing acknowledgments for his unmerited goodness to me; and if I was permitted to add to the catalogue one other blessing, it should be, that my countrymen should learn wisdom and virtue, and in this their day to know the things that pertain to their peace. Farewell.

I am, dear Sir, yours,
Patrick Henry.[50]

Results show that "the letter of Mr. Henry completely turned the guns of Clopton's friends against them. It threw the weight of Mr. Henry's great influence in the district in favor of Marshall. This weight was not all due to Mr. Henry's public services. There were in the district many warm personal friends, and many blood relations. No wonder, therefore, that the letter was pretty well worn out by constant use, before the canvass closed. Marshall was elected by the small majority of 108, and his election was very certainly due to Mr. Henry's letter."[51] Marshall was later appointed Secretary of State, and afterward, Chief Justice.

On February 25, 1799, John Adams, "shaking himself free of his partisan counsellors,—all hot for war with France,—suddenly changed the course of history by sending to the Senate the names of these three citizens, Oliver Ellsworth, Patrick Henry, and William Vans Murray, 'to be envoys extraordinary and ministers plenipotentiary to the French republic, with full powers to discuss and settle, by a treaty, all controversies between the United States and France.' "[52] Mr. Henry declined this offer later in April.

General Washington, at this time sensing the great danger to the Union, turned again to Patrick Henry in an earnest appeal that he come forward and offer for the Legislature. The letter was written from Mount Vernon, January 15, 1799, and was marked (Confidential.)

It would be a waste of time, to attempt to bring to the view of a person of your observation and discernment, the endeavours of a certain party among us, to disquiet the Public mind with unfounded alarms—to arraign every act of the administration—to set the people at variance with their government—and to

[50] Tyler, *Henry*, pp. 409–410–411; *Writings of Washington*, XI, 557–559.

[51] Henry, *Henry*, II, pp. 597–598.

[52] Tyler, *Henry*, pp. 411–412; Henry, *Henry*, II, pp. 623–624.

embarrass all its measures. Equally useless would it be to predict what must be the inevitable consequences of such a policy, if it cannot be arrested.

Unfortunately, and extremely do I regret it, the State of Virginia has taken the lead in this opposition. I have said the *state* because the conduct of its legislature in the eyes of the world, will authorize the expression—& because it is an incontrovertible fact, that the principal leaders of the opposition dwell in it, and because no doubt is entertained, I believe, that with the help of the chiefs in the other states, all the plans are arranged, and systematically pursued by their followers in other parts of the union—though in no state, except Kentucky, that I have heard of, has Legislative countenance been obtained beyond Virginia.

It has been said, that the great mass of the citizens of this state are well affected, notwithstanding, to the general government, and the Union—and I am willing to believe it—but how is this to be reconciled with their suffrages at the Election of Representatives both to Congress and their state legislature; who are men opposed to the first, and by the tendency of their measures would destroy the latter?

One of the reasons assigned is, that the most respectable and best qualified characters among us will not come forward. Easy and happy in their circumstances at home, and believing themselves secure in their liberties and property, they will not forsake them, or their occupations, and engage in the turmoil of public business, or expose themselves to the calumnies of their opponents, whose weapons are detraction.

But at such a crisis as this, when every thing dear and valuable to us is assailed; when this party hang upon the wheels of government as a dead weight, opposing every measure that is calculated for defense and self-preservation, abetting the nefarious views of another nation upon our rights . . . when every act of their own government is tortured, by constructions they will not bear, into attempts to infringe and trample upon the constitution with a view to introduce monarchy.

When the most unceasing and purest exertions were making to maintain a neutrality which had been proclaimed by the executive, approved unequivocally by Congress—by the State legislatures—nay by the people themselves, in various meetings, and to preserve the country in Peace, are charged as a measure calculated to favor Great Britain at the expense of France . . . When measures are systematically and pertinaciously pursued, which must eventually dissolve the union or produce coercion; I say when these things have become so obvious, ought characters who are best able to rescue their country from the pending evil to remain at home? Rather, ought they not to come forward, and by their talents and influence, stand in the breach which such conduct has made on the peace and happiness of this country and oppose the widening of it?

I come now, my good sir, to the object of my letter, which is, to express a hope and an earnest wish, that you would come forward at the ensuing elections (if not for Congress, which you may think would take you too long from home), as a candidate for representative in the General Assembly of this Commonwealth.

There are, I have no doubt, very many sensible men who oppose themselves to the torrent, that carries away others who had rather swim with, than stem it, without an able pilot to conduct them—but these are neither old in legislation, nor well known in the community. Your weight of character and influence in the House of Representatives would be a bulwark against such dangerous sentiments, as are delivered there at present. It would be a rallying point for the timid, and an attraction of the wavering. In a word, I conceive it to be of immense importance at this crisis that you should be there; and I would fain hope that all minor considerations will be made to yield to the measure.[53]

Regardless of health, Patrick Henry could not well ignore this appeal from General Washington. He offered himself at once as a candidate in the coming election for a seat in the House of Delegates, "there to give check, if possible, to the men who seemed to be hurrying Virginia upon violent courses, and the republic into civil war." Consequently, when the news was spread that Patrick Henry, who had not spoken in public for some ten years, was now to come forward from the borders of the grave, at it were, to counsel them once more, it aroused great interest. On the day before the March term of Court in Charlotte County, Mr. Henry left his home by carriage and journeyed the 20 miles to the county seat, and spent the night near the village with a friend.[54] Upon arriving in the village the next morning, he found a large crowd awaiting him. People had come on foot, on horse and in carriage; gathering from the adjoining counties and from Hampden-Sydney College—every mind intent upon what he would have to say. A Baptist clergyman, seeing that a throng was following him about, chided them, saying: "Mr. Henry is not a

[53] Henry, *Henry*, II, pp. 601–602–603–604.

[54] *Ibid.*, op. cit., II, p. 606. "This was doubtless Colonel Joel Watkins, who lived three miles from the county seat."

God." "No," said Mr. Henry, deeply moved by the remark; "No indeed, my friend; I am but a poor worm of the dust—as fleeting and unsubstantial as the shadow of the cloud that flies over yon fields, and is remembered no more."

Mr. Henry took a seat and rested himself on the porch of the tavern facing the court-green from which he would address the people. A student from the college, John Miller of South Carolina, recounted the occasion in after years:

> having learned that the great orator would speak . . . he pushed his way through the gathering crowd, and secured the pedestal of a pillar, where he stood within eight feet of him. He was very infirm, and seated in a chair conversing with some old friends, waiting for the assembling of the immense multitudes who were pouring in from all the surrounding country to hear him. At length he arose with difficulty, and stood somewhat bowed with age and weakness. His face was almost colorless. His countenance was careworn; and when he commenced his exordium, his voice was slightly cracked and tremulous. But in a few moments a wonderful transformation of the whole man occurred, as he warmed with his theme. He stood erect; his eyes beamed with a light that was almost supernatural; his features glowed with the hue and fire of youth; and his voice rang clear and melodious with the intonations of some grand musical instrument whose notes filled the area, and fell distinctly and delightfully upon the ears of the most distant of the thousand gathered before him.[55]

No full account of Mr. Henry's speech, given at this time of imminent danger, is known. No shorthand report was made, but, according to an account in John Randolph's handwriting, and the testimony of scores of good listeners, such as Dr. Archibald Alexander, Dr. John H. Rice, and the Rev. John Robinson, it was as follows:

"He told the people that the late proceedings of the Virginia Assembly had filled him with apprehension and alarm; that they had planted thorns upon his pillow; that the state had quitted the sphere in which she had been placed by the Constitution, and in daring to pronounce upon the validity of Federal laws had gone out of her jurisdiction in a manner not warranted by any authority, and in the highest degree alarming to every considerate man; that such opposition on the part of Virginia to the acts of the General Government must get their enforcement by military power; that

---

[55] Tyler, *Henry*, op. cit., p. 416, Fontaine, MS; Henry, *Henry*, II, p. 607.

this would probably produce civil war; civil war foreign alliances; and that foreign alliances must necessarily end in subjugation to the powers called in. He conjured the people to pause and consider well before they rushed into such a desperate condition, from which there could be no retreat. He painted to their imaginations Washington, at the head of a numerous and well-appointed army, inflicting upon them military execution. 'And where,' he asked, 'Are our resources to meet such a conflict? Where is the citizen of America who will dare to lift his hand against the father of his country, to point a weapon at the breast of the man who has so often led them to battle and victory?' A drunken man in the crowd, John Harvey by name, threw up his arm and exclaimed that 'he dared do it.' 'No,' answered Mr. Henry, rising aloft in all his majesty, 'You dare not do it; in such a parricidal attempt, the steel would drop from your nerveless arm.'[56]

" 'The look and gesture at this moment,' said Dr. Rice, who related the incident, 'gave to these words an energy on my mind unequalled by anything that I have ever witnessed.'

"Mr. Henry, proceeding in his address, asked whether the county of Charlotte would have any authority to dispute an obedience to the laws of Virginia; and he pronounced Virginia to be to the Union what the county of Charlotte was to her.

"Having denied the right of the State to decide upon the constitutionality of Federal laws, he added that it might be necessary to say something of the merits of the Alien and Sedition laws, which had given occasion to the action of the Assembly. He would say of them that they were passed by Congress, and Congress is a wise body. That these laws were too deep for him; they might be right, and they might be wrong. But whatever might be their merits or demerits, it belonged to the people who held the reins over the head of Congress, and to them alone, to say whether they were acceptable or otherwise to Virginians; and that this must be done by way of petition. . . . 'If,' said he, 'I am asked what is to be done when a people feel themselves intolerably oppressed, my answer is ready—*overturn the government.* But do not, I beeseech you, carry matters to this length without provocation. Wait at least until some infringement is

[56] Morgan, *Henry*, op. cit., p. 422, "Dr. J. H. Rice wrote to Wirt, expressing doubt as to whether history should take cognizance of such incidence as this. Things of the kind might be misleading. 'Perhaps they will give an incorrect view of the state of affairs at that period. It was a stormy time, indeed. But many more bitter words would have been spoken, and much more black ink shed, I think, before the people would have fallen to cutting each others throats.' "

made upon your rights that cannot be otherwise redressed; for if ever you recur to another change, you may bid adieu forever to representative government. You can never exchange the present government but for a monarchy. If the Administration have done wrong, let us all go wrong together.'

"Here he clasped his hands and waved his body to the right and left, his auditory unconsciously waving with him. 'Let us,' said he, 'trust God and our better judgment to set us right hereafter. United we stand, divided we fall. Let us not split into factions which must destroy that union upon which our existence hangs. Let us preserve our strength for the French, the English, the Germans, or whoever else shall dare invade our territory, and not exhaust it in civil commotions and intestine wars.' "[57]

After he had completed his speech Mr. Henry felt very weak and had to be carried into the tavern to rest. It was the last time that he would speak in public, and the sentiments of his hearers were expressed by Dr. John H. Rice, who declared: "The sun has set in all his glory." During the applause, another speaker followed him to the stand. He was John Randolph of Charlotte County, younger and inexperienced, making his first bid for a Republican seat in Congress. He began with a hoarseness barely audible, but his voice soon cleared and a rustic in the audience cried out: "I tell you what, the young man is no bug eater neither."[58]

Randolph's full speech is not recorded, but he began by saying, "that he had admired that man more than any one on whom the sun had shone, but that now he was constrained to differ from him *toto coelo*." One writer, Henry Adams, "surmises that it 'could have been only a solemn defense of States' rights; an appeal to State pride and fear; an *ad hominem* attack on Patrick Henry's consistency, and more or less effective denunciation of Federalists in general.' "[59] To this, "Patrick Henry 'made no reply, nor did he again present himself to the people.'[60] There is, how-

[57] *Ibid.*, pp. 422–423; Henry, *Henry*, pp. 607–608–609–610. Wirt, *Henry*, pp. 393–395.

[58] Henry, *Henry*, op. cit., II, p. 611, *Virginia Historical Magazine*, IV., 35, Dr. Rice's account.

[59] Morgan, *Henry*, II, p. 424.

[60] Tyler, *Henry*, op. cit., p. 420 n., J. W. Alexander, *Life of A. Alexander*, pp. 188–189. "About this whole scene have gathered many myths, of which several first appeared in a Life of Henry, in the *New Edinb. Encycl.* 1817; were thence copied into Howe, *Hist. Coll.* Va. 224–225; and have thence been engulfed in that rich mass of unwhipped hyberboles and of unexploded fables still patriotically swallowed by the American public as American history."

ever, a tradition, not improbable, that when Randolph had finished his speech, and had come back into the room where the aged statesman was resting, the latter, taking him gently by the hand, said to him, with great kindness: 'Young man, you call me father. Then, my son, I have something to say unto you: keep justice, keep truth,—and you will live to think differently.' "

The biographer, Morgan, pointed to Henry Adams, who was "impelled to urge that nothing in Henry's life was nobler than his last public act," saying:

"The greatest orator and truest patriot, a sound and consistent democrat, sprung from the people and adored by them—this persistent and energetic opponent of the Constitution, who had denounced its over-swollen powers and its 'awful squint towards monarchy,' now came forward, not for office, nor to qualify or withdraw anything he had ever said, but with his last breath to warn the people of Virginia not to raise their hand against the national government. . . . In the light of subsequent history, there is a solemn and pathetic grandeur in this dying appeal of the old Revolutionary orator."[61]

As to Mr. Henry's views on the alien and sedition acts, certificates of four gentlemen have been given to show that he disapproved of them; that he thought "the laws unconstitutional, particularly the sedition act, and that their operation was harsh in many cases."[62] From the testimonies of those who heard him, it was seen "that his effort was to quiet the minds of the people, and to induce them to follow constitutional methods for the redress of their grievances." His speech was referred to by Dr. Alexander, the president of the college, as "a noble effort, such as could have proceeded from none but a patriotic heart."[63]

Thus did he counsel them to stand united against civil strife. No man had fought harder than he against those powers granted in the Federal Constitution. The bitter effects from the views taken by Madison and Jefferson were seen in the actions of the different states to nullify federal laws, with the ultimate threat of disunion.[64] These were dangerous seas to Patrick Henry. He and Washington had stood together and weathered the storm that had passed. He dreaded further bloodshed, and the country was

---

[61] Morgan, *Henry*, pp. 424–425.

[62] Henry, *Henry*, op. cit., II, pp. 612–613, Charles Campbell, the historian in the Petersburg *Index* for August, 1867.

[63] *Ibid.*, II, p. 613–614.

[64] *Ibid.*, II, pp. 614–615. See the States affected by the Federal Laws.

in no condition for another war. He would not lend his support in such destruction.

Differences between Henry and Jefferson with regard to the Kentucky and Virginia resolutions grew out of their divergent views of the Federal Constitution. "Mr. Jefferson held it to be only a compact between sovereign States each of whom had the right to judge of its infraction, and of the remedy to be resorted to, and if deemed proper, to resort to nullification or secession. Mr. Henry, on the contrary, considered that the United States Constitution created a government under which the people of the United States became one nation, as to the objects embraced in that instrument; and that, as to these, the people of the several States had merged their sovereignty into that of the whole. In his estimation, therefore, the only right left to a state to annul a Federal act or to dissolve the Union was the right of revolution. That this was his construction of the United States Constitution from the beginning, is made plain by his speeches in the Virginia Convention of 1788. In these he declared again and again, that the plan contained in the instrument was that of a consolidated government. With this construction of the Constitution it was adopted by Virginia and made binding on him. And when, ten years afterward, he is found giving it the same construction, he is charged with being an apostate from his former principles. His firm and patriotic adherence to his principles, indeed, compares most favorably with the conduct of Mr. Jefferson, and of his follower, Mr. Madison, in whose political histories serious inconsistencies might be pointed out, if it were worth the while. In truth, however, there was a radical difference between Mr. Henry and Mr. Jefferson, as to what was the foundation on which republican institutions in America must rest to be permanent. Mr. Jefferson based his hope of American liberty upon the success of the principles of the French Revolution. As late as 1799 we find him writing to Judge Stuart: 'The cause of republicanism triumphing in Europe can never fail to do so here in the long run.'[65]

"Instead of trusting American liberty to the mercy of unbridled passions, Mr. Henry looked to the restraining and elevating principles of Christianity as the hope of his country's institutions. 'Righteousness alone can exalt them as a nation,' was his declared belief. Certain it is that Mr. Henry was never conscious of any

---

[65] *Ibid.*, op. cit., II, p. 621, Letter of May 14, 1799, in possession of Hon. A. H. H. Stuart.

change in his political sentiments touching the principles which underlie American institutions. This is made clear by a message to his friend, Judge Tyler, presented in the following extract from a letter of the Judge to Mr. Wirt. He wrote of Henry:

'The close of his life was clouded in the opinion of many of his friends, supposing he was attached to the aristocratic party; but however he might have been misled by founding his opinions by misrepresentations in his aged and infirm state, it was impossible he could be an aristocrat. His principles were too well fixed. . . . I lament that I could not see him before his death; he sent me a message expressing his desire to satisfy me how much he had been misrepresented. Men might differ in ways and means, and not in principles,' said he."[66]

When Patrick Henry returned to his home that evening after giving his speech at Charlotte Courthouse, he was weak and exhausted. This condition continued for several days; he seemed never to regain his strength and finally had to take to his bed. On election day, the first Monday in April, being confined to his room, he was unable to attend the polls, but as was expected, the good people in his district, trusting to his judgment in all matters, elected him to the House by a great majority. John Randolph was also elected. But Mr. Henry was never again to return to his seat in the Virginia legislature. "For, truly, they who, on that March day, at Charlotte Courthouse, had heard Patrick Henry, 'had heard an immortal orator who would never speak again.' "[67] Learning, however, that his mission to France had been confirmed by the Senate, he raised himself in bed long enough to write to President Adams and decline his offer to be Minister to France. In his letter written April 16, 1799, he mentioned the condition of his health, saying:

> I have been confined for several weeks by a severe indisposition, and am still so sick as scarcely to be able to write this. My advanced age and increasing debility compel me to abandon every idea of serving my country, where the scene of operation is so far distant, and her interests call for incessant and long-continued exertion.[68]

Mr. Henry's illness was unlike the spell of malaria he had suffered the past year. This was a condition affecting the intestinal

---

[66] *Ibid.*, op. cit., II, pp. 621–622, MS. See also *Letters and Times of the Tylers*, I, p. 183. The Judge regarded the Federal as the aristocratic party.

[67] Tyler, *Henry*, op. cit., p. 421, Henry Adams.

[68] Henry, *Henry*, II, p. 623.

tract and had developed serious symptoms. His physician and friend, Dr. Cabell of Lynchburg, was summoned and remained with him. In early June, he wrote a short note to his daughter, Martha Fontaine in Henry County, saying, "Dear Patsy, I am very unwell and Dr. Cabell is with me." When she and the other relatives arrived, they found him sitting in his old arm-chair. The daughters, Anne Roane and Betsy Aylett, living beyond Richmond, were delayed. Anne was suddenly taken ill and passed away. Judge Roane on May 24 wrote the following letter telling of his loss:

> The cup of my misery, my dear sir, is now full by the loss of my most amiable, virtuous, and affectionate consort, your dutiful and affectionate daughter.[69]

When this letter reached Red Hill, Mr. Henry's condition had grown steadily worse and the contents of the letter were withheld from him. His illness was known as intussusception,[70] which was fatal in those days, but could be treated today. Fully conscious of his condition and in perfect calm and great solemnity, he said to his loved ones standing around him, "Oh, how wretched should I be at this moment, if I had not made my peace with God!"[71]

From his grandson, Patrick Henry Fontaine, who was present, the following account of his last moments is given:

"On June 6, all other remedies having failed, Dr. Cabell proceeded to administer to him a dose of liquid mercury. Taking the vial in his hand, and looking at it for a moment, the dying man said: 'I suppose, doctor, this is your last resort.' The doctor replied: 'I am sorry to say, governor, that it is. Acute inflammation of the intestines has already taken place; and unless it is removed mortification will ensue, if it has not already commenced, which I fear.' 'What will be the effect of this medicine?' said the old man. 'It will give you immediate relief, or—' the kindhearted doctor could not finish the sentence. His patient took up the word: 'You mean, doctor, that it will give relief or prove fatal immediately?'

The doctor answered: 'You can only live a very short time without it, and it may possibly relieve you.' Then Patrick Henry said, 'Excuse me, doctor, for a few minutes;' and drawing over his

---

[69] Tyler, *Henry*, p. 421, Henry, *Henry*, II, p. 624.

[70] Morgan, *Henry*, p. 426.

[71] Henry, *Henry*, op. cit., II, p. 625; *Evangelical Magazine*, I, 80.

eyes a silken cap which he usually wore, and still holding the vial in his hand, he prayed, in clear words, a simple child-like prayer for his family, for his country, and for his own soul then in the presence of death. Afterward, in perfect calmness, he swallowed the medicine. Meanwhile Dr. Cabell, who greatly loved him, went out upon the lawn, and in his grief threw himself down upon the earth under one of the trees weeping bitterly. Soon, when he had sufficiently mastered himself, the doctor came back to his patient, whom he found calmly watching the congealing of the blood under his finger-nails and speaking words of love and peace to his family, who were weeping around his chair. Among other things, he told them that he was thankful for that goodness of God, which having blessed him all his life, was then permitting him to die without any pain. Finally, fixing his eyes with much tenderness on his dear friend, Dr. Cabell, with whom he had formerly held many arguments respecting the Christian religion, he asked the doctor to observe how great a reality and benefit that religion was to a man about to die. And after Patrick Henry had spoken to his beloved physician those few words in praise of something which, having never failed him in all his life before, did not then fail him in his very last need of it, he continued to breathe very softly for some moments; after which they who were looking upon him, saw that his life had departed."[72]

Thus do we come to the close of the life of the great patriot, whose singular calling it was to lift Americans out of oppression and tyranny to the light of liberty. His challenge is eternal.

"With no pomp or ceremony, but amid the tears of his devoted family and loving neighbors, Patrick Henry was laid to rest in the quiet graveyard at Red Hill, at the foot of the garden." Upon the slab covering his grave were these words, "His fame his best epitaph."*

The *Virginia Gazette* carried a beautiful tribute to his memory. In his will were found these words:

> This is all the inheritance I can give to my dear family. The religion of Christ can give them one which will make them rich indeed.

Found also with his will was a copy of his resolutions against the Stamp Act, to which he "added these memorable words, which cannot be too often recalled by every American citizen:"

---

[72] Henry, *Henry,* op. cit., II, p. 626, Tyler's *Henry,* p. 376, from Fontaine M.S. See also Tyler, *Henry,* edited 1887 by John T. Morse, Jr., pp. 421–422–423.

Whether this will prove a blessing or a curse, will depend upon the use our people will make of the blessings which a gracious God hath bestowed on us. If they are wise, they will be great and happy. If they are of a contrary character, they will be miserable. Righteousness alone can exalt them as a nation. Reader! whoever thou art, remember this; and in thy sphere practice virtue thyself, and encourage it in others.

P. Henry.

*Red Hill, Patrick Henry's last home, together with kitchen, slave quarters, stables, coach house and old well, has been reconstructed and made a memorial by Mr. and Mrs. Eugene B. Casey of Virginia.

APPENDIX:

WILLIAM WIRT HENRY

ON THE CHARACTER AND PUBLIC CAREER OF PATRICK HENRY, WITH COMMENTS UPON MR. JEFFERSON'S LETTERS.

CHARLOTTE COURTHOUSE, VA., November 22, 1867
To the Editor of the Richmond *Dispatch:*

Dear Sir,—Some days after its appearance, my attention was called to an article in your paper of the 25th July last, copied from the Philadelphia *Age*, which purported to be a manuscript of Thomas Jefferson containing reminiscences of Patrick Henry.

The article contained many statements derogatory to the reputation of Mr Henry, in whose vindication I feel it my duty to publish this reply. Although the manuscript contains many misstatements of fact, it is doubtless from the pen of Mr. Jefferson, and is evidently the communication furnished Mr. Wirt while he was preparing the life of Henry—as I notice that author, when referring to Mr. Jefferson as authority, quotes in many instances the very words of the article you published, and in other portions of his work seems to be combatting the charges therein made by Mr. Jefferson. Taking the manuscript, then, to be genuine, I can only account for its existence by remembering that it was penned at a period of Mr. Jefferson's life, when the heat engendered by party strife had fixed in his mind distorted views of his political opponents.

The statement that Mr. Henry first came into public notice as a burgess about the year 1762 is incorrect. He was elected for the first time in May, 1765, and during that month made the attack spoken of upon the proposition for a public loan office. (Wirt's Sketches of Henry, p. 61, et seq.) During the same month the famous resolutions against the Stamp Act were offered by Mr. Henry and passed by the House. Mr. Jefferson states that these resolutions were drawn by George Johnston, a lawyer from the Northern Neck, who seconded them. In reply to this, I need only refer to the statement of Mr. Wirt, (p. 74), that Mr. Henry left amongst his private papers, in his own handwriting, a copy of these resolutions, with an endorsement stating the circumstances under which they were offered, in which endorsement he says: "That alone, unadvised and unassisted, on a blank leaf of an old law book, I wrote the within." This paper was found sealed up and directed to his executors, and comes to us as his dying declaration. It is still in existence at Red Hill.

Mr. Jefferson was at the time a student at William and Mary, and heard the debate; but his statement as to who wrote the resolutions cannot be weighed a moment against the solemn declaration of Mr. Henry. Nor can I credit Mr. Jefferson when he says that Mr. Henry was a very inefficient member of deliberative bodies in ordinary business, and had not accuracy enough of idea in his head to draw a bill on the most simple subject which would bear legal criticism. He was very frequently placed upon important committees. One of these was the standing committee of Correspondence between the Colonies, appointed by the Virginia House of Burgesses the 12th of March, 1773, which was selected from the best material in the Colony, and which led eventually to a Colonial Congress. We have also the testimony of a very able contemporary as to this matter. George Mason, in a letter to Mr. Cockburn, dated Williamsburg, 26th May, 1774, (*Virginia Historical Register*, January, 1850, p. 28), writes: "Whatever resolves and measures are intended for the preservation of our rights and liberties, will be reserved for the conclusion of the session. Matters of this sort here are conducted and prepared with a great deal of privacy, and by very few members, of whom Patrick Henry is the principal. * * * He is by far the most powerful speaker I ever heard. Every word he says not only engages, but commands the attention, and your passions are no longer your own when he addresses them. But his eloquence is the smallest part of his merit. He is, in my opinion, the first man upon this continent, as well in abilities as public virtues; and had he lived in Rome about the time of the first Punic war, when the Roman people had arrived at their meridian glory, and their virtue not tarnished, Mr. Henry's talents must have put him at the head of that glorious commonwealth."

Mr. Jefferson informs us that after his service as Governor, succeeding Mr. Henry, he had no further personal knowledge of him. And yet his most serious charges as to personal conduct refer to subsequent periods. It will be remembered also that Mr. Jefferson never met with him until Mr. Henry was twenty-four years of age.

That Mr. Henry commenced life in very straitened circumstances, is without doubt; but that he ever acted as a bar-keeper, is denied by Mr. Wirt, (p. 37), who obtained his information from the companions of Mr. Henry's youth.

I am entirely satisfied, also, that Mr. Jefferson has misrepresented Mr. Henry's attainments and conduct as a lawyer. He represents him as too lazy to acquire or practice law, never undertaking to draw pleadings if he could avoid it, engaging very unwillingly, but as an assistant, to speak in the cause, making the fee an indispensable preliminary, keeping no accounts, requiring large fees for his services, insatiable in money, and doing so little business in the general court, other than criminal, that it would not pay the expenses of his attendance. I have in my possession Mr. Henry's fee books, commencing in the latter part of 1760, when he first came to the bar, and coming down to 1771, more than one year after he came to the general court. Sixteen pages of these books have been cut out and lost; but estimating that the fees charged upon them average in numbers with those upon the remaining pages . . . I find that Mr. Henry charges fees in 1185 suits, from September, 1760, the commencement of his practice, to the 31st December, 1763, besides many fees for preparing papers out of court. In November, 1763, he was employed in, and in December following he argued, the celebrated Parson's Cause which gave him so great a reputation. Afterwards his business increased rapidly; of which, however, only a small portion was criminal, the great bulk being the ordinary suits of the country, plain actions of debt, etc. In these it is preposterous to suppose he appeared only as an assistant, to speak. So far from his being insatiable, his books show the usual moderate charges of the day, such as have been long since discarded by the profession; and many of his fees appear never to have been collected. Randall, in his *Life of Jefferson,* (vol. 1, p. 47), gives the number of cases in which he (Jefferson) was employed in the earlier years of his practice, as evidence of his great success; but judging Mr. Henry by the same rule, his success was much greater before he had made what is usually represented as his first speech. How he acquired or retained a practice so large, and continually increasing, so perfectly unfit for it as Mr. Jefferson represents him, I am at a loss to understand.

Nor can I reconcile with Mr. Jefferson's statement another fact, mentioned by Mr. Wirt and by Mr. Randall: I mean the public advertisement of Robert C. Nicholas, after he was made treasurer, committing his unfinished business to Mr. Henry. Mr. Nicholas was one of the examiners who signed Mr. Henry's license, and enjoyed the first practice at the bar, according to Mr. Wirt; and Mr. Randall thinks (vol. 1, p. 49, Life of Jefferson), that he committed his practice to Mr. Henry upon the advice of Mr. Jefferson.

The insinuation that Mr. Henry paid for the Leatherwood lands purchased of Mr. Lomax in a discreditable manner—discreditable, as is alleged, because of the depreciated money used in payment—is entirely unjust. The interest of Mr. Lomax was a subject of litigation, and the sworn answer of Mr. Henry in the case is before me, together with the answer of his widow in a suit brought to divide Mr. Henry's estate after his death. By these papers it appears that the purchase was made in 1778 for paper money, and that Mr. Henry sold other lands of equal value in order to pay the purchase money. At the time of the purchase, paper money had depreciated so as to be worth only one-fifth of specie, and that it would further depreciate must have been apparent to all. I find two receipts given by Mr. Lomax, one for five half johannes at 46s., each, dated 30th May 1778; and the other for £500, cash, dated October, 1778, showing that a large portion of the purchase money was paid during the year of the purchase, and at times when the depreciation of the currency had increased but little. What were the dates of the deferred payments I have not ascertained; but whatever they may have been, no stigma can attach to Mr. Henry for paying for land in the very currency he had contracted to pay, and which he was receiving for lands sold by him to meet the purchase.

Mr. Jefferson has endeavored to connect the name of Mr. Henry with the infamous Yazoo speculation. He asserts that about the close of the war Mr. Henry engaged in this speculation, and bought up a great deal of depreciated paper at 2s. and 2s. 6d. in the pound to pay for it; that the Georgia Legislature having declared that transaction fraudulent and void, the depreciated paper which he had bought up was likely to remain on his hands worth nothing, but that Hamilton's funding system came most opportunely to his relief, and raised his paper from 2s. 6d. to 27s. 6d. the pound. The facts are simply as follows:

On the 7th February, 1795, the Georgia Legislature passed an act selling to four companies, viz: the Georgia, the Georgia and Mississippi, the Upper Mississippi, and the Tennessee—about forty million acres of land for the sum of $500,000. These companies paid the money and obtained deeds to the land. It soon became known, however, that the Legislature had been bribed, and the succeeding Legislature, on the 30th January, 1796, declared the grant fraudulent and void. (Garland's *Randolph*, vol. 1, p. 66; and Tucker's *History of the United States*, vol. 2, p. 187.) This transaction became infamous, and was known as the Yazoo speculation; and it is with this that Mr. Jefferson evidently intends to connect Mr. Henry.

I find from Mr. Henry's private papers that late in the year 1789, he, with Judge Paul Carrington, Joel Watkins, Francis Watkins, and some half dozen other gentlemen—all of high character—entered into a co-partnership, which they called the Virginia Yazoo Company, having for their object the purchase of Georgia lands. In 1789 the Georgia Legislature passed an act to sell to the South Carolina, the Virginia Yazoo, and the Tennessee Companies, a portion of her territory. But refusing to take Georgia certificates in payment, and requiring specie instead, the companies could not pay for the land, and their rights were afterwards declared forfeited. (Tucker's *History of the United States*, vol. 2, p. 187.) No improper conduct can be charged on the Virginia Yazoo Company in this transaction. They paid no money, and got no land.

I find a letter from Francis Watkins, the secretary and treasurer of the company, addressed to Mr. Henry, March 7, 1795, that Mr. Scott, the agent of the company in attendance on the Georgia Legislature, had failed to obtain a new grant, while other companies had obtained the lands. Mr. Watkins advised a dissolution of the company forthwith. I have never seen the slightest evidence that Mr. Henry was connected with any other company, nor am I aware that this was ever charged. In further exculpation of the Virginia company, I would add that John Randolph, in the United States Congress, in 1805, assailed with great bitterness the Yazoo speculation and the persons connected with it; yet in 1820, upon the death of Colonel Joel Watkins, one of the Virginia company, Mr. Randolph, long his intimate friend, in writing his obituary, says: "Under the guidance of old-fashioned honesty and practical good sense he accumulated an ample fortune, in which it is firmly believed by all who knew him there was not a dirty shilling."

The only paper which the act of Georgia declaring fraudulent and void the Yazoo speculation could have affected, was the certificates of debt of the State of Georgia held by the companies interested for the purpose of meeting their purchase. And when Mr. Jefferson wrote, he had evidently in his mind that portion of the system urged by Hamilton, whereby the United States assumed the debts of the several states, Georgia among the rest.

The funding and assumption act was approved on the 4th of August, 1790, (*Laws of the United States*, vol. 1, p. 162.) and gave a considerable value immediately to the paper affected by it. (Randall's *Life of Jefferson*, vol. 1, p. 606.) Now, it could not have been possible, as stated by Mr. Jefferson, that the act of Georgia, which passed in 1796, depreciated the paper held by Mr. Henry to 2s. 6d., when the system of Hamilton had been in operation for six years, and had given a greater value to that paper from its commencement; nor could the act of Congress of 1790 have come most opportunely to Mr. Henry's relief in 1796, and raised his paper depreciated by the act of Georgia of that year. The desire to impute a discreditable motive to Mr. Henry has evidently resulted in confounding dates; and the act of Georgia in 1796 is put prior to Hamilton's funding system of 1790.

Mr. Jefferson proceeds to state that Mr. Henry continued hostile to the Federal Constitution after its adoption, and expressed more than any other man his thorough contempt and hatred of General Washington; and that from being the most violent of all anti-Federalists, he was brought over to the new Constitution by the effect of Hamilton's funding system on the depreciated paper he owned; that Hamilton became now his idol; and, abandoning the Republican advocates of the Constitution, the Federal Government on Federal principles became his creed.

I have a number of letters written by Mr. Henry after the adoption of the Constitution, among them letters to Richard Henry Lee while a member of the first United States Senate from Virginia, with whom he was on the most intimate terms, and whose election he had secured over Mr. Madison as the opposing candidate. I find no contempt, hatred, or even unkind feeling, expressed anywhere towards General Washington. Mr. Henry's conduct towards General Washington during his whole life is at variance with the statement; and I cannot believe it, resting upon the evidence of but a single witness, who informs us he had no personal knowledge of Mr. Henry at the time. On the contrary, I find that Chief Justice Marshall, who had opportunities of seeing Mr. Henry during this period, states (in note xviii. to vol. 5, *Life of Washington*) that Mr. Henry was truly the personal friend of General Washington. To the same effect is the testimony of Mr. A. Blair, secretary of the Council of Virginia. (Sparks's *Writings of Washington*, vol. 11, Appendix xviii.) He writes to General Washington June 19, 1799: "I had the honor to qualify for my present office when Mr. Henry commenced the administration of our Revolutionary Government. From that period to the day of his death I have been on the most intimate, and I believe friendly, terms with him. * * * With regard to you, sir, I may say, as he said of Marshall, that *he loved you*, and for the same reason, because you felt and acted as a Republican—as an American."

Mr. Henry's independence of character was too great to permit him ever to make an idol of Hamilton or of any other man. If he could have been induced to idolize Mr. Jefferson, Mr. Jefferson's reminiscences doubtless would have assumed a different hue. So far from permitting the financial system of Hamilton to change his politics, one of the last acts of Mr. Henry's public life was a protest against the very feature of that system which, if Mr. Jefferson is to be believed, put money into Mr. Henry's pocket and made him a political apostate.

In the Virginia Assembly of 1790, the last in which Mr. Henry sat, on the 3rd November, the following resolution was adopted by the House of Delegates:

"*Resolved*, That so much of the act of Congress entitled an act making provision for the debt of the United States as assumes the payment of the State debts is repugnant to the Constitution of the United States, as it goes to the exercise of a power not expressly granted to the General Government."

On the vote adopting this resolution, Mr. Henry's name is with the ayes. (Vide, *Journal of the House of Delegates* for 1790, pp. 35 and 36.)

That Mr. Henry opposed the adoption of the Constitution in its unamended form is true; but that he continued hostile to it afterwards is not true, if he himself is to be believed. Amongst his papers there is a copy, in his own hand, of his reply to General Washington when offered the position of Secretary of State. It is dated October 17, 1795; and after giving his reasons for declining the appointment, which are of a private nature, it continues:

"Believe me, sir, I have bid adieu to the distinction of Federal and anti-Federal ever since the commencement of the present

Government, and in the circle of my friends have often expressed my fears of disunion amongst the States from collision of interest, but especially from the baneful effects of faction.

"The most I can say is, that if my country is destined in my day to encounter the horrors of anarchy, every power of mind and body which I possess will be exerted in support of the government under which I live, and which has been fairly sanctioned by my countrymen.

"I should be unworthy the character of a Republican or an honest man if I withheld from the Government my best and most zealous efforts because on its adoption I opposed it in its unamended form. And I do most cordially execrate the conduct of those men who lose sight of the public interest from personal motives. It is with painful regret that I perceive any occurrences of late have given you uneasiness. Indeed, sir, I did hope and pray that it might be your lot to feel as small a portion of that as the most favored condition of humanity can experience. And if it eventually comes to pass that evil, instead of good, comes out of the public measures you may adopt, I confide that our country will not so far depart from her character as to judge from the events, but give full credit to the motives and decide from these alone. Forgive, sir, these effusions, and permit me to add to them one more, which is an ardent wish that the best rewards which are due to a well-spent life may be yours.

"With sentiments of the most sincere esteem and high regard, I ever am, dear sir, your much obliged and very humble servant,

P. Henry."

(See also letter of P. Henry to General Henry Lee. Sparks's *Writings of Washington*, vol. 10, Appendix xxiii.)

These letters show that Mr. Henry had in good faith carried out the purpose expressed in the last speech he made against the Constitution in the Convention of 1788. He then declared that he would live under it a peaceable citizen, and that he would endeavor to remove its defects in a constitutional way, alluding to the amendments afterwards proposed. (Robertson's *Virginia Debates*, p. 465.) Though opposed to Jay's Treaty and the Alien and Sedition Laws, he yet refused to go with that party which he believed had a tendency to break up the Government. (See his letter to A. Blair, Sparks's *Writings of Washington*, vol. 11, Appendix xviii.) The famous resolutions of the Virginia Legislature of '98 and '99 aroused in his mind the strongest fears lest the country should encounter the horrors of anarchy, and many of the best and wisest of the land shared his apprehensions. It was at the earnest solicitation of General Washington that he determined to offer for a seat in the ensuing Legislature, and redeem the promise contained in the extract above. Different accounts have been given of his speech in the canvass—the last speech he ever made. But a publication made by Mr. Charles Campbell in the Petersburg *Index* of August last settles the question. He publishes the certificates of George Woodson Payne, Mr. Henry's brother-in-law, and of the Rev. Clement Read, Colonel Clement Carrington, and Robert Morton, his countrymen, and gentlemen of high character and intelligence. Three of these gentlemen heard Mr. Henry's last speech, and testify that his effort was to quiet the minds of the people, to persuade them to use constitutional means to remedy their grievances, and thus to prevent a dissolution of the Union; and three of them testify that Mr. Henry disapproved of the Alien and Sedition Laws.

The terms Federalist and anti-Federalist, first used to designate the parties proposing and opposing the Constitution, after its adoption changed their meaning. Before the post-constitutional parties had become defined, which so powerfully convulsed the country, Mr. Henry had retired from public life. He declined a re-election to the Legislature in the spring of 1791. Death prevented his sitting in the session of 1799, and his last speech was the only political speech he made after those parties arose. His letter to Mrs. Aylett in 1796, (Wirt's *Henry*, p. 400) declares that at that time he had not changed his political opinions; and where have we the evidence of his political apostacy at any time? If Mr. Jefferson relies on Mr. Henry's opposition to the resolutions of '98 and '99 to establish his apostacy, the answer is at hand. If the fact that Mr. Henry, after opposing the adoption of the Constitution, opposed the resolutions of '98 and '99, proves his apostacy, the fact that Mr. Madison and Mr. Jefferson, after supporting the adoption of the Constitution, supported the resolutions of '98 and '99, proves their apostacy. If Mr. Jefferson intended to fix the apostacy in the year 1790, the date of Hamilton's funding system, then I answer that the Legislature of Virginia did not look upon Mr. Henry as an apostate. In 1794, Mr. Henry was elected United States Senator, and in 1796 he was elected Governor for the fifth time.

The charge, then, against Mr. Henry of political apostacy from corrupt motives is, I submit, utterly untrue; and his character is untarnished by such ungenerous aspersions, from whatever quarter they may come, or with whatever design they may be uttered.

The statement that "General Washington offered Mr. Henry the position of Secretary of State to flatter him, knowing he would not accept, and was entirely unqualified for it," if true, is more discreditable to General Washington than to Mr. Henry. But it is contradicted by the statement of General Washington contained in the letter offering the position. In that letter he said to Mr. Henry: "It would be uncandid not to inform you that this office has been offered to others; but it is as true that it was from a conviction in my own mind that you would not accept it (until Tuesday last, in a conversation with General Lee, he dropped sentiments which made it less doubtful) that it was not offered first to you. I need scarcely add that if this appointment could be made to comport with your inclination, it would be as pleasing to me as I believe it would be acceptable to the public. With this assurance and with this belief, I make you this offer of it. My first wish is that you would accept it." (Sparks's *Writings of Washington*, vol. 11, p. 81.)

If General Washington's design was to flatter Mr. Henry, or to get from him his political status, surely the answer he received must have been satisfactory.

What, then, must we conclude from the following extract from a letter from General Henry Lee to Mr. Henry, dated the 26th December of the same year, which is before me, remembering that General Lee (according to Mr. Jefferson) was acting as the common friend of General Washington and Mr. Henry? Says General Lee:

"The Senate had disagreed to the President's nomination of Mr. Rutledge, and a vacancy in that important office has taken place. For your country's sake, for your friends' sake, for your family's sake, tell me you will obey a call to it. You know my friendship for you; you know my circumspection; and I trust you know, too, that I should not address you on such a subject without good grounds. Surely, no situation better suits an individual than that will you. You continue at home only on duty. Change of air and exercise will add to your days. The salary excellent and the honor very great. Be explicit in your reply."

How strange that General Washington, so admirable a judge of men, should offer the position of Secretary of State to one who had "no accuracy of idea in his head," and, if General Lee is to be believed, should be willing to appoint the same man Chief Justice of the United States, though he had been always "too lazy to acquire or practice law"! I can only find a parallel to this conduct in that of the State of Virginia towards the same person, which, though abounding in great men at the time, imposed upon Mr. Henry her highest offices during a period of more than twenty years, and continued to proffer them even after they had been steadfastly refused.

That the violence of party spirit, scrupling at no misrepresentation to injure an opponent, did, in some small measure, succeed in alienating from Mr. Henry the affections of his countrymen after his voice was hushed in death, may be true; but it could never have been said with truth "that he sunk to nothing in the estimation of his country." The effect of detraction, however, was ephemeral. Mr. Wirt could write in 1817: "The storm of 1799, thank Heaven, has passed away, and we again enjoy the calm and sunshine of domestic peace. We are able to see with other eyes and to feel with far different hearts. * * * The sentiments now so universally expressed in relation to Mr. Henry evince that the age of party resentment has passed away, and that that of the noblest gratitude has taken its place."

In conclusion, I cannot but express regret that, of the private and confidential communications received by Mr. Wirt, and by him studiously withheld from the public eye, this one, containing rumors and opinions to the disadvantage of Mr. Henry—rumors refuted by other evidence, and opinions overthrown by a large majority of voices, as we are assured by Mr. Wirt himself—should have appeared in print at this late day. (See letter to F. W. Gilmer, Kennedy's *Life of Wirt*, vol. 2, p. 79, which evidently refers to this manuscript.) It cannot but create unpleasant feelings even in the minds of the warmest friends of Mr. Jefferson. Mr. Wirt refused to give publicity to this manuscript, doubtless in accordance with the desire of Mr. Jefferson himself, to whose criticism he submitted his Life of Patrick Henry in manuscript, and by whose advice he published it. (See *Letters of Jefferson and Wirt*, Kennedy's *Life of Wirt*, vol. 1, pp. 407–412.)

WM. WIRT HENRY

INDEX

ABOUT THE AUTHOR

Norine Dickson Campbell is a native of Clarendon County, South Carolina, and makes her home in Hanover County, Virginia, at "South Greenock," Beaverdam. She received her education in the private school of Mrs. Mary M. David in Manning, South Carolina. Her forebear, Colonel Roger Gordon of Scotland, brought the first forty settlers to the Williamsburg Township, South Carolina, in 1732. She is descended from six of the families who made up the Roger Gordon Colony; two of her forebears were from Virginia.

A devotee of history, she had her first article published in her early teens, on the *Battle of Eutaw Springs, South Carolina.* She has since written several historical articles for Virginia and Georgia magazines. From her early student days on, Norine Campbell has had three goals. The first, to restore Patrick Henry to his rightful eminence in American history. The second, to establish Scotchtown, the ancestral Henry home, as a national shrine, complete with colonial gardens and furnishings. This was accomplished in 1958 when Scotchtown was acquired by the Association for the Preservation of Virginia Antiquities, to be administered as a museum by the Scotchtown Committee of the Hanover County Branch of the Association. And the third, to put into permanent form the original documents and new information gathered by the author over more than 25 years of research.

With the publication of PATRICK HENRY: Patriot and Statesman, the final goal has been attained—that of bringing to public attention a definitive biography of this distinguished American.